Andranick S. Tanguiane

Aggregation and Representation of Preferences

Introduction to Mathematical Theory of Democracy

With 63 Figures and 34 Tables

Springer-Verlag
Berlin Heidelberg NewYork
London Paris Tokyo
Hong Kong Barcelona Budapest

Dr. Dr. Andranick S. Tanguiane
Academy of Sciences of the USSR, Computing Centre, 40 Vavilov St.,
Moscow 117333, USSR

Department of Econometrics and Statistics
FernUniversität, Feithstraße 140, Postfach 940, D-5800 Hagen 1, Germany

ISBN-13:978-3-642-76518-6 e-ISBN-13:978-3-642-76516-2
DOI: 10.1007/978-3-642-76516-2

Softcover reprint of the hardcover 1st edition 1991

Typesetting: Camera ready by author;

42/3020-543210 – Printed on acid-free paper

Acknowledgements

This essay, based on my Russian publications, was proposed to be written in English by professor Josef Gruber. He invited me to the University of Hagen, Germany, in December 1988, and the first version of the manuscript was prepared to be read there as lectures. However, my visit to Hagen didn't take place in 1988. Later I revised and enlarged the text to its present state.

I would like to thank professor Gruber for the idea of this work, his great support and help in the preparation of its publication. I acknowledge also my friend Serge Jolkoff for numerous valuable consultations. I am grateful to Mrs. Elke Greber who retyped the manuscript in a camera-ready form, and to Mr. Martin Kohl who contributed to its accomplishment.

Andranick Tanguiane Hagen, 14 December 1990

Contents

Introduction

Aggregation is the conjunction of information, aimed at its compact representation. Any time when the totality of data is described in terms of generalized indicators, conventional counts, typical representatives and characteristic dependences, one directly or indirectly deals with aggregation. It includes revealing the most significant characteristics and distinctive features, quantitative and qualitative analysis. As a result, the information becomes adaptable for further processing and convenient for human perception. Aggregation is widely used in economics, statistics, management, planning, system analysis, and many other fields. That is why aggregation is so important in data processing.

Aggregation of preferences is a particular case of the general problem of aggregation. It arises in multicriteria decision-making and collective choice, when a set of alternatives has to be ordered with respect to contradicting criteria, or various individual opinions. However, in spite of apparent similarity the problems of multicriteria decision-making and collective choice are somewhat different. Indeed, an improvement in some specifications at the cost of worsening others is not the same as the satisfaction of interests of some individuals to the prejudice of the rest. In the former case the reciprocal compensations are considered within a certain entirety; in the latter we infringe upon the rights of independent individuals. Moreover, in multicriteria decision-making one usually takes into account objective factors, whereas in collective choice one has to compare subjective opinions which cannot be measured properly. Generally speaking, most of the conclusions true for collective choice are also valid for multicriteria decision-making, but not the converse. Therefore, a general problem of aggregation of preferences should be formulated for collective choice, and the obtained results can be extended to multicriteria decision-making.

Aggregation of preferences is often realized in terms of goal functions, or utility functions, adopting greater values at better alternatives. Then the choice model turns to an optimization model, based on the search for maxima of the goal function, which allows the use of methods of mathematical programming for its analysis. In this case the task of numerical determination of goal function, commensurating criteria according to their significance, is also brought to the problem of aggregation of preferences.

The problem of aggregation of preferences in its mathematical formulation was raised in the 18th century, when Borda, Condorcet, and Laplace turned their attention to the theory of elections (Black 1958). They discovered some inconsistencies and paradoxes of collective choice and also ascertained that overcoming them was impossible within the bounds of considered prerequisites. The following development of the theory of elections dealt with numerous attempts to solve or to go around these paradoxes. New systems of voting, treaty procedures, complicated rules for setting and counting ratings, marks and estimates were proposed, but all of them turned out to be inacceptable in certain cases. Only in 1950 was it proved that there was no universal way to bring preferences to a reasonable compromise (Arrow 1951). This discovery influenced greatly the theory of choice and related disciplines: Firstly, the search for a universal formula of decision-making came to the end and the concomitant difficulties were understood as principal; secondly, it became clear that any regulated procedure of aggregation of preferences had limited applications; thirdly, the informality of choice was affirmed since the rules of decision-making had to be chosen with respect to the decisions themselves; finally, with the proof of "the impossibility of collective choice", as Arrow had called his result, the concept of provable impossibility came from the foundations of mathematics to the field of its applications.

Arrow's theorem, also known as Arrow's paradox, stated the inconsistency of the following conditions (axioms) of aggregation of preferences formulated for collective choice.

A1. (*Number of Alternatives*). The set of alternatives contains at least three elements.

A2. (*Universality*). The aggregation procedure is defined for all possible combinations of individual preferences.

A3. (*Unanimity*). If all individuals prefer one alternative to another, then the first one is preferable for the collective as a whole.

A4. (*Independence of Irrelevant Alternatives*). The collective preference on any given pair of alternatives is determined only by individual preferences on the given pair of alternatives and is not influenced by changes of individual preferences on other alternatives.

A5. (*Prohibition of Dictatorship*). The collective choice is not determined by the choice of a single individual, called a dictator.

Since the above conditions are inconsistent, any decision-making procedure, obviously, can satisfy only four of them. The first condition specifies the nontrivial case because, for two alternatives, the collective choice problem is solved by a majority rule. The third and the fifth axioms seem to be quite trustworthy. Therefore, Arrow's theorem is commonly interpreted as the inconsistency of the two rest conditions—the universality and the independence of irrelevant alternatives.

Following this interpretation we can classify the later studies in the given field by their relation to Arrow's conditions. For example, attempts to aggregate fixed preferences are associated with the rejection of the universality condition (note that for fixed preferences the independence condition is always true). An alternate interpretation is valid for statistical models of collective choice. Being based on averaging the data, they meet the universality condition but not the independence of irrelevant alternatives. The former studies are represented by the works on independent preferences and their aggregation in terms of separable goal functions (Debreu 1960; Fishburn 1967; Koopmans 1972), the latter studies—by Borda's method of marks with its statistical justification by Laplace (Black 1958).

Arrow's theorem was succeeded by numerous modifications and generalizations (Kelly 1978). At the same time the development of adjacent disciplines—game theory and mathematical economics—caused the emergence of collective choice models with an infinite set of individuals. The interest in infinite models can be explained by the fact that by virtue of mathematical induction all finite structures have similar properties, implying the qualitative concepts of "large" and "small" to be indistinguishable in formal models. Their replacement by the concepts of "finite" and "infinite" provides the model with the required system of signs and rules to use them. Infinite models are common in mechanics where a great quantity of particles is usually described by a continuous medium, or in mathematical economics where the perfect competition is studied on a continuum of traders (Aumann 1964; 1966). Such idealization makes single elements negligible and allows the consideration of only the components commensurable with the whole.

For a collective choice model with an infinite set of individuals it was established that Arrow's axioms were consistent (Fishburn 1970). In particular, it means that the inconsistency of Arrow's axioms is disappearing with the increase in the number of individuals, and that the role of dictator in collective decisions becomes negligible when the number of individuals is large. Kirman and Sondermann (1972) considered the infinite model filled up with "invisible agents"—the points of the Stone–Cech compactification of the set of individuals, and the existence of a dictator, even if "invisible", implying the inconsistency of Arrow's axioms, was reaffirmed. Later it was proposed to

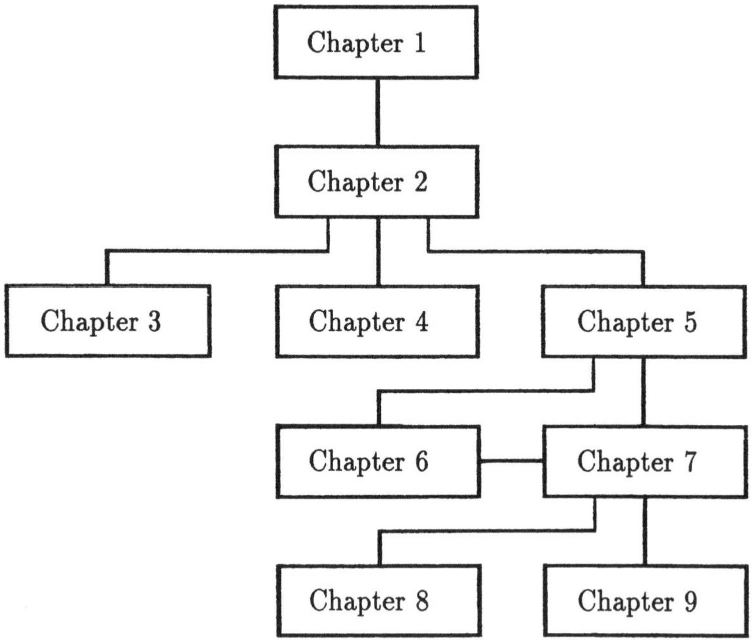

Fig. 1

take into account the coalitions of individuals of positive measure only, and the infinite collective choice model without a dictator was substantiated again (Schmitz 1977; Armstrong 1980; 1985).

The mentioned works are summarized in (Fishburn 1987), but it is still unclear why in certain cases the dictator can be taken into and away from the model without any influence on its other properties. Therefore, one can ask, what is the role of the dictator in the collective choice model, and is the formal consideration adequate to its interpretation. The prohibition of dictatorship must be carefully examined within the context of Arrow's model and, if necessary, revised, together with obtained results, their interpretation and terminology.

The outlined results are taken as a background for our essay. In a sense, we follow these selected problems in collective choice, trying to comprehend them from a single point of view. At the same time, regarding science as a part of culture, we are trying to pay sufficient attention to the traditions in scientific research, successiveness of basic ideas and general analogies.

The structure of the book is shown in fig. 1. Chapters 1 and 2 can be regarded as introductory. The first chapter introduces the problems of collective choice with a series of examples. It shows the role of the concept of preference in collective choice and characterizes the main distinctions of ordinal and cardinal approaches to aggregation of preferences, resulting from different understanding of the nature of preferences. The second chapter deals with the main properties of preferences, formalized by orderings. Since under rather general assumptions preference orderings are represented by goal functions, we introduce the concept of preference, drawing analogy to properties of real-value functions.

In chapters 3 and 4 the two least evident Arrow's axioms are rejected alternately. In the third chapter a model without the universality condition is studied. We consider fixed independent preferences and substantiate an algorithm of construction of collective preference by some minimal data. In the fourth chapter Borda's method of marks, inconsistent with the independence of irrelevant alternatives, is considered. In particular, we derive formulas to estimate the reliability of decision-making recommendations obtained by the method of marks. The problem statement in these chapters meets the established interpretation of Arrow's paradox as the necessity to reject one of Arrow's axioms to make the collective choice rational. The reader will see that the two models may be useful, but require restrictive assumptions, and therefore don't solve the general problem of aggregation of preferences.

In chapters 5 and 6 we consider Arrow's collective choice model. Chapter 6 is specially devoted to the interaction between the models with finite and infinite sets of individuals. In particular, we prove that the collective choice, satisfying axioms A1–A4, is realized by deciding coalitions which form a hierarchy with the dictator at its top level. The difference between finite and infinite models is explained by the properties of deciding hierarchies. In the former the top level of deciding hierarchy always exists, whereas in the latter it can be unattainable. Therefore, it is the deciding hierarchy, not the dictator, which is invariant in the model. Here we also come to the understanding of the dictator as a representative of deciding coalitions and clarify his role in the collective choice model.

In the seventh chapter the prohibition of dictatorship is revised with regard to the interpretation of some dictators as representatives. We show that a dictator can be appointed to express a majority preference in most cases. The interpretation of dictator as representative weakens the categoricity of the conclusions about the "impossibility" of collective choice, and in a sense we can speak about overcoming Arrow's paradox. The paradox can be regarded as the result of an excess of information in the model, which comes into contradiction with itself. In its turn, an excess of information can be caused either by an excess of rules with which the contradictive information is deduced, or by an extended treatment of basic concepts, as in "naive" set theory. The former case is interpreted as the necessity to eliminate one of Arrow's axioms. The latter case leads to the revision of the concept of a dictator, which as we shall prove, is understood in an extended way. In this connection it is recalled that paradoxes of the set theory were overcome by means of a refinement of the concept of a set itself.

To be more precise, we introduce quantitative indicators of representativeness, and prove that with respect to these indicators there always exist dictator-representatives, whom we don't consider as dictators in a proper sense, and to whom we don't extend Arrow's axiom about the prohibition of dictatorship. Thus we obtain the consistency of Arrow's axioms.

However, even for an optimal representative, the part of cases, when his preference contradicts that of a majority, can be quite significant. In 8th chapter we consider a few representatives and delimitate their competence in such a way that decisions of the resulting "cabinet" (named by analogy with the cabinet of ministers) meet a majority preference almost for all situations. On the other hand, in the 9th chapter we study a model of a council—collective representation with no delimitation of competence between its members, making decisions by means of voting.

The formalization of the idea of representativeness is, probably, the main result of our study. Its contribution to the solution of our problems is somewhat similar to the role of Laplace's central limit theorem in quantitative refinements of Bernoulli's law of large numbers, making its applications much more various and precise. By means of the concept of representativeness we manage to distinguish dictators and recognize the ones who are not dictators in a proper sense. We also substantiate such a way of realization of collective choice as giving powers to the elected candidates. Although it is used in all democratic systems, the acceptability of substitution of individual choice, or small group choice, for a collective one is not evident at all. We think that the concept of representativeness can be used for estimation of efficiency of election procedures and rules of decision-making.

Our definition of the dictator, the cabinet, and the council has evident parallels with three forms of political power—the president, the government, and the parliament. Since we consider their capabilities to represent the collective will, we call the direction of our study the mathematical theory of democracy.

Chapter 1

Different Ways of Aggregation of Preferences

1.1 Aggregation of Preferences as a Voting Problem

Collective choice is probably one of the most ancient forms of data aggregation. Usually, it is realized by means of voting. Let us consider advantages and disadvantages of several election procedures based on voting. Some examples are taken from (Black 1958) without special reference.

In the *method of a simple majority* each elector names the candidate he prefers, and the one who gets the greatest number of votes is taken as a winner. This method is quite simple, universal, but in certain cases its justice is questionable. To illustrate it, suppose that there are three candidates A, B, and C and seven electors with the preferences shown in fig. 2, where the candidates

$(A,\ B,\ C)$	3 electors
$(B,\ C,\ A)$	2 electors
$(C,\ B,\ A)$	2 electors

Fig. 2

are arranged in the order of decrease in preference. Thus, three electors prefer A to B and B to C (and A to C respectively), two electors prefer B to C and C to A, and two electors C to B and B to A. Since A gets 3 votes, more than any other candidate, A is elected, yet he is considered worst by a majority of 4 against 3.

According to another well-known *method of an absolute majority*, each elector also names the one candidate he prefers but to be elected a candidate must get no less than half the votes. This method lacks the mentioned disadvantage, but cannot be used in many cases because it blocks any decision which is not backed up by an absolute majority. Thus, in the above example no candidate would be elected. The condition of an absolute majority makes the electors come to an agreement before the voting itself, which may lead far away from the desired compromise. To illustrate it, consider three candidates A, B, and C and 9 electors with the preferences shown in fig. 3. Since candidate C has

$(A,\ B,\ C)$	4 electors
$(B,\ C,\ A)$	3 electors
$(C,\ B,\ A)$	1 elector
$(C,\ A,\ B)$	1 elector

Fig. 3

no chances to be elected, his adherents—the last two electors—will give their votes for A or B, and then A will be elected. Nevertheless, A can hardly be considered as most acceptable, since 4 of 9 electors find him worst. The best compromise seems to be candidate B, who gets only one vote less than A, being put last by only one elector.

To avoid similar situations *single vote elections* are held *in rounds*, when the candidate who gets the fewest votes is excluded from further competition. However, this method is also untrustworthy in certain cases. Consider three candidates A, B, and C and 7 electors whose preferences are shown in fig. 4.

$(A,\ C,\ B)$	3 electors
$(B,\ C,\ A)$	3 electors
$(C,\ A,\ B)$	1 elector

Fig. 4

Obviously, candidate C is excluded after the first round, getting only one vote. Nevertheless, C seems to be the most acceptable candidate. Indeed, C is preferred to A or to B by a majority of 4 against 3. This example also proves the imperfection of another widely used procedure of voting which rejects all candidates, except the two getting the most votes in the first round.

$$\left.\begin{array}{l} \left.\begin{array}{l}(A,\ B)\\(A,\ B)\\(B,\ A)\end{array}\right\}\ (A,\ B) \\ \\ \left.\begin{array}{l}(B,\ A)\\(B,\ A)\\(B,\ A)\end{array}\right\}\ (B,\ A) \\ \\ \left.\begin{array}{l}(B,\ A)\\(A,\ B)\\(A,\ B)\end{array}\right\}\ (A,\ B)\end{array}\right\}\ (A,\ B)$$

Fig. 5

Some other kind of elections in rounds are *indirect elections*, held firstly in separate groups to form an electors board which makes the final choice. This method, commonly used in hierarchical systems, can come into contradiction with a majority rule. To illustrate it, suppose that there are two candidates A and B and 9 electors, divided into three groups, with the preferences shown in fig. 5. Candidate A, getting a majority in the first and in the third group, is elected, yet B gets an absolute majority in direct voting. A similar situation occured at the elections of the president of the USA in 1876, when the candidate of the Republican Party R. Hayes gained a victory over the candidate of the Democratic Party S. Tilden, having got a majority of 185 against 184 in the electors board, yet a minority in popular vote (4 034 000 against 4 285 000). In spite of evident injustice indirect elections are used when it is required to represent independent groups, as in international organizations where different states are equal in rights regardless of their population.

A serious disadvantage of many election procedures is the dependence of the final choice upon voting strategies. Let us demonstrate the strategic aspect of elections with an example of *pairwise voting*, when candidates are voted on by two at a time, and the loser is eliminated from further competition. Consider three candidates A, B, and C and 7 electors with the preferences shown in fig. 6. Here candidate A has the best chance to be elected. Indeed, if the first group of electors consisted of 2 members, the chances of the three candidates would be equal because of the symmetry in preferences. Therefore, the eliminated preference (A, B, C) with candidate A being the best should be deciding. Nevertheless, any candidate can be elected by the given method: The result depends on the couple of candidates chosen for voting in the first

$(A,\ B,\ C)$	3 electors
$(B,\ C,\ A)$	2 electors
$(C,\ A,\ B)$	2 electors

Fig. 6

turn. If A and B are put up first, then B is rejected by 5 votes against 2, and ultimately C will be elected, getting 4 votes against 3 votes for A. Similarly, if A and C are put up first, then B will be elected, and if B and C are voted on in the first turn, then A will be the winner.

Thus no election system of the above-mentioned is quite universal and, as we shall see later, it is inherent not in particular methods of voting, but comes from some fundamental properties of collective choice.

1.2 Aggregation of Preferences by a Majority Rule

The discussed examples show that it is impossible to judge the final decision by voting results only; one must take into consideration some additional information, and this fact was established by the first contributors. As a rule, the structure of individual preferences is quite sufficient, and therefore preference orderings are used in most formal models.

Aggregation of preferences is often realized by a *majority rule.* It prescribes in any couple of alternatives to prefer the one which is preferred by a majority. Note that a majority rule is not so evident as it seems to be at first sight. For example, it can contradict the method of a simple majority. Consider three candidates A, B, and C and 7 electors with the preferences shown in fig. 7. According to a majority rule, the best candidate is B, because he is preferred to A by 4 electors and to C by 5 electors from the 7. On the contrary, if we apply the method of a simple majority, A would be elected.

$(A,\ B,\ C)$	3 electors
$(B,\ A,\ C)$	2 electors
$(C,\ B,\ A)$	2 electors

Fig. 7

(A, B, C)	1 elector
(B, C, A)	1 elector
(C, A, B)	1 elector

Fig. 8

Condorcet was the first who studied a majority rule. He discovered a majority paradox which we illustrate with an example. Let three candidates A, B, and C be arranged in order by 3 electors as shown in fig. 8. Then the collective ordering obtained by a majority rule is cyclic (intransitive). Indeed, A is preferred to B, B is preferred to C, and C to A by 2 votes against 1. With the help of combinatorial analysis Condorcet proved that the part of such "bad" cases increased rapidly with the increase in the number of candidates and electors.

To overcome a majority paradox Condorcet suggested to break cycles in their weakest links, backed up by the lowest majority. To illustrate the Condorcet method, consider three candidates A, B, and C and 7 electors with the preferences shown in fig. 9. Here A is preferred to B and B to C by a majority

(A, B, C)	3 electors
(B, C, A)	2 electors
(C, A, B)	2 electors

Fig. 9

of 5 votes against 2, but C is preferred to A by a majority of 4 against 3. The obtained cyclic order (A, B, C, A) has the weakest link (C, A), backed up by the lowest majority of 4 against 3. Breaking the cycle in this link, we come to the ordering (A, B, C) with candidate A at the first place.

The Condorcet method and especially his approach to the problem influenced greatly the further studies in collective choice. Different procedures of elections were considered on the subject of their applicability under various assumptions. Among later works of that kind we mention (Black 1958), where the applicability of a majority rule is examined. Black suggested a quite natural restriction on individual preferences to avoid cycles in the collective ordering obtained by a majority rule. It is supposed that the alternatives can be linearly ordered in such a way that along this order every individual preference increases until its maximum, determined by the particular individual, and then decreases. For example, technical projects can be arranged by their cost, candidates for president by their degree of radicalism, etc. The only requirement is the existence of a one-dimentional arrangement along which every individual preference has a *single peak*. Black proved that in the case of single-peaked preferences a majority rule gives an acyclic collective preference. There are some other works on how to avoid cycles in orderings obtained by a majority rule, but most of the considered assumptions are much more complex. In a sense Black's result is unique in its clearness.

Several authors attempted to improve on a majority rule, following the approach of Condorcet. The idea to correct the collective ordering, obtained by a majority rule, was proposed in the most explicit form by F. Galton. He suggested correcting the collective preference "in general", trying to find out the acyclic ordering, which is close to the totality of all individual preferences. This so-called *method of median* is based on minimization of summarized distances between given individual preferences and the desired ordering. For that purpose the Hamming distance between Boolean matricies of binary relations is commonly used (the distance is defined to be the number of non-coinciding elements of two matricies). The main difficulty of the method of median is that one must seek the desired ordering among orderings of a particular class which can hardly be described in terms adapted for calculations. Scanning all binary relations is extremely inefficient. For example, in the case of 3 alternatives there are $3! = 6$ linear orderings, but the number of all binary relations, or Boolean matrices of 3×3 size, equals $2^9 = 512$. Note that the enumeration of Boolean matricies of a given class of orderings is an unsolved problem.

Another way to avoid cyclic orderings was proposed by Ch. Dodgson, also known as a writer under the pseudonym Lewis Carroll. In one of his articles on collective choice, reprinted in the book (Black 1958), he introduced the *method of inversions*. An inversion is defined to be a permutation of two alternatives, adjacent in the preference ordering. Obviously, any preference ordering can be brought to any other one by means of a sequence of inversions. For example, the ordering (A, B, C) can be brought to the ordering (B, C, A) by two inversions—by permutation of A and B and then of A and C. Dodgson suggested changing individual preferences with the least total number of inversions to make the majority preference transitive (acyclic). For example, consider candidates A, B, and C and 7 electors with the preferences shown in fig. 10. It is easy to see that a majority rule gives the cyclical ordering (A, B, C, A). To break the cycle one has to change the collective preference either on (A, B), or on (B, C), or on (C, A). The first two changes need inversions in at least two individual preferences. On the other hand, to break the cycle at the link (C, A) one has to make a single inversion in a single individual preference. According to Dodgson, such change is the most acceptable, whence

$(A,\ B,\ C)$	3 electors
$(B,\ C,\ A)$	2 electors
$(C,\ A,\ B)$	2 electors

Fig. 10

we come to the collective ordering (A, B, C).

Note the difference between the method of inversions and the method of Condorcet. Inversions suppose changes in individual preferences, whereas the Condorcet method deals with collective orderings. Dodgson's method takes into account the summarized compulsion, measured by the number of required inversions, whereas the Condorcet method ignores it. Finally, the method of inversions minimizes the sum of primary changes in individual preferences, whereas the Condorcet method mimimizes the number of individuals whose preferences are ignored.

Let us demonstrate the difference between the two methods, modifying the previous example. Introduce two candidates D and E to separate A and C, and two auxiliary candidates F and G to make the collective ordering transitive on the new candidates. Thus, consider candidates $A, B, C, D, E, F,$ and G and 7 electors with the preferences shown in fig. 11. It is easy to see

$(A,\ B,\ D,\ C,\ E,\ F,\ G)$	3 electors
$(B,\ C,\ D,\ E,\ A,\ F,\ G)$	1 elector
$(B,\ C,\ F,\ G,\ A,\ D,\ E)$	1 elector
$(C,\ D,\ E,\ A,\ B,\ F,\ G)$	1 elector
$(C,\ F,\ G,\ A,\ B,\ D,\ E)$	1 elector

Fig. 11

that a majority rule gives the collective order with the only cycle (A, B, C, A). Breaking it by the Condorcet method, we come to the ordering (A, B, C), as in the example illustrated with fig. 9, whence A is to be elected. If we apply the Dodgson method, B or C will be elected. Indeed, to make the collective ordering transitive it is sufficient to permute candidates A and B in preferences of two electors. The same is valid for candidates B and C. To change the order of A and C in any preference one has to make at least three inversions.

The method of inversions can be interpreted as a search for a compromise, when to come to an agreement participants adjust their preferences to each other.

Summing up what has been said, we note that in the early studies in collective choice various approaches to the problem of aggregation of preferences were suggested. It was established that in a general case it was impossible to get a transitive collective preference by a majority rule. To overcome it four ways were proposed:

- To restrict the diversity of individual preferences, e. g. to single-peaked preferences;
- to find a compromise ordering by a formal model, as in the method of median;
- to find a compromise ordering, ignoring the lowest majority, following the Condorcet method;
- to find a compromise ordering, taking into account certain quantitative characteristics of individual preferences to commensurate the degree of merit of alternatives, as in Dodgson's method of inversions.

1.3 Aggregation of Preferences with Account of Degree of Preference

The degree of individual preferences was not taken into account in the previous examples. Nevertheless, the account of it is highly desired especially in the cases when chances of alternatives seem to be equal. Although the measurement of preference is complicated because it cannot be expressed in standard units, there are many practical ways to take into consideration the intensity of preferences from direct numerical estimation to various indirect methods. Aggregation of preferences is realized by means of, say, summation of the estimates, which can hardly be justified formally. A typical example is the entrance examinations to university, when school-leavers are selected by the sums of their marks. Note that it presupposes the interchangability of knowledge in different disciplines, which is not evident. With regard to the lack of justification, such methods must be applied with certain reservations. The main reason is that the input data—the quantitative estimates, characterizing the degree of preference—can never be considered as quite reliable. Furthermore, attention must be paid to the specific disadvantages inherent in every procedure of aggregation of preferences based on quantitative estimation of alternatives, even if the estimation is done in indirect form. Let us illustrate it with the classical method of marks.

$(A,\ B,\ C)$	8 electors
$(B,\ C,\ A)$	7 electors
$(C,\ B,\ A)$	6 electors

Fig. 12

The *method of marks* was proposed in 1770 by J. Ch. de Borda to replace a simple majority rule used by the French Academy of Sciences in elections to its membership. Under this method each elector attributes integer marks to candidates, according to his preference: The last candidate gets 1, next to the last gets 2, etc., and the collective ordering is defined by summarized marks of each candidate. For example, consider three candidates A, B, and C and 21 electors with the preferences shown in fig. 12. Here

the sum of marks of candidate A equals $3 \times 8 + 1 \times 7 + 1 \times 6 = 37$;
the sum of marks of candidate B equals $2 \times 8 + 3 \times 7 + 2 \times 6 = 49$;
the sum of marks of candidate C equals $1 \times 8 + 2 \times 7 + 3 \times 6 = 40$,

whence the collective ordering is (B, C, A) with B being the best. Note that by a simple majority rule A is the best, which seems doubtful.

The main defect of the method of marks, which was mentioned by Borda, is its dependence on strategic behaviour of electors which can result in the win of a mediocre candidate. Indeed, the electors can place the strongest opponents to their favourite candidates at the bottom of their schedules to prevent them from being ahead. Let us trace the intermediate stages of such a struggle with an example. Suppose that there are four candidates A, B, C, and D and 5 electors with the preferences shown in fig. 13. Here candidate A has an

$(A,\ B,\ C,\ D)$	3 electors
$(B,\ A,\ C,\ D)$	2 electors

Fig. 13

evident superiority over any other candidate. Both by a majority rule, or by the method of marks A is the best, B goes next, then C and D. However, B gets superiority over A, if the adherents of B lower their marks of A, intentionally distorting their preferences, as shown in fig. 14. Now the sum of B's marks is greater than that of A. To prevent this the adherents of A also lower their

$(A,\ B,\ C,\ D)$	3 electors
$(B,\ C,\ D,\ A)$	2 electors

Fig. 14

$(A,\ C,\ D,\ B)$	3 electors
$(B,\ C,\ D,\ A)$	2 electors

Fig. 15

marks of B. Ultimately the marks are calculated according to the preferences shown in fig. 15, resulting in the win of C, who is worse than A and B both by a majority rule and by the method of marks (cf. with fig. 13). The method of marks has another disadvantage—the dependence on irrelevant alternatives, or dependence on addition of new alternatives, which is also inherent in Dodgson's method of inversions (cf. with fig. 10–11). It means that the addition of new alternatives—or the consideration of irrelevant alternatives—can change the collective ordering. Let us illustrate it with an example. Suppose that initially there are two candidates A and B and 3 electors with the preferences shown in fig. 16. Both by a majority rule and by the method of marks candidate A

$(A,\ B)$	2 electors
$(B,\ A)$	1 elector

Fig. 16

is superior. Let candidates C and D be introduced in addition to A and B, making the individual preferences as shown in fig. 17. According to a majority rule, A is still superior over B, but according to the method of marks, B is superior. Note that additional candidates (alternatives) can be not real but imaginary, and therefore the considered peculiarity of the method of marks requires special attention.

P. S. de Laplace supposed that the mentioned objectionable properties could be eliminated if the estimation of alternatives could be expressed in real numbers. We shall discuss this possibility in detail in the 4th chapter. Now we only note that in this case there arise new difficulties: On the one hand,

$(A,\ B,\ C,\ D)$	2 electors
$(B,\ C,\ D,\ A)$	1 elector

Fig. 17

an accurate estimation is impossible; on the other hand, the summation of estimates needs justification anyway. This is why the aggregation of preferences with regard to the degree of preference is far from being general-purpose.

1.4 Ordinal and Cardinal Approaches to Aggregation of Preferences

Referring to the above examples, we can distinguish between the two approaches to aggregation of preferences:

- *Ordinal,* when only the orders of alternatives in individual preferences are taken into account, as in a majority rule;
- *cardinal,* when quantitative estimates are attributed to alternatives and the collective preference is determined by them, as in the method of marks.

In the previous sections we have discussed the disadvantages of both approaches. The main ones are the limited applicability of the former and the lack of logical justification for the latter. In this connection some authors attempted to combine the two approaches into a single one.

Black's method is of particular interest. He proposed using a majority rule and breaking cycles with the method of marks, eliminating other alternatives. Let us demonstrate it with an example. Suppose that there are five candidates A, B, C, D, and E and 7 electors with the preferences shown in fig. 18. By the

$(A,\ B,\ C,\ D,\ E)$	3 electors
$(B,\ C,\ A,\ D,\ E)$	1 elector
$(B,\ C,\ D,\ E,\ A)$	1 elector
$(C,\ D,\ E,\ A,\ B)$	2 electors

Fig. 18

$(A,\ B,\ C)$	3 electors
$(B,\ C,\ A)$	2 electors
$(C,\ A,\ B)$	2 electors

Fig. 19

first two lines it is seen that each candidate A, B, C is preferable to D and D to E by a majority. Candidates A, B, C form a cycle and after eliminating candidates D and E we obtain the preferences shown in fig. 19. Here

the sum of marks of candidate A equals $3 \times 3 + 1 \times 2 + 2 \times 2 = 15$;
the sum of marks of candidate B equals $2 \times 3 + 3 \times 2 + 1 \times 2 = 14$;
the sum of marks of candidate C equals $1 \times 3 + 2 \times 2 + 3 \times 2 = 13$,

whence, according to Black's method, we get the ordering (A, B, C, D, E). Note that applying the method of marks directly, we come to another result. Indeed, referring to fig. 18, we obtain that

the sum of marks of candidate A equals $5 \times 3 + 3 + 1 + 2 \times 2 = 23$;
the sum of marks of candidate B equals $4 \times 3 + 3 + 2 + 1 \times 2 = 24$;
the sum of marks of candidate C equals $3 \times 3 + 4 + 4 + 5 \times 2 = 27$;
the sum of marks of candidate D equals $2 \times 3 + 2 + 3 + 4 \times 2 = 19$;
the sum of marks of candidate E equals $1 \times 3 + 1 + 2 + 3 \times 2 = 12$,

whence the collective ordering is (C, B, A, D, E).

A less evident way to combine the two approaches to aggregation of preferences was proposed by Copeland (Copeland 1951; Fishburn 1973). Copeland's method is based on estimation of an alternative by the difference between the number of superior and the number of inferior alternatives to the given one, while superiority or inferiority being understood according to a majority rule. For example, consider five candidates A, B, C, D, and E and 4 electors with the preferences shown in fig. 20. Candidate A is superior to B by a majority of 3 against 1 and he is not inferior to any other candidate, therefore his Copeland's estimate is 1. Candidate B is superior to C, D, and E, but is inferior to A, whence his estimate equals 2. Candidate C is superior to D and inferior to B, therefore his estimate is 0. Copeland's estimates of D and E equal to -1 and -2, respectively. Thus the collective preference calculated according to Copeland's method is (B, A, C, D, E).

At first sight Copeland's method seems to be close to a majority rule. However, his method is sensitive to irrelevant alternatives and therefore cannot

$(A,\ B,\ C,\ D,\ E)$	1 elector
$(A,\ B,\ D,\ C,\ E)$	1 elector
$(E,\ D,\ C,\ A,\ B)$	1 elector
$(B,\ C,\ E,\ D,\ A)$	1 elector

Fig. 20

be regarded as a modification of a majority rule. As with the method of marks, it makes use of the intensities of individual preferences with the only difference that they are taken into account only if they are shared by a majority. Let us prove the sensitivity of Copeland's method to the addition of new alternatives with an example. Revert to fig. 20, adding candidate F, placing him into elector preferences as shown in fig. 21. It is easy to verify that

$(A,\ F,\ B,\ C,\ D,\ E)$	1 elector
$(A,\ F,\ B,\ D,\ C,\ E)$	1 elector
$(E,\ D,\ C,\ A,\ F,\ B)$	1 elector
$(B,\ C,\ E,\ D,\ A,\ F)$	1 elector

Fig. 21

the order of candidates A, B, C, D, E in individual preferences is the same, yet their Copeland's estimates are $2, 1, 0, -1, -2$ respectively, whence the collective preference becomes (A, B, C, D, E) instead of (B, A, C, D, E).

We stress that the condition of independence of irrelevant alternatives suggests the ordinal approach to aggregation of preferences; sensitivity to irrelevant alternatives suggests the cardinal approach, i.e. that we take into account the degree of preference.

We can say that the combined approach to aggregation of preferences originated from attempts to invent a universal method based on a majority rule. Since it was impossible, universal methods turned out to be dependent on irrelevant alternatives. However, there remained a hope to aggregate preferences under some weakened assumptions; particularly, to invent a universal method within the ordinal approach, i.e. satisfying the condition of independence of irrelevant alternatives.

The final negative result was obtained by Arrow (1951). He considered a model with a finite set of individuals who could order arbitrarily a finite set f alternatives according to their preferences. Arrow proved that the following assumptions (axioms) were inconsistent.

A1. (*Number of alternatives*). The set of alternatives contains at least three elements.

A2. (*Universality*). The collective ordering is defined for any combination of individual preferences.

A3. (*Unanimity*). If all individuals prefer one alternative to another, then the first alternative is also preferable in the collective ordering.

A4. (*Independence of Irrelevant Alternatives*). The collective ordering on any couple of alternatives is determined only by the individual preferences on the given couple of alternatives.

A5. (*Prohibition of Dictatorship*). No individual is a dictator, where a dictator is understood to be the individual whose preference always coincides with that of the collective.

Note that in the case of two alternatives both approaches to aggregation of preferences—ordinal, or cardinal—are applicable and a majority rule gives the same results as the method of marks. Therefore only the case stated by A1 is to be considered.

The unanimity axiom is satisfied under both approaches. Obviously, it follows from a majority rule, consequently, meets the ordinal approach. On the other hand, if one alternative has all estimates better than another, then the first one is always superior in the collective preference; consequently, unanimity holds under the cardinal approach as well.

The dictatorship comes into contradiction with the idea of collectivity, therefore, it should be avoided both under ordinal, or cardinal approach.

If conditions A1, A3, A5 are regarded as evident, then the problem is reduced to the consistency of A2 (universality) and A4 (independence of irrelevant alternatives). Taking into account what has been said, the inconsistency of Arrow's axioms A1–A5 can be interpreted as the inconsistency of axioms A2 and A4, i.e. as the impossibility of a universal procedure of aggregation of preferences based on the ordinal approach.

We can conclude that Arrow's paradox extends a majority paradox discovered by Condorcet up to the level of the ordinal approach in general. Therefore, any universal procedure of decision-making uses, perhaps indirectly, certain elements of the cardinal approach. Since the cardinal approach cannot be justified strictly, it implies the imperfection of all universal methods of aggregation of preferences.

1.5 Alternate View at Aggregation of Preferences

In the above sections we have outlined the problem and the early studies which determined the state of thought in collective choice by the middle of the 20th century. Let us make a short resume.

Before the end of the 18th century collective choice was not a scientific discipline. On the eve of the French Revolution the voting problem attracted the attention of a few mathematicians. They developed a "naive" approach to decision-making (we use the word "naive" by analogy with the "naive" set theory preceeding the axiomatic set theory). The naive approach revealed paradoxes which were not solved. On the contrary, these paradoxes were multiplied and extended to more general situations. The naive period of development of collective choice ended with Arrow's paradox which established the inconsistency of certain fundamental principles.

Nevertheless, practice was in a sense in disagreement with theory. Many voting and decision-making procedures proved to be efficient for practical needs, although they were poorly justified. The gap between theory and practice can be explained by that every real situation deals with restrictions ignored in theory. In other words, the paradoxes of collectice choice may result from an excess of information, contradicting itself in formal models, when some significant restrictions are omitted.

In turn an excess of information can be caused either by an excess of rules with which the contradictive information is deduced, or by an extended treatment of basic concepts as in the "naive" set theory. The first possibility was mentioned when we have interpreted Arrow's paradox as the necessity of eliminating one of Arrow's axioms. The second possibility will be discussed in connection with the concept of the dictator which, as we shall show, is understood in an extended way. We shall refine its definition and interpretation, taking into account the degree of representativeness of dictators, i.e. their capability to represent the collective preference. From this standpoint we shall distinguish between proper dictators and dictators-representatives. If we restrict the prohibition of dictatorship to the dictators in the refined sense, Arrow's axioms become consistent. This way we propose to overcome Arrow's paradox. Certainly, we overcome it at the level of interpretation, but not at the level of formal construction, where it remains valid.

To conclude this introductory chapter, we would like to mention that formal analysis on the one hand, and thoroughful interpretation on the other hand, contribute greatly to our understanding of the nature of collective choice and decision-making. Let us make a few methodological remarks on interrelations between theoretical models and their practical applications.

1. To choose a model of aggregation of preferences, it is desirable to have preliminary information about expected alternatives and individual preferences. For example, if there are only a few alternatives, meeting the hypothesis about single-peaked preferences, then a majority rule can be recommended. On the contrary, if a great divergence of opinions is expected, then the method of marks or its modifications can be more efficient.

2. Keeping a method chosen in advance, no compromise decision may be obtained. Unforeseen situations may require changing the rules of aggregation of preferences. In the case of collective choice, it is sometimes better to avoid any regulated procedure of decision-making.

3. One should analyse decisions not with a single but with several models in parallel. The comparison of aggregated preferences obtained by several methods aids refining the statement of the problem, clarifies the goals and intentions.

4. The examples of the present section show that the same individual preferences can be aggregated in different ways with different results. The intuitive acceptability of an aggregated preference depends on particular preferences rather than on a chosen method of aggregation. Therefore the search for an adequate model is nothing else but the formulation of goals. Corrections of optimization model with account of obtaining results help both to find optimal decisions and to realize unconscious intentions.

Summing up what has been said, we conclude that a decision-making model has to consist of two interacting levels with a feedback. At the upper level certain aggregation rules, or their specifications, are chosen; at the lower one the optimal decision is found out. Its analysis can result in corrections of rules at the upper level of the model. To make the rules consistent with the decision, several iterations may be needed.

We think that this scheme is efficient for social choice as well. Indeed, under necessity even political systems are changed. Prices, taxes, laws and other means of social regulation are destined to achieve social goals. Conversely, social goals are revised with regard to economical and political achievements. The interaction between goals and results is necessary in order to make the social choice optimal with respect to the current state of social development.

Chapter 2

Preferences and Goal Functions

2.1 Introductory Remarks

Preferences are usually formalized by means of binary relations. This approach was originally established in mathematical economics and was generalized in theory of measurement. A binary relation can be interpreted as a series of results of pairwise comparisons, and it is one of the reasons, why binary relations are used in theory of choice.

We consider partial, weak, and strict orders, corresponding to different degrees of distinguishability of alternatives in preferences. With regard to the limited accuracy of measurement and perception, only partial orders meet the idea of preference in a strict sense, whereas weak and strict orders should be regarded as certain idealizations of real preferences. However, the use of weak and strict orders is justified by the fact that they can be represented by goal functions, in contrast to partial orders, whose numerical representations are much more complex (Fishburn 1970b).

When a preference order is represented by a goal function, decision-making becomes an optimization problem—the search for maxima of the given goal function under the restrictions, corresponding to budget, resources, technology, etc. The interdependence of different properties of alternatives, caused by physical, econimical, or other constraints is also represented by restrictions. We can say that the desire is opposed to the reality—the goal function to the restrictions, and their interaction determines the optimal decision.

Thus the problem of numerical representation of orderings is of considerable importance for practical purposes. On the other hand, numerical representations allow us to study preferences in habitual functional terms. With regard to these reasons the present chapter introduces the concept of preference from the standpoint of analogy of preferences and real-value functions.

The results of this chapter are published in Russian in (Tanguiane 1979a,

1979b, 1980b, 1988).

2.2 Binary Relations and Orderings

Let us introduce basic definitions.

2.2.1. DEFINITION. A *binary relation* S on a set X is defined to be a set S of ordered pairs (x, y), where $x, y \in X$, or, which is equivalent, a subset S of the Cartesian product $X \times X$. The notation $(x, y) \in S$ is read as "x and y are in relation S". Instead of the notation $(x, y) \in S$ the notation xSy is also used.

2.2.2. DEFINITION. A binary relation S on a set X is said to be

reflexive if $(x, x) \in S$ for every $x \in X$;

irreflexive if $(x, x) \notin S$ for every $x \in X$;

symmetric if $(x, y) \in S$ implies $(y, x) \in S$ for every $x, y \in X$;

asymmetric if $(x, y) \in S$ implies $(y, x) \notin S$ for every $x, y \in X$;

anti-symmetric if $(x, y) \in S$ and $(y, x) \in S$ implies $x = y$ for every $x, y \in X$;

transitive if $(x, y) \in S$ and $(y, z) \in S$ implies $(x, z) \in S$ for every $x, y, z \in X$;

negatively transitive if $(x, y) \notin S$ and $(y, z) \notin S$ implies $(x, z) \notin S$ for every $x, y, z \in X$;

connected if $x, y \in X$ implies $(x, y) \in S$, or $(y, x) \in S$, or both;

weakly-connected if $x, y \in X$ and $x \neq y$ implies either $(x, y) \in S$, or $(y, x) \in S$.

Binary relations, satisfying some of the above properties, can be defined by means of their complements. It is stated by the following proposition.

2.2.3. PROPOSITION (A Duality Principle for Binary Relations). *Let two binary relations S_1 and S_2 on a set X be bound up by the condition*

$$S_2 = \{(x, y) : (x, y) \in X \times X,\ (y, x) \notin S_1\},$$

which is equivalent to

$$S_1 = \{(x, y) : (x, y) \in X \times X,\ (y, x) \notin S_2\}.$$

Then

1. *S_1 is reflexive if and only if S_2 is irreflexive;*

2. *S_1 is symmetric if and only if S_2 is symmetric;*

3. *S_1 is asymmetric if and only if S_2 is connected;*

4. *S_1 is anti-symmetric if and only if S_2 is weakly-connected;*

5. *S_1 is transitive if and only if S_2 is negatively transitive.*

We omit the trivial proof of this proposition.

Now we define three types of binary relations, to which we refer in our study as to *preferences.*

2.2.4. DEFINITION. A *partial order* is defined to be an asymmetric transitive binary relation.

2.2.5. DEFINITION. A *weak order* is defined to be an asymmetric negatively transitive binary relation.

2.2.6. DEFINITION. A *strict order* is defined to be an asymmetric, negatively transitive, and weakly-connected binary relation.

For these three orders the belonging $(x, y) \in P$ to the order P is said to be "x is preferable to y"; we shall also use the notation $x \succ y$, or $y \prec x$. The *indifference* is the notbelonging to the relation, i.e. $(x, y) \notin P$ and $(y, x) \notin P$ simultaneously. In this case it is said to be "x is indifferent to y", which is also written as $x \sim x$.

The *dual relation* to P is defined to be

$$R = \{(x, y) : (x, y) \in X \times X, (x, y) \notin P\}.$$

If P is a preference, R is interpreted as the *preference or indifference.* The notation $(x, y) \in R$ is read as "x is preferred or indifferent to y". Sometimes it is written as $x \succeq y$, or $y \preceq x$.

According to proposition 2.2.3, the relation R can be defined not by means of relation P but directly. Note that the concept of strict order is dual to the concept of *linear order.*

Let us give simple examples of preferences, which will be useful in the sequel.

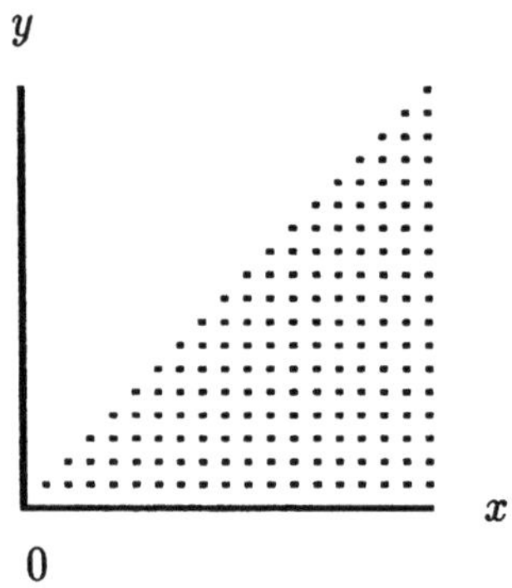

Fig. 22

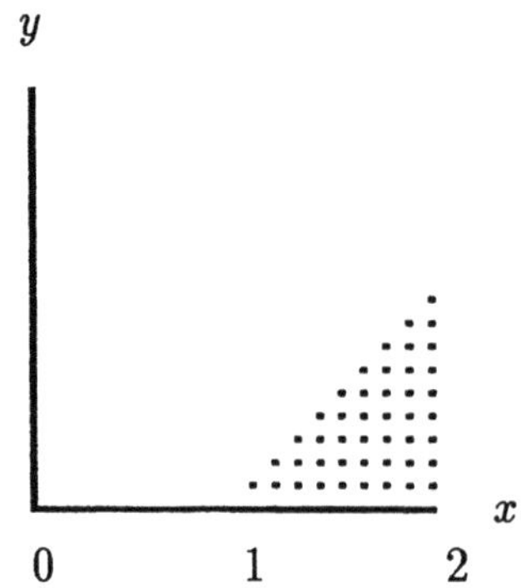

Fig. 23

2.2.7. EXAMPLE. The relation "to be greater than" on of the set of real numbers **R** is a strict order, consequently, a preference. In our designations it can be written down as

$$P = \{(x,y) : (x,y) \in \mathbf{R} \times \mathbf{R},\ x > y\},$$

and the dual relation "to be greater or equal" (which is a linear order) can be written down as

$$R = \{(x,y) : (x,y) \in \mathbf{R} \times \mathbf{R},\ x \geq y\}.$$

This example is illustrated in fig. 22.

2.2.8. EXAMPLE. Let **R** be the set of real numbers and P be the relation, which distinguishes sufficiently remote points:

$$P = \{(x,y) : (x,y) \in \mathbf{R} \times \mathbf{R},\ x > y + 1\}$$

(fig. 23). Then P is a partial order, but not a weak order. Indeed, P is not negatively transitive, since $(2,1) \notin P$ and $(1,0) \notin P$, yet $(2,0) \in P$. Note that the indifference defined with respect to P lacks transitivity. It can be interpreted as the result of inaccuracy of measurement (in the given case the accuracy is within 1), or poor perception capability to distinguish close factors.

2.2.9. EXAMPLE. If X consists of two elements at least, then the relation

$$P = \{(a,x) : x \in X,\ x \neq a\}$$

for any fixed $a \in X$ is a weak order, consequently, a preference with the element a being the best, and all the rest elements of X being inferior to a and

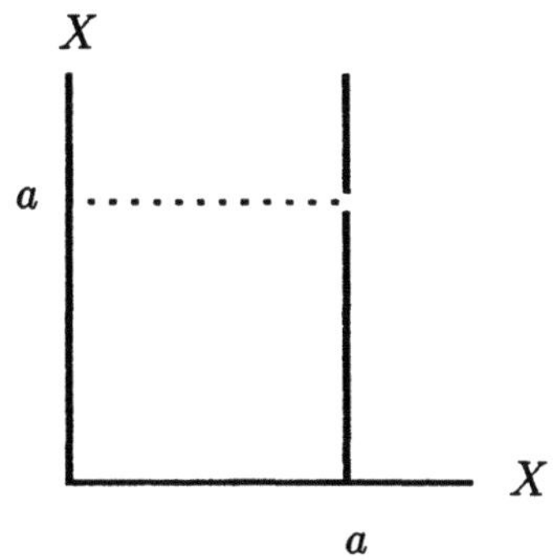

Fig. 24

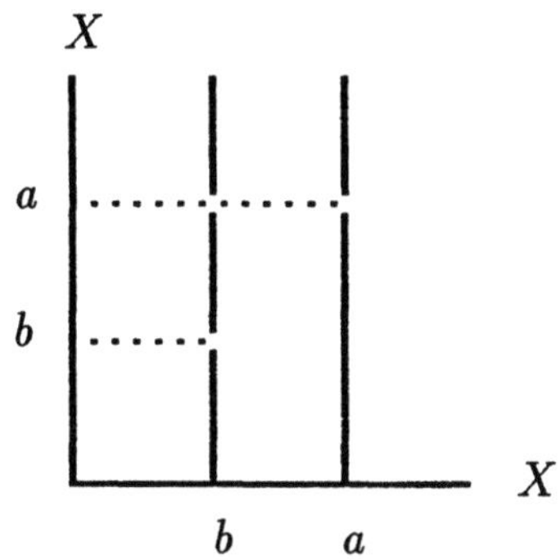

Fig. 25

indifferent to each other. This preference, shown in fig. 24, we shall denote $(a,\ x\dots)$, where the comma separates the classes of indifferent alternatives, and $x\dots$ designates the class of elements indifferent to x.

2.2.10. EXAMPLE. If X consists of three elements at least, then for any two unequal $a, b \in X$ the relation

$$P = \{(a,x) : x \in X,\ x \neq a\} \cup \{(b,x) : x \in X,\ x \neq a, b\}$$

is a weak order, consequently, a preference with the element a being the best, b being the second best, and all the rest elements being inferior to a and b and indifferent to each other. This preference, shown in fig. 25, we shall denote $(a, b,\ x\dots)$. The designation (a, b, c) means that a is preferable to b and c, and b is preferable to c.

2.2.11. EXAMPLE. The trivial relation

$$P = \emptyset$$

(the empty set) for any set X is a weak order, consequently, a preference, meaning the total indifference on X. The dual relation is

$$R = X \times X.$$

Let us enumerate simple properties of partial and weak orders.

2.2.12. PROPOSITION (Properties of Partial Orders). *Let P be a partial order on X and R be dual to P. Then for arbitrary $x, y, z \in X$ it holds:*

1. *$(x,y) \in P$ implies $(x,y) \in R$;*
2. *$(x,y) \in P$ and $(y,z) \in R$ implies $(x,z) \in R$;*
3. *$(x,y) \in R$ and $(y,z) \in P$ implies $(x,z) \in R$;*
4. *$(x,y) \notin P$ and $(y,z) \notin R$ implies $(x,z) \in P$;*
5. *$(x,y) \notin R$ and $(y,z) \notin P$ implies $(x,z) \in P$;*
6. *$(x,y) \notin R$ and $(y,z) \notin R$ implies $(x,z) \in P$;*
7. *$(x,y) \in P$ implies either $(x,z) \in P$, or $(z,y) \in R$;*
8. *$(x,y) \in P$ implies either $(x,z) \in R$, or $(z,y) \in P$.*

2.2.13. PROPOSITION (Properties of Weak Orders). *Let P be a weak order on X and R be dual to P. Then for arbitrary $x, y, z \in X$ it holds:*

1. *$(x,y) \in P$ implies $(x,y) \in R$;*
2. *$(x,y) \in P$ and $(y,z) \in R$ implies $(x,z) \in P$;*
3. *$(x,y) \in R$ and $(y,z) \in P$ implies $(x,z) \in P$;*
4. *$(x,y) \in R$ and $(y,z) \in R$ implies $(x,z) \in R$;*
5. *$(x,y) \notin P$ and $(y,z) \notin R$ implies $(x,z) \notin R$;*
6. *$(x,y) \notin R$ and $(y,z) \notin R$ implies $(x,z) \notin R$;*
7. *$(x,y) \notin R$ and $(y,z) \notin P$ implies $(x,z) \notin R$;*
8. *$(x,y) \in P$ impies either $(x,z) \in P$, or $(z,y) \in P$.*

Now we formulate a test for weak orders.

2.2.14. PROPOSITION (A Test for Weak Orders). *Every weak order is at the same time a partial order. The converse holds if and only if the indifference, determined by the given order, is an equivalence, i.e. a reflexive, symmetric, and transitive binary relation.*

PROOF. Let P be a weak order on X. By items 1 and 3 of proposition 2.2.13 the relation P is transitive, whence P is a partial order. Let us show that the indifference $\sim$ defined with respect to P is an equivalence. If $x \sim y$ for some $x, y \in X$, then $(x,y) \notin P$ and $(x,y) \notin P$, i.e. $y \sim x$, which proves that the indifference is symmetric. Since P is asymmetric, P is irreflexive, and $(x,x) \notin P$ for every $x \in X$, whence $x \sim x$, which proves that the indifference is reflexive. Finally, if $x \sim y$ and $y \sim z$ for some $x, y, z \in X$, then we have $(x,y) \notin P$, $(y,x) \notin P$, $(y,z) \notin P$, $(z,y) \notin P$. Taking into account that P is negatively transitive, we obtain $(x,z) \notin P$ and $(z,x) \notin P$, i.e. $x \sim z$, which proves the transitivity of indifference.

Now we shall show that if P is a partial order on X and the induced indifference $\sim$ is transitive, then P is negatively transitive, whence P is a weak order. Let R be dual to P and $(x,y) \notin P$, $(y,z) \notin P$ for some $x, y, z \in X$, which implies $(y,x) \in R$, $(z,y) \in R$. Since by item 1 of proposition 2.2.12 we have $P \subset R$, four cases are possible:

$$\begin{array}{llll} (y,x) \in P, & (z,y) \in P; & & \\ (y,x) \in R, & (y,x) \notin P, & (z,y) \in P; & \\ (y,x) \in P, & (z,y) \in R, & (z,y) \notin P; & \\ (y,x) \in R, & (y,x) \notin P, & (z,y) \in R, & (z,y) \notin P. \end{array}$$

For the first case by transitivity we obtain $(z,x) \in P$, whence by asymmetry $(x,z) \notin P$. Taking into account items 2 and 3 of proposition 2.2.12, we obtain for the second and third cases that $(z,x) \in R$, whence by definition of R we get $(x,z) \notin P$. Finally, the fourth case means that $y \sim z$ and $x \sim y$. Since the indifference is transitive, we obtain $x \sim z$, whence $(x,z) \notin P$, as required.

The following property of partial orders we shall use in the sequel.

2.2.15. PROPOSITION (The Intersection Property of Partial Orders). *The set-theoretical intersection of an arbitrary set of partial orders on X is also a partial order on X.*

We omit the trivial proof of the proposition. Note that it is not true for weak orders.

2.2.16. EXAMPLE (No Intersection Property for Weak Orders). Let $X = \{x, y, z\}$. Define two weak orders on X, putting

$$P_1 = (x, y, z) = \{(x,y), (y,z), (x,z)\},$$
$$P_2 = (y, z, x) = \{(y,z), (z,x), (y,x)\}.$$

Then

$$P = P_1 \cap P_2 = \{(x, y)\}$$

is not a weak order. Indeed, $(y, x) \notin P$ and $(x, z) \notin P$, yet $(y, z) \in P$ in contradiction to the negative transitivity of weak orders.

We mention the fact established by E. Szpilrajn (Szpilrajn 1930; Fishburn 1970b).

2.2.17. THEOREM (About the Extendability of a Partial Order to a Strict Order). *Under the axiom of choice each partial order on a given set can be extended to a strict order on the given set.*

This theorem also implies that partial orders are extendable to weak orders. Taking into account proposition 2.2.14, we can interpret partial orders as preferences, which are indefinite, or revealed worse than that described by weak orders. The indefinitness can be characterized by the number (cardinality) of possible extensions to weak orders, similarly to the dimension of an order understood to be the number of its linear extensions.

2.3 Continuous Orderings

In this section we suppose that the set X where the preferences are defined is a topological space.

2.3.1 DEFINITION. A partial order P on a topological space X is said to be *continuous*, if P as a subset of $X \times X$ is open with respect to the product topology.

Note the difference between this topological definition of continuity of an order and the set-theoretical definition, assuming the absence of empty intervals (jumps). These definitions are equivalent for connected spaces, but in the case of disconnected space a topologically continuous partial order can have jumps and therefore be discontinuous from the set-theoretical point of view. Similarly, a continuous function adopts all intermediate values on a connected domain of definition, but can have jumps between separate components of its argument. Further we shall revert to the analogy between continuous orders and functions.

Now we introduce another definition of topological continuity of orders, valid, however, only for weak orders.

2.3.2. PROPOSITION (An Equivalent Definition of Topological Continuity for Weak Orders). *A weak order P on a topological space X is continuous in the sense of definition* 2.3.1 *if and only if for every $x^0 \in X$ the sets*

$$\{x : x \in X,\ (x, x^0) \in P\}$$

and

$$\{x : x \in X,\ (x^0, x) \in P\}$$

are open in X. If relation R is dual to P, then the above condition is equivalent to that the sets

$$\{x : x \in X,\ (x, x^0) \in R\}$$

and

$$\{x : x \in X,\ (x^0, x) \in R\}$$

are closed for every $x^0 \in X$.

PROOF. At first, let P be continuous in the sense of definition 2.3.1 and let $x^0 \in X$. We shall show that the set

$$O = \{x : x \in X,\ (x, x^0) \in P\}$$

is open. If O is empty it is open. Suppose that there exists an element $x \in O$. Since P is open in $X \times X$ and $(x, x^0) \in P$, there exist neighborhoods $U(x)$ and $U(x^0)$ of points x and x^0, respectively, such that $U(x) \times U(x^0) \subset P$, i.e. $(x', x^0) \in P$ for all $x' \in U(x)$. Therefore, each element $x \in O$ is contained in O with its neighborhood, as required. One can prove similarly that the set

$$\{x : x \in X,\ (x^0, x) \in P\}$$

is also open.

Now let P be a weak order and the sets

$$\{x : x \in X,\ (x, x^0) \in P\}$$

and

$$\{x : x \in X,\ (x^0, x) \in P\}$$

be open for every $x^0 \in X$. We shall prove that P is open in $X \times X$. It is sufficient to show that for every $(x, y) \in P$ there are certain neighborhoods U and V of points x and y, respectively, such that $U \times V \subset P$. Firstly suppose that there is $x^0 \in X$ such that $(x, x^0) \in P$ and $(x^0, y) \in P$. Put

$$U = \{z : z \in X,\ (z, x^0) \in P\}$$

and

$$V = \{z : z \in X,\ (x^0, z) \in P\}.$$

By our assumption U and V are open, and for every $(z', z'') \in U \times V$ we have $(z', x^0) \in P, (x^0, z'') \in P$, whence by virtue of transitivity $(v', z'') \in P$. Therefore, $U \times V \subset P$, as required. Finally suppose that there is no $x^0 \in X$ such that $(x, x^0) \in P$ and $(x^0, y) \in P$. Define the open sets

$$U = \{z : z \in X,\ (z, y) \in P\}$$

and

$$V = \{z : z \in X,\ (x, z) \in P\}.$$

Since by assumption

$$U \cap V = \emptyset,$$

we obtain

$$U \subset V^c = \{z : z \in X,\ (x, z) \in P\} = \{z : z \in X,\ (z, x) \in R\},$$

and similarly

$$V \subset U^c = \{z : z \in X,\ (y, z) \in R\}.$$

Thus for every $(z', z'') \in U \times V$ we have $(z', x) \in R$ and $(y, z'') \in R$. Since $(x, y) \in P$ and P is a weak order, by items 2–3 of proposition 2.2.13 we obtain $(z', z'') \in P$. Therefore, $U \times V \subset P$.

The proved equivalence of the two definitions of continuity of preferences is not valid for partial orders, which are not weak orders.

2.3.3. EXAMPLE (No Equivalence of Two Definitions of Continuity for Partial Orders). Let X consist of the two convergent sequences

$$y_n = 3 - 1/n \underset{n\to\infty}{\longrightarrow} y_0 = 3$$

and

$$z_n = 1 - 1/n \underset{n\to\infty}{\longrightarrow} z_0 = 1.$$

Let each y_i be preferable to all z_j, except for the cases $i = j \neq 0$. In other words, define the relation

$$P = \{(y_0, z_0)\} \cup \{(y_i, z_j) : i \neq j;\ i, j = 0, 1, \ldots\}$$

shown in fig. 26. Obviously, P is asymmetric and transitive, consequently, P is a partial order. For every y_i the set

$$\{x : x \in X,\ (x, y_i) \in P\}$$

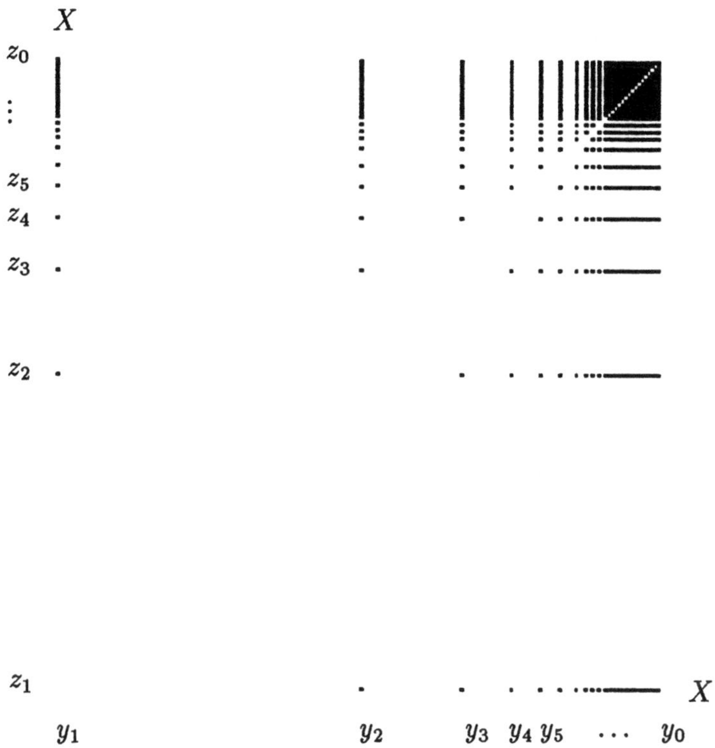

Fig. 26

is empty, and the set

$$\{x : x \in X,\ (y_i, x) \in P\}$$

coincides with the sequence

$$\{z_0\} \cup \{z_n\},$$

lacking, may be, a single point other than z_0. Therefore the sets

$$\{x : x \in X,\ (x, y_i) \in P\}$$

and

$$\{x : x \in X,\ (y_i, x) \in P\}$$

are open for every y_i. Similarly, for every z_i the sets

$$\{x : x \in X,\ (x, z_i) \in P\}$$

and

$$\{x : x \in X,\ (z_i, x) \in P\}$$

are also open. However, P as a subset of $X \times X$ is not open with respect to the product topology. Indeed, for all $n = 1, 2, \ldots$ we have

$$(y_n, z_n) \notin P,$$

yet

$$(y_n, z_n) \underset{n\to\infty}{\longrightarrow} (y_0, z_0) \in P.$$

The difference between the two definitions of continuity of orders (formulated in definition 2.3.1 and proposition 2.3.2) is the following. The former assumes that if one alternative is preferable to another, then the same holds for all pairs of alternatives close to the given two. The latter concerns fluctuations of only one alternative, while the other is supposed to be fixed. As shown by the above example, the transitivity of indifference is essential to derive the former definition from the latter (to separate alternatives into preference classes).

Now we shall examine the analogy between continuous orders and continuous real-value functions. It turns out that some well-known properties of functions have order rather than functional origin.

2.3.4. PROPOSITION (About the Intermediate Value). *Let a partial order P be continuous on a topological space X and let R be dual to P. Suppose that I is a connected subset of X and let $x_1, x_2 \in I$, $y \in X$ be such that $(x_1, y) \in R$ and $(y, x_2) \in R$. Then there exists $x_3 \in I$ such that x_3 is indifferent to y* (fig. 27).

PROOF. Define the sets

$$I_1 = I \cap \{x : x \in X,\ (x, y) \in R\}$$

and

$$I_2 = I \cap \{x : x \in X,\ (y, x) \in R\}.$$

Since P is continuous, I_1 and I_2 are closed subsets of I; they are not empty, because $x_1 \in I_1$ and $x_2 \in I_2$; finally

$$I = I_1 \cup I_2$$

(otherwise there exists $x \in I$ such that $(x, y) \notin R$ and $(y, x) \notin R$, consequently, $(y, x) \in P$ and $(x, y) \in P$ in contradiction to asymmetry of P). Since I is connected, there exists

$$x_3 \in I_1 \cap I_2,$$

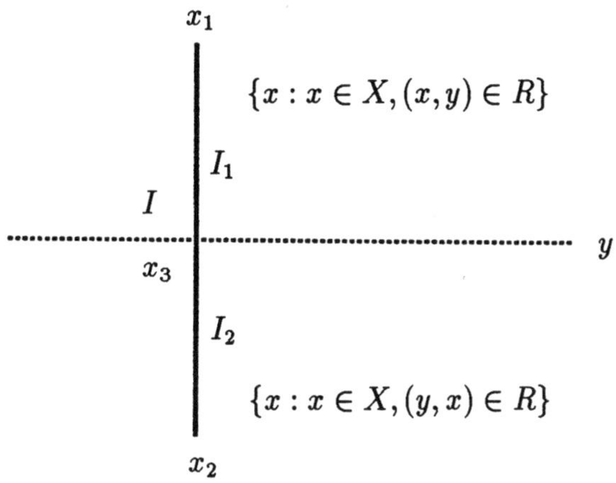

Fig. 27

which is obviously indifferent to y.

The following propositions, proving the analogy between continuous orders and functions, are valid for weak orders only.

2.3.5. PROPOSITION (On Attaining Maxima and Minima on a Compactum). *Let P be a continuous weak order on a compactum X and let R be dual to P. Then there exist both minimal and maximal elements in X, i.e. $m, M \in X$ such that $(x, m) \in R$ and $(M, x) \in R$ for any $x \in X$.*

PROOF. For each $x \in X$ define $M(x)$ to be the set of all preferable or indifferent to x elements, i.e.

$$M(x) = \{x' : x' \in X,\ (x', x) \in R\},$$

which is closed by continuity of P. We shall show that the family of sets $M(x)$ has the finite intersection property. Indeed, if $M(x_1), \ldots, M(x_n)$ is a finite collection of sets of the given family, then by transitivity of R (item 5 of proposition 2.2.3) we obtain that among $x_1, \ldots, x_n$ there is a maximal element x_k. Obviously,

$$x_k \in \bigcap_{i=1}^{\infty} M(x_i).$$

Since X is a compactum, the intersection of all sets $M(x)$ is not empty, containing a certain element M, which is obviously the maximal element in X

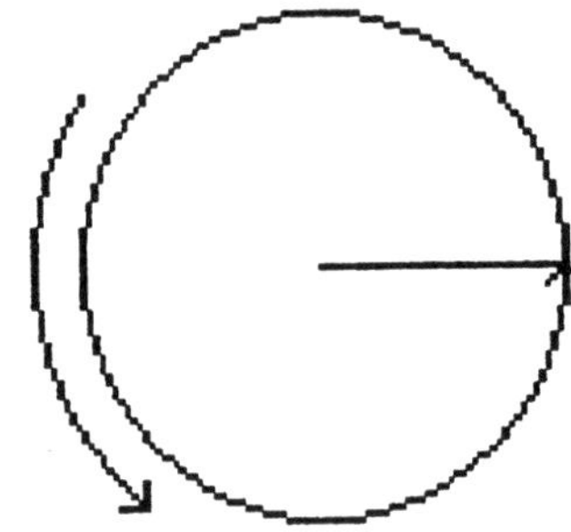

Fig. 28

with respect to R. The existence of the minimal element is proved similarly.

The above proposition is not valid for partial orders, which are not weak orders. Moreover, the concept of maximal and minimal elements with respect to a partial order becomes indefinable even for a compactum. Let us explain it with an example.

2.3.6. EXAMPLE (No Maxima and Minima for a Continuous Partial Order on a Compactum). Let X be the circumference $[0; 2\pi)$. Define the relation "to be greater than" for $x \neq 0$ only, i.e. put

$$P = \{(x, y) : x, y \in X,\ 0 < y < x < 2\pi\}$$

(fig. 28). Relation P is obviously asymmetric and transitive, consequently, P is a partial order. The point 0 is indifferent to any other point, whence the indifference is not transitive. By proposition 2.2.14 we obtain that P is not a weak order. Note that P is continuous on the compactum X (because P is open in $X \times X$), having neither minimal, nor maximal elements on $(0; 2\pi)$. The only possible minimum could be 0, indifferent to any other element, but it could be the maximum as well. Since P is not a total indifference, it is not reasonable to combine maximum and minimum at a single element.

2.3.7. PROPOSITION (About a Dense Subset Filling up Intervals). *Let P be a continuous weak order on a connected space X and let S be dense in X. Then for every $x, y \in X$ such that $(x, y) \in P$ there exists an element $s \in S$ such that $(x, s) \in P$ and $(s, y) \in P$.*

PROOF. Since the weak order P is continuous, the sets

$$U = \{z : z \in X,\ (z, y) \in P\}$$

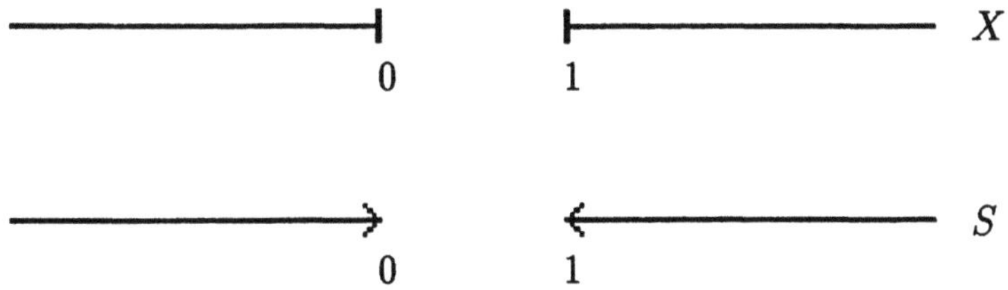

Fig. 29

and

$$V = \{z : z \in X,\ (x, z) \in P\}$$

are open neighborhoods of x and y respectively. It is easy to see that

$$X = U \cup V.$$

Indeed, if $z \in X$, then by item 8 of proposition 2.2.13 either $(x, z) \in P$, or $(z, y) \in P$, consequently, either $z \in U$, or $z \in V$. Since X is connected,

$$U \cap V \neq \emptyset.$$

Moreover, $U \cap V$ is open, and therefore there exists the required element

$$s \in S \cap U \cap V.$$

The following two examples show that both the connectedness of X and the assumption that the order P is weak are essential for the validity of the above proposition.

2.3.8. EXAMPLE. Let X be the set of real numbers except the interval $(0; 1)$. Let P be the strict order "to be greater than" on X, which is obviously continuous. Let a dense subset S to be X except the two boundary points 0 and 1 (fig. 29). It is easy to see that there is neither element $s \in S$ such that $0 < s < 1$, nor even element $s \in S$ such that $0 \leq s \leq 1$.

2.3.9. EXAMPLE. Let X be the set of real numbers. Let P be the partial order on X defined in example 2.2.8:

$$P = \{(x, y) : x, y \in X,\ x > y + 1\},$$

which is obviously continuous. Define dense set $S = X$. Then for the points 0 and 2 there is no element $s \in S$ such that $(2, s) \in P$ and $(s, 0) \in P$, because otherwise we should have $2 > s + 1$ and $s > 1$, whence $1 > s > 1$, which is impossible by virtue of transitivity of relation $>$.

2.3.10. PROPOSITION (About the Reconstruction of a Continuous Weak Order by its Restriction to a Dense Subset). *Let two continuous weak orders P_1 and P_2 coincide on a dense subset S of a connected space X. Then they coincide on the whole of X.*

PROOF. We shall show that $(x, y) \in P_1$ for some $(x, y) \in X$ implies $(x, y) \in P_2$. By proposition 2.3.7 there is an element $s \in S$ such that $(x, s) \in P_1$ and $(s, y) \in P_1$, and also an element $t \in S$ such that $(s, t) \in P_1$ and $(t, y) \in P_1$ (fig. 30). Define the sets

$$U = \{z : z \in X,\ (z, s) \in P_1\}$$

and

$$V = \{z : z \in X,\ (t, z) \in P_1\},$$

which are open neighborhoods of points x and y, respectively. Note that their closures have an empty intersection

$$[U] \cap [V] = \emptyset,$$

and for all $s' \in S \cap U$ and $t' \in S \cap V$ it holds $(s', s) \in P_1$ and $(t, t') \in P_1$. By virtue of our assumption we obtain $(s', s) \in P_2$ and $(t, t') \in P_2$. According to item 1 of proposition 2.2.13, we have

$$S \cap U \subset \{z : z \in X,\ (z, s) \in P_2\} \subset \{z : z \in X,\ (z, s) \in R_2\}$$

and

$$S \cap V \subset \{z : z \in X,\ (t, z) \in P_2\} \subset \{z : z \in X,\ (t, z) \in R_2\},$$

where R_2 is dual to P_2. Since relation P_2 is continuous, the sets

$$\{z : z \in X,\ (z, s) \in R_2\}$$

and

$$\{z : z \in X,\ (t, z) \in R_2\}$$

are closed. Therefore,

$$[S \cap U] \subset \{z : z \in X,\ (z, s) \in R_2\}$$

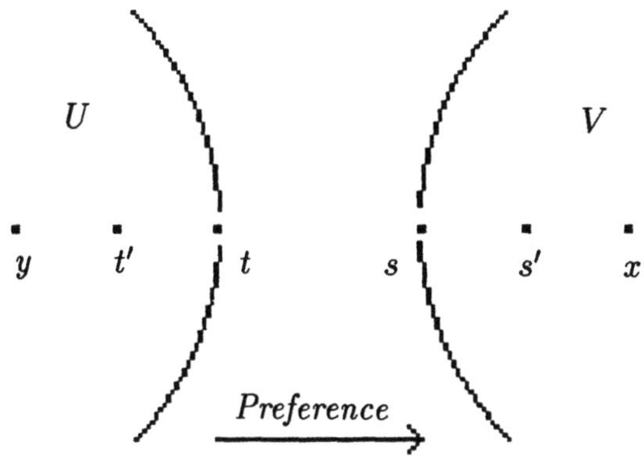

Fig. 30

and

$$[S \cap V] \subset \{z : z \in X,\ (t, z) \in R_2\}.$$

Since $x \in [S \cap U]$ and $y \in [S \cap V]$, we obtain $(x, s) \in R_2$ and $(t, y) \in R_2$. By our assumption $(s, t) \in P_1$ implies $(s, t) \in P_2$, and by virtue of items 2–3 of proposition 2.2.13 we get the required $(x, y) \in P_2$.

Similarly, one can prove that $(x, y) \in P_2$ implies $(x, y) \in P_1$ for any $x, y \in X$.

The following examples demonstrate that the connectedness of X and the condition that P_1 and P_2 are weak orders are essential for the validity of the above proposition.

2.3.11. Example. Let X be the set of real numbers except the interval $(0; 1)$. Let P_1 be the relation "to be greater than" and P_2 coincide with P_1 except for the pair $(1, 0)$, not belonging to P_2, i.e. let points 0 and 1 be indifferent with respect to P_2. Obviously, P_1 and P_2 are continuous weak orders, coinciding on dense subset $S \subset X$, where S is the set of real numbers except the segment $[0; 1]$. Since X is not connected, the statement of proposition 2.3.10 is not fulfilled.

2.3.12. Example. Let X be the segment $[0; 1]$ and S be the half-open interval $(0; 1]$. Let P_1 be the relation "to be greater than" and P_2 coincide with P_1 on S, but let the point 0 be indifferent to all others with respect to P_2. Obviously, P_1 and P_2 are continuous partial orders on the connected space X, and P_1 is a weak order, coinciding with P_2 on the dense subset S. Nevertheless,

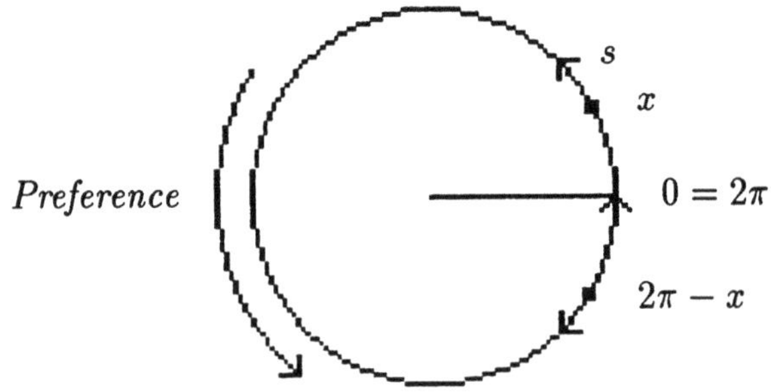

Fig. 31

P_1 doesn't coincide with P_2 over the whole of X.

The above propositions prove that a continuous weak order can be reconstructed by its restriction to a dense subset of its domain of definition. Nevertheless, to construct a continuous weak order on a space X it is not sufficient to define a continuous weak order on its dense subset, because no continuous extension to X may exist. Similarly, a continuous function is reconstructable by its restriction to a dense subset of its domain of definition, but can have no continuous extension to its closure (as $y = 1/x$). Tipical problems arise at the points of discontinuity of the first and second genus, the analogies with which we illustrate with the following examples.

2.3.13. Example (Order Discontinuity of the First Genus). Let X be the circumference $[0; 2\pi)$. Let its dense subset S be the same circumference except point 0 (fig. 31). Define P to be the relation "to be greater than" on S, which is obviously continuous. We shall prove that there is no continuous extension of P to a continuous weak order P' on X. Assume the contrary, i.e. that there exists such P'. If $P' = P$, then the point 0 is indifferent to all other points with respect to P'. In this case, as shown by example 2.3.6, the relation P' is not a weak order, against the assumption. Therefore, $P' \neq P$ and, consequently, there is an element $s \in S$ such that either $(s, 0) \in P'$, or $(0, s) \in P'$. Consider the first possibility. Since P' is continuous, there exists an open neigborhood U of the point 0 such that

$$U = \{x : x \in X,\ (s, x) \in P'\}.$$

Since X is a circumference, U contains all points sufficiently close to 2π. If x is sufficiently small, then

$$(s, 2\pi - x) \in P'.$$

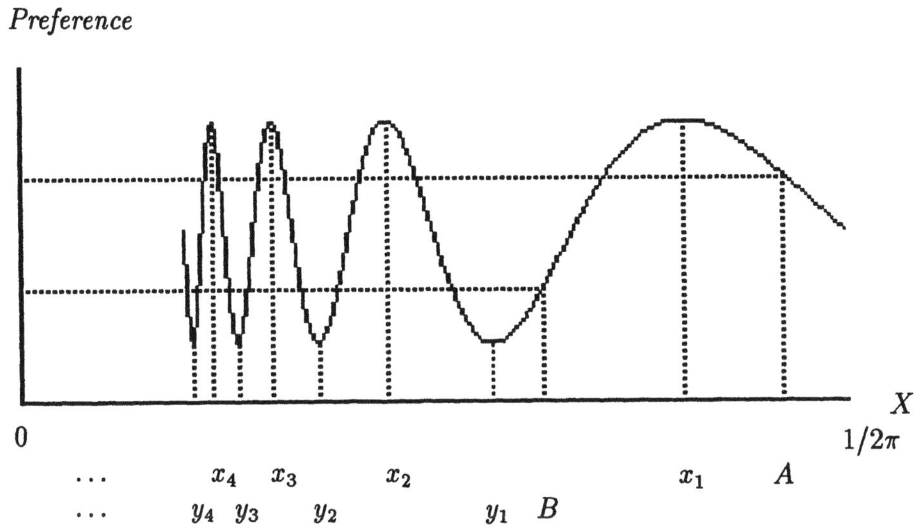

Fig. 32

On the other hand, if x is sufficiently small, then $2\pi - x > s$, whence by definition of P and P' we have

$$(2\pi - x, s) \in P',$$

in contradiction to the asymmetry of P'. The second possibility $(0, s) \in P'$ is brought to contradiction in the same way.

In the above example we draw analogy to a point of discontinuity of a function, when both left-hand and right-hand limits exist, but don't equal. Now we shall consider the case, when these limits don't exist either.

2.3.14. Example (Order Discontinuity of the Second Genus). Let X be the segment $[0; 1/2\pi]$ and S be the half-open interval $(0; 1/2\pi]$, which is dense in X. Define a weak order on S to be

$$P = \{(x, y) : x, y \in S, \ \sin\frac{1}{x} > \sin\frac{1}{y}\}$$

(fig 32). Since the sets

$$\{x : x \in S, \ \sin\frac{1}{x} > \sin\frac{1}{x^0}\}$$

and

$$\{x : x \in S, \ \sin\frac{1}{x^0} > \sin\frac{1}{x}\}$$

are open in S for every $x^0 \in S$, the weak order P is continuous on S. We shall show that there is no continuous weak order on X, coinciding with P on S. Assume the contrary, i.e. that there exists such a weak order P'. Let R' be dual to P'. Define two sequences

$$x_n = (\pi/2 + 2\pi n)^{-1} \underset{n\to\infty}{\longrightarrow} 0,$$

and

$$y_n = (3\pi/2 + 2\pi n)^{-1} \underset{n\to\infty}{\longrightarrow} 0.$$

Put

$$A = (2\pi + \pi/6)^{-1},$$

and

$$B = (3\pi + \pi/6)^{-1}.$$

Note that

$$(x_n, A) \in P' \subset R'$$

and

$$(B, y_n) \in P' \subset R'$$

for all $n = 1, 2 \ldots$. Since by assumption P' is continuous on X, the sets

$$\{x : x \in X, \ (x, A) \in R'\}$$

and

$$\{x : x \in X, \ (B, x) \in R'\}$$

are closed, whence we obtain that $(0, A) \in R'$ and $(B, 0) \in R'$. By transitivity of R' (item 3 of proposition 2.2.13) we have $(B, A) \in R'$, and therefore $(A, B) \notin P'$ in contradicition to $(A, B) \in P$.

To end the section we conclude that the proved properties of continuous weak orders make them similar to continuous functions, which is convinient for their analysis and applications in decision-making models. In the next section the mentioned analogy will be deepened by numerical representations of weak orders.

2.4 Numerical Representation of Orderings

One of the main problems in utility theory, where preferences are studies, is the representation of orders by real-value order-preserving functions. These functions are called *preference functions, objective functions, goal functions, utility functions,* or *monotone functions.*

2.4.1. DEFINITION. A *goal function* of a weak order (preference) P on a set X is defined to be a real-value function $f(x)$ such that

$$f(x) > f(y) \text{ if and only if } (x, y) \in P$$

for every $x, y \in X$.

Actually we have introduced a goal function in example 2.3.14, having defined a weak order by means of a real-value function $\sin \frac{1}{x}$. Generally speaking, any real-value function on a given set induces a weak order on it. It implies that partial orders, which are not weak orders, cannot be represented by goal functions. Their numerical representations are much more complex, like vector-functions, mappings into the set of intervals, etc.

To be represented by a goal function, a weak order must have properties similar to properties of real numbers. Let us give a simple example of an order, which cannot be represented by a goal function.

2.4.2. EXAMPLE (An Order Unrepresentable by a Goal Function). Consider the *lexicographic order* on the plane, defined by the rule

$$(x', y') \succ (x'', y'') \text{ if either } x' > x'', \text{ or } x' = x'' \text{ and } y' > y''$$

(fig. 33). The lexicographic order cannot be represented by a goal function, otherwise for every x it would be

$$f(x, 0) < f(x, 1),$$

what implies the existence of an uncountable family of disjoint intervals on the real line. Since each interval contains a rational number, it is impossible.

By virtue of proposition 2.2.14 every weak order P on X separates X into disjoint classes of indifferent elements. Obviously, these classes are strictly ordered. Therefore we can reduce the problem of numerical representation of a weak order to the problem of numerical representation of the associated strictly ordered quotient set. Thus we come to the following proposition.

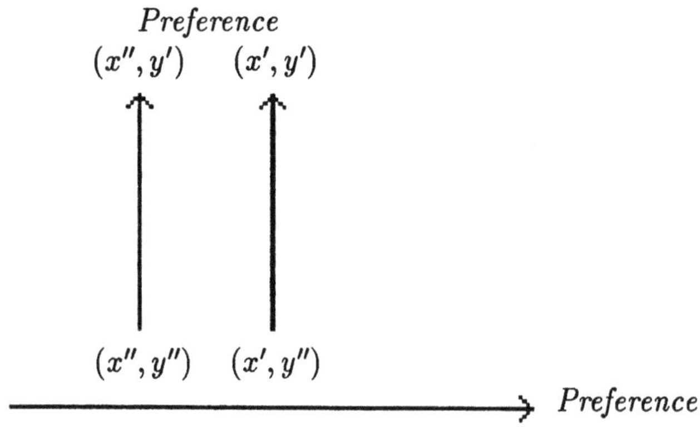

Fig. 33

2.4.3. Proposition (On Reduction of Numerical Representation Problem). *A continuous weak order can be represented by a continuous goal function if and only if there exists a goal function on its strictly ordered quotient set, continuous with respect to the topology induced by the strict order.*

Now we shall prove the representation theorem, formulated for strict orders. Taking into account what has been said, it solves the representation problem for weak orders as well.

2.4.4. Theorem (About the Existence of a Goal Function). *Let X be a strict, or in dual terms linear ordered set, regarded as a topological space with the topology induced by the given strict order $\succ$. Then the following conditions are equivalent:*

1. *There exists a goal function on X.*

2. *There exists a monotone homeomorphism from X into the interval $(0;1)$.*

3. *The topology on X induced by the strict order has a countable base.*

4. *X as a topological space is separable and has no more than a countable set of jumps (empty intervals).*

Proof. We shall state the following implications:

$$2 \Rightarrow 1 \Rightarrow 4 \Rightarrow 2,$$
$$2 \Rightarrow 3 \Rightarrow 4 \Rightarrow 2.$$

Obviously, 2 implies 1 and 3.

We show that condition 1 implies 4. Let a mapping $f : X \to (0;1)$ be monotone. Put

$$Y = f(X).$$

Since Y is a subset of the set of real numbers, Y has a countable dense subset $S \subset Y$. Then the inverse image $f^{-1}(S)$ is a countable dense subset of X. Indeed, the monotone mapping $f(x)$ is a one-to-one correspondence. Since the image $f(A)$ of every interval $A \subset X$ is an interval in Y, it follows that $f^{-1}(s) \in A$ for $s \in S \cap f(A)$. If X had an uncountable set of jumps, then the monotone mapping $f(x)$ would transfer it into an uncountable set of disjoint real intervals, which is impossible (cf. with example 2.4.2).

We show that condition 3 implies condition 4. The existence of a countable dense subset in X follows from the countability of the base. We shall prove that the set of jumps is countable. For each jump, which is an empty interval

$$(a;b) = \{x : x \in X,\ a \prec x,\ x \prec b\},$$

define an open neighborhood of point a to be

$$U(a) = \{x : x \in X,\ x \prec b\}.$$

Let

$$O(a) \subset U(a)$$

be a neighborhood of point a in the countable base. Since the interval $(a;b)$ is empty, $O(a)$ doesn't contain points succeeding a. Therefore if $(a';b')$ and $(a'';b'')$ are two empty intervals, where $a' \neq a''$, then the associated neighborhoods $O(a')$ and $O(a'')$ in the countable base are different. This implies that the number of jumps cannot exceed the cardinality of the base.

We show that condition 4 implies condition 2. Define S to consist of the points of a dense countable subset of X, the endpoints of empty intervals, and also the first and the last elements of X, if there are any in X. By condition 4 set S is countable, and we can index it by positive integers:

$$S = \{s_1, s_2, \ldots\}.$$

We shall construct a mapping $f(d)$ of some subset D of dyadic rational points in the interval $(0;1)$ onto the set S.

By D^n we denote the set of dyadic rational fractions in the interval $(0;1)$ of the form $m/2^n$, i.e.

$$D^1 = \{1/2\},$$

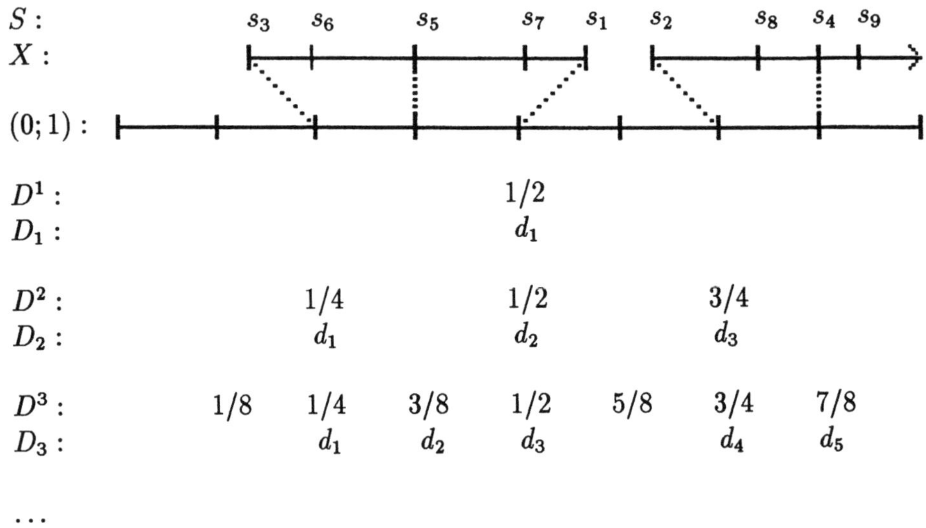

Fig. 34

$$D^2 = \{1/4, 1/2, 3/4\},$$

$$\dots$$

We shall construct D and $f(d)$ by induction on n, eliminating from D^n some points and defining $f(d)$ on the remainder $D_n \subset D^n$ (fig. 34).

1⁰. Put

$$D_1 = D^1,$$

and

$$f(1/2) = s_1$$

2⁰. Suppose that $D_n \subset D^n$ and the order-preserving mapping $f : D_n \to S$ are already constructed. Let

$$d_1 < \dots < d_M$$

be the points making up D_n.

If there is $s \in S$ such that

$$s \prec f(d_1),$$

then we choose it to have the minimal index in S and put

$$f(1/2^{n+1}) = s,$$

otherwise we exclude from D^{n+1} all the points less than d_1.

For each $m = 1, \ldots, M-1$ we proceed as follows. If there is $s \in S$ such that

$$f(d_m) \prec s \prec f(d_{m+1}),$$

then we choose it to have the minimal index in S and put

$$f(d_m + 1/2^{n+1}) = s,$$

otherwise we exclude from D^{n+1} all the points between d_m and d_{m+1}.

If there is $s \in S$ such that

$$f(d_M) \prec s,$$

then we choose it to have the minimal index in S and put

$$f(d_M + 1/2^{n+1}) = s,$$

otherwise exclude from D^{n+1} all the points greater than d_M.

We form D_{n+1} from the points of the D^{n+1} left after these exclusions together with the points of D_n. The order-preserving mapping $f : D_{n+1} \to S$ is defined at the present and all previous inductive steps.

We define

$$D = \bigcup_{n=1}^{\infty} D_n.$$

We show that $f(d)$ maps D onto the whole of S. Assume the contrary, and suppose s_k to be the element of S with the minimal index among that ones, which haven't the inverse image in D. Then either

$$s_k \prec s_i$$

for all $i = 1, \ldots, k-1$, or

$$s_k \succ s_i$$

for all $i = 1, \ldots, k-1$, or

$$s_i \prec s_k \prec s_j,$$

where s_i and s_j are adjacent with respect to the order $\prec$ among that ones, indicies of which are less than k. Since by assumption s_k is the element of S with the minimal index among that ones, which haven't the inverse image in D, elements s_i and s_j have their inverse images in D_n for certain n. But then it is s_k that is picked up at the $(n+1)$st inductive step as the element of S with the minimal index among the ones lying between s_i and s_j (or as the extreme element with respect to all elements that have been picked up earlier), against the assumption.

Now we determine the set $Y \subset (0;1)$ which is homeomeomorphic to X. Consider an arbitrary point $x \in X \setminus S$. By definition of S the point x is neither an extreme element of X, nor an endpoint of empty interval. Therefore, the set

$$A = \{s : s \in S,\ s \prec x\}$$

has no maximal element, and the set

$$B = \{s : s \in S, x \prec s\}$$

has no minimal element, which is also valid for their inverse images $f^{-1}(A)$ and $f^{-1}(B)$. Since $f^{-1}(A)$ and $f^{-1}(B)$ are bounded sets of real numbers, there exist the upper bound

$$y = \sup f^{-1}(A)$$

and the lower bound

$$z = \inf f^{-1}(B),$$

where obviously

$$y \leq z.$$

We show that

$$y = z.$$

If not, then there would exist a dyadic rational number d such that

$$y < d < z,$$

whence d is not used in the construction of D_n for all n. Being a dyadic rational number, $d \in D^n$ for certain n, hence, there exist d'—the maximal, and d''—the minimal elements of D_n, picked up in our construction, such that

$$d' < d < d''.$$

But then $(f(d'); f(d''))$ is an empty interval in S, which is impossible, because it is a neighborhood of x in X and, consequently, must contain at least one point of the dense subset S. The obtained contradiction proves that $y = z$, and we can define $f(y) = x$. Thus the order-preserving one-to-one mapping $y = f^{-1}(x)$ from the set X into the interval $(0;1)$ is defined.

We put

$$Y = f^{-1}(X).$$

Let us show that both $f(y)$ on Y, and $f^{-1}(x)$ on X are continuous. By construction the inverse image of every interval in X is also an interval in Y.

Hence, the mapping $f(y)$ is continuous. To prove the continuity of the inverse mapping $f^{-1}(x)$, it sufficies to show that $f(U)$ is open for every

$$U = \{y : y \in Y,\ a < y < b\},$$

where $0 \leq a < b \leq 1$. If y is the minimal, but not the maximal element in U, then there exist $y' \in U$ and the dyadic rational number d, not used in the construction of D, such that

$$a < d < y < y'.$$

Repeating just adduced arguments, we obtain that $f(y)$ is either the first element of X, or the right-hand endpoint of some empty interval. Therefore, the half-open interval $[f(y); f(y'))$ is open in X, whence $f(y)$ is contained in $f(U)$ together with its neigborhood. Similarly, if y is maximal, but not minimal element of U, then $f(y)$ is contained in $f(U)$ together with a half-open interval, which is open in X. Finally, if y is the only element in U, then $f(y)$ is an isolated point in X and is itself open. Thus for each point $y \in U$ its image $f(y)$ is contained in $f(U)$ together with its neighborhood. Hence, $f(U)$ is open, as required.

The above theorem is a generalized version of known results. The problem of the existence of a monotone real-value function on an ordered set was posed by Cantor (1895). Sufficient conditions for representation of a weak order on a connected topological space, obtained in (Eilenberg 1941), were refined by Debreu (1954; 1964). For convex sets the representation problem was solved by Fishburn (1983). In our formulation we make an accent on that the existence of a goal function depends not so much on topological properties of given space, as on the properties of the ordering itself, more precisely, on the properties of its quotient set. Indeed, the quotient set can be regarded as a topological space with the order topology independently of whether some topology is defined on the basic set. Topological properties are essential, only when we are interested in the continuity of the goal function. In this case the topology on the quotient set induced by the strict order must be included into the quotient topology induced by the topology on the basic set. Thus we separate the problem of existence of a goal function and the problem of its continuity.

To end the section let us illustrate that the conditions of the above theorem are essential. Even such strong restrictions, as the compactness and the separability are not sufficient for the existence of a goal function, if conditions 3 and 4 are not satisfied.

2.4.5. EXAMPLE. Consider the *two arrows space*—the strictly ordered topological space, consisting of continuum of pairs of points, ordered lexicographically. In other words, let space X consist of the couples (x, y), where x

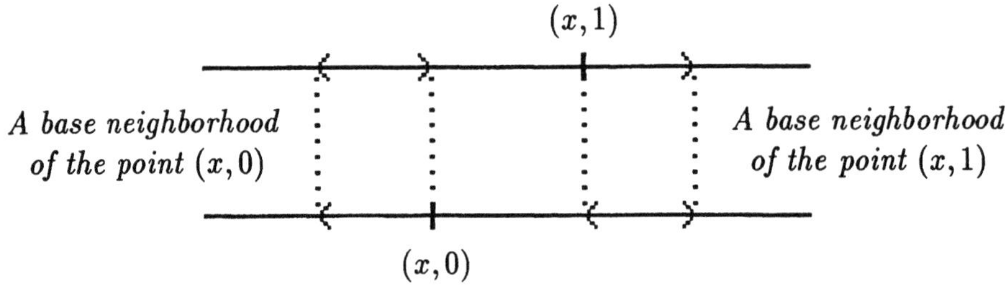

Fig. 35

runs through the segment [0; 1] and y adopts the values 0, or 1, ordered by the rule:

$$(x', y') \succ (x'', y'') \text{ if either } x' > x'', \text{or } x' = x'' \text{ and } y' > y''.$$

The base neighborhoods are shown in fig. 35. The two arrows space is a separable compactum in the order topology, induced by the defined order (Alexandroff & Urysohn 1929). However, it hasn't a countable base. By condition 3 we obtain that it is impossible to define a goal function, representing the given order. We could verify it directly, following the reasons from example 2.4.2.

Now suppose that for the same topological space we define another order on X, for every irrational x putting $(x, 0)$ and $(x, 1)$ to be indifferent, i.e. eliminating corresponding pairs of couples $((x, 1), (x, 0))$ from the initial order. It is easy to see that the obtained relation is a weak order with a countable set of jumps. Also note that its quotient set is different than that of the two arrows space, and that the new relation can be represented by a goal function, which doesn't follow from classical results of Debreu (1954; 1964) and Fishburn (1983).

Chapter 3

Aggregation of Fixed Independent Preferences

3.1 Introductory Remarks

According to the established interpretation of Arrow's theorem, the collective choice is rational, if we give up one of Arrow's axioms A1–A5. The rejection of axiom A1 implies the consideration of two alternatives, when no paradoxes of voting arise, the ordinal and the cardinal approaches are equivalent, and a majority rule is acceptable in every respect. Since the problem of aggregation of preferences becomes trivial, we do not analyse this case. We also retain the unanimity axiom A3 as quite evident. Therefore we shall reject alternately axiom A2 (universality), A4 (independence of irrelevant alternatives), and later A5 (prohibition of dictatorship).

Giving up the universality principle (A2) in the present chapter, we assume that individual preferences are fixed (a partial restriction of the universality condition we also consider in chapter 7). By theorem 2.4.4 in a quite general case both individual and collective orderings can be represented by numerical goal functions. If we suppose that collective goal function $f(x)$ is a function of individual utilities, then the task is reduced to the construction of the collective goal function

$$f(x) = f(u_1(x), \dots, u_n(x)) = f(u_1, \dots, u_n),$$

where

$$u_i = u(x),$$

are utility functions of individuals $i = 1, \dots, n$ on the set of alternatives X.

The unanimity condition (A3) means that

$$u_i' < u_i'' \text{ for all } i = 1, \dots, n$$

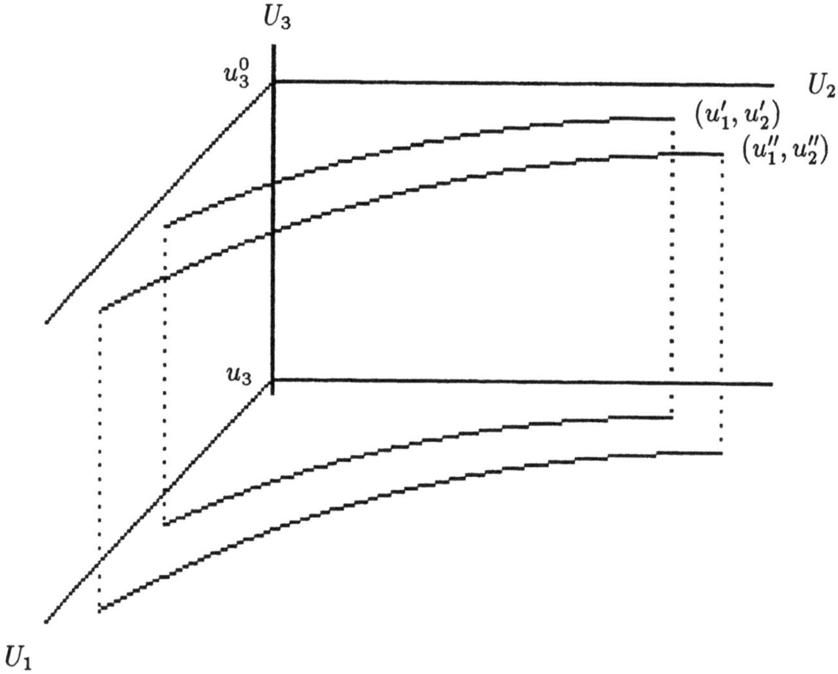

Fig. 36

implies

$$f(u_1', \ldots, u_n') < f(u_1'', \ldots, u_n'').$$

Since axiom A4 supposes the existence of at least two situations, it is meaningless for fixed preferences. Axiom A5 implies that at least two arguments u_i, u_j of the function $f(u_1, \ldots, u_n)$ are significant, i.e. an increment of each implies the increment of the function.

Since our consideration turns out to be trivial, we need additional assumptions for the analysis of the given model. We shall strengthen axiom A3 up to the Pareto principle, whence we shall deduce the strict monotonicy of the goal function $f(u_1, \ldots, u_n)$ with respect to every argument. We shall also assume the independence of individual preferences (other than the independence in axiom A4 for varying individual preferences).

The independence of fixed individual preferences is in a sense a generalization of the Pareto principle, according to which an improvement for one individual with no worsening for others is a global improvement for the collective as a whole. In other words, it is meaningful to speak about a global improvement obtained with respect to a single individual utility. The independence is nothing else, but the assumption that it is meaningful to speak about global improvements with respect to each pair of individual utilities, understood equally for arbitrary fixed levels of others. We can say that every coalition of two individuals has its own preference with the same indifference curves at any two different levels of other utilities (fig. 36). The dependence implies distortions in these preference, while shifting the plane $U_1 \times U_2$ up and down the axis U_3. Let us give a strict definition.

3.1.1. DEFINITION. Let preferences of n individuals on a set of alternatives X be represented by the goal functions

$$u_i = u_i(x), \; i = 1, \ldots, n,$$

and the collective preference be represented by the goal function

$$f(x) = f(u_1(x), \ldots u_n(x)) = f(u_1, \ldots, u_n).$$

Preferences of individuals 1 and 2 are called *independent* if

$$f(u_1', u_2', u_3^0, \ldots, u_n^0) < f(u_1'', u_2'', u_3^0, \ldots, u_n^0)$$

for certain u_1', u_2', u_1'', u_2'' and $u_3^0, \ldots, u_n^0$ implies

$$f(u_1', u_2', u_3, \ldots, u_n) < f(u_1'', u_2'', u_3, \ldots, u_n)$$

for arbitrary $u_3, \ldots, u_n$. The independence of other pairs of preferences is defined similarly.

It is known that the pairwise independence of preferences under rather general assumptions is equivalent to that the collective goal function is *additive*, or *separable*, i.e. has the form

$$f(u_1, \ldots, u_n) = f_1(u_1) + \ldots + f_n(u_n).$$

Additive goal functions are often used in models, and a series of computational methods is developed for them to solve problems of mathematical programming (Hadley 1964). During the last half-century a few axiomatic theories have been proposed to represent preferences by additive goal functions. The discussion of the related questions goes back to the thirties (Ramsey 1931). Later it has been continued in the context of econometric modelling (Leontief 1947; Samuelson 1948; Von Neumann & Morgenstern 1947) and is still topical in our days. The topological conception of additivity was formulated by G. Debreu (1960). An algebraic approach, based on Hölder's theorem on ordered groups, was developed in (Krantz Luce Suppes & Tversky 1971). A survey on the approaches to the problem is given in (Fishburn & Keeney 1974). Also note that the multiplication goal function (Keeney 1974) is almost the same. In fact, taking its logarithm, we come to the summation, preserving the order information.

A considerable attention is paid in literature to practical construction of goal functions, which has applications in quality control and expert judgements. Heuristic methods of construction of additive goal functions are described and classified in Fishburn (1967), where 24 methods are listed. However, all these methods have a common disadvantage, lacking the uniqueness in the determination of the goal function. To be justified, every procedure for the construction of a goal function must be backed at least by an estimation of its accuracy.

Before we study the problem from this point of view, let us make some remarks on the nature of additive goal functions. In the simpliest case the additive goal function is a weighted sum of individual utilities

$$f(u) = f(u_1, \ldots, u_n) = \sum_{i=1}^{n} C_i u_i,$$

where weight coefficients C_i are constant. The use of goal functions of this form gives satisfactory results, even if the form of the goal function cannot be properly justified. It can be explained by the following reasons.

Let $f(u) = f(u_1, \ldots, u_n)$ be an unknown goal function. If we assume its differentiability at a certain point $u^0 = (u_1^0, \ldots, u_n^0)$, then

$$\begin{aligned} f(u) &= f(u^0) + \sum_{i=1}^{n} \frac{\partial f(u^0)}{\partial u_i}(u_i - u_i^0) + o(u - u^0) \\ &= C_0 + \sum_{i=1}^{n} C_i u_i + o(u - u^0), \end{aligned}$$

where

$$C_0 = f(u^0) - \sum_{i=1}^{n} \frac{\partial f(u^0)}{\partial u_i} u_i^0$$

and

$$C_i = \frac{\partial f(u^0)}{\partial u_i}, \quad i = 1, \ldots, n,$$

are constants, and $o(u - u^0)$ is an infinitesimal term of higher exponent than $u - u^0$. Since a goal function is defined up to a monotone transformation, the constant C_0 can be omitted, and we can take its approximation

$$f(u) \approx \sum_{i=1}^{n} C_i u_i.$$

Note that constants

$$C_i = \frac{\partial f(u^0)}{\partial u_i}, \; i = 1, \ldots, n,$$

depend on the choice of the point u^0, therefore, the goal functions of the form $\sum_{i=1}^n C_i u_i$ can be used (except for special cases), only if the considered alternatives do not differ greatly with respect to individual utilities (criteria).

The way of determination of the weight coefficients $C_1, \ldots, C_n$ is also noteworthy. Since the goal function admits the multiplication by a positive constant, it is sufficient to determine the ratios C_i/C_j, where $i, j = 1, \ldots, n$. In turn it is sufficient to consider the ratios C_i/C_j for the pairs (i, j), forming a tree with vertices $1, \ldots, n$, like C_i/C_j, where $j = 2, \ldots, n$. It is easy to see that such trees always consist of $n - 1$ pairs. Further, every ratio C_i/C_j can be determined by the conditions of compensation of utilities for ith and jth individuals only. In other words, we use the indifference curves, which are the level curves of the goal function for the coalition of ith and jth individuals, given by the sum $C_i u_i + C_j u_j$.

Similar reasons are also valid for the construction of the additive goal function, which is nothing else but a weighted sum of individual utilities with variable weight coefficients.

Results of the present chapter are published in Russian in (Tanguiane 1979a; 1980b; 1981c; 1982b; 1982c).

3.2 Construction of Approximation of Additive Goal Function

The aggregation of independent preferences can be realized by a simple algorithmic procedure. We pay the main attention to its consistency, convergence, and to restrictions on the initial data. We use minimal knowledge about preferences, and refer to order information only. Taking into account possible applications, it is essential that the aggregated preference is obtained as a goal function, which is convenient for further optimization analysis.

We shall realize the construction of collective goal function on a space of individual utilities, which is n-dimensional ($n \geq 2$) parallelepiped

$$U = U_1 \times \ldots \times U_n = [a_1; b_1] \times \ldots \times [a_n; b_n],$$

where $[a_i; b_i]$ are segments, $a_i < b_i$, $i = 1, \ldots, n$. Assume that there exists a collective preference on U—a weak order $\prec^f$ (with dual relation $\preceq^f$), represented by an additive goal function

$$f(u_1, \ldots, u_n) = f_1(u_1) + \ldots + f_n(u_n),$$

where $f_i(u_i)$, $i = 1, \ldots, n$, are continuous and increasing, but the weak order $\prec^f$ itself is not known.

Assume that two *compensation curves* (curves of compensation of individual utilities, indifference curves) M_1 and M_2—the level curves of the function $f_1(u_1) + f_2(u_2)$— are given in the coordinate plain $U_1 \times U_2$ (fig. 37).

Also assume that a compensation curve M_i—the level curve of the function $f_1(u_1)+f_i(u_i)$—is given in each coordinate plane $U_1 \times U_i$, $i = 3, \ldots, n$ (fig. 38). Suppose that the curve M_i passes through the vertices (a_1, b_i) and (b_1, a_i) of the rectangle $U_1 \times U_i$ for every $i = 2, \ldots, n$, as shown in fig. 37–38 (otherwise the points a_i and b_i can be chosen appropriately, diminishing, if necessary, the parallelepiped U). Let M_1 correspond to the level of the goal function $f_1(u_1) + f_2(u_2)$ lower than that of M_2, implying M_1 to be below M_2 in fig. 37.

By these n compensation curves we can construct an approximation $\prec^g$ of the unknown weak order $\prec^f$ by means of the following algorithmic procedure.

1. In the plane $U_1 \times U_2$ construct a "staircase" between the two curves M_1 and M_2—a polygonal line of horizontal and vertical segments with endpoints on M_1 and M_2, beginning at the point (b_1, a_2) (fig. 37). Let

$$a_1 \leq s_1^0 < s_1^1 < \ldots < s_1^K = b_1$$

be the coordinates of the verticies of this polygonal line at the axis U_1.

2. Define an increasing piecewise linear function $g_1(u_1)$ on U_1 such that

$$g_1(a_1) = 0$$

and

$$g_1(s_1^k) = \epsilon + k$$

for every $k = 0, \ldots, K$, where $\epsilon = 0$ if $s_1^0 = a_1$, and $0 < \epsilon < 1$ if $a_1 < s_1^0$, i.e. if the upper "stair" is incomplete (fig. 37).

3. On each axis U_i, $i = 2, \ldots, n$, determine the sequence

$$a_i = s_i^0 < s_1^1 < \ldots s_i^K \leq b_i$$

such that

$$(s_i^k, s_i^{K-k}) \in M_i$$

for all $k = 0, \ldots, K$ (fig. 38).

4. For each $i = 2, \ldots, n$ define an increasing piecewise linear functions $g_i(u_i)$ on U_i, putting

$$g_i(s_i^k) = k,$$

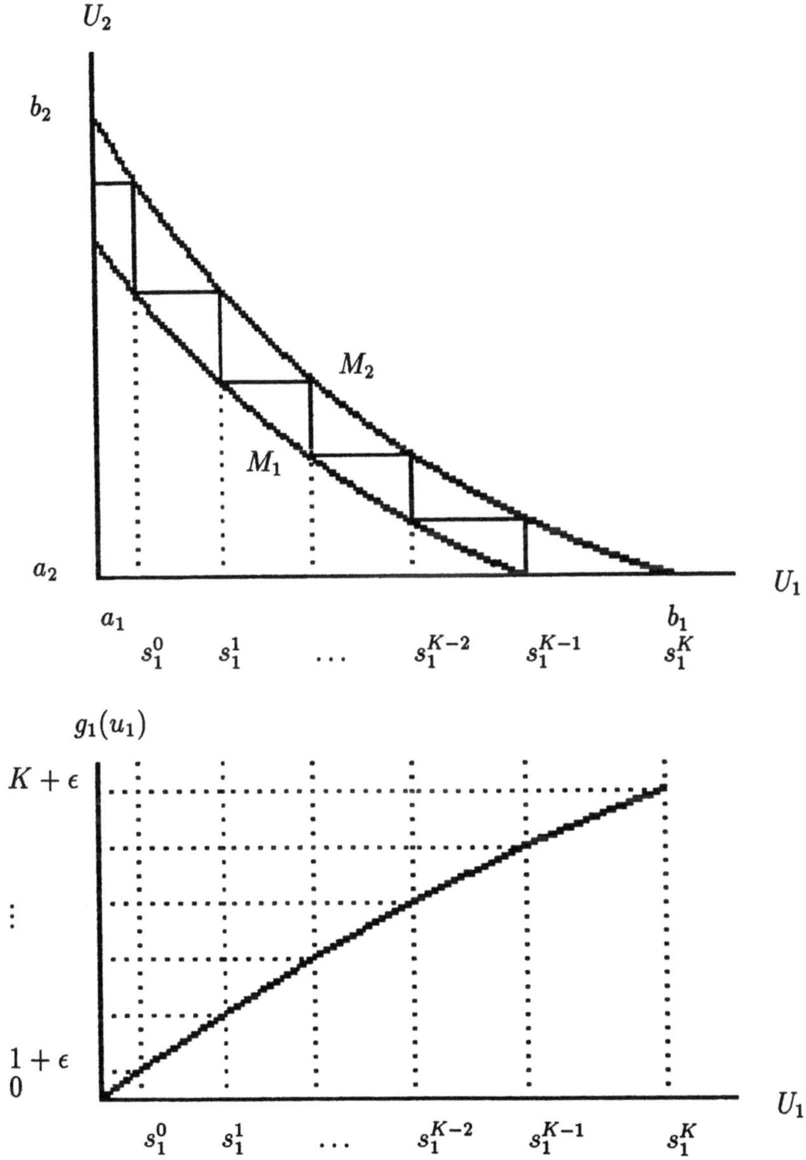

U_2
b_2
M_2
M_1
a_2
U_1
a_1
b_1
s_1^0 s_1^1 ... s_1^{K-2} s_1^{K-1} s_1^K
$g_1(u_1)$
$K+\epsilon$
$1+\epsilon$
0
U_1
s_1^0 s_1^1 ... s_1^{K-2} s_1^{K-1} s_1^K

Fig. 37

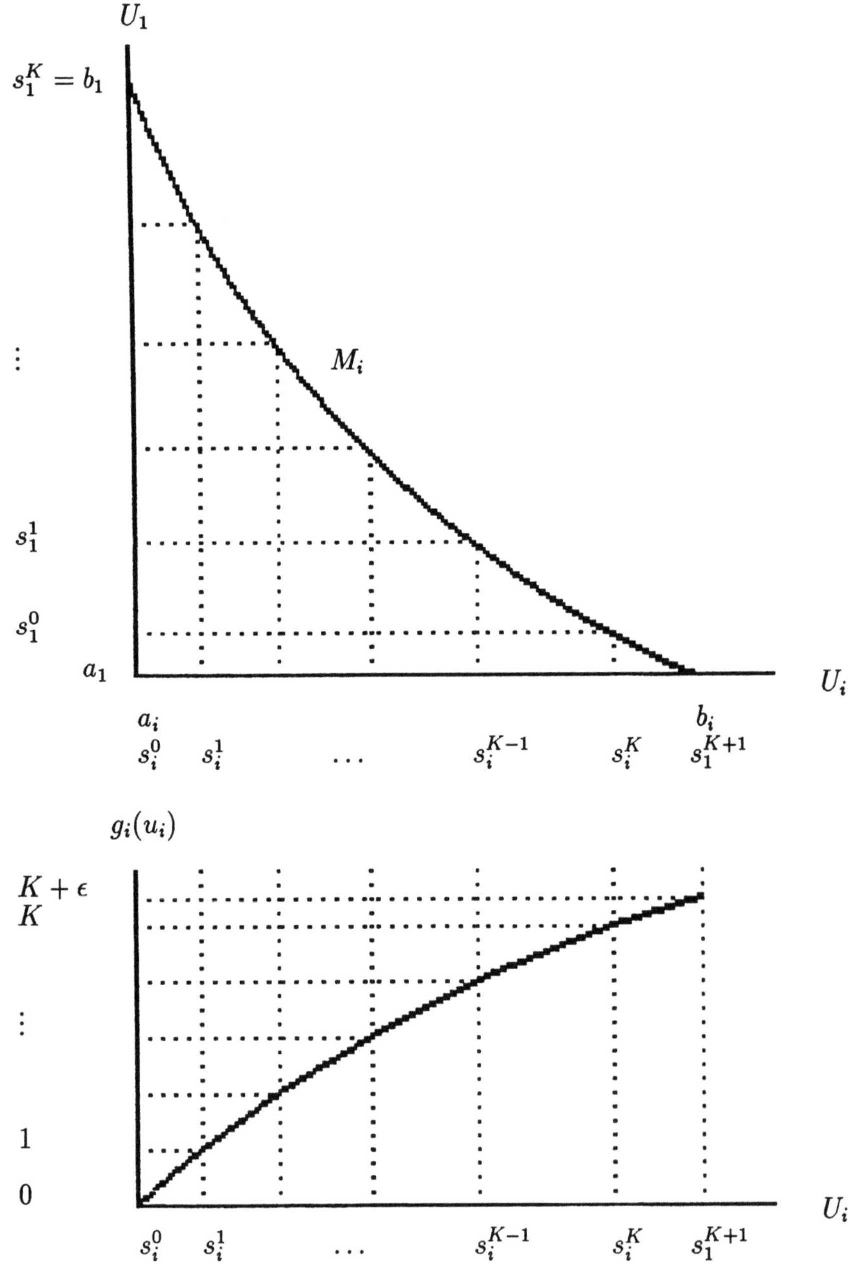

U_1
$s_1^K = b_1$
M_i
s_1^1
s_1^0
a_1
U_i
a_i
b_i
s_i^0 s_i^1 ... s_i^{K-1} s_i^K s_1^{K+1}
$g_i(u_i)$
$K + \epsilon$
K
1
0
U_i
s_i^0 s_i^1 ... s_i^{K-1} s_i^K s_1^{K+1}

Fig. 38

$k = 0, \ldots, K$, and

$$g_i(b_i) = K + \epsilon,$$

where ϵ is the same as in item 2 (fig. 38).

5. Define weak order $\prec^g$ on U by the additive goal function

$$g(u) = g(u_1, \ldots, u_n) = g_1(u_1) + \ldots + g_n(u_n),$$

which is obviously continuous and increasing with respect to every variable.

The idea of the given algorithm is the following. Assuming the existence of the unknown additive goal function, we can normalize it so that its values at the compensation curves M_1 and M_2 would differ by 1. Then each horizontal segment of the polygonal line constructed in item 1 corresponds to the increment of the goal function $f_1(u_1) + f_2(u_2)$ by one, with the increment of $f_1(u_1)$ only, since u_2 is constant. This is reflected by item 2. Items 3 and 4 are based on the observation that if the function $f_1(u_1)$ increases by 1 at a certain interval on axis U_1, then the function $f_i(u_1)$ decreases by 1 at the corresponding interval on axis U_i—to retain constant the sum $f_1(u_1) + f_i(u_i)$ along the compensation curve M_i.

By the way note that the number K of points of the segmentation $s_1^0, s_1^1, \ldots, s_1^K \in U_1$ is always finite, otherwise the continuous function $f_1(u_1)$ would be unbounded on the segment $[a_1; b_1]$, which is impossible.

A formal justification of the algorithm is given in the next section.

3.3 Accuracy of Approximation of Additive Goal Function

Since goal functions are defined up to monotone transformations, it is senseless to estimate the distance between them in common functional metrics. We define the distance between goal functions as the distance between the associated weak orders. In our case the orders $\preceq^f, \preceq^g$ are close subsets of compactum $U_1 \times \ldots \times U_n \times U_1 \times \ldots \times U_n$ with common Eucleadian metrics ρ. Therefore, we can use the *Hausdorff distance* d, which is defined for closed subsets A and B of a compactum, as following (Engelking 1977, p. 370):

$$d(A, B) = \max\{\sup_{a \in A} \inf_{b \in B} \rho(a, b); \sup_{b \in B} \inf_{a \in A} \rho(a, b)\}.$$

To estimate the closeness of binary relations we shall refer to the *oscillation of a function* (Shilov 1973), with which we characterize the compensation curves $M_2, \ldots, M_n$. For example, consider a weak order on rectangle

$Y \times Z = [a; b] \times [c; d]$, represented by a continuous increasing goal function $f = f(y, z)$. Then each level curve of the function $f(y, z)$ is a graph of some decreasing continuous function

$$z = m(y),$$

the oscillation of which is

$$\omega_m(\rho) = \sup_{y',y'' \in Y : |y'-y''| \leq \rho} | m(y') - m(y'') | .$$

It is known that the oscillation is a continuous nondecreasing function, defined for all $\rho \geq 0$ and equal to zero at the point 0.

Now we can estimate the distance between the original unknown goal function $f_1(u_1) + \ldots + f_n(u_n)$ and its approximation $g_1(u_1) + \ldots + g_n(u_n)$.

3.3.1. THEOREM (About the Accuracy of Approximation of a Separable Goal Function). *Under the restrictions of the construction from the previous section the Hausdorff distance between $\preceq^f$ and $\preceq^g$ satisfies the inequality*

$$d(\preceq^t, \preceq^g) < 3n \max\{\rho, \omega_2(\rho), \ldots, \omega_n(\rho)\},$$

where ω_i are the oscillations of the compensation curves $M_i \in U_1 \times U_i$, considered as functions of u_1, $i = 2, \ldots, n$, and ρ is the horizontal distance between M_1 and M_2, i.e.

$$\rho = \sup_{y',y'' \in U_1 : (y,z) \in M_1, (y'',z) \in M_2, z \in U_2} | y' - y'' | .$$

PROOF. Put $s_1^{-1} = a_1$ and $s_1^{K+1} = b_i$ for every $i = 2, \ldots, n$. Put

$$S_1 = \{s_1^{-1}, s_1^0, \ldots, s_1^K\}$$

and

$$S_i = \{s_i^0, s_i^1, \ldots, s_i^{K+1}\}$$

for every $i = 2, \ldots, n$. Let

$$S = S_1 \times \ldots \times S_n,$$

i.e. S is the set of nodes of the network in the parallelepiped U, through which the level hypersurfaces of the goal function $f_1(u_1) + \ldots + f_n(u_n)$ and of its approximation $g_1(u_1) + \ldots + g_n(u_n)$ pass. The only uncertainty is inherent in the boundary nodes of the network with first coordinates equal to s_1^{-1}, or ith coordinates equal to s_i^{K+1}. When the upper stair constructed in the first item of the algorithm is incomplete, the values of the goal functions at these boundary points are not determined accurately, but estimated within $0 < \epsilon < 1$.

The idea of the following proof is based on the observation that S divides U into $n(K+1)$ small parallelepipeds, in vertices of which the values of the goal functions $f(u)$ and $g(u)$ are equal. By strict monotonicity of the goal functions $f(u)$ and $g(u)$ the level hypersurfaces, passing through the vertices of such a parallelepiped, cannot come out of it, which implies that their difference is bounded by its size. All other level hypersurfaces are constrained by these reference hypersurfaces, hence their deviations can be estimated. Finally, the estimation of the distance between the preferences $\preceq^f$ and $\preceq^g$ is derived from the estimation of maximal deviations of the reference level hypersurfaces of the two preferences.

Before we continue the proof, let us formulate an auxiliary proposition.

3.3.2. LEMMA (About the Ordering of the Nodes of the Network). *Let*

$$s^k = (s_1^{k_1}, \ldots, s_n^{k_n}) \in S,$$
$$s^m = (s_1^{m_1}, \ldots, s_n^{m_n}) \in S.$$

Then $k_1 + \ldots k_n + n \leq m_1 + \ldots + m_n$ *implies* $s^k \preceq^f s^m$ *and* $s^k \preceq^g s^m$.

PROOF. Normalize the additive goal function $f_1(u_1) + \ldots + f_n(u_n)$ to make

$$f_i(a_i) = 0$$

for every $i = 1, \ldots, n$ and

$$f_1(s_1^K) = f_1(s_1^{K-1}) + 1.$$

Then by our construction we have

$$f_1(s_1^{k_1}) = k_1 + \epsilon$$

for all $k_1 = 0, \ldots, K$, where $\epsilon = 0$ if $a_1 = s_1^0$, and $0 < \epsilon < 1$ if $a_1 < s_1^0$. Hence,

$$f_i(s_i^{k_1}) = k_i$$

for all $k_i = 0, \ldots, K$, and

$$f_i(b_i) = K + \epsilon$$

for all $i = 2, \ldots, K$. Thus,

$$k_1 \leq f_1(s_1^{k_1}) \leq k_1 + 1$$

for any $s_1^{k_1} \in S_1$, and

$$k_i - 1 \le f_i(s_i^{k_i}) \le k_i$$

for any $s_i^{k_i} \in S_i$, $i = 2, \dots, n$. Therefore,

$$k_1 + \dots + k_n - n - 1 \le f_1(s_1^{k_1}) + \dots + f_n(s_n^{k_n}) \le k_1 + \dots + k_n + 1$$

for any $(s_1^{k_1}, \dots, s_n^{k_n}) \in S$.

Hence,

$$f(s^k) \le k_1 + \dots + k_n + 1,$$

and

$$m_1 + \dots + m_n - n + 1 \le f(s^m).$$

Since by assumption

$$k_1 + \dots + k_n + n \le m_1 + \dots + m_n,$$

we obtain

$$f(s^k) \le f(s^m),$$

or $s^k \preceq^f s^m$. The same is valid for $\preceq^g$, hence $s^k \preceq^g s^m$, as required.

PROOF OF THE THEOREM. For every $i = 1, \dots, n$ denote

$$h_i = \max_{s_i^{k_i} \in S_i} \{ | s_i^{k_i} - s_i^{k_i - 1} | \},$$

and put

$$h = \max\{h_1, \dots, h_n\}.$$

Let $u = (u_1, \dots, u_n) \in U$ and $v = (v_1, \dots, v_n) \in U$ be such that $u \preceq^f v$. We shall show that there exist $s^k, s^m \in S$ such that

$$\rho(u, s^k) \le (n + \sqrt{n})h,$$
$$\rho(v, s^m) \le (n + \sqrt{n})h,$$

where ρ is the distance in n-dimensional Eucleadian space E^n, and $s^k \preceq^g s^m$. For this purpose we take $s^{k'}, s^{m'} \in S$ such that $u \in [s^{k'}; s^{k'+e}]$ and $v \in [s^{m'-e}; s^{m'}]$, where $[s^{k'}; s^{k'+e}]$ denotes the small parallelepiped with diagonal vertices $k' = (k_1', \dots, k_n')$ and $k' + e = (k_1' + 1, \dots, k_n' + 1)$, i.e.

$$[s^{k'}; s^{k'+e}] = \{u = (u_1, \dots, u_n) : s_i^{k_i'} \le u_i \le s^{k_i'+1}, \ i = 1, \dots, n\}$$

(fig. 39). The parallelepiped $[s^{m'-e}; s^{m'}]$ is defined similarly. Since $\preceq^f$ is strictly monotone,

$$s^{k'} \preceq^f u \preceq^f s^{k'+e}$$

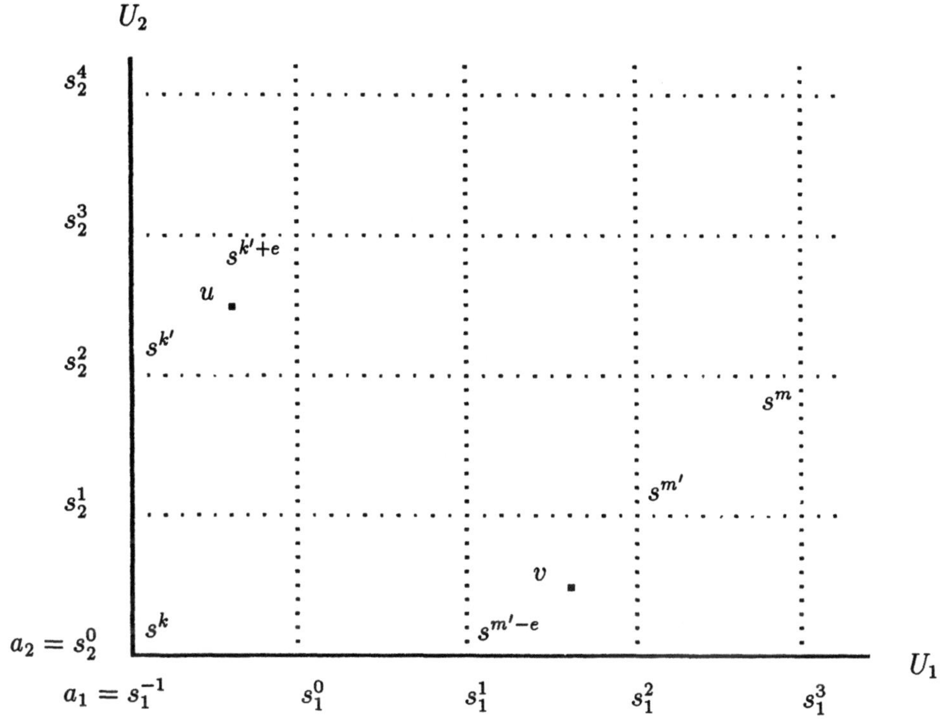

Fig. 39

and

$$s^{m'-e} \preceq^f v \preceq^f s^{m'}.$$

Note that $s^{k'} \preceq^f s^{m'}$ (otherwise $v \preceq^f s^{m'} \prec^f s^{k'} \preceq^f u$, hence by 2.2.13 $v \prec^f u$, against the assumption). Therefore,

$$k_1' + \ldots + k_n' - n \leq m_1' + \ldots + m_n'$$

(otherwise $m_1' + \ldots + m_n' + n < k_1' + \ldots + k_n'$, consequently, by increase of $f(u_1, \ldots, u_n)$ with respect to every u_i and lemma 3.3.2 we come to $s^{m'} \prec^f s^{k'}$ against the obtained realition). Define

$$k = (k_1, \ldots, k_n)$$

such that

$$k_i \leq k_i', \ i = 1, \ldots n,$$

and

$$k_1 + \ldots + k_n = k_1' + \ldots + k_n' - n.$$

If there is no such k, put

$$k = (-1, 0, \dots, 0),$$

i.e. let

$$s^k = a = (a_1, \dots, a_n).$$

Similarly, define

$$m = (m_1, \dots, m_n)$$

such that

$$m'_i \leq m_i, \ i = 1 \dots, n,$$

and

$$m_1 + \dots + m_n = m'_1 + \dots + m'_n + n.$$

If there is no such m, put

$$m = (K, K+1, \dots, K+1),$$

i.e. let

$$s^m = b = (b_1, \dots, b_n).$$

If $s^k = a$, or $s^m = b$, then by increase of g we get $s^k \prec^g s^m$, otherwise, taking into account the above proof and the definition of k and m, we have

$$k_1 + \dots + k_n = k'_1 + \dots + k'_n - n \leq m'_1 + \dots + m'_n = m_1 + \dots + m_n - n,$$

hence, by lemma 3.3.2 we obtain $s^k \preceq^g s^m$.

According to our construction,

$$\begin{aligned} \rho(u, s^k) &\leq \rho(u, s^{k'}) + \rho(s^{k'}, s^k) \\ &\leq (h_1^2 + \dots + h_n^2)^{1/2} + nh \\ &\leq \sqrt{n}h + nh \\ &= (n + \sqrt{n})h. \end{aligned}$$

Similarly,

$$\rho(v, s^m) \leq \rho(v, s^{m'}) + \rho(s^{m'}, s^m) \leq (h_1^2 + \dots + h_n^2)^{1/2} + nh \leq (n + \sqrt{n})h.$$

Conversely, for any $u, v \in U$ such that $u \preceq^g v$ there exist $s^k, s^m \in S$ such that

$$\begin{aligned} \rho(u, s^k) &\leq (n + \sqrt{n})h, \\ \rho(v, s^m) &\leq (n + \sqrt{n})h, \end{aligned}$$

and $s^k \preceq^f s^m$. Therefore, the Hausdorff distance between $\preceq^f$ and $\preceq^g$ in E^{2n} is not greater than

$$[h^2(n + \sqrt{n})^2 + h^2(n + \sqrt{n})^2]^{1/2} = \sqrt{2}\, h(n + \sqrt{n}) \leq \sqrt{2}\, h2n < 3nh.$$

Finally, note that $h_1 \leq \rho$ and $h_1 \leq \omega_i(h_1)$ for every $i = 2, \ldots, n$, whence

$$h \leq \max\{\rho, \omega_2(\rho), \ldots, \omega_n(\rho)\},$$

as required.

If $\rho \to 0$, then $\omega_i(\rho) \to 0$, for all $i = 2, \ldots, n$, and we get an arbitrary accurate approximations of the unknown ordering $\preceq^f$. Since continuous weak orders on U are closed subsets of $U \times U \subset \mathbf{E}^{2n}$ and the Hausdorff distance is not a pseudometric, but a metric, the unknown weak order $\preceq^f$ can be uniquely reconstructed as a limit of its approximations. Thus we obtain the uniqueness theorem.

3.3.3. PROPOSITION (The Uniqueness Theorem). *Consider a parallelepiped in n-dimensional* ($n \geq 2$) *Eucleadian space:*

$$U = U_1 \times \ldots \times U_n = [a_1; b_1] \times \ldots \times [a_n; b_n],$$

where $a_i < b_i$, $i = 1, \ldots, n$. *Suppose that there exists a weak order on* U, *which can be represented by an additive goal function* $f_1(u_1) + \ldots + f_n(u_n)$, *where* $f_1(u_1)$ *are continuous and increasing for every* $i = 1, \ldots, n$. *Suppose that compensation curves* M_i*—the level curves of the functions* $f_1(u_1) + f_i(u_i)$, *passing through the points* (a_1, b_i) *and* (b_1, a_i)*—are given in the coordinate planes* $U_1 \times U_i$ *for every* $i = 2, \ldots, n$, *and that a sequence of compesation curves* $\{M_1^k : k = 1, 2, \ldots\}$, *converging to the compensation curve* M_2, *is given in the coordinate plane* $U_1 \times U_2$. *Then the original weak order can be uniquely reconstructed from this data.*

Note that to reconstruct a weak order uniquely, it is necessary to know an infinite number of compensation curves on at least one coordinate plane. Let us show it with an example.

3.3.4. EXAMPLE (The Insufficiency of a Finite Number of Compensation Curves to Reconstruct an Additive Goal Function). Let m be a positive integer. We define a continuous increasing function $f(t)$ on the segment $[0; 2m]$ by the rule:

$$f(t) = [t - (2p - 1)]^3 + (2p - 1) \text{ if } 2p - 2 \leq t \leq 2p, \; p = 1, 2, \ldots, m.$$

The graph of the function $f(t)$ for $m = 2$ is shown in fig. 40.

Consider the parallelepiped

$$U = U_1 \times \ldots \times U_n = [0; 2m] \times \ldots \times [0; 2m],$$

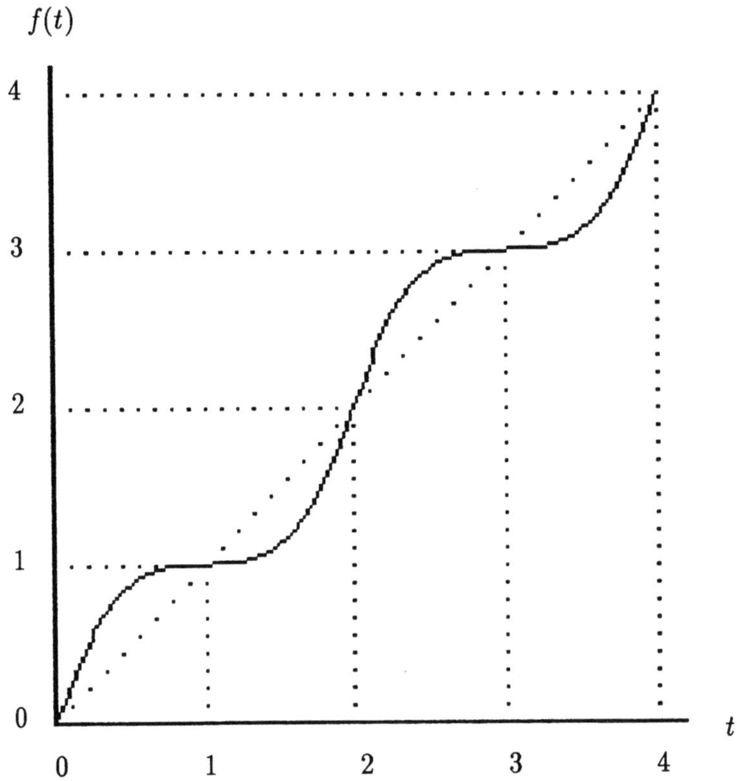

Fig. 40

and define a weak order on it by the goal function $f(u_1) + \ldots + f(u_n)$. We shall show that in each coordinate plane $U_i \times U_j$ the straight lines

$$u_i + u_j = 2p, \ p = 1, \ldots, m,$$

are the level curves of the function $f(u_i)+f(u_j)$ (fig. 41). Indeed, since $f(t)$ on $[0; 2m]$ is composed of the reiterated curve $f(t)$ defined on $[0; 2]$, the compensation curves on $[0; 2m] \times [0; 2m]$ are also composed of reiterated compensation curves on the square $[0; 2] \times [0; 2]$. Consequently, it is sufficient to show that the goal function $f(u_i) + f(u_j)$ is constant along the line $u_i + u_j = 2$. In fact,

$$f(u_i) + f(2 - u_i) = (u_i - 1)^3 + 1 + (2 - u_i - 1)^3 + 1 = 2,$$

as required. Consider another weak order on U with the continuous increasing additive goal function $u_1 + \ldots + u_n$. Obviously, the mentioned stright lines are also compensation curves of this ordering in each coordinate plane.

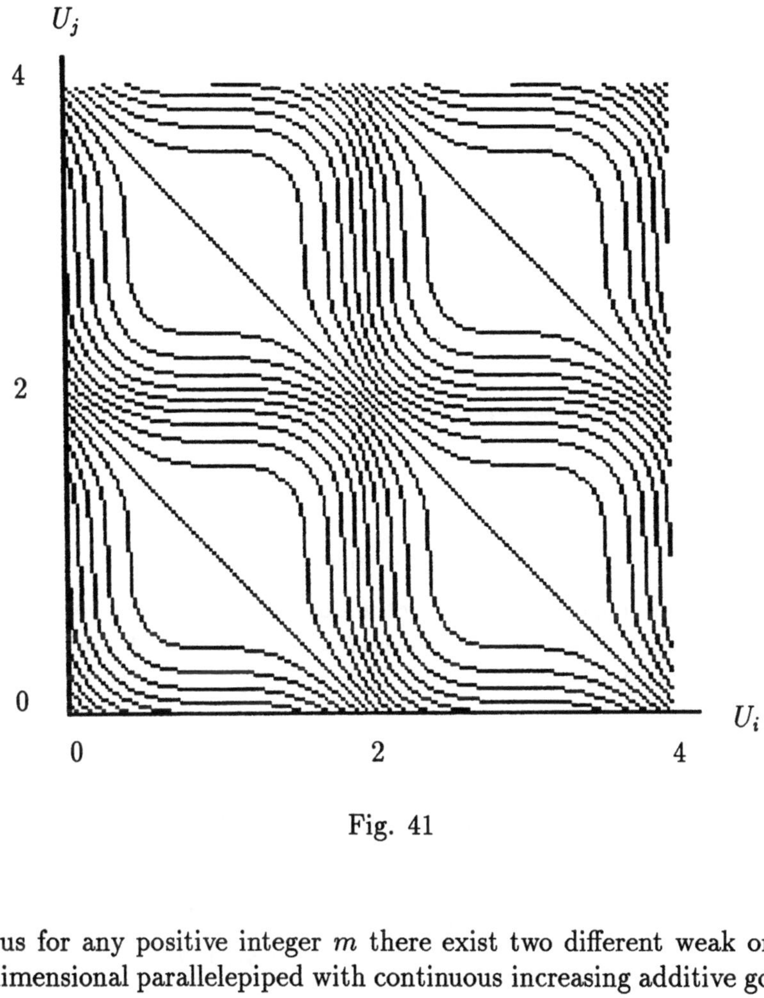

Fig. 41

Thus for any positive integer m there exist two different weak orders on an n-dimensional parallelepiped with continuous increasing additive goal functions, having m common compensation curves in each coordinate plane.

3.4 Applicability of the Construction of Additive Goal Function

The essential condition of theorem 3.3.1 is the existence of the unknown additive goal function, which becomes apparent in that the curves $M_i \subset U_1 \times U_i$, $i = 2, \ldots, n$, are the level curves of a certain function of the form $f_1(u_1) + f_i(u_i)$, defined on $U_1 \times U_i$. In this connection the question arises, whether arbitrary curves, for example, drawn by an expert, are compatible with this assumption?

The positive answer is given by the following theorem.

3.4.1. THEOREM (About the Admissibility of Arbitrary Compensation Curves). *Let the curves*

$$M_i \subset U_1 \times U_i, \ i = 2, \dots, n,$$

be the graphs of continuous decreasing functions

$$g_i : U_1 \to U_i,$$

and the curve

$$M_1 \subset U_1 \times U_2$$

be the graph of a continuous decreasing function

$$g_1 : [a_1; c] \to U_2,$$

where $a_1 < c < b_1$ and

$$g_1(u_1) < g_2(u_1)$$

for all $u_1 \in [a_1; c]$. Then there exist continuous increasing functions $f_1(u_1), \dots, f_n(u_n)$ on the segments $U_1, \dots, U_n$, respectively, such that M_1 and M_2 are the level curves of the function $f_1(u_1) + f_2(u_2)$, and M_i are the level curves of the functions $f_1(u_1) + f_i(u_i)$, $i = 3, \dots, n$.

PROOF. Construct a "staircase" between the curves M_1 and M_2 as shown in fig. 42, i.e. determine a positive integer K and two collections of $K+1$ points each on U_1 and U_2 :

$$\{a_1 = s_1^{-1} \le s_1^0 < \dots < s_1^{K-1} = c < s_1^K = b_1\} \subset U_1,$$
$$\{a_2 = s_2^0 < \dots < s_2^K \le s_2^{K+1} = b_2\} \subset U_2.$$

Such construction is possible and unambignuous, since the functions $g_1(u_1)$ and $g_2(u_1)$ are continuous and decreasing. The number K is finite, because $g_1(u_1) < g_2(u_1)$ for all $u_1 \in [a_1; c]$ implies

$$\inf_{y', y'' \in U_1 : (y', z) \in M_1, (y'', z) \in M_2, z \in U_2} | y' - y'' | = \epsilon > 0.$$

Hence, the differences $s_1^k - s_1^{k-1} > \epsilon$ for every k; consequently, K cannot be infinite.

Define continuous increasing functions $f_1(u_1)$ on U_1 and $f_2(u_2)$ on U_2 such that

$$f_1(u_1) + f_2(u_2) = 0 \quad \text{if } (u_1, u_2) \in M_1,$$
$$f_1(u_1) + f_2(u_2) = 1 \quad \text{if } (u_1, u_2) \in M_2.$$

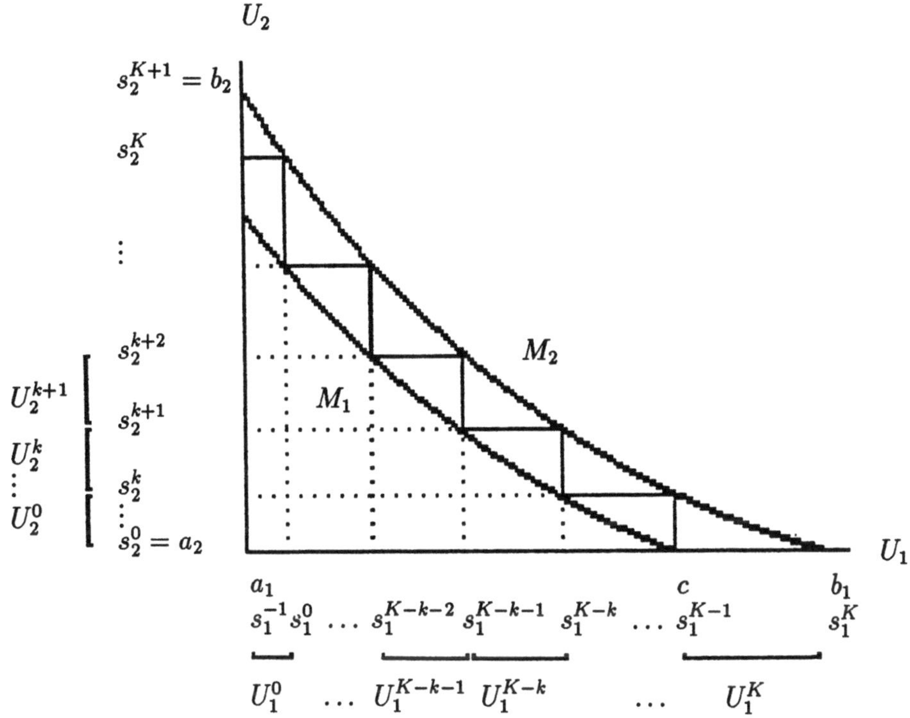

Fig. 42

For every $k = 0, \dots, K$ denote

$$U_1^k = [s_1^{k-1}; s_1^k]$$

and

$$U_2^k = [s_2^k; s_2^{k+1}].$$

The following construction we make by induction on k.

1. Define a continuous increasing function $f_1(u_1)$ on U_1^K such that

$$f_1(s_1^{K-1}) = 0,$$
$$f_1(s_1^K) = 1.$$

Since $g_2(u_1) \in U_2^0$ for $u_1 \in U_1^K$, the continuous increasing function

$$f_2(u_2) = 1 - f_1(g_2^{-1}(u_2))$$

is defined for all $u_2 \in U_2^0$. Obviously,

$$f_2(s_2^0) = 1 - f_1(g_2^{-1}(s_2^0)) = 1 - f_1(s_1^K) = 0,$$

and

$$f_2(s_2^1) = 1 - f_1(g_2^{-1}(s_2^1)) = 1 - f_1(s_1^{K-1}) = 1.$$

If $u_1 \in U_1^K$ and $(u_1, u_2) \in M_2$, then

$$f_1(u_1) + f_2(u_2) = f_1(u_1) + f_2(g_2(u_1)) = f_1(u_1) + 1 - f_1(g_2^{-1}(g_2(u_1))) = 1.$$

2. Suppose that for a non-negative integer $k < K$ the continuous increasing functions $f_1(u_1)$ on U_1^{K-k} and $f_2(u_2)$ on U_2^k, satisfying the conditions

$$\begin{aligned} f_1(s_1^{K-k-1}) &= -k, \\ f_1(s_1^{K-k}) &= 1 - k, \\ f_2(s_2^k) &= k, \\ f_2(s_2^{k-1}) &= k + 1, \end{aligned}$$

are already constructed, and also

$$\begin{aligned} f_1(u_1) + f_2(u_2) &= 0 \quad \text{if } (u_1, u_2) \in M_1, \\ f_1(u_1) + f_2(u_2) &= 1 \quad \text{if } (u_1, u_2) \in M_2. \end{aligned}$$

3. Since $g_1(u_1) \in U_2^k$ for $u_1 \in U_1^{K-k-1}$, by the previous item the continuous increasing function

$$f_1(u_1) = -f_2(g_1(u_1))$$

is defined for all $u_1 \in U_1^{K-k-1}$, and

$$\begin{aligned} f_1(s_1^{K-k-2}) &= -f_2(g_1(s_1^{K-k-2})) = -f_2(s_2^{K+1}) = -k - 1, \\ f_1(s_1^{K-k-1}) &= -f_2(g_1(s_1^{K-k-1})) = -f_2(s_2^k) = -k. \end{aligned}$$

Since $g_2(u_1) \in U_2^{k+1}$ for $u_1 \in U_1^{K-k-1}$, the continuous increasing function

$$f_2(u_2) = 1 - f_1(g_2^{-1}(u_2))$$

is defined for all $u_2 \in U_2^{k+1}$, and

$$\begin{aligned} f_2(s_2^{k+1}) &= 1 - f_1(g_2^{-1}(s_2^{k+1})) = 1 - f_1(s_1^{K-k-1}) = 1 + k, \\ f_2(s_2^{k+2}) &= 1 - f_1(g_2^{-1}(s_2^{k+2})) = 1 - f_1(s_1^{K-k-2}) = k + 2. \end{aligned}$$

If $u_1 \in U_1^{K-k-1}$ and $(u_1, u_2) \in M_1$, then

$$f_1(u_1) + f_2(u_2) = f_1(u_1) + f_2(g_1(u_2)) = -f_2(g_1(u_1)) = 0.$$

If $u_1 \in U_1^{K-k-1}$ and $(u_1, u_2) \in M_2$, then

$$f_1(u_1) + f_2(u_2) = f_1(u_1) + f_2(g_2(u_1)) = f_1(u_1) + 1 - f_1(g_2^{-1}(g_2(u_1))) = 1.$$

This way the continuous increasing functions $f_1(u_1)$ on U_1 and $f_2(u_2)$ on U_2 can be constructed.

For every $i = 3, \ldots, n$ define the continuous increasing function

$$f_i(u_i) = 1 - f_1(g_1^{-1}(u_i))$$

on U_i. Obviously, if $(u_1, u_i) \in M_i$, then

$$f_1(u_1) + f_i(u_i) = f_1(u_1) + f_i(g_i(u_1)) = f_1(u_1) + 1 - f_1(g_1^{-1}(g_i(u_i))) = 1,$$

as required.

Note that the algorithm described in section 3.2 can be modified in different ways. For example, if it is not convinient to oppose the first individual to others, the utility comparisons can be carried out for other pairs of individuals. However, for our purposes it is necessary to transfer the segmentation of U_1 and U_2 obtained by means of the "staircase" to every other axis. For that purpose it sufficies to follow a certain tree of pairs of individuals, transferring the obtained segmentation to every axis by corresponding compensation curves. The estimation of accuracy of approximation of the collective preference may become complicated, since to estimate h in the proof of theorem 3.3.1 we have to consider compositions of oscillations. Say, if the compensation curves are given in the planes $U_{i-1} \times U_i$, $i = 2, \ldots, n$, and $\omega_i(\rho)$ is the oscillation of M_i as a function from U_{i-1} into U_i, $i = 2, \ldots, n$, then the estimation of accuracy of the constructed preference is

$$3n \max\{\rho, \omega_2(\rho), \omega_3(\omega_2(\rho)), \ldots, \omega_n(\omega_{n-1}(\ldots(\omega_2(\rho))\ldots))\}.$$

Also note another modification of the algorithm of construction of an additive goal function. Instead of the first step of the algorithm one has to do the following.

1a. Define $c = s_2^1 \in U_2$ and $s_1^{K-1} \in U_1$ to make (s_1^{K-1}, c) and (b_1, a_2) indifferent with respect to collective preference. Then define $s_1^{K-2} \in U_1$ to make (s_1^{K-2}, c) and (s_1^{K-1}, a_2) indifferent with respect to collective preference, etc. (fig. 43). This way the segmentation

$$\{s_1^0, s_1^1, \ldots, s_1^K\} \subset U_1$$

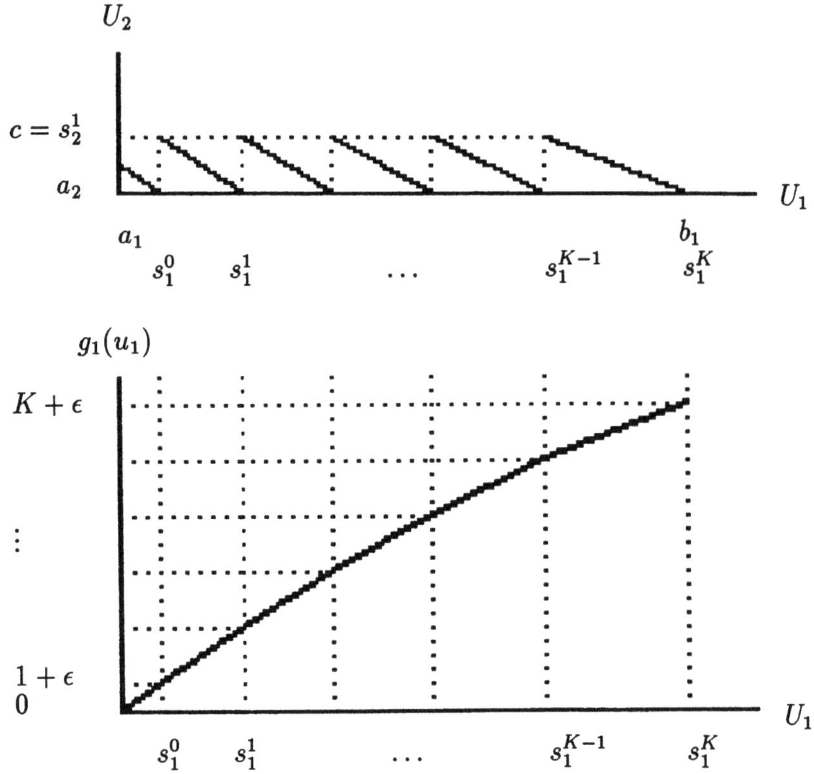

Fig. 43

is determined so that the first component $f_1(u_1)$ of the unknown goal function $f_1(u_1)+\ldots+f_n(u_n)$ increases by the same value on every segment $[s_1^i; s_1^{i+1}]$, $i = 1,\ldots,K-1$.

All other steps of the algoritm are the same as in section 3.2. By theorem 3.3.1 the Hausdorff distance between the weak orders $\preceq^f$ and $\preceq^g$ is less than $3nh$, where h is the length of the maximal segment $[s_1^{k_i}; s_1^{K_i-1}]$ and the maximum is taken over all k_i and i. Since additive goal function increases by 1 along each of these segments, and is uniformly continuous on the parallelepiped U, we obtain that h converges to zero, if $s_2^1 - s_2^0$ tends to zero, i.e. if $c \to a_2$. It is important that convergence of the whole procedure is determined by convergence of a single parameter varied and measured with ease.

To conclude the section, let us formulate a remarkable fact, which characterizes properties of compensation curves and properties of continuous de-

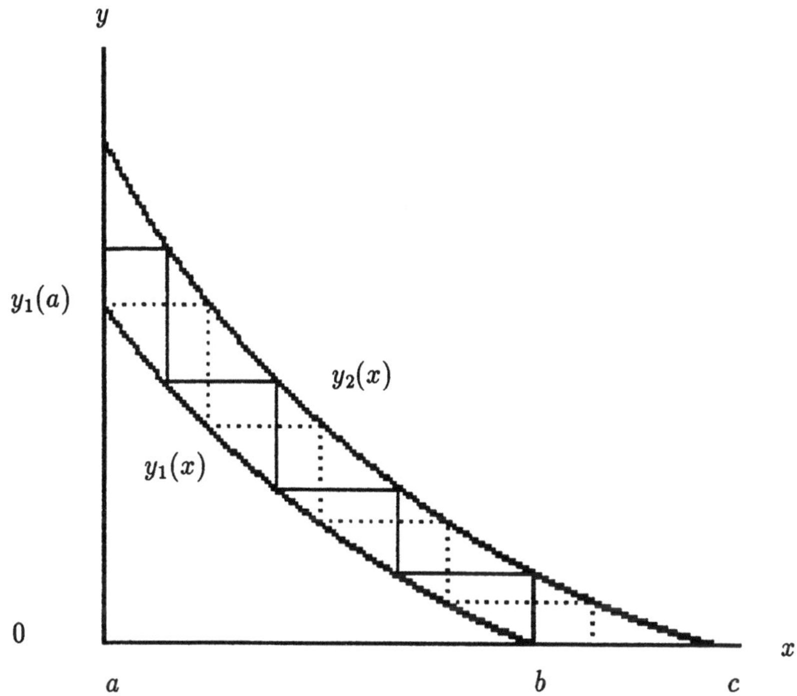

Fig. 44

creasing functions in general.

3.4.2. Proposition (The Equality of the Number of "Stairs" between Two Curves). *Let $a < b < c$. Consider two continuous decreasing functions $y = y_1(x)$ on the segment $[a; b]$ and $y = y_2(x)$ on the segment $[a; c]$ such that $y_1(x) < y_2(x)$ on $[a; b]$ and $y_1(b) = y_2(c) = 0$. Between the graphs of the functions $y_1(x)$ and $y_2(x)$ construct two polygonal lines of vertical and horizontal segments as shown in* fig. 44*—the first one beginning at the point $(b; 0)$ and drawn by the continuous line, the second one beginning at the point $(a, y_1(a))$ and denoted by the dotted line. Then the number of stairs of the first and second line are equal.*

Proof. By theorem 3.4.1 there exist continuous increasing functions $f_1(x)$ on the segment $[a; c]$ and $f_2(y)$ on the segment $[0; y_2(0)]$ such that

$$f_1(x) + f_2(y_1(x)) = 0 \quad \text{if } x \in [a; b],$$
$$f_1(x) + f_2(y_2(x)) = 1 \quad \text{if } x \in [a; c]$$

and

$$f_1(b) = 0, \quad f_1(c) = 1.$$

Consider the first polygonal line, beginning at the point $(b, 0)$. Each its horizontal segment, may be, with the only exception for the last one, provides the increase of the function $f_1(x)$ by 1. If K_1 is the number of horizontal edges of the first line, then

$$-K_1 \leq f_1(a) < -K_1 + 1.$$

Applying the same arguments for the second line, we obtain

$$-K_2 \leq f_1(a) < -K_2 + 1,$$

where K_2 is the number of horizontal edges of the second line. Hence, $K_1 = K_2$, as required.

3.5 Notes on Interpretation

The consideration of additive goal functions is more habitual in the context of multicriteria decision-making. In multicriteria decision-making it is not necessary to interpret and to justify individual utilities, intermediate in the process of the determination of the collective preference by individual ones. As mentioned in section 3.1, the individual utility is a result of the first stage of aggregation. Instead of individual utilities the multicriteria decision-making deals usually with physical parameters, measured by standard units. Therefore each alternative x is characterized not by a collection of individual utilities $(u_1(x), \dots, u_n(x))$, but is identified with a vector of specifications $(u_1, \dots, u_n)$, the meaning of which is quite clear. The independence of individual preferences corresponds to the independence of specifications, i.e. to that it is meaningful to speak about the improvement with respect to one or several specifications; the only important restriction is that these improvements should be understood equally for any fixed values of other specifications. To illustrate the difference between independent and "dependent" specifications, we give a slightly modified example from (Winterfeldt & Fisher 1975).

3.5.1. EXAMPLE (The Dependent and Independent Preferences). Consider two specifications of a car: Length of the body, and type of the steering gear (mechanical or hydraulic). If the car body is not very large—up to 4.5 meters long, then the larger car is always preferable regardless of the type of the steering gear. In this case the specification "length of the body" is independent of another. If we consider cars, differing in length greatly—up to 6 meters, then our preference can depend on the type of steering gear. Indeed, a large car with a mechanical steering gear is not quite safe, and the smaller car is preferable if the steering gear is not hydraulic but mechanical. Therefore, we can write down:

$$\begin{aligned}\text{(6m, hydraulic steering gear)} &\succ \text{(4m, hydraulic steering gear);}\\ \text{(6m, mechanical steering gear)} &\prec \text{(4m, mechanical steering gear).}\end{aligned}$$

In this case the specification "length of the body" is not independent of the type of steering gear.

In the above example the violation of independence arises because a new factor—the safety—is taken into account. The violation of independence means the qualitative revision of specifications, which is natural under great deviations of parameters, but is not typical for their small alterations. For close objects the independence of specifications is highly probable, since the alternatives are regarded from the same point of view and with account of the same criteria. In this connection recall the arguments from section 3.1 about the approximation of differentiable goal functions by a weighted sum of individual utilities within a neighborhood of a given point. As in the above example, remote (in the space of specifications, individual utilities) points cannot be estimated by the goal function like the weighted sum of coordinates. Thus only for similar alternatives, located close to each other in the specification space, the independence of factors is a likelihood hypothesis. Sometimes it is possible to classify alternatives and to assume the independence of preferences within these classes.

In conclusion, note that when the number of individuals (specifications) is 2, and the collective goal function is monotone with respect to individual utilities, the pairwise independence of preferences holds trivially. As we have mentioned in section 3.1, under rather general assumptions the pairwise independence implies the representability of the collective preference by an additive goal function of individual utilities. Therefore one can expect that in this trivial case the collective goal function can always be brought to the additive form. However, it is not true, since for that purpose only non-trivial independence is needed (arising in the case of 3 or more individuals).

3.5.2. Example (No Additive Goal Function for Two Independent Preferences). Consider the space of two individual utilities

$$U = U_1 \times U_2 = [0;2] \times [0;2].$$

Define a strictly increasing continuous weak order on U by the goal function

$$g(u) = g(u_1, u_2) = \begin{cases} u_1 + u_2 & \text{if } u_1 + u_2 \leq 2, \\ f(u_1) + f(u_2) & \text{if } u_1 + u_2 \geq 2. \end{cases}$$

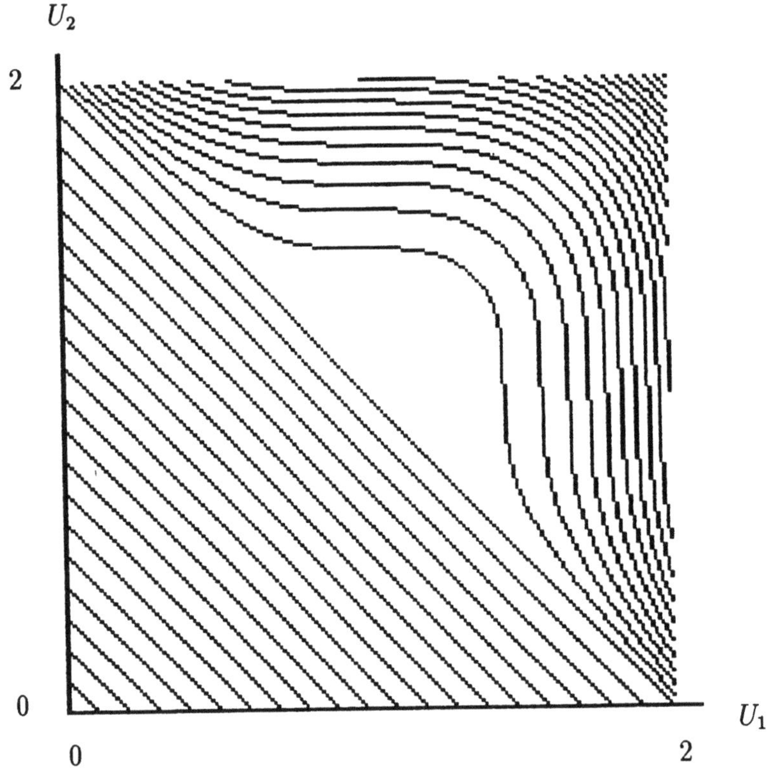

Fig. 45

where $f(t)$ is the same as in example 3.3.4. Its level curves are shown in fig. 45. We shall prove that the given weak order (increasing, continuous and defined on a connected subset of the Eucleadian plane) cannot be represented by an additive goal function on U. In fact, by the uniqueness theorem 3.3.3 if such an additive goal function exists, it can be reconstructed uniquelly by the compensation curve

$$M_2 = \{(u_1, u_2) : u_1 + u_2 = 2\}$$

and the sequence of compensation curves

$$M_1^k = \{(u_1, u_2) : u_1 + u_2 = 2 - 1/k\}, \ k = 1, 2, \dots .$$

However, there exists another weak order on U, compatible with the given data, namely, represented by the goal function $u_1 + u_2$. The contradiction with the uniqueness theorem proves that the weak order represented by the goal function $g(u)$ cannot be represented by an additive goal function on U (note that $g(u)$ is additive in each of two subsets of U, but not on the whole of U.

Chapter 4

Accounting Degree of Preference in Aggregation

4.1 Introductory Remarks

In the present chapter we continue the study of aggregation of preferences without one of axioms A1–A5, begun in chapter 3. As mentioned in chapter 1, the rejection of axiom A4 (independence of irrelevant alternatives) allows taking into account such an important factor, as the degree of preference. It is desirable in multicriteria decision-making, when one has to compare estimates from partial criteria with regard both to their significance, and the difference between the estimates obtained. If the estimation is done by man, as in collective choice, the determinition of the degree of preference meets difficulties, since it cannot be measured in standard units.

The desire to measure the degree of preference is influenced by the tradition to find the mean value with the help of summation. Collective choice and multicriteria decision-making are not exceptions to this approach. However, the application of arithmetical rules is justified only to values with precise numerical meaning, but, generally speaking, it is not inherent in subjective preferences. Nevertheless, a majority rule is based on summation of votes, in the method of marks the alternatives are ordered according to the sums of their places in individual schedules. Here the search for a compromise decision is analogous to finding the center of gravity for a system of massive points. The significance of a criterium can be associated with the arm length, and the estimate of an alternative (the degree of preference), with the mass of a point.

However, in contrast to objective physical measurements, the measurement of the degree of preference requires indirect methods, since direct numerical estimation is rather subjective. Beside relativity and uncertainty, the direct estimation results in strategic struggle, examples of which we have examined in chapter 1. The application of indirect methods sometimes allows to simplify the procedure of estimation itself, makes it more reliable, and prevents it from the influence of subjective and behaviourial moments.

Consider an indirect method of comparison of the degree of preference of two individuals (Mirkin 1974, p. 136). Let A and B be two competitive projects, estimated by two experts, while one of them prefers A, and the other B. To reveal whose preference is stronger, the experts are asked to judge an additional project C. Suppose that the first expert has the preference order (A, B, C), and the second (B, C, A), having put B between A and B. On these grounds we conclude that the preference of the second expert is stronger, therefore his opinion should be taken as deciding. Certainly, it can happen that for the second expert all the three projects are almost equivalent, whereas the first one distinguishes them considerably. Nevertheless, if the second expert doesn't distinguish A and B, the third project will be most likely put outside the small preference interval between A and B. However, if one expert locates between the two basic alternatives 100, and another 99 additional alternatives, the difference seems not to be significant.

The mathematical problem of estimation of the degree of preferences can be posed in terms of probability analysis of such situations. By the method of marks we formulate the likelihood hypothesis that the more alternatives are located between the given two, the stronger is the preference. Then we estimate the fiducial probability of this hipothesis. Such approach implies a new interpretation of sensibility of the method of marks to the addition of irrelevant alternatives: We use it to estimate the degree of preference and to characterize the reliability of the results obtained by the method of marks.

Usually statistical methods are applied to aggregation of preferences under the assumption that individual preferences are "distorted observations" of a collective preference. In this case the problem is brought to error analysis. In contrast to that we don't treat individual preferences as deviations of a single random variable, which sould be averaged. On the contrary, we analyse them to get some meaningful information.

The results of the chapter are published in Russian in (Tanguiane 1985).

4.2 Method of Marks

Recall that the method of marks was proposed by Borda in 1770 (Black 1958). The alternatives are estimated by the sums of places (ranks) in the individual orderings, and the ones getting better sums are considered best. Note that the method of marks satisfies all Arrow's axioms except the condition of independence of irrelevant alternatives. Indeed, it is defined for any finite set of alternatives, i.e. A1 is true. It can be applied to every combination of individual preferences (weak orders) with no fear that the obtained collective ordering will be intransitive (cyclic)—since it is represented numerically, it is obviously a weak order. Therefore A2 is also valid. The unanimity principle (A3) holds, because if one alternative is preferable to another in every individual preference, then its sum of places (ranks) is also better. Finally, simple examples show that decisions obtained by the method of marks are not dictatorial. Indeed, if there was a dictator, his ranks would contribute to the sums of ranks more than the ranks of all other individuals. Since it is not true, the method of marks meets the prohibition of dictatorship (A5). Therefore the method of marks is quite suitable for our analysis of aggregation of preferences without axiom A4.

The first formal justification of the method of marks was proposed by Laplace. He supposed that the most questionable point was the integer-valueness of estimates in individual schedules. If individuals could estimate alternatives proportionally to their preferences, say, by real numbers from the interval $(0;1)$, then the degree of preference would have much more precise quantitative meaning, justifying further calculations. Assuming such estimation possible in a probability model, Laplace showed that the integer-value estimation leads to similar decision-making results. To give the mathematical formulation, we introduce some designations.

Let each individual estimate m alternatives by real numbers from the interval $(0;1)$ proportionally to his preference so that better alternatives are associated with greater estimates. Such estimates we call *latent*, since they are not specified in individual schedules. Nevertheless, we assume their existence, even if individuals fail to determine them precisely.

For a given individual consider a collection of his latent estimates of m alternatives, reordered according to their growth

$$0 \leq u_{(m,1)} \leq \ldots \leq u_{(m,m)} \leq 1,$$

where $u_{(m,k)}$ denotes the latent estimate of the alternative, standing at the kth place from the bottom of the individual's schedule. According to Laplace, this collections of reordered latent estimates can be identified with an ordered sample of a random variable u, equidistributed in the interval $(0;1)$, or with a sample of a single m-dimensional random vector

$$u = (u_1, \ldots, u_m),$$

equidistributed in its domain of definition

$$D = \{u : u = (u_1, \ldots, u_m),\ 0 \leq u_1 \leq \ldots \leq u_m \leq 1\}.$$

The mathematical expectation of the random vector u coincides with the center of gravity of D, which is

$$u^0 = (\frac{1}{m+1}, \dots, \frac{m}{m+1}).$$

Thus on average every individual estimates the alternatives by the integer-value ratio $1 : 2 : \dots : m$, as in the method of marks. By the law of large numbers, when there is many individuals, the sum of latent estimates of each alternative is close to the sum of averaged integer-value estimates. Therefore, the more individuals participate in the procedure, the better is the performance of the method of marks.

The assumption of the equidistribution of random variable u is justified by the tradition, established in mathematical statistics. It is custom to derive probability formulas for the equidistribution, and extend them to a general case, substituting the differential $dF(x)$ for dx, where $F(x)$ is an appropriate distribution function.

Certainly, the difference between the averaged integer-value estimates and latent real-value estimates can influence the final result. Let us examine it under the assumption that the latent estimates are equidistributed. First of all we recall the definition of Euler's beta-function

$$B(p,q) = \int_0^1 x^{p-1}(1-x)^{q-1}dx = \frac{(p-1)!(q-1)!}{(p+q-1)!}. \tag{4.2.1}$$

The incomplete beta-function is defined to be

$$I_x(p,q) = \frac{1}{B(p,q)} \int_0^x x^{p-1}(1-x)^{q-1}dx. \tag{4.2.2}$$

We shall also use the binomial representation of the incomplete beta-function

$$I_x(k, m-k+1) = \sum_{j=k}^{m} C_m^j x^j (1-x)^{m-j} \tag{4.2.3}$$

(Kendall & Stuart 1958). The incomplete beta-function can be regarded as a distribution function of a random variable ξ with the mathematical expectation

$$\mathsf{E}\xi = \frac{p}{p+q}, \tag{4.2.4}$$

and the dispersion

$$\mathsf{D}\xi = \frac{pq}{(p+q)^2(p+q+1)}. \tag{4.2.5}$$

4.2.1. Proposition (The Distribution of the Degree of Preference). *Let*

$$0 \le u_{(m,1)} \le \dots u_{(m,m)} \le 1$$

be an ordered sample of a random variable u, *equidistributed in the interval* $(0;1)$. *Then the length* $\xi_{(m,k)}$ *of random interval* $(u_{(m,i)}; u_{(m,i+k)})$, *interpreted as the difference between the degree of preference of ith and* $(i+k)$*th alternatives in the individual schedule, is a random variable, beta-distributed in the invertal* $(0;1)$ *with the density*

$$p_{(m,k)}(x) = \frac{m!\,x^{k-1}(1-x)^{m-k}}{(k-1)!(m-k)!} = I'_x(k, m-k+1),$$

the mathematical expectation

$$\mathsf{E}\xi_{(m,k)} = \frac{k}{m+1},$$

and the dispersion

$$\mathsf{D}\xi_{(m,k)} = \frac{k(m+1-k)}{(m+1)^2(m+2)}.$$

The proof of this proposition one can find in (Kendall & Stuart 1958).

Note that the above proposition characterizes the degree of preference by the number of alternatives, placed between the given two, while this characteristic does not depend on whether this latent estimates are close to left-, or right-hand end of the interval $(0;1)$.

We shall apply this proposition to the method of marks, with which the maximal likelihood hypothesis about the collective preference is formulated. Let us calculate the fiducial probability for the recommendations obtained by the method of marks.

4.2.2. Theorem (About the Method of Marks). *Consider* n *individuals,* m *alternatives, and let two alternatives* A *and* B *be singled out. By integers* a_j *and* b_j *denote the places of alternatives* A *and* B *in the ordering of the* j *th individual, numbered from the bottom of his schedule. Let individuals be independent (in the probability sense), and let the latent estimates of each be equidistributed. Then the probability of that "alternative* A *is worse than* B*" is approximated as follows:*

$$\mathsf{P}\{\sum_{j=1}^{n} u_{j(m,a_j)} < \sum_{j=1}^{n} u_{j(m,b_j)}\} \approx \frac{1}{\sqrt{2\pi}} \int_{-\infty}^{z} e^{-t^2/2} dt, \tag{4.2.6}$$

where

$$z = \frac{-\sqrt{m+2}\sum_{j=1}^{n}(a_j - b_j)}{\sqrt{\sum_{j=1}^{n} \mid a_j - b_j \mid (m+1- \mid a_j - b_j \mid)}}.$$

PROOF. We have to estimate the probability

$$\mathsf{P}\{\sum_{j=1}^{n}(u_{j(m,a_j)} - u_{j(m,b_j)}) < 0\}.$$

By proposition 4.2.1 the differences

$$u_{j(m,a_j)} - u_{j(m,b_j)}$$

are beta-distributed random variables $\xi_{(m,|a_j-b_j|)}$ with factors ± 1, depending on the sign of their mathematical expectations

$$\mathsf{E}(u_{j(m,a_j)} - u_{j(m,b_j)}) = \frac{a_j - b_j}{m+1}$$

for $j = 1, \ldots, n$. Therefore, their dispersions are equal to

$$\mathsf{D}(u_{j(m,a_j)} - u_{j(m,b_j)}) = \frac{(m+1- \mid a_j - b_j \mid) \mid a_j - b_j \mid}{(m+1)^2(m+2)}, \; j = 1, \ldots, n.$$

It is easy to see that all assumptions of the central limit theorem are satisfied. Consequently, the difference between the sums of the latent estimates of alternatives A and B is almost normally distributed with the mathematical expectation

$$\mu = \frac{1}{m+1}\sum_{j=1}^{n}(a_j - b_j)$$

and the dispersion

$$\sigma^2 = \frac{1}{(m+1)^2(m+2)}\sum_{j=1}^{n}(m+1- \mid a_j - b_j \mid) \mid a_j - b_j \mid.$$

Putting

$$z = -\frac{\mu}{\sigma} = \frac{-\sqrt{m+2}\sum_{j=1}^{n}(a_j - b_j)}{\sqrt{\sum_{j=1}^{n} \mid a_j - b_j \mid (m+1- \mid a_j - b_j \mid)}},$$

we bring the calculation of the desired probability to the standard integral (4.2.6).

Note that we can estimate the accuracy of the obtained approximation. The accuracy of the approximated probabilities given by the central limit theorem is always within $\pm c_0\epsilon_n$ (Zolotarev 1986), where $c_0 < 0.7655$ and ϵ_n is Lyapunov ratio (the sum of the third absolute central moments of the given random variables divided by the dispersion of their sum power 3/2). The latter can be expressed in terms of the incomplete beta-functions, evaluated either with the help of special tables (Pearson 1968), or directly—by application of binomial representation of the incomplete beta-function. If the number of individuals is not very large, this estimation may be rather rough. In this case we can recommend to apply the techniques of refined estimation in terms of pseudomoments (Zolotarev 1986).

4.3 Certainty of Predominance of One Preference over Another

Revert to the problem about two experts from section 4.1. The formula for the distribution of latent estimates allows calculating the fiducial probability of the hipothesis that the preference of the expert who places more additional alternatives between the given two is stronger than that of the expert who places between them fewer additional alternatives.

4.3.1. THEOREM (About the Predominance of One Preference over Another). *Let $\xi_{(m,k)}$ and $\xi_{(m,l)}$ be independent random variables, distributed in the interval $(0;1)$ with the beta-densities $p_{(m,k)}(x)$ and $p_{(m,l)}(x)$, respectively. Then the probability of that the first random variable is greater than the second one is calculated by the formula*

$$\begin{aligned} \mathsf{P}\{\xi_{(m,k)} > \xi_{(m,l)}\} &= \frac{1}{B(k,m-k+1)} \sum_{j=l}^{m} C_m^j\, B(k+j, 2m-k-j+1) \\ &= \frac{(m!)^2}{(k-1)!(m-k)!(2m)!} \sum_{j=l}^{m} \frac{(k+j-1)!(2m-k-j)!}{j!(m-j)!}. \end{aligned}$$

PROOF. Taking into account formulas (4.2.1), (4.2.2), and proposition 4.2.1, we obtain

$$\begin{aligned} \mathsf{P}\{\xi_{(m,k)} > \xi_{(m,l)}\} &= \iint_{0\le y<x\le 1} p_{(m,k)}(x)p_{(m,l)}(y)\, dx\, dy \\ &= \int_0^1 p_{(m,k)}(x) I_x(l, m-l+1)\, dx \end{aligned}$$

$$\begin{aligned}
&= \int_0^1 \frac{x^{k-1}(1-x)^{m-k}}{B(k,m-k+1)} \sum_{j=l}^{m} C_m^j x^j (1-x)^{m-j} dx \\
&= \frac{1}{B(k,m-k+1)} \sum_{j=l}^{m} C_m^j \int_0^1 x^{k+j-1}(1-x)^{2m-k-j} dx \\
&= \frac{1}{B(k,m-k+1)} \sum_{j=l}^{m} C_m^j B(k+j, 2m-k-j+1) \\
&= \frac{(m!)^2}{(k-1)!(m-k)!(2m)!} \sum_{j=l}^{m} \frac{(k+j-1)!(2m-k-j)!}{j!(m-j)!},
\end{aligned}$$

as required.

In appendix we give the fiducial probabilities calculated by the above formula for $m = 3, \ldots, 20$ and $k \leq l = 1, \ldots, m-1$.

4.4 Notes on Interpretation

In this section we show how to use the derived formulas.

4.4.1. EXAMPLE (Significance of the Difference between the Sums of Marks). Consider three candidates A, B, and C and 21 individuals with the preferences shown in fig. 46 (cf. with the example from section 1.3). According

(A, B, C)	8 electors
(B, C, A)	7 electors
(C, B, A)	6 electors

Fig. 46

to the method of marks, the best is candidate B (49 marks), the next best is C (40 marks) and the last is A (37 marks). Estimate the significance of these distinctions by the formula from theorem 4.2.2. For that purpose we calculate the probabilities that corresponding sums of latent estimates are ordered in the same way. Let u^A, u^B, u^C be the sums of latent estimates of candidates A, B, C respectively. In the designations of theorem 4.2.2 we have, for example,

$$u^A = \sum_{j=1}^{21} u_{j(3,a_j)}.$$

Applying theorem 4.2.2, we obtain:

$$\begin{aligned} \mathsf{P}\{u^A < u^B\} &\approx 0.999, \\ \mathsf{P}\{u^A < u^C\} &\approx 0.809, \\ \mathsf{P}\{u^C < u^B\} &\approx 0.994, \end{aligned}$$

whence the distinctions between candidates A and B, and between C and B can be regarded as significant, but not between A and C. Thus with a high reliability we get the ordering $(B, A \sim C)$, whereas the ordering (B, C, A), obtained by direct application of the method of marks, cannot be taken as quite reliable.

Note that this way of thought can be applied to quality control, when it is needed to distinguish between the integral quality of analoguous products by the orderings obtained from partial criteria (specifications).

4.4.2. EXAMPLE (Revealing the Predominance of One Preference over Another). Let two experts consider m alternatives, among which we are interested in A and B. Suppose that the first expert places $k-1$ alternatives between A and B, and the second expert places $l-1$ alternatives. The question arises, what is the reliability of the statement that the preference of the first expert is stronger (and therefore his opinion should be taken as deciding)? From the standpoint of our model we have to determime the probability that the interval between the first expert's latent estimates of A and B is greater than that of the second expert. In the formulation of theorem 4.3.1 this probability is denoted by $\mathsf{P}\{\xi_{(m,k)} > \xi_{(m,l)}\}$. Therefore, we can calculate it by formula of the theorem, or refer to the tables from appendix 1.

Our consideration can be extended to a procedure, when new alternatives are presented successively until the predominance of one preference over another hasn't been revealed with the required reliability.

Consider the case of contraversal opinions, when one expert prefers A, yet another prefers B. Suppose that we want to reveal the predominant preference with the reliability 95%. At first, let three additional alternatives be presented, and let the first expert place two of them between A and B, whereas the second only one. For $m = 5$ (2 basic alternatives +3 additional alternatives) we have $k-1 = 2$, $l-1 = 1$. Referring to table A.1.3, we find that the reliability of the predominance of the preference of the first expert is 74%, which is insufficient. Suppose that another 7 alternatives are added to the 5 considered. Let the first expert put between A and B totally 8, and the second 4 additional alternatives. Then we have $m = 12$, $k-1 = 8$, $l-1 = 4$. Referring to table A.1.10, we find that the reliability of the preference predominance is 95%. Thus we can state with the required reliability that the preference of the first expert is stronger, whence his opinion should be deciding.

Chapter 5

General Model of Aggregation of Preferences

5.1 Introductory Remarks

In this chapter we accomplish the study of the model of aggregation of preferences, discarding one of Arrow's axioms. Now we give up the prohibition of dictatorship. We shall obtain corollaries for the models of Arrow (1951), Fishburn (1970a), Kirman and Sondermann (1972). In section 7 we shall introduce probability measures to characterize quantitatively the elements of the model, and so we shall also generalize the models of Armstrong (1980; 1985) and Schmitz (1977). The works of the named authors deal with the same axioms, but their interpretations are different. It comes from the fact that Arrow's model assumes finite, and the others infinite, set of individuals.

For a model with a finite set of individuals Arrow showed that some quite natural conditions inevitably imply the existence of a dicator—an individual, whose preference determines collective choice regardless of that of others. Fishburn weakened the categoricity of Arrow's result. He stated that there are infinite models of collective choice without a dictator. Kirman and Sondermann took an attempt to explain the difference between the conclusions of Arrow and Fishburn. They supplemented the infinite model with so called "invisible agents", and under the assumption of finite number of alternatives proved the existence of a dictator, even if "invisible"—just in the spirit of Adam Smith's dictum on free competition, which he had called "an invisible hand". According to conclusions of Kirman and Sondermann, the dictatorial origin is present both in finite and infinite models, but in the latter in an indirect form, when it becomes apparent through individuals, grouping around the "invisible dictator".

Following ideas of Kirman and Sondermann, we introduce a concept of a deciding hierarchy. We consider interrelations between aggregating operators (social welfare functions, or social ordering functions) and deciding hierarchies, prove that each aggregating operator is determined by a certain deciding hierarchy, and establish that this correspondence is one-to-one (a bijection). A similar result was formulated by Armstrong (1980), but with inaccuracies in assumptions and demonstration (Tanguiane 1981b, Armstrong 1985).

As one could expect, the dictator turns out to be nothing else but the upper level of the deciding hierarchy. The difference between the conclusions of Arrow and Fishburn is explained, consequently, by the fact that in the finite model the upper level of deciding hierarchy always exists, whereas in the infinite model it can be unattainable. The completion of the collective choice model with the agents, heading all hierarchies, gives the theorem of Kirman and Sondermann about "invisible" dictators, valid, to the point, not only for finite but for arbitrary set of alternatives.

The algebraic language seems to be most suitable for our purposes. By means of abstraction we restrict our consideration to most fundamental properties and causal relationships. In particular, we reveal certain invariants of algebraic model, i.e. the properties invariable under isomorphisms. It results in the conclusion that not the dictator but the deciding hierarchy is the concept, relevant to our consideration. Indeed, only the latter is the model's invariant, whereas the dictator can appear and disappear under its isomorphisms.

In the algebraic model the set of alternatives is provided with a coalition structure, formalized by a Boolean algebra. Such a structure describes the differentiation of individuals by preferences. The case studied by Arrow, Fishburn, and Kirman and Sondermann, when all combinations of individual preferences are allowed, means that nothing is known about the grouping of individuals by preferences. In our model this assumption is realized by the Boolean algebra of all subsets of the set of individuals. Non-discrete algebras are associated with restrictions on grouping of individuals by preferences, but not on the preferences themselves.

The grouping of individuals by preferences may be identified with a system of classifiers: We can suppose that the individuals, belonging to the same communities, have similar preferences. It is easy to see that each system of classifiers corresponds to a certain Boolean algebra of subsets of the set of individuals with the operations of union, intersection and complementation. For example, one can consider groups of individuals with high education, or not (the subset and its complement), with high, or secondary professional education (the union of subsets), with secondary professional education and at the same time whith high education (the intersection of subsets). Thus an algebraic approach allows to represent a given collective as a set of interacting groups, uniting individuals with similar preferences.

Note that the first description of coalitions by means of binary classifiers was proposed in (Lyapunov & Malenkov 1962). Boolean algebras (and σ-algebras) have been used for the description of coalition sets by Aumann (1964; 1966), Aumann and Shapley (1974), Richter (1971), and in applications to collective choice models by Schmitz (1977), Armstrong (1980), and Tanguiane (1979b; 1979c; 1980a).

The results of the section are published in Russian (Tanguiane 1979b; 1979c; 1980a; 1981b).

5.2 Aggregating Operators and Deciding Hierarchies

In the given section we define basic concepts of the collective choice model.

Let X be a non-empty *set of alternatives*. By $\mathcal{P}$ we denote the set of all partial orders on X, which we call the *set of preferences*.

Let V be a non-empty *set of individuals* and $\mathcal{A}$ be a coalition Boolean algebra on V, i.e. a non-empty set of subsets of the set V, containing all finite unions, intersections and complements of the subsets, denoted by $\cup, \cap$, $(.)^c$. The main properties of Boolean algebras are set out in (Sikorski 1964). Every element of algebra $\mathcal{A}$ is said to be a *coalition*; the unit of algebra $\mathcal{A}$ (the whole of V) is said to be the *collective*.

The states of the collective are the combinations of individual preferences, compatible with the Boolean algebra, meaning that all individuals with the same preferences on a pair of alternatives form a coalition.

5.2.1. DEFINITION. A mapping $f : V \to \mathcal{P}$, providing each individual $v \in V$ with some preference $f(v)$ on X, is called a *situation*, if it meets the *measurability condition:*

$$\{v : v \in V,\ (x, y) \in f(v)\} \in \mathcal{A}$$

for any couple of alternatives $x, y \in X$. By $f(A)$ we denote the *unanimity preference of a non-empty coalition* A (or strong Pareto preference), i.e.

$$f(A) = \bigcap_{v \in A} f(v),$$

Obviously, the *unanimity preference of the collective* is

$$f(V) = \bigcap_{v \in V} f(v).$$

The *set of all situations* on V into $\mathcal{P}$ we denote by F.

The above measurability condition is precisely Aumann's requirement of measurability (Aumann 1964), extended from a σ-algebra to an arbitrary Boolean algebra. The degree of restrictiveness of the given condition depends on the choice of coalition algebra, which characterizes the allowed diversity in individual preferences. The lack of restrictions, as in the models of Arrow, Fishburn, and Kirman and Sondermann, corresponds to the algebra of all subsets of the set of individuals, for which the measurability condition holds for all combinations of individual preferences. Therefore, the algebraic approach is a generalization of the traditional discrete approach.

Also note that since by proposition 2.2.15 the intersection of any number of partial orders is a partial order, the unanimity preference of a coalition in the above definition is always a partial order.

Let us formulate *Arrow's axioms* in our designations.

A1. (*Number of alternatives*). X contains no less than 3 elements.

A2. (*Universality*). For any situation $f \in F$ there exists a collective preference $\sigma(f) \in \mathcal{P}$. If all preferences $f(v)$ of all individuals $v \in V$ are weak orders, then the corresponding collective preference $\sigma(f)$ is also a weak order.

A3. (*Unanimity*). $f(V) \subset \sigma(f)$ for every situation $f \in F$.

A4. (*Independence of Irrelevant Alternatives*). If two situations $f, g \in F$ coincide on a couple of alternatives $(x, y) \in X \times X$, i.e.

$$f(v) \cap \{(x, y)\} = g(v) \cap \{(x, y)\}$$

for all individuals $v \in V$, then the associated collective preferences coincide on this couple of alternatives, i.e.

$$\sigma(f) \cap \{(x, y)\} = \sigma(g) \cap \{(x, y)\}.$$

A5. (*Prohibition of Dictatorship*). There is no *dictator*, i.e. an individual $v \in V$ such that $\sigma(f) = f(v)$ for all situations $f \in F$.

5.2.2. DEFINITION. A mapping $\sigma : F \to \mathcal{P}$, satisfying axioms A1–A4, is said to be an *aggregating operator*, or *social welfare function*.

Before we introduce the next definition, recall that an order $\succeq$ on a set H is called a *direction*, if the following conditions hold:

1. Reflexivity ($A \succeq A$ for each $A \in H$).

2. Transitivity ($A \succeq B$ and $B \succeq C$ implies $A \succeq C$ for every $A, B, C \in H$).

3. Anti-symmetry ($A \succeq B$ and $B \succeq A$ implies $A = B$ for every $A, B \in H$).

4. The existence of a common superior (for any two $A, B \in H$ there exists an element $C \in H$ such that it is superior or equal to A and B, i.e. $C \succeq A$ and $C \succeq B$).

5.2.3. DEFINITION. A *hierarchy* $(H, \succeq)$ is defined to be a non-empty set of non-empty coalations $H \subset \mathcal{A} \setminus \{\emptyset\}$ and a direction $\succeq$ on H "to be superior in the hierarchy or equal" if:

1. Coalations, inferior in the hierarchy, express preferences of the superior coalations (even if not completely), i.e. $A \succeq B$ for $A, B \in H$ implies $f(B) \subset f(A)$ for all situations $f \in F$.

2. Coalitions, expressing preferences of some coalitions of the hierarchy, belong to the hierarchy as inferior coalitions, i.e. $A \in H$, $B \in \mathrm{A} \setminus \{\emptyset\}$ and $f(B) \subset f(A)$ for all situations $f \in F$ implies $B \in H$ and $A \succeq B$.

3. The hierarchy is maximal, i.e. it is not a part of any larger hierarchy $(H', \succeq')$ such that $H \subset H'$, $H \neq H'$, and $\succeq$ coincides with $\succeq'$ on H.

To characterize the concept of hierarchy in algebraic terms, recall that an *ultrafilter* is a non-empty set H of non-zero elements of a Boolean algebra $\mathcal{A}$ such that:

1. $A \in H$, $A \subset B$, $B \in \mathcal{A}$ implies $B \in H$.

2. $A, B \in H$ implies $A \cap B \in H$.

3. For any $A \in \mathcal{A}$ either $A \in H$, or $A^c \in H$.

The concept of ultrafilter is dual to the concept of *maximal ideal.* Recall that an atom is an undividable non-zero element $A \in \mathcal{A}$, i.e. $B \subset A$, $B \in \mathcal{A} \setminus \{\emptyset\}$ implies $B = A$. An ultrafilter is called *principal* if there exists an atom $A \in \mathcal{A}$ such that

$$H = \{B : B \in \mathcal{A},\ A \subset B\}.$$

An ultrafilter is called *fixed* if the intersection of all its elements is not empty, otherwise it is called *free*.

5.2.4. DEFINITION. A non-empty coalition $A \in \mathcal{A} \setminus \{\emptyset\}$ is called *deciding* under aggregating operator σ if for all situations $f \in F$ it expresses (even if incompletely) the collective preference, i.e.

$$f(A) \subset \sigma(f).$$

The hierarchy, which consists of deciding coalitions under aggregating operator σ, is called *deciding* under the aggregating operator σ.

5.2.5. PROPOSITION (The Interpretation of Ultrafilters as Hierarchies). *Ultrafilters of the coalition Boolean algebra are the only hierarchies. If $(H, \succeq)$ is a hierarchy, then $A \succeq B$ for $A, B \in H$ if and only if $A \subset B$.*

PROOF. Let $(H, \succeq)$ be a hierarchy. We shall show that H is an ultrafilter. By definition H is a non-empty set of non-zero elements of algebra $\mathcal{A}$.

Firstly, we ascertain that $A \succeq B$, where $A, B \in H$, implies $A \subset B$. Indeed, let $A \succeq B$ for $A, B \in H$. Fix a non-empty preference P on X (example 2.2.9). Define the situation

$$f(v) = \begin{cases} P & \text{if } v \in B, \\ \emptyset & \text{if } v \notin B. \end{cases} \tag{5.2.1}$$

If we suppose that $A \not\subset B$, then

$$f(B) = P \not\subset \emptyset = f(A) \tag{5.2.2}$$

against item 1 of definition 5.2.3.

Conversely, suppose that $A \subset B$ for $A, B \in H$. Then, obviously, $f(B) \subset f(A)$ for each situation $f \in F$, and by item 2 of definition 5.2.3 we have $A \succeq B$.

Secondly, $A \in H$, $B \in \mathcal{A}$ and $A \subset B$ implies $B \in H$. Indeed, if $A \subset B$, then $f(B) \subset f(A)$ for all situations $f \in F$, and, applying item 2 of definition 5.2.3, we obtain that $B \in H$.

Thirdly, $A, B \in H$ implies $A \cap B \in H$. Since $\succeq$ is a direction on H, there exists a coalition $C \in H$ such that $C \succeq A$ and $C \succeq B$. Then $C \subset A$ and $C \subset B$. Consequently, $C \subset A \cap B$, whence by already proved $A \cap B \in H$.

At last, the 3rd item in the definition of ultrafilter is equivalent to the 3rd item of definition 5.2.3, which means the maximality of the hierarchy.

Now let H be an ultrafilter. For coalitions $A, B \in H$ put $A \succeq B$ if and only if $A \subset B$. Obviously, $\succeq$ is a direction on H. We shall prove that $(H, \succeq)$ is a hierarchy.

If $A \succeq B$ for $A, B \in H$, then $A \subset B$ and $f(B) \subset f(A)$ for all situations $f \in F$, therefore item 1 of definition 5.2.3 is true.

To prove item 2 suppose that $f(B) \subset f(A)$ for $A \in H$, $B \in \mathcal{A} \setminus \{\emptyset\}$ for all situations $f \in F$. Fix a not-empty preference P on X (example 2.2.9) and define situation f as in (5.2.1). If we suppose that $A \not\subset B$ we get (5.2.2), against the assumption. Therefore, $A \subset B$, and since H is an ultrafilter, $B \in H$, as required.

As mentioned above, the maximality of hierarchy is equivalent to the 3rd item of definition of ultrafilter.

5.3 Bijection Theorem

After we have defined the basic concepts of the model, we establish the relation between the aggregating operators and the hierarchies.

5.3.1. THEOREM (About the Bijection). *For any aggregating operator σ the set of all deciding coalitions forms a deciding hierarchy (ultrafilter of the coalition Boolean algebra). Conversely, each hierarchy (ultrafilter) determines a certain aggregating operator, for which the given hierarchy is deciding. The correspondence between the aggregating operators and the deciding hierarchies is one-to-one. If σ is an aggregating operator and H is the associated deciding hierarchy, then the aggregating operator is determined by the rule:*

$$\sigma(f) = \bigcup_{A \in H} f(A)$$

for every situation $f \in F$.

To prove the theorem we formulate three auxiliary propositions (Kirman & Sondermann 1972).

5.3.2. LEMMA (A Test for Deciding Coalitions). *A coalition $A \in \mathcal{A}$ is deciding under aggregating operator σ if and only if there exist a couple of alternatives $x, y \in X$ and a situation $f \in F$ such that*

$$(x, y) \in f(A),$$
$$(y, x) \in f(A^c),$$
$$(x, y) \in \sigma(f).$$

In other words, a coalition is deciding if and only if it is deciding for a certain situation on a certain couple of alternatives despite of opposite preference of its complement.

PROOF. If A is a deciding coalition, then $(x,y) \in f(A)$ implies $(x,y) \in \sigma(f)$ for any pair of alternatives $x,y \in X$ for any situation $f \in F$. Therefore, obviously, if $(x,y) \in f(A)$ and $(y,x) \in f(A^c)$ for a certain couple of alternatives $x,y \in X$ for a certain $f \in F$, then $(x,y) \in \sigma(f)$. Thus the formulated condition is necessary.

Let us prove that it is sufficient. Suppose that

$$(x,y) \in f(A),$$
$$(y,x) \in f(A^c),$$
$$(x,y) \in \sigma(f)$$

for a certain couple of alternatives $x,y \in X$ and a certain situation $f \in F$. We shall prove that A is a deciding coalition.

1. At first, we establish that

   $$(x,y) \in g(A),$$
   $$(y,x) \in g(A^c)$$

   implies

   $$(x,y) \in \sigma(g)$$

   for an arbitrary situation $g \in F$. Indeed, the required fact follows from the assumption and axiom A4 (fig. 47.1).

2. Let us show that

   $$(x,z) \in g(A),$$
   $$(z,x) \in g(A^c)$$

   implies

   $$(x,z) \in \sigma(g)$$

   for any alternative $z \in X$, $z \neq x$ for an arbitrary situation $g \in F$. If $z = y$, then the required fact follows from item 1. Taking into account A1, suppose that $z \neq y$. Referring to example 2.2.10, define situation h such that

   $$(x,y,z) \in h(A),$$
   $$(y,z,x) \in h(A^c)$$

   (fig. 47.2). By item 1 we get $(x,y) \in \sigma(h)$. By A3 we have $(y,z) \in \sigma(h)$, hence, by transitivity (A2) we obtain $(x,z) \in \sigma(h)$. Applying A4 to g and h, we deduce $(x,z) \in \sigma(h)$.

$$
\begin{array}{llllll}
 & & \overbrace{\qquad\qquad}^{A} & \overbrace{\qquad\qquad}^{A^c} & & \\
1. & f: & (x,y) & (y,x) & & \Rightarrow (x,y) \in \sigma(f) \\
 & g: & (x,y) & (y,x) & & \Rightarrow (x,y) \in \sigma(g) \\
 & & & & & \\
2. & h: & (x,y,z) & (y,z,x) & \Rightarrow (x,y,z) \in \sigma(h) & \Rightarrow (x,z) \in \sigma(h) \\
 & g: & (x,z) & (z,x) & & \Rightarrow (x,z) \in \sigma(g) \\
 & & & & & \\
3. & i: & (w,x,z) & (z,w,x) & \Rightarrow (w,x,z) \in \sigma(i) & \Rightarrow (w,z) \in \sigma(i) \\
 & g: & (w,z) & (z,w) & & \Rightarrow (w,z) \in \sigma(g) \\
 & & & & & \\
4. & j: & (w,z,u) & (z,u,w) & \Rightarrow (w,z,u) \in \sigma(j) & \Rightarrow (w,u) \in \sigma(j) \\
 & g: & (w,u) & (u,w) & & \Rightarrow (w,u) \in \sigma(g)
\end{array}
$$

Fig. 47

3. Let us show that

$$(w,z) \in g(A),$$
$$(z,w) \in g(A^c)$$

implies

$$(w,z) \in \sigma(g)$$

for any couple of alternatives $w, z \in X$, $z \neq x$, for an arbitrary situation $g \in F$. If $w = x$, then the required fact follows from item 2. Suppose that $w \neq x$. Define a situation $i \in F$ such that

$$(w,x,z) \in i(A),$$
$$(z,w,x) \in i(A^c)$$

(fig. 47.3). By item 2 we get $(x,z) \in \sigma(i)$, and by A3 we have $(w,x) \in \sigma(i)$, whence by transitivity (A2) we obtaine $(w,x) \in \sigma(i)$. Applying A4 to situations i and g, we deduce $(w,z) \in \sigma(i)$.

4. Let us show that

$$(w,u) \in g(A),$$
$$(u,w) \in g(A^c)$$

implies

$$(w, u) \in \sigma(g)$$

for any couple of alternatives $w, u \in X$ for an arbitrary situation $g \in F$. If $u \neq x$, the required fact follows from item 3. If $u = x$, then by A1 there exists $z \in X,\ z \neq x, w$. Define a situation $j \in F$ such that

$$(w, z, u) \in j(A),$$
$$(z, u, w) \in j(A^c)$$

(fig. 47.4). By A3 we get $(z, u) \in \sigma(j)$, and by item 3 we have $(w, z) \in \sigma(j)$, whence by transitivity (A2) we obtain $(w, u) \in \sigma(j)$. Applying A4 to situations j and g, we deduce $(w, u) \in \sigma(g)$.

5. At last we show that A is a deciding coalition under σ, i.e.

$$(w, z) \in g(A)$$

implies

$$(w, z) \in \sigma(g)$$

for any couple of alternatives $w, z \in X$ for an arbitrary situation $g \in F$. By A1 there exists $u \in X,\ u \neq w, z$. Define a situation $k \in F$ such that

$$\begin{array}{ll} (w, u, z) \in k(v) & \text{if } v \in A, \\ (u, w, z) \in k(v) & \text{if } v \notin A \text{ and } (w, z) \in g(v), \\ (u, z, w) \in k(v) & \text{if } v \notin A \text{ and } (z, w) \in g(v), \\ (u, w) \in k(v) & \text{if } v \notin A,\ (w, z) \in g(v) \text{ and } (z, w) \notin g(v) \end{array}$$

(fig. 48). Since $(w, u) \in k(A)$ and $(u, w) \in k(A^c)$, by item 4 we get $(w, u) \in \sigma(k)$, and by A3 we get $(u, z) \in \sigma(k)$; whence by transitivity (A2) we have $(w, z) \in \sigma(k)$. Applying A4 to situations g and k, we deduce $(w, z) \in \sigma(g)$.

5.3.3. LEMMA (Ultrafilter-Like Arrangement of Deciding Coalitions). *Let σ be an aggregating operator. Then the set of all deciding coalitions (under σ) is an ultrafilter of Boolean algebra $\mathcal{A}$.*

PROOF. Since by A3 the whole of V is a deciding coalition, and by definition deciding coalitions are non-zero elements of $\mathcal{A}$, the deciding coalitions under σ form a non-empty set of non-zero elements of the Boolean algebra $\mathcal{A}$. Let us verify the items of definition of ultrafilter.

$$\begin{array}{lllll} k: \overbrace{(w,u,z)}^{A} & \overbrace{(u,w,z)\ (u,z,w)\ (u,w\sim z)}^{A^c} & \Rightarrow (w,u,z)\in\sigma(k) & \Rightarrow (w,z)\in\sigma(k) \\ g: (w,z) & (w,z) \quad (z,w) \quad (w\sim z) & & \Rightarrow (w,z)\in\sigma(g) \end{array}$$

Fig. 48

1. If A is a deciding coalition and $A \subset B$, where $B \in \mathcal{A}$, then B is also a deciding coalition. Indeed, then $f(B) \subset f(A) \subset \sigma(f)$ for any situation $f \in F$.

2. Let A and B be deciding coalitions. We shall show that $A \cap B$ is also a deciding coalition. Fix three alternatives $x, y, z \in X$ (by A1) and define a situation $f \in F$ such that

$$\begin{aligned} (x,y,z) &\in f(v) \quad \text{if } v \in A\cap B,\\ (z,x,y) &\in f(v) \quad \text{if } v \in A\cap B^c,\\ (y,z,x) &\in f(v) \quad \text{if } v \notin A \end{aligned}$$

(fig. 49). Since A, B are deciding coalitions, and $(x,y) \in f(A)$, $(y,z) \in f(B)$, we have $(x,y) \in \sigma(f)$ and $(y,z) \in \sigma(f)$, whence by transitivity (A2) we obtain $(x,y) \in \sigma(f)$. Since

$$\begin{aligned} (x,z) &\in f(A\cap B),\\ (z,x) &\in f((A\cap B)^c), \end{aligned}$$

by lemma 5.3.2 we get that $A \cap B$ is a deciding coalition. Note that $A \cap B \neq \emptyset$, otherwise $(z,x) \in f(V)$ and by A3 $(z,x) \in \sigma(f)$, against the asymmetry of $\sigma(f)$ (A2).

3. We shall show that if $A \in \mathcal{A}$, then either A, or A^c is a deciding coalition. Fix three alternatives $x, y, z \in X$ and define a situation $f \in F$ such that

$$\begin{aligned} (x,y,z) &\in f(A)\\ (z,x,y) &\in f(A^c), \end{aligned}$$

while all individual preferences being weak orders (example 2.2.10). By A3 we have $(x,y) \in \sigma(f)$. Since all individual preferences $f(v)$ are weak orders, by A2 we have that $\sigma(f)$ is also a weak order. By item 8 of proposition 2.2.13 either $(x,z) \in \sigma(f)$, or $(z,y) \in \sigma(f)$. Then by lemma 5.3.2 in the first case the deciding coalition is A and in the second A^c, as required.

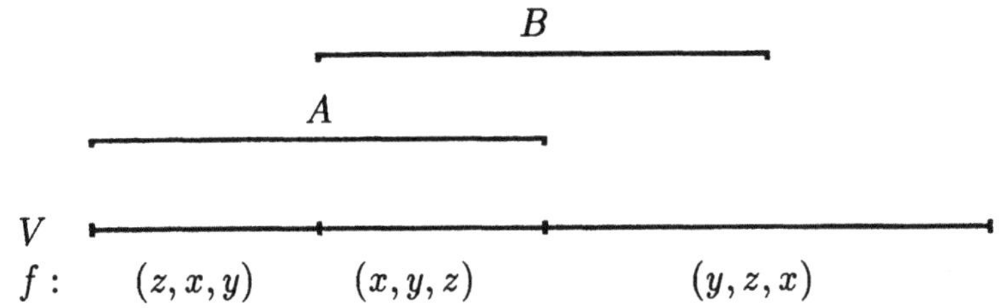

Fig. 49

5.3.4. LEMMA (About the Preference of a Hierarchy). *Let H be an ultrafilter. Fix a situation $f \in F$ and put*

$$\sigma(f) = \bigcup_{A \in H} f(A).$$

Then $\sigma(f)$ is a partial order, and if preferences $f(v)$ of all individuals $v \in V$ are weak orders, then $\sigma(f)$ is also a weak order.

PROOF. Obviously, $\sigma(f)$ is a binary relation on X.

Let us show that $\sigma(f)$ is asymmetric. Suppose that $(x,y) \in \sigma(f)$ and $(y,x) \in \sigma(f)$ for some $x, y \in X$. Then there exist elements of ultrafilter $A, B \in H$ such that $(x,y) \in f(A)$ and $(y,x) \in f(B)$. Since H is an ultrafilter,

$$A \cap B \neq \emptyset,$$

yet

$$(x,y) \in f(A \cap B),$$
$$(y,x) \in f(A \cap B),$$

which is impossible, because by proposition 2.2.15 $f(A \cap B)$ is a partial order, consequently, it is asymmetric.

Let us show that $\sigma(f)$ is transitive. If $(x,y) \in \sigma(f)$ and $(y,z) \in \sigma(f)$ for some $x, y, z \in X$, then there exist elements of ultrafilter $A, B \in H$ such that $(x,y) \in f(A)$ and $(y,z) \in f(B)$. Since $f(A \cap B)$ is a partial order, by transitivity $(x,z) \in f(A \cap B)$. Since $A \cap B \in H$, we obtain $(x,z) \in \sigma(f)$, as required.

Now we show that if all preferences $f(v)$ of all individuals $v \in V$ are weak orders, then $\sigma(f)$ is also a weak order. For that purpose it is sufficient to test

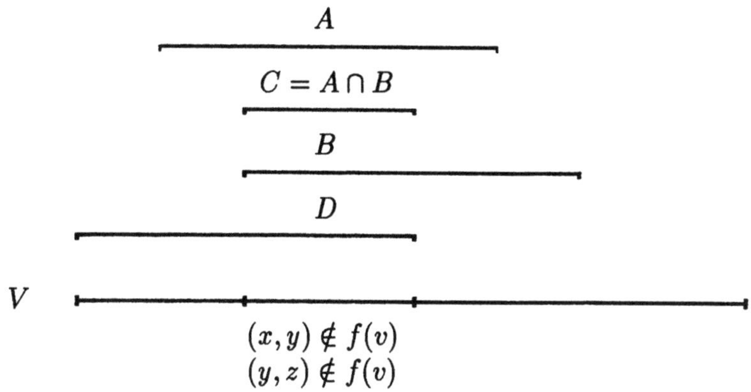

Fig. 50

its negative transitivity. At first note that by the measurability condition for any given $x, y \in X$ we have

$$\{v : v \in V,\ (x, y) \in f(v)\} \in \mathcal{A}.$$

Therefore,

$$(x, y) \in \sigma(f) \text{ if and only if } \{v : v \in V,\ (x, y) \in f(v)\} \in H. \tag{5.3.1}$$

Let $(x, y) \notin \sigma(f)$ and $(y, z) \notin \sigma(f)$ for some $x, y, z \in X$. Denote

$$\begin{aligned} A &= && \{v : v \in V,\ (x, y) \notin f(v)\}, \\ B &= && \{v : v \in V,\ (y, z) \notin f(v)\}, \\ C &= A \cap B = && \{v : v \in V,\ (x, y) \notin f(v),\ (y, z) \notin f(v)\}, \\ D &= && \{v : v \in V,\ (x, z) \notin f(v)\} \end{aligned}$$

(fig. 50). Since $f(v)$ are negatively transitive for all $v \in V$, we have $C \subset D$. By (5.3.1) we obtain $A \in H$, $B \notin H$. Since H is an ultrafilter, we have $C \in H$, consequently, $D \in H$, whence $D^c \notin H$. By (5.3.1) we get $(x, y) \notin \sigma(f)$, i.e. $\sigma(f)$ is negatively transitive, as required.

Proof of the theorem. The first statement of the theorem follows from lemma 5.3.3. Let us prove the second statement of the theorem.

Let H be an ultrafilter. Put

$$\sigma(f) = \bigcup_{A \in H} f(A)$$

for every situation $f \in F$. By lemma 5.3.4 the mapping $\sigma : F \to \mathcal{P}$ satisfies A2. Since $V \in H$, axiom A3 holds. Axiom A4 holds trivially. Since

$$f(A') \subset \bigcup_{A \in H} f(A) = \sigma(f)$$

for all $A' \in H$ and $f \in F$, the ultrafilter H consists of deciding coalitions. Therefore H is a deciding hierarchy, which proves the second statement of the theorem.

To prove the third statement, it is sufficient to show that if H is the ultrafilter of deciding coalitions under aggregating operator σ, then

$$\sigma(f) = \bigcup_{A \in H} f(A)$$

for every situation $f \in F$. Since all coalitions from H are deciding,

$$\bigcup_{A \in H} f(A) \subset \sigma(f)$$

for every situation $f \in F$. The converse inclusion we shall prove by contradiction. Assume that there exist a couple of alternatives $x, y \in X$ and a situation $f \in F$ such that

$$(x,y) \in \sigma(f),$$
$$(x,y) \notin \bigcup_{A \in H} f(A).$$

By the measurability condition

$$B = \{v : v \in V,\ (x,y) \in f(v)\} \in \mathcal{A},$$
$$C = \{v : v \in V,\ (y,x) \in f(v)\} \in \mathcal{A}.$$

By assumption $B \notin H$. If $C \in H$, then $(y,x) \in \sigma(f)$, and by asymmetry $(x,y) \notin \sigma(f)$, against the assumption, hence $C \notin H$. Since H is an ultrafilter, $B^c \in H$ and $C^c \in H$. Therefore

$$A = B^c \cap C^c \in H,$$

particularly, $A \neq \emptyset$. Referring to example 2.2.9, define the situation

$$g(v) = \begin{cases} \emptyset & \text{if } v \in A, \\ \{(x,z) : z \neq x,\ z \in X\} & \text{if } v \in B, \\ \{(y,z) : z \neq y,\ z \in X\} & \text{if } v \in C \end{cases}$$

(fig. 51). Applying A4 to situation f and g, we obtain $(x,y) \in \sigma(g)$. According to A1, there exists $z \in X,\ z \neq x, y$. By A2 $\sigma(g)$ is a weak order, whence by item 8 of proposition 2.2.13 either $(x,z) \in \sigma(g)$, or $(z,y) \in \sigma(g)$. Consider each case separately.

$$\begin{array}{llll} & \overbrace{A = B^c \cap C^c} & \overbrace{B} & \overbrace{C} \\ f: & (x \sim y) & (x, y) & (y, x) \\ g: & (x \sim y \sim z) & (x, y \sim z) & (y, x \sim z) \\ h: & \{(y, x)\} & (x, y \sim z) & (y, x \sim z) \\ i: & \{(z, x)\} & (x, y \sim z) & (y, x \sim z) \\ j: & \{(y, z)\} & (x, y \sim z) & (y, x \sim z) \end{array}$$

Fig. 51

1. Let $(x, z) \in \sigma(g)$. Define the situation

$$h(v) = \begin{cases} \{(y, x)\} & \text{if } v \in A, \\ g(v) & \text{if } v \notin A \end{cases}$$

(fig. 51). Applying A4 to situations g and h, we obtain $(x, z) \in \sigma(h)$. Since $A \in H$, we obtain $(y, x) \in \sigma(h)$. By transitivity (A2) we have $(y, z) \in \sigma(h)$. Define the situation

$$i(v) = \begin{cases} \{(z, x)\} & \text{if } v \in A, \\ g(v) & \text{if } v \notin A \end{cases}$$

(fig. 51). Since $A \in H$, we have $(z, x) \in \sigma(i)$. Applying A4 to $h(v)$ and $i(v)$, we obtain $(y, z) \in \sigma(i)$. By transitivity we have $(y, x) \in \sigma(i)$. Applying A4 to situations g and i, we obtain $(y, x) \in \sigma(g)$, which is impossible, because $\sigma(g)$ is asymmetric (by A2), yet we proved that $(x, y) \in \sigma(g)$.

2. Let $(z, y) \in \sigma(g)$. Applying A4 to situations g and h, we obtain $(z, y) \in \sigma(h)$. Since $(y, x) \in \sigma(h)$, by transitivity (A2) we have $(z, x) \in \sigma(h)$. Define the situation

$$j(v) = \begin{cases} \{(y, z)\} & \text{if } v \in A, \\ g(v) & \text{if } v \notin A \end{cases}$$

(fig. 51). Since $A \in H$, we get $(y, z) \in \sigma(j)$. Applying A4 to situations h and j, we obtain $(z, x) \in \sigma(j)$. By transitivity (A2) we have $(y, x) \in \sigma(j)$. Applying A4 to situations g and j, we obtain $(y, x) \in \sigma(g)$, which is impossible, because $\sigma(g)$ is asymmetric (by A2), yet we proved that $(x, y) \in \sigma(g)$.

The obtained contradictions proves the inclusion

$$\sigma(f) \subset \bigcup_{A \in H} f(A),$$

as required.

In the above proof we used preferences like $\{(x,y)\}, \{(z,x)\}$, and $\{(y,z)\}$, which are not weak orders (except for the case when the set of alternatives consists of two elements). The use of partial orders, which are not weak orders, is essential to establish a one-to-one correspondence between aggregating operators and ultrafilters. Using weak orders only, as in most works on collective choice, we could establish a surjection from the set of aggregating operators onto the set of ultrafilters (Kirman & Sondermann 1972), but not a bijection. That is why we have extended the concept of a situation to all partial orders, making a reservation for weak orders in our formulation of axiom A2. Further discussion of related questions will be continued at the end of the chapter.

5.4 Theorems of Arrow and Fishburn

The central concept in Arrow's theory of collective choice is the dictator. The dictator is understood to be the individual, determining collective choice, i.e. whose preference coincides with that of the whole collective despite of preferences of other individuals. The definition of the dictator is given in axiom A5.

5.4.1. Proposition (Dictators as Fixing Points of Ultrafilters). *An individual $v \in V$ is a dictator if and only if the ultrafilter of deciding coalitions H is fixed, being determined by v, i.e.*

$$H = H_v = \{A : A \in \mathcal{A},\ v \in A\}.$$

Proof. Take an arbitrary point $v \in V$. Denote the ultrafilter, all elements of which contain v, by

$$H_v = \{A : A \in \mathcal{A},\ v \in A\}.$$

We shall show that

$$f(v) = \bigcup_{A \in H_v} f(A) \tag{5.4.1}$$

for every situation $f \in F$. At first let $(x,y) \in f(v)$ for certain $x, y \in X$. By the measurability condition,

$$B = \{w : w \in V,\ (x,y) \in f(w)\} \in \mathcal{A},$$

and, obviously, $v \in B$, whence $B \in H_v$. Therefore

$$(x,y) \in f(B) \subset \bigcup_{A \in H_v} f(A).$$

Now suppose that

$$(x,y) \in \bigcup_{A \in H_v} f(A)$$

for certain $x, y \in X$. Then there exists a coalition $B \in H_v$ such that $(x,y) \in f(B)$, therefore, $(x,y) \in f(w)$ for all $w \in B$, particularly, $(x,y) \in f(v)$. Thus (5.4.1) is proved.

Let σ be an aggregating operator and H be the ultrafilter, corresponding to H by theorem 5.3.1. If $v \in V$ is a dictator under σ, then by (5.4.1) we have

$$\sigma(f) = f(v) = \bigcup_{A \in H_v} f(A)$$

for every situation $f \in F$. Then by theorem 5.3.1 we have $H_v = H$. Conversely, if H_v is a fixed ultrafilter for a certain $v \in V$, then by theorem 5.3.1 and (5.4.1) for every situation $f \in F$ we have

$$\sigma(f) = \bigcup_{A \in H_v} f(A) = f(v),$$

i.e. v is the dictator under σ.

Let us formulate a simple corollary, following from the above proposition.

5.4.2. Corollary (Uniqueness of the Dictator). *The number of dictators under an arbitrary aggregating operator does not exceed one if and only if the coalition Boolean algebra is a reduced field of sets, i.e. for any two $v, w \in V$ there exists an element $A \in \mathcal{A}$ such that $v \in A$ and $w \in A^c$.*

Now we can prove the theorems of Arrow and Fishburn.

5.4.3. Corollary (Arrow's Theorem). *Let the set of individuals be finite, and all combinations of individual preferences be allowed. Then under any aggregating operator there exists a dictator, and therefore axioms* A1–A5 *are inconsistent.*

Proof. Since all combinations of individual preferences are allowed, the coalition algebra is the algebra of all subsets of a finite set, where every ultrafilter is fixed. By proposition 5.4.1 we obtain the required fact.

5.4.4. COROLLARY (Fishburn's Theorem). *Let the set of individuals be infinite, and all combinations of individual preferences be allowed. Then there exists an aggregating operator without a dictator, and therefore axioms* A1–A5 *are consistent.*

PROOF. Since all combinations of individual preferences are allowed, the coalition algebra is the algebra of all subsets of an infinite set, where (under the axiom of choice) free ultrafilters exist. By proposition 5.4.1 there exist aggregating operators, under which there are no dictators. It implies the consistence of axioms A1–A5.

5.5 Representation of Model of Aggregation of Preferences

Now we are going to give a pure algebraic definition of the collective choice model. We shall show that the same model can be defined on different sets of individuals. Indeed, there are no reasons to distinguish between collective choice models with, say, five independent individuals, or five groups of agents with identical preferences. A general case, however, is not so evident. To characterize similar models we use the concept of isomorphism and represent each class of isomorphic (similar) models by the one, realized on a 'good' set of individuals.

First of all recall how to construct the *Stone representation of a Boolean algebra* (Sikorski 1964).

Let V' be the set of all ultrafilters of Boolean algebra $\mathcal{A}$. For each element $A \in \mathcal{A}$ denote by $h(A)$ the set of ultrafilters from V', which contain the element A. Then the class $\mathcal{A}'$ of all sets $h(A)$, where $A \in \mathcal{A}$, is a reduced field of subsets of V', and h is an isomorphism of $\mathcal{A}$ onto $\mathcal{A}'$. The family $\mathcal{A}'$ one can consider as a base of some topology on V'. Under this topology V' is a totally disconnected compactum, the clopen sets of which are elements of $\mathcal{A}'$. All ultrafilters of algebra $\mathcal{A}'$ are fixed and are determined by points of V'. If H and H' are associated ultrafilter of algebras $\mathcal{A}$ and $\mathcal{A}'$, respectively, then

$$H = \bigcap_{A' \in H'} A'.$$

By F' denote the set of situations on V' (for the same set of preferences $\mathcal{P}$ and isomorphic algebra of coalitions $\mathcal{A}'$). The fixed ultrafilter of algebra $\mathcal{A}$, determined by point $v \in V$, is denoted by H_v.

5.5.1. THEOREM (On the Representation of a Collective Choice Model). *Let V' be the Stone compactum of algebra $\mathcal{A}$ with the algebra $\mathcal{A}'$ of clopen* *subsets, isomorphic to $\mathcal{A}$ (the space of ultrafilters of algebra $\mathcal{A}$). Then there are bijections between the sets of situations $F = \{f\}$ on V and $F' = \{f'\}$ on V', and between the sets of aggregating operators $\Sigma = \{\sigma\}$ on F and $\Sigma' = \{\sigma'\}$ on F' such that the preferences of corresponding operators $\sigma \in \Sigma$ and $\sigma' \in \Sigma'$ on corresponding situations $f \in F$ and $f' \in F'$ coincide, i.e.*

$$\sigma(f) = \sigma'(f').$$

Before we prove the theorem, we formulate the following proposition.

5.5.2. LEMMA (A Test for Equality of Situations). *If $f'_1, f'_2 \in F'$ coincide on all fixed ultrafilters, i.e.*

$$f'_1(H_v) = f'_2(H_v)$$

for all $v \in V$, then they are equal, i.e.

$$f'_1(H) = f'_2(H)$$

for all $H \in V'$.

PROOF. Assume the contrary, i.e. that there exist $x, y \in X$ and $H_0 \in V'$ such that either $(x,y) \in f'_1(H_0)$ and $(x,y) \notin f'_2(H_0)$, or $(x,y) \notin f'_1(H_0)$ and $(x,y) \in f'_2(H_0)$. Since the latter case is brought to the former by renumbering the situations, we shall examine the first possibility only. By the measurability condition there exist $A'_1, A'_2 \in \mathcal{A}'$ such that $(x,y) \in f'_1(H)$, where $H \in V'$, if and only if $H \in A'_1$ and $H \notin A'_2$. Therefore, $A'_1 \cap A'^c_2 \neq \emptyset$ and, consequently, there exists a coalition $A \in \mathcal{A}$ such that $h(A) = A'_1 \cap A'^c_2$. Let $v \in A$. Then $H_v \in A'_1 \cap A'^c_2$, hence $(x,y) \in f'_1(H_v)$ and $(x,y) \notin f'_2(H_v)$, against the assumption.

PROOF OF THE THEOREM. Define a mapping $\varphi : F \to F'$, associating each situation $f \in F$ with a situation $f' = \varphi(f) \in F'$ by the following rule:

$$f'(H) = \bigcup_{A: A \in H} f(A) \tag{5.5.1}$$

for all $H \in V'$. By lemma 5.3.4 $f'(H)$ is a partial order for each $H \in V'$. We shall show that mapping $f' : V' \to \mathcal{P}$ satisfies the measurability condition. Let $x, y \in X$. By the measurability condition for f there exists an element $A \in \mathcal{A}$ such that $(x,y) \in f(v)$ if and only if $v \in A$. Then $(x,y) \in f'(H)$ if and only if $A \in H$, i.e. $H \in h(A)$, as required. Thus f' is a situation, and indeed $\varphi : F \to F'$.

If $f' = \varphi(f)$, then by (5.4.1) we have $f(v) = f'(H_v)$ for every $v \in V$. Consequently, any two unequal situations from F are associated with some two unequal situations F', which means that φ is a one-to-one correspondece of F into F'.

Let us show that φ is a surjection. Let $f' \in F'$. Put $f(v) = f'(H_v) \in \mathcal{P}$ for each $v \in V$. We shall prove that the mapping $f : V \to \mathcal{P}$ is a situation, i.e. satisfies the measurability condition. Let $x, y \in X$. By the measurability condition for f' there exists an element $A' \in \mathcal{A}'$ such that $(x, y) \in f'(H)$ if and only if $H \in A'$. It means that $(x, y) \in f'(H_v)$, where $v \in V$, if and only if $H_v \in A'$, or, which is equivalent, $A \in H_v$, where $h(A) = A'$, i.e. $v \in A$, as required. Thus f is a situation. Now we shall prove that $\varphi(f) = f'$. If $f'' = \varphi(f)$, then by (5.4.1) we have $f''(H_v) = f(v)$ for all $v \in V$. Since by construction of f we have $f'(H_v) = f(v)$, by lemma 5.5.2 we obtain $f'' = f'$.

At last we prove that if $f' = \varphi(f)$, then $f(A) = f'(h(A))$ for any non-zero coalition $A \in \mathcal{A}$. Indeed, on the one hand,

$$f(A) \subset \bigcap_{H:A\in H} \bigcup_{B\in H} f(B) = \bigcap_{H\in h(A)} f'(H) = f'(h(A)).$$

On the other hand, for any non-zero coalition $A \in \mathcal{A}$ there exists $v \in A$, consequently, $h(A)$ contains at least one fixed ultrafilter H_v. Hence,

$$f'(h(A)) = \bigcap_{H\in h(A)} f(H) \subset \bigcap_{H_v\in h(A)} f'(H_v) = \bigcap_{v\in A} f'(v) = f(A).$$

Thus we have constructed a one-to-one correspondence φ between the sets of situations F and F'. Moreover, every two corresponding situations have the same preferences at the coalitions, associated by isomorphism h. Since by theorem 5.3.1 aggregating operators are completely determined by preferences of coalitions, the rule

$$\sigma'(f') = \sigma(f),$$

where $f \in F$, $f' \in F'$, $f' = \varphi(f)$, determines the required one-to-one correspondence between the sets of aggregating operators Σ' on F' and Σ on F.

It follows from the theorem that any collective choice model can be transferred to the Stone space of the given coalition Boolean algebra. One can conclude that just an abstract Boolean algebra, but not its realization as a field of sets on a concrete set of individuals determines the properties of the collective choice model. Isomorphic models can be defined for different sets of individuals, even of unequal cardinality.

5.5.3. DEFINITION. Fix a set of alternatives X with the associated set of preferences $\mathcal{P}$. An *algebraic collective choice model* is defined to be a triplet $(\mathcal{A}, F, \sigma)$, where $\mathcal{A}$ is a Boolean algebra of coalitions, F is the set of situations, defined on the set of all ultrafilters of $\mathcal{A}$ and σ is an aggregating operator. Two algebraic collective choice models $(\mathcal{A}, F, \sigma)$ and $(\mathcal{A}', F', \sigma')$ are called *isomorphic* if there is an isomorphism h of algebra $\mathcal{A}$ onto algebra $\mathcal{A}'$ and a one-to-one correspondence $\varphi : F \to F'$ such that

$$f' = \varphi(f)$$

implies

$$f(A) = f'(h(A))$$

for all non-zero $A \in \mathcal{A}$ and

$$\sigma'(f') = \sigma(f).$$

5.5.4. PROPOSITION (A Test for Isomorphic Models). *Let $(\mathcal{A}, F, \sigma)$ and $(\mathcal{A}', F', \sigma')$ be two algebraic collective choice models, defined for the same set of alternatives X with the associated set of preferences $\mathcal{P}$. Let H be the ultrafilter of algebra $\mathcal{A}$, corresponding to σ by theorem* 5.3.1, *and H' be the ultrafilter of algebra $\mathcal{A}'$, corresponding to σ'. These models are isomorphic if and only if there exists an isomorphism h from algebra $\mathcal{A}$ onto algebra $\mathcal{A}'$, transmitting H into H', i.e. such that*

$$H' = h(H).$$

PROOF. Note that isomorphic algebras have the same Stone representation and apply theorem 5.5.1.

Thus under isomorphisms of collective choice models the deciding hierarchies are transmitted into the deciding hierarchies, i.e. the deciding hierarchy is an algebraic invariant of the model. The dictator is not invariant with respect to isomorphisms of the model.

5.5.5. EXAMPLE. Consider a set of 6 individuals $V = \{1, \ldots, 6\}$ with a Boolean algebra of coalitions, generated by 5 atoms $\{1\}, \ldots, \{4\}, \{5, 6\}$. Define aggregating operator by deciding hierarchy. Fix the ultrafilter, all elements of which contain atom $\{5, 6\}$. Obviously, there are two dictators—individuals 5 and 6. The Stone representation of the given Boolean algebra is a discrete space of 5 points, where each atom consists of a single point. Therefore the collective choice mode, isomorphic to the given one, has a single dictator instead of two.

Since the number of dictators may vary in isomorphic models, the dictator is not an algebraic invariant. Moreover, since there are infinite Boolean algebras with free ultrafilters, there is a collective choice model with no dictator. However, in its Stone representation all ultrafilters are fixed, hence the dictator can be taken into and away from the model under its isomorphisms.

5.6 Topological Formulation of Model of Aggregation of Preferences

In this section we use some concepts and facts of general topology set out in (Kelley 1955; Engelking 1977; Arhangelskii & Ponomarev 1974).

Recall that if $S \subset X \times X$ is a binary relation on X, then its *characteristic function* is defined to be the two-value function

$$\chi_S(x,y) = \begin{cases} 1 & \text{if } (x,y) \in S, \\ 0 & \text{if } (x,y) \notin S. \end{cases}$$

We consider the set of binary relations on X as a topological space of their characteristic functions with the *topology of pointwise convergence*. A *base clopen neighborhood O of a binary relation $S \subset X \times X$* consists of the binary relations $S' \subset X \times X$, which coincide with the given one on a finite set of couples of alternatives

$$T = \{(x_1, y_1), \ldots, (x_n, y_n)\} \subset X \times X,$$

i.e.

$$O = O_T(S) = \{S' : S' \subset X \times X,\ S' \cap T = S \cap T\}.$$

Obviously, a *prebase clopen neighborhood* is the base neighborhood $O_T(S)$, where

$$T = \{(x,y)\} \subset X \times X,$$

i.e. consists of a single couple of alternatives $\{(x,y)\}$. Thus the set of binary relations on X is identified with the Tihonov product $\{0,1\}^{X \times X}$, or, if X is infinite, with the generalized Cantor discontinuum $D^{X \times X}$. Under this topology the set of partial orders (preferences), as well as the set of weak orders, is closed in $D^{X \times X}$ (Armstrong 1980).

5.6.1. PROPOSITION (Compactness of the Set of Preferences). *The set of all partial orders (preferences) on X is closed in $D^{X \times X}$ and therefore is a compactum.*

PROOF. Suppose that $P \in [\mathcal{P}]$. We shall prove that $P \in \mathcal{P}$.

At first we shall show that P is asymmetric. Let $(x,y) \in P$ for some $x, y \in X$, $x \neq y$. Put

$$T = \{(x,y),(y,x)\}$$

and consider the neighborhood

$$O_T(P) = \{S' : S' \subset X \times X,\ S' \cap T = P \cap T\}. \tag{5.6.1}$$

Since $P \in [\mathcal{P}]$, there exists a certain partial order $P' \in O_T(P) \cap \mathcal{P}$, i.e. $P' \cap T = P \cap T$. Since $(x,y) \in P$, we obtain $(x,y) \notin P$, as required.

Now we shall show that P is transitive. Let $(x,y) \in P$ and $(y,z) \in P$ for some $x, y, z \in X$. Put

$$T = \{(x,y),(y,z),(x,z)\},$$

and consider the neighborhood $O_T(P)$. Since $P \in [\mathcal{P}]$, there exists a certain partial order $P' \in O_T(P) \cap \mathcal{P}$, i.e. $P' \cap T = P \cap T$. Since $(x,y) \in P$ and $(y,z) \in P$, we also have $(x,y) \in P'$ and $(y,z) \in P'$, whence by transitivity $(x,z) \in P'$. Since $P' \cap T = P \cap T$, we obtain $(x,z) \in P$, as required.

Beside the set of preferences, we also topologize the set of individuals V, which we consider as a space with the base of clopen subsets, which are elements of the coalition Boolean algebra $\mathcal{A}$.

5.6.2. PROPOSITION (The Equivalence of Measurability and Continuity of Situations). *A mapping $f : V \to \mathcal{P}$ satisfies the measurability conditions (is a situation) if and only if it is continuous.*

PROOF. At first we shall prove that the measurability condition implies the continuity. Let $f : V \to \mathcal{P}$ be a situation. To prove its continuity, it is sufficient to show that $f^{-1}(O_T(P))$ is open for an arbitrary $P \in \mathcal{P}$ and its arbitrary prebase neighborhood $O_T(P)$, where $T = \{(x,y)\}$ for some $x, y \in X$. Since $T = \{(x,y)\}$, only two mutually exclusive cases are possible: Either

$$f^{-1}(O_T(P)) = \{v : v \in V,\ (x,y) \in f(v)\},$$

or

$$f^{-1}(O_T(P)) = \{v : v \in V,\ (x,y) \notin f(v)\} = \{v : v \in V,\ (x,y) \in f(v)\}^c,$$

which by the measurability are elements of $\mathcal{A}$, i.e. clopen subsets of V.

Now let a mapping $f : V \to \mathcal{P}$ be continuous. Consider an arbitrary couple of alternatives $x, y \in X$. Obviously,

$$U = \{P : P \in \mathcal{P},\ (x,y) \in P\}$$

is a clopen subset of $\mathcal{P}$, consequently,

$$f^{-1}(U) = \{v : v \in V,\ (x,y) \in f(v)\}$$

is a clopen subset of V, and therefore an element of $\mathcal{A}$, as required.

The set F of all situations we regard as a space with the topology of pointwise convergence. Under this topology a *base neighborhood of a situation* $f \in F$ is the set of the situations $f' \in F$ such that some finite set of individuals $W \subset V$ has preferences close to the given ones. In other words, a base neighborhood of a situation $f \in F$ is determined by a finite set of individuals

$$W \subset V,$$

a finite family of finite collections of couples of alternatives

$$T_W = \{T_w \subset X \times X : w \in W\},$$

where each $T_w \subset X \times X$ is finite, and is defined to be

$$U_{W,T_W}(f) = \{f' : f' \in F,\ f'(w) \cap T_w = f(w) \cap T_w,\ w \in W\}.$$

As in the case of binary relations, it is much easier to define the topology in F, referring to the prebase. A *prebase neighborhood of a situation* $f \in F$ is the set of the situations $f' \in F$, under which some individual $w \in V$ (i.e. $W = \{w\}$) has the same preference, on a given pair of alternatives $T_w = \{(x,y)\}$, i.e.

$$U_{w,(x,y)}(f) = \{f' : f' \in F,\ f'(w) \cap \{(x,y)\} = f(w) \cap \{(x,y)\}\}$$

for some $w \in V$ and $x, y \in X$.

5.6.3. PROPOSITION (About the Continuity of Aggregating Operators). *Every aggregating operator is a continuous mapping from the space of situations into the space of preferences.*

PROOF. To prove the continuity of an aggregating operator σ, it is sufficient to show that $\sigma^{-1}(O_T(P))$ is open in F for an arbitrary preference P and its arbitrary prebase neighborhood $O_T(P)$, where $T = \{(x,y)\}$ for some $x, y \in X$.

Consider the representation of the model, where each aggregating operator is determined by a certain dictator. Let w be the dictator under our aggregating operator σ. Define the situation

$$f(v) = P \text{ for all } v \in V.$$

Then

$$\begin{aligned}\sigma^{-1}(O_T(P)) &= \{f' : f' \in F,\ f'(w) \cap T = P \cap T\}\\ &= \{f' : f' \in F,\ f'(w) \cap T = f(w) \cap T\}\\ &= U_{w,(x,y)}(f)\end{aligned}$$

is a prebase neighborhood of the situation f, which is open.

At last, the set Σ of aggregating operators on the space of situations F we also regard as a space with the topology of pointwise convergence. A *base neighborhood of an aggregating operator* σ_0 is the set of aggregating operators $\sigma \in \Sigma$ such that on a finite set of situations $G \subset F$ they have preferences close to the given aggregated preferences. In other words, a base neighborhood of an aggregating operator $\sigma_0 \in \Sigma$ is determined by a finite set of situations

$$G \subset F,$$

a finite family of finite collections of couples of alternatives

$$T_G = \{T_g : T_g \subset X \times X,\ g \in G\},$$

where each $T_g \subset X \times X$ is finite, and is defined to be

$$O_{G,T_G}(\sigma_0) = \{\sigma : \sigma \in \Sigma,\ \sigma(g) \cap T_g = \sigma_0(g) \cap T_g,\ g \in G\}.$$

It is easy to see that a *prebase neighborhood of an aggregating operator* $\sigma_0 \in \Sigma$ is the set of aggregating operators $\sigma \in \Sigma$ such that for a given situation $g \in F$ (i.e. $G = \{g\}$) they have preferences, which coincide on a given pair of alternatives (x, y), i.e.

$$O_{g,(x,y)}(\sigma_0) = \{\sigma : \sigma \in \Sigma,\ \sigma(g) \cap \{(x,y)\} = \sigma_0(g) \cap \{(x,y)\}\}.$$

5.6.4. THEOREM (A Topological Formulation of the Bijection Theorem). *The space Σ of aggregating operators is homeomorphic to the space V' of ultrafilters of the coalition Boolean algebra. If the coalition algebra is the set of all subsets of set V, the space Σ of aggregating operators is homeomorphic to* *the Stone–Cech compactification of the space of individuals.*

PROOF. Let us prove the first statement of theorem 5.6.4. Let V' be the Stone compactum—the space of ultrafilters of the Boolean algebra $\mathcal{A}$. By theorem 5.3.1, there exists a one-to-one correspondence $\varphi : V' \to \Sigma$. To show that φ is a homeomorphism it is sufficient to ascertain that φ is continuous (since V' is a compactum, any continuous one-to-one correspondence is a homeomorphism). In turn for that purpose it is sufficient to show that the preimage of an element of the prebase of Σ is open in V'. Let $O_{g,(x,y)}(\sigma_0)$ be an arbitrary element of the prebase of Σ and H_0 be the ultrafilter, associated with σ_0 by theorem 5.3.1. Again by theorem 5.3.1, taking an arbitrary aggregating operator $\sigma \in \Sigma$, denote the associated ultrafilter by H. Then

$$\begin{aligned}
&\varphi^{-1}(O_{g,(x,y)}(\sigma_0)) = \\
&= \varphi^{-1}(\{\sigma : \sigma \in \Sigma,\ \sigma(g) \cap \{(x,y)\} = \sigma_0(g) \cap \{(x,y)\}\}) \\
&= \{H : H \in V',\ \bigcup_{A \in H} g(A) \cap \{(x,y)\} = \bigcup_{A \in H_0} g(A) \cap \{(x,y)\}\}.
\end{aligned}$$

Let g' be a mapping on V', associated with g on V by the rule (5.5.1), i.e.

$$g'(H) = \bigcup_{A \in H} g(A)$$

for all $H \in V'$. Then we continue the above equalities

$$\begin{aligned}
&\{H : H \in V',\ \bigcup_{A \in H} g(A) \cap \{(x,y)\} = \bigcup_{A \in H_0} g(A) \cap \{(x,y)\}\} = \\
&= \{H : H \in V',\ g'(H) \cap \{(x,y)\} = g'(H_0) \cap \{(x,y)\}\} \\
&= g'^{-1}(O_{(x,y)}(g'(H_0))),
\end{aligned}$$

where $O_{(x,y)}(g'(H_0))$ is a prebase neighborhood of preference $g'(H_0)$. Since by theorem 5.5.1 the mapping g' is a situation, by proposition 5.6.2 it is continuous. Then $g'^{-1}(O_{(x,y)}(g'(H_0)))$ is open in V'. Hence $\varphi^{-1}(O_{g,(x,y)}(\sigma_0))$ is open in V, as required.

To prove the second statement of theorem 5.6.4, it is sufficient to note that when the coalition Boolean algebra is the set of all subsets of the set of individuals, its Stone representation (the space of ultrafilters) is at the same time the Stone–Cech compactification of the set of individuals. Taking into account the first statement of theorem 5.6.4, we immediately obtain the second.

5.6.5. COROLLARY (Theorem of Kirman and Sondermann). *Let the set of individuals be infinite and all combinations of individual preferences be allowed. Then the set of individuals can be compactified by "invisible" individuals such*

Dictatorial aggregating operators	$\{\sigma_\alpha\}$	$\longrightarrow$	σ_0	Nondictatorial aggregating operator
	$\Updownarrow$		$\Updownarrow$	
"Visible" dictators	$\{v_\alpha\}$	$\longrightarrow$	v_0	"Invisible" dictator

Fig. 52.

that under each aggregating operator there will be a dictator, may be "invisible". Hence, axioms A1–A5 *are inconsistent.*

PROOF. Since all combinations of individual preferences are allowed, the coalition algebra is the algebra of all subsets of the set of individuals. By theorem 5.6.4 the space of aggregating operators is homeomorphic to the Stone–Cech compactification of the set of individuals, the points of the growth of which are called invisible agents. Since the set of all preferences is a compactum (proposition 5.6.1), every situation is continuous (proposition 5.6.2) and any continuous mapping of a given space into a compactum can be extended to its Stone–Cech compactification (these "invisible" agents can be regarded as "limit" individuals with "limit" preferences). Since each ultrafilter of the Stone space is fixed, the corresponding ultrafilter of clopen sets in the Stone–Cech compactification of the set of individuals is also fixed (by homeomorphism), hence, there always exists a dictator (proposition 5.4.1), as required.

Note that nondictatorial aggregating operators are the accumulation points to dictatorial ones. Indeed, by theorem 5.3.1 associate a nondictatorial aggregating operator σ_0 with an "invisible" dictator v_0 from the Stone–Cech compactification βV of the set of individuals V (fig. 52).

Let $\{v_\alpha\} \subset V$ be a direction, converging to v_0 in βV, and for every α denote by σ_α an aggregating operator, associated with v_α by theorem 5.3.1. Since the compactified space of individuals is homeomorphic to the space of aggregating operators, the direction $\{\sigma_\alpha\}$ converges to σ_0. Thus we have proved that dictatorial aggregating operators are dense in the space of aggregating operators.

Instead of Stone–Cech compactification, defined for a completely regular topological space (that is the reason why we have restricted our consideration to the discrete space of individuals), one can use the compactification of Wallman type, defined for much more wide class of topological spaces. Without going into topological details we give the following generalization of the theorem of Kirman and Sondermann.

5.6.6. PROPOSITION (About the Extension of a Collective Choice Model). *Let $\mathcal{A}$ be a coalition Boolean algebra on the set of individuals V. Then there exists a topological space V' (Hausdorff if algebra $\mathcal{A}$ is reduced) and algebra $\mathcal{A}'$ of its clopen subsets such that:*

1. *V' is an extension of V, i.e. $V \subset V'$ and V is dense in V';*
2. *Algebra $\mathcal{A}'$ is an extension of algebra $\mathcal{A}$ to the whole of V', i.e. the restriction of $\mathcal{A}'$ to V is $\mathcal{A}$, and $\mathcal{A}'$ is isomorphic to $\mathcal{A}$;*
3. *Each situation f' on V' is an extension of some situation f on V;*
4. *For any aggregating operator on F' there exists a dictator.*

PROOF. Add all free ultrafilters of algebra $\mathcal{A}$ to the set of individuals V and denote the new set by V'. For each $A \in \mathcal{A}$ denote by $h(A)$ the set A itself and also all free ultrafilters, containing A. Then the class $\mathcal{A}'$ of all sets $h(A)$, where A runs over $\mathcal{A}$, is an algebra of subsets of the set V'. Obviously, V is dense in V under the topology generated by the base $\mathcal{A}'$ of clopen sets in V'. Since V is dense in V', the restriction of $\mathcal{A}'$ to V is isomorphic to $\mathcal{A}$. By construction every ultrafilter of $\mathcal{A}'$ is fixed, therefore, by proposition 5.4.1 for any aggregating operator on F' there exists a dictator. At last, each situation $f \in F$ on V is extended to V' by the rule (5.5.1). Since the two algebras $\mathcal{A}$ and $\mathcal{A}'$ are isomorphic, the given rule establishes a one-to-one correspondence between F and F'.

The omitted details of the above proof one can restore easily, following the proof of theorem 5.5.1. The only difference is that now we don't identify inseparable individuals; for example, a non-trivial undividable coalition (atom) is not replaced by a single point, as in example 5.5.5, but is still represented by several individuals.

Summing up what has been said, we can conclude that the analysis of the concept of aggregating operator is reduced to the analysis of ultrafilters of coalition Boolean algebra (theorem 5.3.1) and thereupon to properties of points of the Stone compactum (theorems 5.5.1 and 5.6.4). As a result, the nature of some known results becomes clear: The theorems of Arrow and Fishburn are explained by the properties of ultrafilters of finite, or infinite Boolean algebras, the theorem of Kirman and Sondermann, by the embedding of spaces of individuals. The formal constructions is interpreted in terms of deciding hierarchies headed by dictators.

5.7 Notes on Interpretation

In most works on collective choice only weak orders are considered as preferences. As mentioned at the end of section 2.1, partial orders, which are not weak orders, can be interpreted as insufficiently revealed preferences, or as preferences with a poor distinguishing capability, causing intransitivity of indifference (cf. example 2.2.8.)

5.7.1. DEFINITION. We call a situation $g \in F$ *distinguishing* if all preferences $g(v)$ of all individuals $v \in V$ are weak orders. The set of all distinguishing situations we denote by G.

In the collective choice model we can restrict our consideration to distinguishing situations only. All axioms and definitions are the same with the only exception for the dictator.

5.7.2. DEFINITION (For the Model Restricted to Distinguishing Situations Only). An individual $v \in V$ is said to be a *dictator* under aggregating operator σ, if he expresses the collective preference for all distinguishing situations, i.e.

$$g(v) \subset \sigma(g)$$

for all $g \in G$.

Most of the above results remain valid under this definition. However, the correspondence between aggregating operators and ultrafilters is no longer a bijection. The set of aggregating operators falls into classes with common ultrafilters of deciding coalitions. Each such class has a minimal element, which we call a base aggregating operator.

5.7.3. DEFINITION. An aggregating operator σ is called a *base aggregating operator* if there is no other aggregating operator σ_1 such that $\sigma_1(g) \subset \sigma(g)$ for a certain distinguishing situation $g \in G$.

5.7.4. PROPOSITION (A Test for Base Aggregating Operators). *An aggregating operating σ is a base aggregating operator, if and only if it is determined* *by the rule:*

$$\sigma(g) = \bigcup_{A \in H} g(A)$$

for each distinguishing situation $g \in G$, where H is an ultrafilter of deciding coalitions.

PROOF. The required fact follows immediately from lemmas 5.3.2–5.3.4, valid also for the model restricted to distinguishing situations.

5.7.5. PROPOSITION (The Bijection Disproof). *Let σ be an aggregating operator and $x_0 \in X$. Then the rule*

$$\sigma_1(g) =$$
$$= \begin{cases} \sigma(g) & \text{if there is no } x \in X \text{ such that } (x_0, x) \notin \sigma(g) \text{ and } (x, x_0) \notin \sigma(g), \\ \sigma(g) \cup \{(x_0, x) : (x_0, x) \notin \sigma(g), (x, x_0) \notin \sigma(g), x \neq x_0, x \in X\} & \text{otherwise} \end{cases}$$

for every distinguishing situation $g \in G$ determines an aggregating operator, which is not a base aggregating operator. The effect of operator σ_1 is the following: If alternative x_0 is indifferent to some others in the preference $\sigma(g)$, it is declared superior among them in the preference $\sigma_1(g)$.

PROOF. Obviously, $\sigma_1(g)$ is an asymmetric binary relation on X for any distinguishing situation $g \in G$. If $(x, y) \notin \sigma_1(g)$ and $(y, z) \notin \sigma_1(g)$ for some $g \in G$ and $x, y, z \in X$, then $(x, y) \notin \sigma(g)$ and $(y, z) \notin \sigma(g)$, hence, $(x, z) \notin \sigma(g)$ by negative transitivity of $\sigma(g)$. If $x \neq x_0$, then $(x, z) \notin \sigma_1(g)$. If $x = x_0$, then $(x, y) \notin \sigma_1(g)$ implies $(y, x) \in \sigma(g)$. Since $(y, z) \notin \sigma(g)$, and $\sigma(g)$ is a weak order, by item 8 of proposition 2.2.13 we have $(z, x) \in \sigma(g)$. Therefore, $(x, z) \notin \sigma_1(g)$, i.e. $\sigma_1(g)$ is negatively transitive. Thus A2 holds. The validity of A3 and A4 is obvious.

A revision is also needed for proposition 5.5.4. Now the existence of isomorphism of two algebras with the correspondence of deciding hierarchies is necessary, but not sufficient for the isomorphism of models. Indeed, by proposition 5.7.4 for the same coalition algebra and the same deciding hierarchy there exist at least two different aggregating operators.

For the model, defined originally for distinguishing situations only, we can introduce a concept of *stability*, understood as the extendability of the aggregating operator to the set of other "indistinguishing" situations. There are two reasons in favour of such definition of stability.

Firstly, the loss of information on individual preferences does not affect essentially the performance of aggregating operator. Indeed, it is still defined, and if the informational loss doesn't relate to the dictatorial preference, the collective preference is not affected at all, otherwise the variation of collective preference doesn't exceed the variation of dictatorial preference. In other words, an increment of argument doesn't result in a great variation of operator.

Secondly, partial orders, which are not weak orders, may appear in the model as a result of deviations from the initial coalition structure, when coalitions are divided into smaller ones (the union of coalitions has no undesired consequences). To explain it, suppose that a coalition's preference is a weak order. Let its few individuals change their preferences. It means that the given coalition is divided into smaller ones. However, even if they have weak order preferences, the original coalition as a whole may have no longer a weak order preference (cf. example 2.2.16).

Under such understanding of stability, only base aggregating operators are stable, i.e. which are completely determined by deciding hierarchies. Note that the inextendability of non-base aggregating operators to "indistinguishing" situations is the idea of the proof of theorem 5.3.1.

5.7.6. PROPOSITION (The Role of Deciding Hierarchies in Stable Collective Choice). *The collective choice is stable, i.e. an aggregating operator σ is extendable to the set of "indistinguishing" situations if and only if σ is a base aggregating operator, i.e. is determined by some deciding hierarchy.*

PROOF. If σ is a base aggregating operator, then by proposition 5.7.4 it is determined by some deciding hierarchy, hence by theorem 5.3.1 σ can be defined for all, but not only for distinguishing situations.

Now let σ be a non-base aggregating operator. Let us show that it cannot be extended to the set of indistinguishing situations. Assume the contrary, i.e. that it can be extended. Then by lemmas 5.3.2–5.3.4 there exists an ultrafilter H such that

$$\bigcup_{A \in H} f(A) \subset \sigma(f)$$

for all situations $f \in F$, and by proposition 5.7.4 there exist a distinguishing situation $f \in G$ and a couple of alternatives (x, y) such that

$$(x, y) \in \sigma(f),$$
$$(x, y) \notin \bigcup_{A \in H} f(A).$$

The remainder of the proof follows the proof of theorem 5.3.1, which comes to contradiction.

Another noteworthy observation is the analogy of the obtained results with the theory of linear continuous functionals. The set of situations can be regarded as a space of continuous mappings of the set of individuals into the Boolean ring of binary relations on the set of alternatives. In turn the set of aggregating operators can be regarded as a space of continuous mappings of the space of situations into the same Boolean ring of binary relations. We can say that the space of situations is conjugated to the space of individuals, and the set of aggregating operators is the second conjugated space. From this point of view theorems 5.3.1, 5.5.1 and 5.6.5 prove the reflexivity of the space of individuals (i.e. each element of the second conjugated space is identified with a certain element of the basic space). Although the mentioned analogy is not precise (the set of preferences is not invariant with respect to the operation of symmetric difference, and therefore preferences do not form a Boolean ring), it helps to comprehend the interaction of different components of the collective choice model.

Chapter 6

Aggregation of Infinite Set of Preferences

6.1 Introductory Remarks

The replacement of a finite models by an infinite one is a common method in theoretical studies. Certain phenomena, not observed in the finite model, are revealed in the infinite model, and the conclusions are extended to the finite case, being interpreted as tendencies, inherent in the model's enlargement. The use of infinite models is justified, when one deals with the qualitative analysis. The concepts of "finite" and "infinite" together with the rules to use them give a means to formalize the qualitative concepts of "large" and "small". We should stress that the concepts of infinite and unboundedness are not equivalent. The boundedness in an infinite nodel can be assumed in terms of compactness-like properties.

Recall that infinite models are widely used in physics and mechanics. Now they are also used in mathematical economics and game theory. For example, Edgeworth's hypothesis on the coincidence of a core of economy with the set of its equilibria is proved for an infinite set of agents. The infinite model is justified by a limit theorem, describing how the growth in the number of agents in a finite model leads to the continuum model with the desired property.

Collective choice models with infinite sets of individuals are studied in (Armstrong 1980; Fishburn 1970a; Kirman & Sondermann 1972; Naumov 1978). However, these models lack an appropriate justification for their interpretation. In the present section we fill up this gap, and go on with the analysis of the infinite model. In particular we compare direct and indirect aggregation of preferences (as direct and indirect elections), which turn out to be equivalent in finite, but not in infinite case. Since indirect, or successive aggregation is a common way of data processing, this problem is of general interest.

Results of the present chapter are published in Russian (Tanguiane 1979c; 1981a; 1982a).

6.2 Imbeddings of Models of Aggregation of Preferences

In this section we define how to understand the increase in the number of individuals in the collective choice model, i.e. how to superimpose models with different numbers of individuals.

6.2.1. DEFINITION. An algebraic collective choice model $(\mathcal{A}, F, \sigma)$ is said to be *isomorphically imbedded* in an algebraic collective choice model $(\mathcal{A}', F', \sigma')$, defined for the same set of alternatives with the associated set of preferences, if there exists an isomorphism φ from algebra $\mathcal{A}$ into $\mathcal{A}'$ such that

$$\sigma(f) \subset \sigma'(f')$$

for all *corresponding situations* $f \in F$, $f' \in F'$, i.e. such that

$$f'(\varphi(A)) = f(A)$$

for all non-zero coalitions $A \in \mathcal{A}$. If algebra $\mathcal{A}$ is a subalgebra of algebra $\mathcal{A}'$ and φ is the identity mapping, we shall say that the first model is *imbedded* in the second.

Note that if the isomorphism φ in definition 6.2.1 is a surjection, we come to the isomorphism of models in the sense of definition 3.5.3. Indeed, then we have

$$\sigma(f) = \sigma'(f')$$

for all corresponding situations $f \in F$, $f' \in F'$. Now take the ultrafilters $H \subset \mathcal{A}$ and $H' \subset \mathcal{A}'$, associated with the aggregating operators σ and σ' by theorem 5.3.1. By the next proposition 6.2.2 we obtain $\varphi(H) = H'$, whence

$$\sigma(f) = \bigcup_{A \in H} f(A) = \bigcup_{A \in H} f'(\varphi(A)) = \bigcup_{A' \in H'} f'(A') = \sigma'(f'),$$

as required.

The isomorphic imbedding means that the set of individuals of the first model is placed into the set of individuals of the second model, retaining the coalion structure, extending the situations, while not affecting the collective preference. Before we give a strict formulation, recall that a *homomorhism* φ

from a Boolean algebra $\mathcal{A}$ on a set V into a Boolean algebra $\mathcal{A}'$ on a set V' is said to be *induced by a pointwise mapping* ψ of the set V' into the set V if

$$\varphi(A) = \psi^{-1}(A)$$

for any $A \in \mathcal{A}$. For example, if algebra $\mathcal{A}$ is *perfect*, i.e. every its ultrafilter is fixed, then each homomorphism from $\mathcal{A}$ into $\mathcal{A}'$ is induced by a pointwise mapping (Sikorski 1964).

6.2.2. PROPOSITION (About the Correspondence of Deciding Hierarchies). *Let $(\mathcal{A}, F, \sigma)$ and $(\mathcal{A}', F', \sigma')$ be two algebraic collective choice models, defined for the same set of alternatives with the associated set of preferences. Let $H \subset \mathcal{A}$ and $H' \subset \mathcal{A}'$ be the ultrafilters, associated with the aggregating operators σ and σ' by theorem* 3.3.1. *Then the first model is isomorphically imbedded in the second one if and only if there exists an isomorphism φ from algebra $\mathcal{A}$ into algebra $\mathcal{A}'$ such that*

$$\{\varphi(A) : A \in H\} \subset H', \tag{6.2.1}$$

and if such isomorphism exists it coincides with the isomorphism from definition 6.2.1.

PROOF. At first suppose that model $(\mathcal{A}, F, \sigma)$ is isomorphically imbedded in model $(\mathcal{A}', F', \sigma')$, i.e. there exists an isomorphism φ from algebra $\mathcal{A}$ into algebra $\mathcal{A}'$ such that $\sigma(f) \subset \sigma'(f')$ for all corresponding situations $f \in F$ and $f' \in F'$. Let us prove (6.2.1). Assume the contrary, i.e. that there exists an element $A \in H$ such that $\varphi(A) \notin H'$. Fix two alternatives $x, y \in X$ and define the corresponding situations

$$f(v) = \begin{cases} \{(x,y)\} & \text{if } v \in A, \\ \{(y,x)\} & \text{if } v \notin A \end{cases} \tag{6.2.2}$$

and

$$f'(v') = \begin{cases} \{(x,y)\} & \text{if } v' \in \varphi(A), \\ \{(y,x)\} & \text{if } v' \notin \varphi(A). \end{cases} \tag{6.2.3}$$

Since $A \in H$ and $(\varphi(A))^c \in H'$, by theorem 5.3.1 we have $(x,y) \in \sigma(f)$ and $(y,x) \in \sigma'(f')$. Since φ is an isomorphism, $\varphi(B) \neq \emptyset$ for any coalition $B \in \mathcal{A} \setminus \{\emptyset\}$. Since f and f' are corresponding situations, $\sigma(f) \subset \sigma'(f')$. In particular, $(x,y) \in \sigma'(f')$, against the asymmetry of $\sigma'(f')$. The obtained contradiction proves (6.2.1).

Now let φ be an isomorphism from algebra $\mathcal{A}$ into algebra $\mathcal{A}'$, satisfying (6.2.1). Then for corresponding situations $f \in F$, $f' \in F'$ by theorem 5.3.1 we have

$$\sigma(f) = \bigcup_{A \in H} f(A) = \bigcup_{A \in H} f'(\varphi(A)) \subset \bigcup_{A' \in H'} f'(A') = \sigma'(f'),$$

from which we conclude that the first model is isomorphically imbedded in the second one.

6.2.3. PROPOSITION (About the Correspondence of Individuals). *Let $(\mathcal{A}, F, \sigma)$ and $(\mathcal{A}', F', \sigma')$ be two algebraic collective choice models defined for sets of individuals V and V', respectively, for the same set of alternatives X. If the first model is isomorphically imbedded in the second and the isomorphism φ from definition* 6.2.1 *is induced by a pointwise mapping ψ from V' into V, then*

$$\sigma(f) = \sigma'(f')$$

for all situations $f \in F$, $f' \in F'$ such that

$$f(\psi(v')) = f'(v') \text{ for all } v' \in V'. \tag{6.2.4}$$

Conversely, if there exists a mapping ψ from V' into V, inducing an isomorphism from algebra $\mathcal{A}$ into algebra $\mathcal{A}'$, such that

$$\sigma(f) = \sigma'(f')$$

for all situations $f \in F$, $f' \in F'$, satisfying the condition (6.2.4), *then the first model is isomorphically imbedded in the second one.*

PROOF. Denote by H and H' the ultrafilters, associated with the aggregating operators σ and σ' by theorem 5.3.1.

At first suppose that model $(\mathcal{A}, F, \sigma)$ is isomorphically imbedded in model $(\mathcal{A}', F', \sigma')$, and let the isomorphism φ from definition 6.2.1 be induced by a pointwise mapping ψ from the set V' into V. Let situations $f \in F$, $f' \in F'$ satisfy condition (6.2.4). We shall show that $\sigma(f) = \sigma'(f')$. Note that for any non-zero $A \in \mathcal{A}$ the set $\{v' : v' \in V, \ \psi(v') \in A\}$ is not empty, consequently,

$$f(A) = \bigcap_{v \in A} f(v) \subset \bigcap_{v' \in \varphi(A)} f'(\psi(v')) = f'(\varphi(A)).$$

Therefore, by theorem 5.3.1 and proposition 6.2.2 we obtain

$$\sigma(f) = \bigcup_{A \in H} f(A) \subset \bigcup_{A \in H} f'(\varphi(A)) \subset \bigcup_{A' \in H'} f'(A') = \sigma'(f'),$$

as required.

To prove the converse inclusion, suppose that $(x, y) \in \sigma'(f')$ for some $x, y \in X$. By theorem 5.3.1 $(x, y) \in f'(A')$ for a certain $A' \in H'$. Since f' is a situation, by the measurability condition we have

$$B' = \{v' : v' \in V', \ (x, y) \in f'(v')\} \in \mathcal{A},$$

and since H' is an ultrafilter and $A' \subset B'$, then also $B' \subset H'$. Since f is a situation,

$$B = \{v : v \in V,\ (x, y) \in f(v)\} \in \mathcal{A}.$$

It is easy to see that $\psi(v') \in B$ if and only if $v' \in B'$, therefore, $\varphi(B) = B'$. At the same time $(x, y) \in f(B)$ and $B \in H$ (otherwise, since H is an ultrafilter, it would be $B^c \in H$, and by proposition 6.2.2 we would have $\varphi(B^c) = B'^c \in H'$, which is impossible, because by the above proof $B' \in H'$). Hence,

$$(x, y) \in \bigcup_{A \in H} f(A) = \sigma(f),$$

as required.

Now let φ be an isomorphism from $\mathcal{A}$ into $\mathcal{A}'$, induced by a mapping ψ from V' into V such that $\sigma(f) = \sigma'(f')$ for all situations $f \in F$, $f' \in F'$, satistying (6.2.4). By proposition 6.2.2 to prove the isomorphic imbedding of the first model in the second one, it is sufficient to verify that

$$\{\varphi(A) : A \in H\} \subset H'.$$

We shall prove it by contradiction. Assume that there exists $A \in H$ such that $\varphi(A) \notin H'$. Since H' is an ultrafilter, $(\varphi(A))^c \in H'$. Fix $x, y \in X$ and define the corresponding situations $f \in F$, $f' \in F'$ as in (6.2.1) and (6.2.2). It is easy to see that

$$f(\psi(v')) = f'(v')$$

for all $v' \in V'$, therefore, according to the assumtion of the proposition,

$$\sigma(f) = \sigma'(f').$$

By theorem 5.3.1 we have $(x, y) \in \sigma(f)$ and $(y, x) \in \sigma'(f')$, yet by the first part of the proof $(x, y) \in \sigma'(f')$, against the asymmetry of $\sigma'(f')$. The obtained contradiction accomplishes the proof.

Now we can define strictly the *number of individuals in an algebraic collective choice model.* An algebraic collective choice model is called *finite* or *infinite*, depending on whether finite or infinite is the coalition algebra. Since the same algebra (up to isomorphisms) can be realized on different sets of individuals, we identify their number with the lowest cardinality of a dense subset, which for a finite algebra coincides with the number of its atoms, called *participants.*

6.2.4. PROPOSITION (About the Embedding in a Greater Model). *Every finite algebraic collective choice model can be isomorphically imbedded in any algebraic collective choice model, defined for the same set of alternatives, with a greater or equal number of participants, or infinite.*

PROOF. Recall that a family T of non-zero disjoint elements of algebra $\mathcal{A}$ is called a *partitioning* if their union is the unity of algebra $\mathcal{A}$. Let $(\mathcal{A}, F, \sigma)$ be an algebraic collective choice model with n participants and $(\mathcal{A}', F', \sigma')$ be a model defined for the same set of alternatives, but infinite, or with m participants, where $m \geq n$. Then, obviously, there exist partitionings $T \subset \mathcal{A}$ and $T' \subset \mathcal{A}'$ of n elements each. Let $H \subset \mathcal{A}$ and $H' \subset \mathcal{A}'$ be the ultrafilters, associated with the aggregating operators σ and σ' by theorem 5.3.1. Since the partitionings are finite, there exist certain $A \in T$ and $A' \in T'$ such that $A \in H$ and $A' \in H'$. Let φ be a one-to-one correspondence between T and T' such that $\varphi(A) = A'$. Since T is a generator family (as a family of atoms of a finite algebra), by the theorem about the extension to homomorphisms (Sikorski 1964), φ can be extended to an isomorphism φ from algebra $\mathcal{A}$ into algebra $\mathcal{A}'$, while, obviously, $\{\varphi(A) : A \in H\} \subset H'$. Then by proposition 6.2.2 model $(\mathcal{A}, F, \sigma)$ is isomorphically imbedded in model $(\mathcal{A}', F', \sigma')$, as required.

Now we define sequential imbeddings of algebraic collective choice models.

6.2.5. DEFINITION. Let N be the set of all positive integers. A sequence $\{(\mathcal{A}_n, F_n, \sigma_n)\}$ of algebraic collective choice models defined for the same set of alternatives is called a *sequence of (isomorphically) imbedded models* if each model $(\mathcal{A}_n, F_n, \sigma_n)$ is (isomorphically) imbedded in the next model $(\mathcal{A}_{n+1}, F_{n+1}, \sigma_{n+1})$, where $n \in N$.

The representation theorem for Boolean algebras allows proving the following important proposition.

6.2.6. PROPOSITION (Realization of a Sequence of Isomorphically Imbedded Models on the Same Set of Individuals). *For any sequence $\{(\mathcal{A}_n, F_n, \sigma_n)\}$ of isomorphically imbedded algebraic collective choice models defined for the same set of alternatives there exists a sequence $\{(\mathcal{A}'_n, F'_n, \sigma'_n)\}$ of imbedded models such that for each $n \in N$ the two models $\{(\mathcal{A}_n, F_n, \sigma_n)\}$ and $\{(\mathcal{A}'_n, F'_n, \sigma'_n)\}$ are isomorphic* (fig. 53).

PROOF. We shall construct the inductive limit of the given sequence of collective choice models.

For each $n \in N$ by $\varphi_{n,n}$ denote the identity isomorphism from algebra $\mathcal{A}_n$ onto itself; by $\varphi_{n+1,n}$ the isomorphism (as in definition 6.2.1) from algebra $\mathcal{A}_n$ into algebra $\mathcal{A}_{n+1}$, and for any $m, n \in N$, where $m > n$, denote by $\varphi_{m,n}$ the

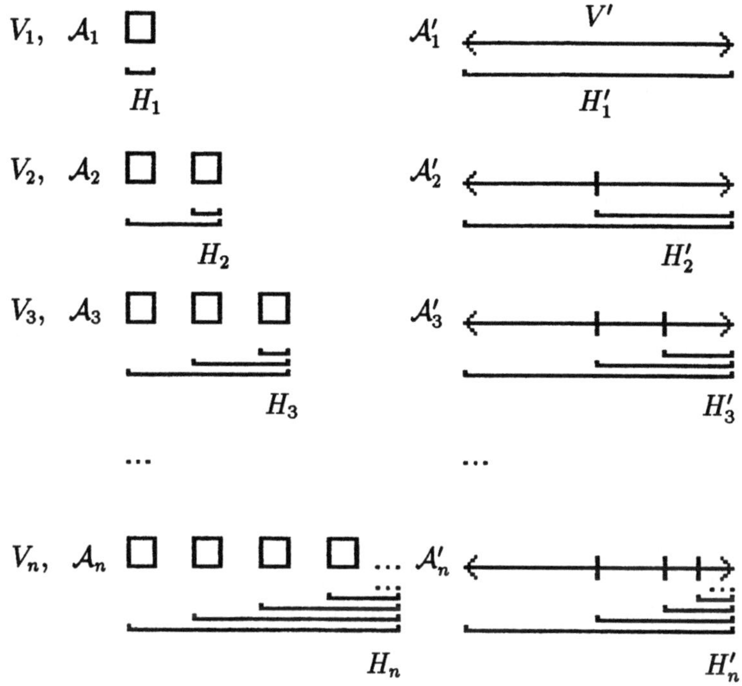

Fig. 53

composition of isomorphisms

$$\varphi_{m,n} = \varphi_{m,m-1} \circ \varphi_{m-1,m-2} \circ \cdots \circ \varphi_{m+1,n},$$

which is obviously an isomorphism from algebra $\mathcal{A}_n$ into algebra $\mathcal{A}_m$. Consider the set

$$\mathcal{A} = \bigcup_{n=1}^{\infty} \mathcal{A}_n = \{A : A \in \mathcal{A}_n, n \in N\},$$

and define the equivalence $\sim$ on $\mathcal{A}$, declaring equivalent the elements $A \in \mathcal{A}_m$ and $B \in \mathcal{A}_n$, where $m, n \in N$, if and only if $\varphi_{k,m}(A) = \varphi_{k,n}(B)$, where $k = \max\{m, n\}$. Define Boolean operations on the quotient set

$$\mathcal{A}' = \mathcal{A} \,|_{\sim} .$$

Let $A', B' \in \mathcal{A}'$ and $A \in \mathcal{A}_m, B \in \mathcal{A}_n$ be representitatives of the classes A' and B', respectively. Their union define to be the class from $\mathcal{A}'$ with the representative $\varphi_{k,m}(A) \cup \varphi_{k,n}(B) \in \mathcal{A}_k$, where $k = \max\{m, n\}$; their intersection—the class from $\mathcal{A}'$ with the representative $\varphi_{k,m}(A) \cap \varphi_{k,n}(B) \in \mathcal{A}_k$, where

$k = \max\{m, n\}$; the complement to $A' \in \mathcal{A}'$ we define to be the class from $\mathcal{A}$ with the representitative $A^c \in \mathcal{A}_m$. By the representation theorem (Sikorski 1964) the Boolean algebra $\mathcal{A}'$ can be realized on a certain set V'. Note that for each $n \in N$ the set $\mathcal{A}'_n$ of classes from $\mathcal{A}'$ with the representitatives from $\mathcal{A}_n$ forms a subalgebra of algebra $\mathcal{A}'$, isomorphic to algebra $\mathcal{A}_n$. Indeed, the mapping h_n, which associates each element $A \in \mathcal{A}_n$ with the class $h_n(A) \in \mathcal{A}'$ containing A as its representitative, is an isomorphism.

Now for each $n \in N$ we can construct a model $(\mathcal{A}'_n, F'_n, \sigma'_n)$, which is isomorphic to the model $(\mathcal{A}_n, F_n, \sigma_n)$. Define set of situations F'_n for the given set of alternatives, set of individuals V', and coalition algebra $\mathcal{A}'_n$. According to theorem 5.3.1, determine the aggregating operator σ'_n by the ultrafilter

$$H'_n = \{h_n(A) : A \in H_n\} \subset \mathcal{A}'_n.$$

Then by proposition 6.2.2 the model $(\mathcal{A}'_n, F'_n, \sigma'_n)$ is isomorphic to the model $(\mathcal{A}_n, F_n, \sigma_n)$.

Finally, we shall show that for each $n \in N$ the model $(\mathcal{A}'_n, F'_n, \sigma'_n)$ is imbedded in the model $(\mathcal{A}'_{n+1}, F'_{n+1}, \sigma'_{n+1})$. By construction $\mathcal{A}'_n \subset \mathcal{A}'_{n+1}$. By virtue of proposition 6.2.2 it sufficies to verify the inclusion $H'_n \subset H'_{n+1}$. Let $A' \in H'_n$. Then by construction $h_n^{-1}(A') \in H_n$. Since the model $(\mathcal{A}_n, F_n, \sigma_n)$ is isomorphically imbedded in the model $(\mathcal{A}'_{n+1}, F'_{n+1}, \sigma'_{n+1})$, it follows from proposition 6.2.2 that $\varphi_{n+1,n}(h_n^{-1}(A')) \in H_{n+1}$. By construction

$$H'_{n+1} \in A'' = h_{n+1}(\varphi_{n+1,n}(h_n^{-1}(A'))).$$

Since elements $h_n^{-1}(A')$ and $\varphi_{n+1,n}(h_n^{-1}(A'))$ are equivalent, they belong to the same class from $\mathcal{A}'$, i.e. $A'' = A'$, hence, $A' \in H'_{n+1}$, as required.

From propositions 6.2.4, 6.2.6 we derive the following important corollary.

6.2.7. COROLLARY (The Realization of a Sequence of Models with Increasing Number of Participants on a Single Set of Individuals). *For any sequence* $\{(\mathcal{A}_n, F_n, \sigma_n)\}$ *of finite algebraic collective choice models with increasing number of participants and defined for the same set of alternatives there exists a sequence* $\{(\mathcal{A}'_n, F'_n, \sigma'_n)\}$ *of imbedded algebraic collective choice models such that for each* $n \in N$ *the models* $(\mathcal{A}_n, F_n, \sigma_n)$ *and* $\{(\mathcal{A}'_n, F'_n, \sigma'_n)\}$ *are isomorphic.*

This way all our consideration is reduced to a single set of individuals with refining partitionings, atoms of which determine coalition algebras. The increase in the number of participants is nothing else but the division of atoms. It is easy to see that one part of dictator becomes a dictator in the refined coalition structure.

6.3 Limit Theorem

Thus models of collective choice with unequal numbers of participants are associated with different algebras of coalitions, consequently, with different spaces of states, which are sets of situations. Therefore the question arises: How can we analyse the convergence of a sequence of mappings (in our given case, a sequence of aggregating operators) with different domains of definition?

A similar problem arises, when a numerical function is approximated at discrete points. An addition of new points results in that we obtain a sequence of functions with extending domains of definition. However, their coincidence at common argument values allows considering such a sequence as approximations of the given function.

As shown in the previous section, an addition of new participants is equivalent to addition of new coalitions. Therefore, we can start from a given infinite set of individuals, which is successively divided into more and more small coalitions, which are called participants. At the same time each situation of the infinite model is approximated by situations of finite models, which are locally constant mappings from the set of individuals into the set of preferences, similar to step-functions, approximating a continuous numerical function. Owing to the refinement of coalitions, situations of the finite models come closer to situations of the infinite model. Therefore, the convergence of aggregating operators should be understood as the continuity of a certain aggregating operator in the infinite model with respect to the sequences of situations from the finite models, approximating the situations of the infinite model. Propositions 6.2.6 and 6.2.7 follow this approach, reducing the consideration of a sequence of finite models with increasing number of participants to the consideration of models, realized on the same set of individuals. Consequently, without loss of generality we can define the convergence of models only for the models realized on the same set of individuals. However, it is desirable to give a topological interpretation of the construction, similar to the topological formulation of algebraic model in section 3.6.

To define the *convergence of a sequence of Boolean algebras*, consider the set 2^V of all subsets of the set of individuals V. Each Boolean algebra $\mathcal{A} \subset 2^V$ is associated with a certain characteristic (two value) function $\chi_{\mathcal{A}} : 2^V \to \{0,1\}$ such that

$$\chi_{\mathcal{A}}(A) = \begin{cases} 1 & \text{if } A \in \mathcal{A}, \\ 0 & \text{if } A \notin \mathcal{A}. \end{cases}$$

We consider the set of all Boolean algebras on V as a topological space of their characteristic functions with the topology of pointwise convergence. A *base clopen neighborhood of Boolean algebra* $\mathcal{A}$ consists of all Boolean algebras $\mathcal{A}'$ on V, which coincide with $\mathcal{A}$ on a finite set of subsets of V, i.e. a base neighborhood $O_{\mathcal{B}}(\mathcal{A})$ of a Boolean algebra $\mathcal{A}$ on V is determined by a finite set of subsets $\mathcal{B} \subset 2^V$. It is defined to be

$$O_{\mathcal{B}}(\mathcal{A}) = \{\mathcal{A}' \subset 2^V : \mathcal{A}' \cap \mathcal{B} = \mathcal{A} \cap \mathcal{B}\}.$$

A *prebase neighborhood of Boolean algebra* $\mathcal{A}$ consists of the Boolean algebras $\mathcal{A}'$, which coincide with $\mathcal{A}$ on a single subset $A \subset V$ (then $\mathcal{B} = \{A\}$), i.e. all of them either do, or don't include A as an element:

$$O_A(\mathcal{A}) = \{\mathcal{A}' \subset 2^V : \mathcal{A}' \cap \{A\} = \mathcal{A} \cap \{A\}\}.$$

In terms of sequences of algebras it means that a *sequence of Boolean algebras* $\{\mathcal{A}_n\}$ on V *converges to Boolean algebra* $\mathcal{A}$ if for any subset $A \subset V$ there exists number m such that $\mathcal{A}_n$ coincide with $\mathcal{A}$ on A since m, i.e. $\mathcal{A}_n \cap \{A\} = \mathcal{A} \cap \{A\}$ for all $n > m$.

6.3.1. PROPOSITION (About the Convergence of Situations). *Consider a sequence of Boolean algebras* $\{\mathcal{A}_n\}$ *defined on the same set of individuals* V *and converging to Boolean algebra* $\mathcal{A}$ *on* V. *Let* $\{F_n\}$ *and* F *be the sets of situations defined for the same set of alternatives* X *and the given algebras, respectively. Then for each situation* $f \in F$ *there exists a direction of situations*

$$\mathcal{F} = \{f_\alpha : f_\alpha \in \bigcup_{n=1}^{\infty} F_n, \ \alpha \in \Lambda\},$$

converging to f *with respect to the topology of pointwise convergence.*

PROOF. Recall that a subbase is a subset of base, which is also a base in the topology. A subbase neighborhood of situation $f \in F$ under the topology of pointwise convergence is determined by a finite set of individuals

$$W \subset V,$$

and an indexed finite family of pairs of alternatives

$$T = \{(x_1, y_1), \ldots, (x_k, y_k)\}.$$

The subbase neighborhood of f is defined to be

$$U_{W,T}(f) = \{f' : f' \in F, \ f'(w) \cap T = f(w) \cap T, \ w \in W\}.$$

Let us construct a situation $f_T \in F_m$ for some m, which coincides with f on the set of pairs of alternatives T, i.e.

$$f_T(v) \cap T = f(v) \cap T$$

for all $v \in V$. Obviously, this situation will belong to the neighborhood $U_{W,T}(f)$. By the measurability condition

$$\{v : v \in V, (x_i, y_i) \in f(v)\} \in \mathcal{A}$$

for all $i = 1, \ldots, k$. Consider the minimal subalgebra $\mathcal{A}' \subset \mathcal{A}$ generated by these sets. Since $\mathcal{A}'$ is finite, it is atomic; let

$$A_1, \ldots, A_l$$

be all its atoms. Note that preferences $f(v)$ of individuals from each atom are constant, particularly

$$f(v) \cap T = f(w) \cap T$$

for all $v, w \in A_i$ for all $i = 1, \ldots, l$. Since by assumption the sequence of algebras $\{\mathcal{A}_n\}$ converges to $\mathcal{A}$, there exists a positive integer m such that $A_i \in \mathcal{A}_n$, where $i = 1, \ldots, l$, for all $n \geq m$. Now define a situation $f_T \in F_m$, putting

$$f_T(v) = f(A_i) \text{ if } v \in A_i, \ i = 1, \ldots, l.$$

Obviously, the situation f_T satisfies the measurability condition with respect to $\mathcal{A}_m$, consequently, it satisfies the measurability condition with respect to all $\mathcal{A}_n$, where $n \geq m$, and coincides with f on the set of pairs of alternatives T.

Thus for each subbase neighborhood $U_{W,T}(t)$ of situation $f \in F$ there exists a situation

$$f_T \in \bigcup_{n=1}^{\infty} F_n$$

such that $f_T \in U_{W,T}(f)$. Since the finite collections of alternatives $T \subset X \times X$ are directed by inclusion, and by the above construction $T_1 \subset T$ implies $f_{T_1} \in U_{W,T}(f)$, the family of situations

$$\mathcal{F} = \{f_T : T \subset X \times X, \ T \text{ is finite}\}$$

is a direction, converging to f, as required.

The proved fact substantiates the following definition.

6.3.2. Definition. Let $\{(\mathcal{A}_n, F_n, \sigma_n)\}$ be a sequence of algebraic collective choice models defined for the same set of individuals V and for the same set of alternatives X. It is said to *converge* to algebraic collective choice model $(\mathcal{A}, F, \sigma)$ defined for the same sets V and X if:

1. The sequence of Boolean algebras $\{\mathcal{A}_n\}$ converges to $\mathcal{A}$ with respect to the topology of pointwise convergence.

2. For each situations $f \in F$ there exists a direction of approximating situations

$$\mathcal{F} = \{f_\alpha : f_\alpha \in \bigcup_{n=1}^{\infty} F_n, \ \alpha \in \Lambda\},$$

converging to f with respect to the topology of pointwise convergence.

3. The sequence of aggregating operators $\{\sigma_n\}$ converges to σ with respect to the topology of pointwise convergence. In prebase terms it means that for any pair of alternatives (x, y), any situation $f \in F$, and any direction

$$\mathcal{F} = \{f_\alpha : f_\alpha \in \bigcup_{n=1}^{\infty} F_n, \ \alpha \in \Lambda\} \to f$$

the collective preference $\sigma(f)$ on the given pair of alternatives equals to the preferences $\sigma_n(f_\alpha)$, where $f_\alpha \in F_n$ for all sufficiently large n and superior α, i.e.

$$\sigma_n(f_\alpha) \cap \{(x, y)\} = \sigma(f) \cap \{(x, y)\}.$$

Now we shall formulate the main result of the section.

6.3.3. THEOREM (The Limit Theorem). *Every sequence of embedded collective choice models with finite increasing numbers of participants converges to an infinite collective choice model with a countable coalition algebra, and the limit model is unique for the given sequence of models. Conversely, for each infinite collective choice model with a countable coalition algebra there exists a sequence of imbedded collective choice models with finite increasing numbers of participants, which converges to the given model.*

PROOF. Let $\{(\mathcal{A}_n, F_n, \sigma_n)\}$ be a sequence of imbedded collective choice models with finite increasing numbers of participants (atoms), defined on the same set of individuals V and for the same set of alternatives X. We shall construct an infinite model $(\mathcal{A}, F, \sigma)$, to which the given sequence converges. Put

$$\mathcal{A} = \bigcup_{n=1}^{\infty} \mathcal{A}_n.$$

It is easy to see that $\mathcal{A}$ is an infinite countable Boolean algebra, containing all algebras $\mathcal{A}_n$ as its subalgebras, and that sequence $\{\mathcal{A}_n\}$ converges to $\mathcal{A}$ with respect to the topology of pointwise convergence.

Let F be the set of situations for the constructed Boolean algebra $\mathcal{A}$ and the set of all preferences on X. To determine the limit aggregating operator we shall construct an ultrafilter in $\mathcal{A}$.

For each n denote by $H_n \subset \mathcal{A}_n$ the ultrafilter, associated with the aggregating operator σ_n by theorem 5.3.1. Put

$$H = \bigcup_{n=1}^{\infty} H_n,$$

and let us verify that H is an ultrafilter of algebra $\mathcal{A}$. Indeed, H is a non-empty set of non-zero elements of $\mathcal{A}$. We show that if $A \in H$, $B \in \mathcal{A}$, $A \subset B$, then $B \in H$. In fact, there are numbers m, n such that $A \in H_m$, $B \in \mathcal{A}_n$. Put $k = \max\{m, n\}$. By proposition 6.2.2 we have $H_m \subset H_k$, consequently, $A \in H_k$, and since $\mathcal{A}_n \subset \mathcal{A}_n$, we obtain $B \in \mathcal{A}_n$. Since H_k is an ultrafilter, $B \in H_k$, whence $B \in H$, as required. Now we show that if $A, B \in H$, then $A \cap B \in H$. In fact, there exist numbers m, n such that $A \in H_m$ and $B \in H_n$. Put $k = \max\{m, n\}$. Repeating the above arguments, we obtain that $A, B \in H_k$, consequently, $A \cap B \in H_k$, whence $A \cap B \in H$. Finally, we show that if $A \in H$, then either $A \in H$, or $A^c \in H$. Indeed, there exists number n such that $A \in \mathcal{A}_n$, and since H_n is an ultrafilter, either $A \in H_n$, or $A^c \in H_n$, hence, either A, or A^c belongs to H, as required.

Thus H is an ultrafilter of the algebra $\mathcal{A}$. By theorem 5.3.1 it is associated with a certain aggregating operator σ. Let us show that the sequence of aggregating operators $\{\sigma_n\}$ converges to σ in the sense of definition 6.3.2. Fix an arbitrary pair of alternatives (x, y), a situation $f \in F$, and a direction

$$\mathcal{F} = \{f_\alpha : f_\alpha \in \bigcup_{n=1}^{\infty} F_n,\ \alpha \in \Lambda\},$$

converging to f. By the measurability condition

$$B = \{v : v \in V,\ (x, y) \in f(v)\} \in \mathcal{A}.$$

By our construction $B \in \mathcal{A}_n$ for all sufficiently large n. Consequently, one of the coalitions B, or B^c belongs to all the ultrafilters H_n. Since the direction $\mathcal{F}$ converges to f, we have

$$f_\alpha(v) \cap \{(x, y)\} = f(v) \cap \{(x, y)\}$$

for all $v \in V$ for all superior $\alpha \in \Lambda$. Therefore, for all sufficiently large n and sufficiently superior α we obtain

$$\sigma_n(f_\alpha) \cap \{(x, y)\} \quad = \quad \bigcup_{A_n \in H_n} f_\alpha(A_n) \cap \{(x, y)\}$$

$$\begin{aligned} &= f(B) \cap \{(x,y)\} \\ &= \bigcup_{A \in H} f(A) \cap \{(x,y)\} \\ &= \sigma(f) \cap \{(x,y)\}, \end{aligned}$$

as required.

The existence of a direction of situations, converging to each situation $f \in F$, satisfying item 2 of definition 6.3.2, follows directly from proposition 6.3.1, therefore all items of definition 6.3.2 hold for the model $(\mathcal{A}, F, \sigma)$.

Let us show that the limit of the sequence of collective choice models $(\mathcal{A}_n, F_n, \sigma_n)$ is unique. In fact, if algebra $\mathcal{A}'$ on V differs from algebra $\mathcal{A}$, then there exists a subset $A \subset V$ such that $\{A\} \cap \mathcal{A}' \neq \{A\} \cap \mathcal{A}$, therefore, the sequence $\{\mathcal{A}_n\}$ doesn't converge to $\mathcal{A}'$. Since the limit algebra $\mathcal{A}$ is unique, the set of situation F is also unique. Finally, if σ' is an aggregating operator on F other than σ, then there exist a situation $f \in F$ and a pair of alternatives $x, y \in X$ such that

$$\{(x,y)\} \cap \sigma(f) \neq \{(x,y)\} \cap \sigma'(f),$$

yet by definition 6.3.2 it means that the sequence $\{\sigma_n\}$ doesn't converge to σ.

Now let $(\mathcal{A}, F, \sigma)$ be an infinite collective choice model defined for a set of individuals V and a set of alternatives X with the associated set of preferences. Let the coalition algebra $\mathcal{A}$ be countable. We shall construct a sequence of imbedded collective choice models $\{(\mathcal{A}_n, F_n, \sigma_n)\}$ on the same set of individuals for the same set of alternatives with finite increasing numbers of participants, converging to the model $(\mathcal{A}, F, \sigma)$.

To begin with, we construct a sequence of imbedded finite subalgebras of $\mathcal{A}$ with increasing number of atoms, converging to $\mathcal{A}$. Since algebra $\mathcal{A}$ is countable, it can be numbered. Let

$$\mathcal{A} = \{A_1, \ldots, A_i, \ldots\}.$$

The sequence of Boolean algebras $\{\mathcal{A}_n\}$ we define by induction.

1^0. Let $\mathcal{A}_1$ be the two-element subalgebra of algebra $\mathcal{A}$, consisting of zero and unit of $\mathcal{A}$ (i.e. the empty set and the whole of V).

2^0. Suppose that the finite algebras $\mathcal{A}_k$ are already constructed for all positive integers $k \leq n$ for a certain positive integer n so that $\mathcal{A}_1 \subset \ldots \subset \mathcal{A}_n$ and $\mathcal{A}_k \neq \mathcal{A}_{k+1}$, where $k = 1, \ldots, n-1$.

Since subalgebra $\mathcal{A}_n$ is finite, there exists coalition A_{i_n} with the minimal index i_n such that $A_{i_n} \notin \mathcal{A}_n$. Define subalgebra $\mathcal{A}_{n+1}$ as the minimal subalgebra of $\mathcal{A}$, containing all elements of $\mathcal{A}_n$ and the element A_{i_n}. Subalgebra $\mathcal{A}_{n+1}$ is finite, as generated by a finite set of generators, and $\mathcal{A}_n \subset \mathcal{A}_{n+1}$, while $\mathcal{A}_n \neq \mathcal{A}_{n+1}$.

Since the algebra $\mathcal{A}$ is infinite, the induction will not stop at a finite step, therefore, we obtain a sequence $\{\mathcal{A}_n\}$, which exhausts the algebra $\mathcal{A}$, consequently, converges to $\mathcal{A}$.

For each coalition subalgebra $\mathcal{A}_n$ denote the associated set of situations by F_n.

For each positive integer n we determine aggregating operator σ_n on the set of situations F_n by an ultrafilter. To construct this ultrafilter, consider the ultrafilter H in algebra $\mathcal{A}$ associated with the aggregating operator σ by theorem 5.3.1. For each n put

$$H_n = H \cap \mathcal{A}_n.$$

We shall ascertain that H_n is an ultrafilter of algebra $\mathcal{A}$. Indeed, H_n is a non-empty subset of non-zero elements of algebra $\mathcal{A}_n$ (non-empty, since it contains the unit of algebra $\mathcal{A}_n$—the set V). We show that if $A \in H_n$, $B \in \mathcal{A}_n$, $A \subset B$, then $B \in H_n$. Indeed, then $A \in H$, $B \in \mathcal{A}$, and since H is an ultrafilter, $B \in H$. At the same time $B \in \mathcal{A}_n$, therefore, $B \in H_n$, as required. We show that if $A, B \in H_n$, then $A \cap B \in H_n$. Indeed, $A, B \in H$, and since H is an ultrafilter, $A \cap B \in H$; at the same time $A \cap B \in \mathcal{A}_n$, therefore, $A \cap B \in H_n$, as required. As last, we show that if $A \in \mathcal{A}_n$, then either $A \in H_n$, or $A^c \in H_n$. Indeed, then $A \in \mathcal{A}$, and since H is an ultrafilter, either $A \in H$, or $A^c \in H$; at the same time $A, A^c \in \mathcal{A}$, therefore, either $A \in H_n$ or $A^c \in H_n$, as required. Thus we have stated that H_n is an ultrafilter of the algebra $\mathcal{A}_n$ for each n. By theorem 5.3.1 each ultrafilter H_n is associated with a certain aggregating operator σ_n on F_n. Since by construction $H_n \subset H_{n+1}$ for each n, by proposition 6.2.2 the model $(\mathcal{A}_n, F_n, \sigma_n)$ is imdedded in the model $(\mathcal{A}_{n+1}, F_{n+1}, \sigma_{n+1})$ for each n. Therefore, $\{(\mathcal{A}_n, F_n, \sigma_n)\}$ is a sequence of imbedded collective choice models with finite increasing numbers of participants. By the first part of the proof it converges to the model $(\mathcal{A}, F, \sigma)$.

It follows from corollary 6.2.7 and theorem 6.3.3 that any sequence of finite collective choice models with increasing numbers of participants converges to a certain infinite model with a countable coalition algebra, and conversely, each infinite collective choice model with a countable coalition algebra is a limit of a certain sequence of finite collective choice models with increasing numbers of participants.

Recall that each countable Boolean algebras is isomorphic to the field of clopen subsets of a certain closed subset of the Cantor discontinuum (Sikorsky 1964; p. 26). Consequently, there exists a continuum of isomorphic types of countable Boolean algebras. On the other hand, all finite collective choice models with equal numbers of participants are isomorphic. Therefore, the diversity of the limit models is caused only by the way the finite models are imbedded into each other. It is analogous to the construction of point sets on the line: All finite sets with equal number of points are discrete and isomorphic, but countable sets differ in the arrangement and in the number of accumulation points.

Let us illustrate alternate ways of increase in the number of participants with an example. By the way we shall see how the dictator transfers his functions to the deciding hierarchy, which results in his disappearance.

6.3.4. EXAMPLE (Two Types of Imbedding of Models and Disappearing of the Dictator). Consider an infinite set of individuals—the set V of dyadic-irrational points of the interval $(0;1)$ (a point of the interval $(0;1)$ is said to be *dyadic-irrational* if it is not of the form $m/2^n$, where m and n are positive integers). Let X be an arbitrary set of alternatives, containing 3 elements at least. We shall divide V into coalitions in two ways, constructing two sequences of imbedded collective choice models $\{(\mathcal{A}_n, F_n, \sigma_n)\}$ and $\{(\mathcal{A}'_n, F'_n, \sigma'_n)\}$. Each of the models $(\mathcal{A}_n, F_n, \sigma_n)$ and $(\mathcal{A}'_n, F'_n, \sigma'_n)$ will have 2^n participants, consequently, they will be isomorphic. However their limit models will differ: One will have atomic, another atomless coalition algebra.

Let $\mathcal{A}_0$ be the two-element Boolean algebra, composed of the empty set and the whole of V.

Define $\mathcal{A}_1$ to be the algebra, generated by the atoms

$$A_1^0 = (0;1/2) \cap V; \;\; A_1^1 = (1/2;1) \cap V,$$

and $\mathcal{A}_2$ to be the algebra, generated by the atoms

$$A_2^0 = (0;1/2) \cap V; A_2^1 = (1/2;3/4) \cap V; A_2^2 = (3/4;7/8) \cap V; A_2^3 = (7/8;1) \cap V;$$

etc. (fig. 54 left).

We increase the number of participants by dividing the last atom into two, then the last one into two again, and so on.

The sequence $\{\mathcal{A}'_n\}$ differs from $\{\mathcal{A}_n\}$ in that we divide into two not only the last, but each atom of the coalitions algebra. Thus, $\mathcal{A}'_0$ and $\mathcal{A}'_1$ we define in the same way as $\mathcal{A}_0$ and $\mathcal{A}_1$, but $\mathcal{A}'_2$ we define to be the algebra generated by the atoms

$$A_2^{0'} = (0;1/4) \cap V; A_2^{1'} = (1/4;1/2) \cap V; A_2^{2'} = (1/2;3/4) \cap V; A_2^{3'} = (3/4;1) \cap V$$

(fig. 54 right).

It is easy to see that the algebra $\mathcal{A}$ on V, to which the sequence of algebras $\{\mathcal{A}_n\}$ converges, is isomorphic to the field of finite subsets of the set of all positive integers and their complements. The algebra $\mathcal{A}'$ on V, to which the sequence of algebras $\{\mathcal{A}'_n\}$ converges, is isomorphic to the field of clopen subsets

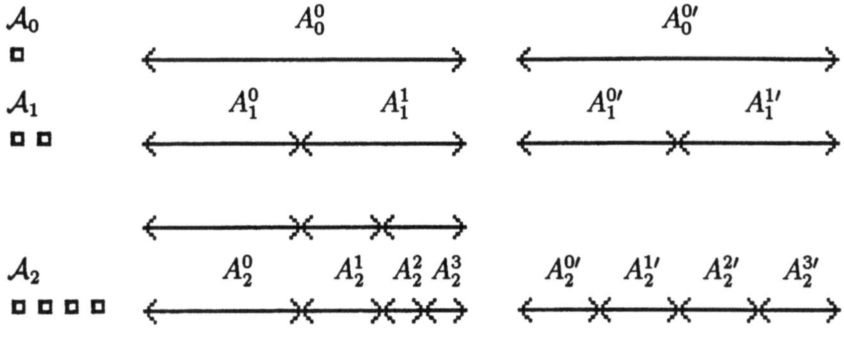

Fig. 54

of the Cantor discontinuum. Thus two limit coalition algebras are obtained by different imbedding of the same finite models.

Now let us determine aggregating operators. Taking into account theorem 5.3.1, is sufficies to determine deciding hierarchies. Since we deal with finite algebras, where each ultrafilter is fixed, it suffices to determine dictators. In each model let the dictator be the last atom of the coalition algebra. Then the bases of ultrafilters of deciding coalitions in the both limit models consist of the last atoms of algebras $\{\mathcal{A}_n\}$ and $\{\mathcal{A}'_n\}$, i.e. of atoms $A_n^{2^n-1}$ in the first of the limit models, and of atoms $A_n^{2^n-1\prime}$ in the second. Since dyadic-rational points are eliminated, these ultrafilters are free, i.e. there are no dictators under aggregating operators σ and σ', although there are dictators in the representations of the models (by theorem 5.5.1) and their extensions (by proposition 5.6.6).

It is noteworthy that representation and extension of the first limit model $(\mathcal{A}, F, \sigma)$ are different. Indeed, the representation of $\mathcal{A}$ is nothing else, but the set N of all positive integers, comactified by the "infinity" point ∞, with the algebra $\mathcal{A}$ of all finite subsets of N and their complements in $N \cup \{\infty\}$. The dictator of the model is the point ∞. The extension of V consists of the initial set of individuals—the dyadic-irrational points of interval $(0; 1)$, supplemented with the "invisible dictator"—the point 1. On the contrary, representation and extension of the second limit model $(\mathcal{A}', F', \sigma')$ are the same. They are isomorphic to the Cantor discontinuum and can be regarded as the initial set of individuals V, supplemented with two-points, inserted instead of the eliminated dyadic-rational points, while the first of each being the upper bound of the preceding points, and the second being the lower bound of all the succeeding points. The "invisible dictator" under σ' is also the limit point 1.

Now let us trace how the dictatorial functions are transferred to the deciding hierarchy, which replaces the dictator in the limit model. For example, consider the above-defied model $(\mathcal{A}_n, F_n, \sigma_n)$ for some n. Let $f_n \in F_n$ be such that the decision "x is preferred fo y" is made by the dictator alone despite of all other individuals, i.e. put $(x,y) \in f_n(A_n^{2^n-1})$ and $(x,y) \notin f_n(A_n^k)$ for all $k = 0, \ldots, 2^n - 2$. If we consider the same situation f_n in the next model $(\mathcal{A}_{n+1}, F_{n+1}, \sigma_{n+1})$, then the same decision "x is preferred to y" is made not by the dictator alone but by a certain coalition from the deciding hierarchy. In fact, the coalition $A_n^{2^n-1}$, being an atom in algebra $\mathcal{A}_n$, is no longer an atom in algebra $\mathcal{A}_{n+1}$. Thus the dictator is divided into two participants, only one of which becomes a dictator.

A simple calculation illustrates how the part of properly dictatorial decisions decreases with the growth of the number of participants. Let X be a finite set of alternatives. Fix $x, y \in X$ and denote by p the ratio of the number of preferences on X, containing the pair (x,y), to the number of all preferences on X. The value p can be understood as the probability that the pair (x,y) belongs to a randomly chosen preference. Note that by symmetry the value of p does not depend on (x,y) but is determined by the number of preferences on X, i.e. by the number of alternatives. Let us evaluate the part of the outcomes when the pair (x,y) belongs to the dictatorial preference, while not belonging to other preferences. If n is the number of participants (individuals), then it equals to $p(1-p)^{n-1}$. The part of the outcomes when the pair (x,y) does not belong to the dictatorial preference but belongs to every other preference equals to $(1-p)p^{n-1}$. Hence, the part of the outcomes (situations) when the decision on a given pair of alternatives is *properly dictatorial* (made by a dictator alone despite of the preferences of all other individuals) is equal to

$$d = p(1-p)^{n-1} + p^{n-1}(1-p).$$

Since $0 < p < 1$, the part of properly dictatorial decisions on a given pair of alternatives tends to 0 with increase in the number of participants.

Now let us evaluate the part of the outcomes when the dictatorial preference differs from every other preference not on a single pair of alternatives but in whole. Let q be inverse to the number of preferences on X, interpreted as the probability of random choice of the given preference. Then the part of the outcomes when the dictatorial preference is unique, i.e. does not coincide with any other preference, equals to

$$D = (1-q)^{n-1}.$$

Since $0 < q < 1$, the part of properly dictatorial decisions on a given pair of alternatives tends to 0 with increase in the number of participants.

In the following example we evaluate d and D for the simpliest case.

6.3.5. EXAMPLE (The Part of Properly Dictatorial Decisions). Let X consist of three alternatives, i.e. $X = \{x, y, z\}$. Enumerate all partial orders on X :

$$P_1 = \{\emptyset\};$$
$$P_2 = \{(x,y)\};\ P_3 = \{(x,z)\};\ P_4 = \{(y,x)\};$$
$$P_5 = \{(y,z)\};\ P_6 = \{(z,x)\};\ P_7 = \{(z,y)\};$$
$$P_8 = \{(x,y),(x,z)\};\ P_9 = \{(x,z),(y,z)\};\ P_{10} = \{(y,x),(y,z)\};$$
$$P_{11} = \{(y,x),(z,x)\};\ P_{12} = \{(z,x),(z,y)\};\ P_{13} = \{(z,y),(x,y)\};$$
$$P_{14} = \{(x,y),(y,z),(x,z)\};\ P_{15} = \{(x,z),(z,y),(x,y)\};$$
$$P_{16} = \{(y,x),(x,z),(y,z)\};\ P_{17} = \{(y,z),(z,x),(y,x)\};$$
$$P_{18} = \{(z,x),(x,y),(z,y)\};\ P_{19} = \{(z,y),(y,x),(z,x)\}.$$

From the above list we can see that $q = 6/19$ and $p = 1/19$. The numerical values of d and D are shown in Table 6.3.6.

6.4 Sequential Aggregation of Preferences

In the present section two ways of aggregation of preferences are compared. The first one is the *direct aggregation*, studied in the previous sections. The second one is the *indirect*, or *sequential aggregation*, analogous to indirect voting, when the set of individuals is divided into groups with their own local group preferences, to which a unifying aggregating operator is applied. We prove that such indirect aggregation can be substituted by a certain direct aggregation. The converse is valid for a countable coalition algebra, i.e. for a reasonable idealization of finite model. For Boolean algebras of higher cardinality there exist direct aggregating operators, which can be substituted by no sequential aggregating operators.

6.4.1. DEFINITION. A *grouping* T is defined to be a family of subsets of the set of individuals V, dense in $\mathcal{A}$, i.e. such that for any coalition $A \in \mathcal{A}$ there exists an element $E \in T$, for which $A \cap E \neq \emptyset$. The elements of grouping T are called *groups.* The *local coalition structure* of a group $E \in T$ is the restriction of algebra $\mathcal{A}$ to E, i.e.

$$\mathcal{A}_E = \{A \cap E : A \in \mathcal{A}\}$$

(which is a Boolean algebra (Sikorski 1964; p. 31)). A *local situation in the group* $E \in T$ is a mapping

$$f_E : E \to \mathcal{P},$$

6.3.6.TABLE. Characteristics of Dictatorial Decisions in the Collective Choice Model with Three Alternatives.

The number of participants (n)	The part of properly dictatorial decisions on a pair of alternatives (d)	The part of outcomes, when the dictatorial preference is unique (D)
2	0.4321	0.9474
3	0.2161	0.8975
4	0.1227	0.8503
5	0.0760	0.8055
6	0.0495	0.7631
7	0.0331	0.7231
8	0.0224	0.6849
9	0.0152	0.6489
10	0.0104	0.6147
11	0.0071	0.5824
12	0.0049	0.5517
13	0.0033	0.5227
14	0.0023	0.4952
15	0.0016	0.4691
16	0.0011	0.4444
17	0.0007	0.4210
18	0.0005	0.3989
19	0.0003	0.3779
20	0.0002	0.3580
21	0.0002	0.3391
22	0.0001	0.3213
23	0.0001	0.3044
24	0.0001	0.2884
25	0.0000	0.2732
26	0.0000	0.2588
27	0.0000	0.2452
28	0.0000	0.2323
29	0.0000	0.2201
30	0.0000	0.2085
...		
184	0.0000	0.0001
185	0.0000	0.0000

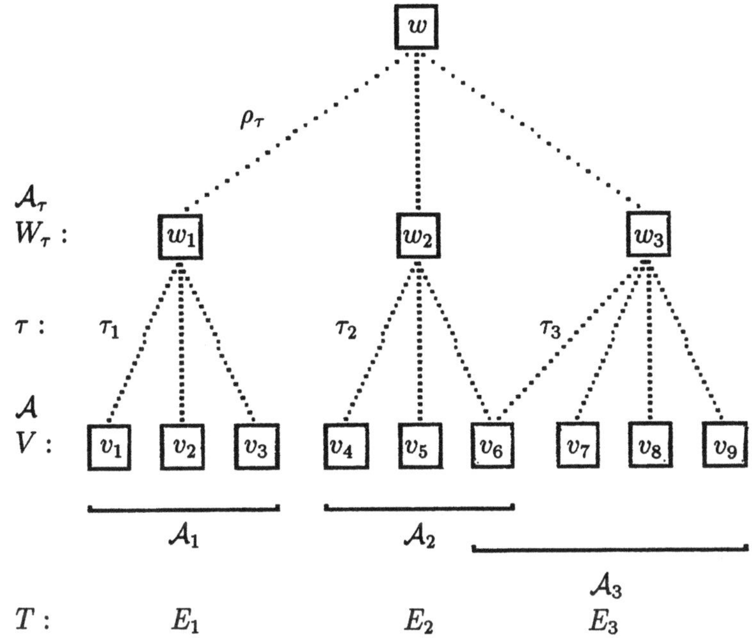

Fig. 55

satisfying the measurability condition with respect to algebra $\mathcal{A}_E$. Denote the set of all situations in group $E \in T$ by F_E. An *assignment* under grouping T is an indexed set

$$\tau = \{\tau_E : E \in T\}$$

of *local aggregating operators*

$$\tau_E : F_E \to \mathcal{P}.$$

An ultrafilter H_E of algebra $\mathcal{A}_E$ such that

$$\tau_E(f_E) = \bigcup_{A_E : A_E \in H_E} f_E(A_E)$$

for all $f_E \in F_E$, is called a *local deciding hierarchy* under τ_E. A *local dictator* of group $E \in T$ under assignment τ is the dictator under τ_E (fig. 55).

Thus the grouping is the union of individuals for the first stage of aggregation of preferences. In a general case an individual can belong to many groups—by analogy with the representative systems of Murakami (Murakami 1966; Fishburn 1973). The condition of density of grouping means that groups represent interests of all coalitions, since each coalition has a representative in a certain group. The initial coalition structure remains the same within the groups. Indeed, the way of aggregation of preferences should not distort the initial information, as the coalition structure, characterizing the diversity in individual preferences. Note that the determination of group preference is identical to the determination of collective preference in our general model.

6.4.2. PROPOSITION (Restriction of Situations to Groups). *Consider a group $E \subset V$. Denote the restriction of $\mathcal{A}$ to E by*

$$\mathcal{A}_E = \{A \cap E : A \in \mathcal{A}\}.$$

Then the restriction f_E of any situation $f \in F$ to E is measurable with respect to the algebra $\mathcal{A}_E$, consequently, f_E is a local situation in the group E.

The proof is trivial.

6.4.3. PROPOSITION (Restriction of Ultrafilters to Groups). *Consider $E \subset V$. Denote the restriction of $\mathcal{A}$ to E by $\mathcal{A}_E$. Then for any ultrafilter H_E of algebra $\mathcal{A}_E$ there exists the only ultrafilter H of algebra $\mathcal{A}$, the restriction to E of which coincides with H_E, i.e.*

$$H_E = \{A \cap E : A \in H\}.$$

Conversely, if H is an ultrafilter of algebra $\mathcal{A}$ such that $A \cap E \neq \emptyset$ for all $A \in H$, then the restriction of H to E is an ultrafilter of algebra $\mathcal{A}_E$.

PROOF. To begin with, let H_E be an ultrafilter of the algebra $\mathcal{A}_E$. Put

$$H = \{A : A \in \mathcal{A},\ A \cap E \in H_E\}.$$

We shall show that H is an ultrafilter of algebra $\mathcal{A}$. Obviously, H is a non-empty set of non-zero elements of algebra $\mathcal{A}$. If $A \in H$, $B \in \mathcal{A}$ and $A \subset B$, then $A \cap E \in H_E, B \cap E \in \mathcal{A}_E$, and $A \cap E \subset B \cap E$. Since by assumption H_E is an ultrafilter, we have $B \cap E \in H_E$, whence $B \in H$. If $A, B \in H$, then $A \cap E \in H_E$, and $B \cap E \in H_E$. Since by assumption H_E is an ultrafilter,

$$(A \cap E) \cap (B \cap E) = (A \cap B) \cap E \in H_E,$$

whence $A \cap B \in H$. If $A \in \mathcal{A}$, then, since by assumption H_E is an ultrafilter either $A \cap E \in H_E$, or $A^c \cap E \in H_E$, hence, either $A \in H$, or $A^c \in H$. Thus H is an ultrafilter of algebra $\mathcal{A}$, and also

$$\{A \cap E : A \in H\} = H_E.$$

If H' is another ultrafilter of algebra $\mathcal{A}$ such that $\{A \cap E : A \in H'\} = H_E$, then, obviously, $H' \subset H$, and since H' is maximal, $H' \subset H$. Consequently, the ultrafilter with the given property is unique.

Now let H be an ultrafilter of algebra $\mathcal{A}$ such that $A \cap E \neq \emptyset$ for all $A \in H$. We shall show that $H_E = \{A \cap E : A \in H'\}$ is an ultrafilter of the algebra $\mathcal{A}_E$. By assumption H_E is a non-empty set of non-zero elements of $\mathcal{A}_E$. Let $A_E \in H_E$, $B_E \in \mathcal{A}_E$, and $A_E \subset B_E$. We shall show that $B_E \in H_E$. By assumption there exist $A \in H$ and $B_E \in \mathcal{A}_E$ such that $A_E = A \cap E$ and $B_E = B \cap E$. Since $A_E \subset B_E$, we have

$$B_E = A_E \cup B_E = (A \cap E) \cup (B \cap E) = (A \cup B) \cap E.$$

Since $A \subset A \cup B$ and H is an ultrafilter, $A \cup B \in E$, hence, $B_E \in H_E$, as required. If $A_E \in H_E, B \in H_E$, then $A_E = A \cap E$ and $B_E = B \cap E$ for certain $A, B \in H$, therefore,

$$A_E \cap B_E = (A \cap E) \cap (B \cap E).$$

Since H is an ultrafilter, $A \cap B \in H$, hence, $A_E \cap B_E \in H_E$. If $A_E \in \mathcal{A}_E$, then $A_E = A \cap E$ for certain $A \in \mathcal{A}$, and since H is an ultrafilter, either $A \in H$, or $A^c \in H$. Hence, either $A_E = A \cap E \in H_E$, or $A_E^c = A^c \cap E \in H_E$. Thus H_E is an ultrafilter of algebra $\mathcal{A}_E$, as required.

According to proposition 6.4.3, local hierarchies in any group can be identified with hierarchies in the whole collective. In the representation of the model such hierarchies are determined by points of the closure of the given group. Indeed, the Stone spaces of quotient algebras are precisely (up to homomorphisms) the close subsets of the Stone space of the Boolean algebra (Sikorski 1964; p. 32).

Now we shall formalize the second stage of aggregation—the union of group preferences.

It is easy to see that each assignment τ induces a certain Boolean algebra on the set of groups T. Let $\mathcal{H}_\tau$ be the set of local deciding hierarchies under the assignment τ. By proposition 6.4.3 $\mathcal{H}_\tau$ is a set of ultrafilters of algebra $\mathcal{A}$. For each element $A \in \mathcal{A}$ by $h_\tau(A)$ denote the set of all ultrafilters $H \in \mathcal{H}_\tau$ such that $A \in H$. Then the class $\mathcal{A}_\tau$ of all sets $h_\tau(A)$, where $A \in \mathcal{H}$, is a Boolean algebra on $\mathcal{H}_\tau$, and h_τ is a homomorphism of $\mathcal{A}$ onto $\mathcal{A}_\tau$ (Sikorski 1964; p. 23). Now we can transfer algebra $\mathcal{A}_\tau$ from the set of local deciding hierarchies in groups to the set of groups themselves. Define *supercoalitions* (prefix "super" indicates at the relation to the second level of the model) to be the subsets $S \subset T$ such that $\{H_E : E \in S\} \in \mathcal{A}_\tau$. We shall denote the *supercoalition algebra* on the set of groups T under the assignment τ by the same character $\mathcal{A}_\tau$, as the associated algebra on the set of ultrafilters $\mathcal{H}_\tau$.

The described construction is quite clear for the respresentation of the model, where the assignment τ is associated with the *set of local dictators* $W_\tau \subset V$. The algebra $\mathcal{A}_\tau$ turns out to be the restriction of $\mathcal{A}$ to W_τ.

6.4.4. DEFINITION. Let $\mathcal{H}_\tau = \{H_E : E \in T\}$ be the set of local deciding hierarchies under the assigment τ. A set of groups $A_\tau \subset T$ is called a *supercoalition*, if there exists a coalition $A \in \mathcal{A}$ such that

$$A_\tau = \{E : E \in T, A \in H_E\}.$$

The Boolean algebra of supercoalitions under the assignment τ is denoted by $\mathcal{A}_\tau$. A *supersituation* under the assignment τ is a mapping $g_\tau : T \to \mathcal{P}$, measurable with respect to the supercoalition algebra $\mathcal{A}_\tau$. The set of supersituations under τ is denoted by G_τ. A *unifying aggregating operator* is an aggregating operator $\rho_\tau : G_\tau \to \mathcal{P}$.

The reference to the assignment in definition 6.4.4 is necessary, since the assignment determines all components of the upper level of the model. Let us show it with an example, illustrating how the assignment can affect the supercoalition algebra.

6.4.5. EXAMPLE (The Dependence of Supercoalition Algebra on the Assignment). Identify a countable set of individuals with the set N of all positive integers. Suppose that the coalition algebra is the set of all finite subsets of even numbers and their complements. Let T be the grouping, each group of which consists of two successive numbers—one odd and one even. Define the first assignment to make even numbers to be local dictators, and the second assignment to make the odd numbers to be local dictators. It is easy to see that under the first assignment the supercoalition algebra is isomorphic to the algebra of finite subsets of N and their complements, but under the second assignment it becomes isomorphic to the algebra of all subsets of N.

Let τ be an assignment and f be a situation on V. By proposition 6.4.2 for every group $E \in T$ the restriction of f to E is a local situation f_E in the group E, therefore, one can define a mapping $\tau(f) : T \to \mathcal{P}$ so that

$$\tau(f) = \tau(f, E) = \tau_E(f_E)$$

for all $E \in T$ and all $f \in F$, where τ_E is the local aggregating operator for the group E under the assignement τ, and f_E is the restriction of f to E. Thus for each situation we define preferences of all groups.

6.4.6. PROPOSITION (On the Compatibility of Situations with Supersituations). *Let τ be an assignment and f be a situation on V. Then the mapping $\tau(f) : T \to \mathcal{P}$ is measurable with respect to the supercoalition algebra $\mathcal{H}_\tau$ and, consequently, is a supersituation.*

PROOF. Let $x, y \in X$. We shall show that

$$A_\tau = \{E : E \in T,\ (x,y) \in \tau_E(f_E)\} \in \mathcal{A}_E,$$

where $\tau_E \in \tau$, and f_E is the restriction of the situation f to E for every $E \in T$. By the measurability condition for f we have

$$A = \{v : v \in V,\ (x,y) \in f(v)\} \in \mathcal{A}.$$

Note that by theorem 5.3.1 we have $(x,y) \in \tau_E(f_E)$ if and only if $v \in A$ and $\in H_E$, hence,

$$A_\tau = \{E : E \in T,\ A \in H_E\},$$

which means that $A_\tau \in \mathcal{A}_\tau$.

6.4.7. PROPOSITION (On the Compatibility of Group and Unifying Aggregating Operators). *Let $\tau(f)$ be an assignment and ρ_τ be a unifying aggregating operator. Then the rule*

$$\sigma(f) = \rho_\tau(\tau(f)),$$

where $f \in F$, determines an aggregating operator $\sigma : F \to \mathcal{P}$.

PROOF. We shall verify Arrow's axioms A1–A4 for the operator σ, supposing that they are valid for goup and unifying aggregating operators. By the previous proposition $\tau(f)$ is a supersituation for any situation $f \in F$. If the preference $f(v)$ of every individual $v \in V$ is a weak order, then by A2 the preferences $\tau(f,E)$ of all groups $E \in T$ are also weak orders.Therefore, by A2 $\rho_\tau(\tau(f))$ is a weak order, i.e. σ satisfies A2. Let us verify A3. Consider $f \in F$. Obviously, $f(V) \subset f(E)$. By virtue of A3 we have $f_E(E) \subset \tau_E(f_E)$, where f_E is the restriction of f to E. Hence,

$$f(V) \subset \bigcap_{E \in T} \tau_E(f_E) = \tau(f,T).$$

Since by A3 we have

$$\tau(f,T) \subset \rho_\tau(\tau(f)) = \sigma(f),$$

we obtain $f(V) \subset \sigma(f)$. Let us verify A4. Let two situations $f, g \in F$ coincide on a pair of alternatives (x,y). By A4 we have that $\tau(f,E)$ and $\tau(g,E)$ coincide on (x,y) for every group $E \in T$, and then by A4 we obtain that $\rho_\tau(\tau(f))$,

$\rho_\tau(\tau(g))$ also coincide on (x, y), i.e. $\sigma(f)$ and $\sigma(g)$ coincide on (x, y), as required.

The above proposition justifies the consideration of the superposition

$$\sigma = \rho_\tau \circ \tau$$

of assignment τ and unifying aggregating operator ρ_τ. This superposition turns out to be an aggregating operator, satisfying axioms A1–A4. The aggregating operators of this form we shall call *sequential.*

6.4.8. THEOREM (About Sequential Aggregation of Preferences). *Fix an assignment τ and consider a family of sequential aggregating operators of the form*

$$\sigma = \rho_\tau \circ \tau.$$

Then in the representation of the model the dictators under various σ are precisely the points of the closure of the set of local dictators, and the "global" dictator under σ always equals to the "unifying" dictator under ρ_τ.

PROOF. As we have mentioned above, in the representation of the model the supercoalition algebra $\mathcal{A}_\tau$ is the restriction of the algebra $\mathcal{A}$ to the set of local dictators W_τ, i.e.

$$\mathcal{A}_\tau = \mathcal{A}_{W_\tau} = \{A_{W_\tau} : A_{W_\tau} = A \cap W_\tau,\ A \in \mathcal{A}\}.$$

At first let $w \in [W_\tau]$. We shall define a unifying aggregating operator ρ_τ such that w will be a dictator under the sequential aggregating operator $\sigma = \rho_\tau \circ \tau$. Denote by H the ultrafilter, determined by the point w, i.e. put

$$H = \{A : A \in \mathcal{A},\ w \in A\}.$$

By assumption $A \cap W_\tau \neq \emptyset$ for any coalition $A \in H$, therefore, by proposition 6.4.3 we have that

$$H_{W_\tau} = \{A \cap W_\tau : A \in H\}$$

is an ultrafilter of the algebra $\mathcal{A}_{W_\tau} = \mathcal{A}_\tau$. By theorem 5.3.1 it is associated with a certain unifying aggregating operator ρ_τ. Let us verify that H is a deciding hierarchy under $\sigma = \rho_\tau \circ \tau$. We shall show that $f(A) \subset \sigma(f)$ for all $f \in F$ and $A \in H$. Obviously, $f(A) \subset f(w)$ for all $v \in W_\tau \cap A$, and since by assumption

$$A_\tau = A \cap W_\tau \in H_{W_\tau},$$

we obtain

$$f(A) \subset \bigcap_{v \in W_\tau \cap A} f(v) = \tau(f, A_\tau) \subset \rho_\tau(\tau(f)) = \sigma(f).$$

Thus we have shown that H is a deciding hierarchy under σ, and therefore w is the dictator under σ, as required.

Now let $\sigma = \rho_\tau \circ \tau$ be a sequential aggregating operator with dictator $w \in V$. We shall show that $w \in [W_\tau]$. Assume the contrary, i.e. $w \notin [W_\tau]$. Since V is a totally disconnected compactum, there exists a neighborhood $A \in \mathcal{A}$ of the point w such that $A \cap [W_\tau] = \emptyset$. Let P be a not-empty preference on X, say, from example 2.2.9. Define a situation $f \in F$, putting

$$f(v) = \begin{cases} \emptyset & \text{if } v \in A, \\ P & \text{if } v \notin A. \end{cases}$$

Since $A^c \in H_E$ for all $E \in T$, where H_E are the local deciding hierarchies of groups $E \in T$ under the assignment τ, extended by proposition 6.4.3 to ultrafilters of $\mathcal{A}$, then

$$P \subset \tau(f, E)$$

for all $E \in T$, and by A3 we get

$$P \subset \rho_\tau(\tau(f)) = \sigma(f).$$

On the other hand, since $w \in A$ and w is the dictator under σ, we get $\sigma(f) = \emptyset$. The obtained contradiction proves that $w \in [W_\tau]$.

Finally, we show that the dictator $w \in V$ under the sequential aggregating operator $\sigma = \rho_\tau \circ \tau$ coincides with the dictator under the unifying aggregating operator ρ_τ. Let w be the dictator under the aggregating operator σ. Then

$$H = \{A : A \in \mathcal{A},\ w \in A\}$$

is the deciding hierarchy under σ. By the first part of the proof

$$H_{W_\tau} = \{A \cap W_\tau : A \in H\} = \{A \cap W_\tau : w \in A\}$$

is a deciding hierarchy under a certain unifying aggregating operator $\tilde{\rho_\tau}$ such that $\sigma = \tilde{\rho_\tau} \circ \tau$. Let us show that $\tilde{\rho_\tau} = \rho_\tau$. Assume the contrary, i.e. that there is a supersituation $g \in G_\tau$ such that $\tilde{\rho_\tau}(g) \neq \rho_\tau(g)$. We shall define a situation $f \in F$ such that $\sigma(f) \neq \rho_\tau(\tau(f))$, against the above proof. Since $\tilde{\rho_\tau}(g) \neq \rho_\tau(g)$ there exist $x, y \in X$ such that $(x, y) \in \tilde{\rho_\tau}(g)$ and $(x, y) \notin \tilde{\rho_\tau}(g)$ (the case $(x, y) \notin \tilde{\rho_\tau}(g)$ and $(x, y) \in \tilde{\rho_\tau}(g)$ is analogous). By the measurability condition there exist supercoalitions $A_\tau, B_\tau \in \mathcal{A}_\tau$ such that $(x, y) \in g(E)$ if and only if $E \in A_\tau$, and $(y, x) \in g(E)$ if and only if $E \in B_\tau$. Then there exist coalitions $A, B \in \mathcal{A}$ such that

$$A_\tau = \{E : E \in T,\ A \in H_E\}$$

and

$$B_\tau = \{E : E \in T,\ B \in H_E\},$$

where H_E are local deciding hierarchies of groups $E \in T$ under the assignment τ—ultrafilters of the algebra $\mathcal{A}$. Define a situation $f \in F$, putting

$$f(v) = \begin{cases} \{(x,y)\} & \text{if } v \in A, \\ \{(y,x)\} & \text{if } v \in B, \\ \emptyset & \text{if } v \in (A \cup B)^c. \end{cases}$$

Then

$$\tau(f,E) = \begin{cases} \{(x,y)\} & \text{if } E \in A, \\ \{(y,x)\} & \text{if } E \in B, \\ \emptyset & \text{if } E \in (A_\tau \cup B_\tau)^c. \end{cases}$$

Applying A4 to supersituations $\tau(f)$ and g, we obtain that $(x,y) \in \tilde{\rho_\tau}(\tau(f))$, i.e. $\sigma(f) \neq \tilde{\rho_\tau}(\tau(f))$, as required. Thus $\tilde{\rho_\tau} = \rho_\tau$, and therefore H_{W_τ} is the deciding hierarchy under the unifying aggregating operator ρ_τ. Since $[W_\tau]$ is the Stone space of algebra $\mathcal{A}_{W_\tau}$ (Sikorski 1964; p. 32) and $w \in [A_{W_\tau}]$ for all $A_{W_\tau} \in \mathcal{A}_{W_\tau}$, we obtain that w is the dictator under the unifying aggregating operator ρ_τ, as required.

The following proposition gives a sufficient condition of the substitution of a sequential aggregating operator for a direct aggregating operator. To formulate it, recall that an ultrafilter H is said to have *a countable base* if it contains a countable family $H' \subset H$ such that for every $A \in H$ there is $B \in H'$ such that $B \subset A$.

6.4.9. Proposition (A Sufficient Condition of Substitution of a Sequential Aggregating Operator for a Direct One). *Let the deciding hierarchy H associated with aggregating operator σ be an ultrafilter with a countable base. Then for any grouping T there exists an assignment τ such that $\sigma = \rho_\tau \circ \tau$.*

Proof. According to proposition 6.4.8, it suffices to consider the representation of the model with the dictator w under σ and to verify that there exists a set of local dictators W_τ such that $w \in [W_\tau]$. If there exists a group $E \in T$ such that $w \in [E]$, define an assignment τ such that the local dictator of the group E would be w and all other local dictators take arbitrarily. Now suppose that $w \notin [E]$ for all $E \in T$. Let

$$H' = \{A_1, \ldots, A_n, \ldots\}$$

be the countable base of the ultrafilter H. We shall define the set of local dictators by induction on n.

1⁰. Since T is dense in $\mathcal{A}$, there exists an element $E_1 \in T$ such that $E_1 \cap A_1 \neq \emptyset$. Put $w_1 \in E_1 \cap A_1$.

2⁰. Suppose that we have already determined the groups $E_1, \ldots, E_n$ with the local dictators $w_1, \ldots, w_n$ such that $w_i \in A_i$ for all $i = 1, \ldots, n$. Note that

$$O = A_{n+1} \cap [E_1]^c \cap \ldots \cap [E_n]^c$$

is open. Since $w \in A_{n+1}$ and by assumption $w \notin [E]$ for all $E \in T$, the set O is not empty. Since T is dense in $\mathcal{A}$, there exists $E_{n+1} \in T$ such that $E_{n+1} \cap O \neq \emptyset$. Put $w_{n+1} \in E_{n+1} \cap O$.

For the groups, which are not occupied in the inductive process, define local dictators arbitrarily. Since $w_n \in A_n$ for all $n = 1, 2, \ldots$ and $\{A_n\}$ is the countable base of ultrafilter H, we have $w \in [\{w_n\}] \subset [W_\tau]$, as required.

From the above proposition we derive an important corollary.

6.4.10. Corollary (About the Equivalence of Direct and Sequential Aggregation of Preferences for a Countable Coalition Algebra). *For a collective choice model with a countable algebra of coalitions any sequential aggregating operator is equivalent to a certain direct aggregating operator. Conversely, for any direct aggregating operator and any grouping there exists an equivalent sequential aggregating operator defined for the given grouping.*

Let us show that the countability of the base of ultrafilter is an essential condition of proposition 6.4.9. Before we give a counterexample, we recall some topological facts (Arhangelskii & Ponomarev 1974; Kelley 1957; van Douwen 1978).

A completely regular topologial space is called *pseudocompact* if every countable real-value function on it is bounded. A family $\mathcal{B}$ of open sets of a topological space V is called a *π-base* if for every open set $O \subset V$ there exists an element $B \in \mathcal{B}$ such that $B \subset O$. A point $w \in \beta V \setminus V$, where βV denotes the Cech–Stone compactification of a completely regular space V, is called *remote* if $w \notin [A]_{\beta V}$ for every nowhere dense $A \subset V$. It is known that if V is not pseudocompact and has a countable π-base, then there exist $2^{\mathcal{C}}$ remote points in $\beta V \setminus V$, where $\mathcal{C}$ is the cardinality of continuum.

6.4.11. Example (The Unequivalence of Direct and Sequential Aggregation of Preferences). Let us identify the set of individuals with the Cantor discontinuum on the segment $[0; 1]$ except point 0. Let the coalition algebra $\mathcal{A}$ be the set of clopen subsets of V. We shall verify that the Cech–Stone compactification βV of the space V is the Stone space of algebra $\mathcal{A}$. Let V' be the set of all ultrafilters of algebra $\mathcal{A}$ with the topology of Stone compactum. Identify V with the set of fixed ultrafilters of $\mathcal{A}$. Then V is dense in V'. We shall show that V' is the Cech–Stone compactification of V. For that purpose it sufficies to verify that if L and M are disjunct closed subsets of V, then their closures in V' are also disjunct (Arhangelskii & Ponomarev 1974). Since V is a Lindelöf space and ind $V = 0$, then also Ind $V = 0$ (Aleksandrov 1977), therefore, there exists a clopen neighborhood $A \in \mathcal{A}$ of the closed set L such that $A \subset (V \setminus M)$. By definition of the topology of Stone compactum

$$A' = \{v' : v' \in V',\ A \in v'\},$$

and

$$A'^c = \{v' : v' \in V',\ A^c \in v'\}$$

are clopen subsets of V'. Since $L \subset A'$ and $M \subset A'^c$, we have $[L]_{V'} \subset A'$ and $[M]_{V'} \subset A'^c$, therefore,

$$[L]_{V'} \cap [M]_{V'} = \emptyset,$$

as required. As a subspace of the real line, V is completely regular and has a countable base, consequently, a countable π-base. Since the real-value function $f(v) = 1/v$ is not bounded on V, the space V is not pseudocompact. Therefore, there exists a remote point $w \in V' \setminus V$.

Now define aggregating operator σ by the dictator, which is the remote point $w \in V' \setminus V$. Consider the grouping

$$T = \{E_n : E_n = [1/2^n; 1/2^{n-1}] \cap V,\ n = 1, 2, \ldots\}.$$

Note that

$$V = \bigcup_{n=1}^{\infty} E_n$$

and that E_n is open for every n, therefore, under every assignment τ the set of local dictators W_τ is nowhere dense in V. Since w is a remote point, we have $w \notin [W_\tau]_{V'}$, whence by theorem 6.4.8 the aggregating operator σ is equivalent to no sequential aggregating operator defined for the given grouping.

6.5 Reduction of Model and Notes on Interpretation

The representation of collective choice model simplifies proofs and make them more clear but, as a rule, implies an increase in the cardinality of the set of individuals. For example, the Stone representation of the algebra of all subsets of the set of all positive integers has the cardinality $2^{\mathcal{C}}$, where $\mathcal{C}$ is the cardinality of continuum. Obviously, in this case we can consider a countable dense set of individuals, but in a general case the reduction to a dense subset of individuals has to be justified.

6.5.1. PROPOSITION (On the Reduction of Collective Choice Model). *Let a subset $S \subset V$ be dense in the coalition algebra $\mathcal{A}$. Denote by $\mathcal{A}_S$ the restriction of $\mathcal{A}$ to S and by F_S the set of the situations on S measurable with respect to $\mathcal{A}_S$. Then for every aggregating operator $\sigma : F \to \mathcal{P}$ there exists an aggregating operator $\rho : F_S \to \mathcal{P}$ such that*

$$\sigma(f) = \rho(f_S)$$

for any situation $f \in F$ and its restriction $f_S \in F_S$ to S, while algebraic models $(\mathcal{A}, F, \sigma)$ and $(\mathcal{A}_S, F_S, \rho)$ being isomorphic.

PROOF. Consider S as a grouping, each group being a single point of S, i.e. put

$$T = \{E : E = \{s\},\ s \in S\},$$

and apply theorem 6.4.8. Since each group consists of a single point, the only possible set of local dictators is the set S itself. By theorem 6.4.8 the dictators under σ and ρ coincide, and this is realizable, since S is dense in V.

In order not to overburden the collective choice model with redundant individuals, we can reduce their number to the minimal cardinality of dense subsets, called the *density* of the coalition algebra. Its important property is the invariance with respect to isomorphisms—in contrast to the cardinality of the set of individuals. Thus, in example 6.4.11 is suffices to restrict all the consideration to a countable set of individuals, say, to the end points of empty intervals.

It is noteworthy that the possibility to reduce the collective choice model to the model with a countable set of individuals does not imply that it can be considered as an idealization of a finite model with a large number of participants. In fact, according to the limit theorem, the necessary and sufficient condition for that is the countability of the coalition Boolean algebra. To the point, theorems of Fishburn and Kirman and Sondermann, are formulated for the algebra of all subsets of an infinite set of individuals, which is uncountable. Therefore, we cannot substantiate them strictly from the standpoint of our limit theorem. However, we can propose a slight modification of Fishburn's and Kirman–Sondermann's theorems, considering a countable set of individuals with a countable algebra. For example, we can consider the field of finite subsets of a countable set and their complements. Such versions of these theorems imply the same conclusions and are compatible with our limit theorem.

Summing up what has been said, the simpliest infinite collective choice model is the model with a countable set of individuals with a countable Boolean algebra of coalitions. However, we distinguish two cases, arising in the reduced collective choice model. In the first case the reduction can entail no loss of information on individual preferences; in the second case the information is partially lost. Let us illustrate it with two examples.

6.5.2. EXAMPLE (No Loss of Information on Individual Preferences in the Reduced Model). Identify the set of individuals V with the Cantor discontinuum. In other words, an individual v is identified with an infinite string of 0 and 1, which we denote by

$$v = v_1 \dots v_n \dots ,$$

where $v_i = 0, 1;\ i = 1, \dots, n$. The coalition Boolean algebra is generated by the sets of the form

$$A_n = \{v \in V : v_1 \dots v_n 000 \dots \leq v \leq v_1 \dots v_n 111 \dots\},$$

where $\leq$ is the lexicographic order on the sequences of 0 and 1. Suppose that the set X of alternatives is finite. Then the set of preferences is also finite, and by the measurability condition every situation determines a finite partitioning of coalition algebra such that all individuals from each its coalition have the same preference. In other words, every situation is a locally constant mapping of V into $\mathcal{P}$. Now consider a reduction of the set of individuals to a countable dense subset $S \subset V$. Let S consist of the points

$$s = v_1 \dots v_n 000 \dots ,$$
$$s = v_1 \dots v_n 111 \dots ,$$

where $v_i = 0, 1;\ i = 1, \dots, n$, and n runs over all positive integers. It is easy to see that under our assumptions all individual preferences are represented by certain coalitions, or by certain individuals in the reduced model. Thus all individuals are represented in every situation, and we have no loss of information on individual preferences.

6.5.3. EXAMPLE (The Loss of Information on Individual Preferences in the Reduced Model). Let the set of individuals and the coalition algebra be like in the previous example, but the set of alternatives be countable:

$$X = \{x_1, x_2, \dots\}.$$

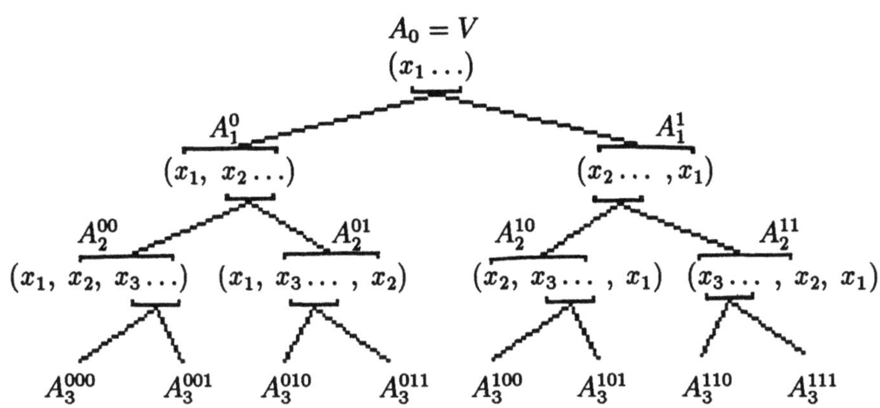

Fig. 56

Since the measurability condition restrains the preference diversity on pairs of alternatives only, there exist situations, when each individual has the preference different from others. Let us construct such a situation f.

For each individual $v = v_1 \dots v_m \dots \in V$ define $f(v)$ to be a strict order such that $(x_m, x_n) \in f(v)$, where $m < n$ are positive integers, if and only if $v_m = 0$. The construction of f is shown in fig. 56. At first V is divided into two coalitions

$$A_1^0 = \{v : v = 0v_2 \dots\} = \{v : v \in V, v_1 = 0\},$$
$$A_1^1 = \{v : v = 1v_2 \dots\} = \{v : v \in V, v_1 = 1\}.$$

Using the designation of examples 2.2.9 and 2.2.10, put

$$f(A_1^0) = (x_1,\ x_2 \dots);$$
$$f(A_1^1) = (x_2 \dots\ ,\ x_1),$$

where $(x_1,\ x_2 \dots)$ denotes the weak order with x_1 being the most preferable and x_2 being indifferent to all other alternatives; $(x_2 \dots\ ,\ x_1)$ denotes the weak order with x_1 being the least preferable and x_2 being indifferent to all other alternatives. At the second stage the coalition A_1^0 is divided into two coalitions

$$A_1^{00} = \{v : v \in V, v = 00v_3 \dots\} = \{v : v \in V, v_1 = 0, v_2 = 0\},$$
$$A_2^{01} = \{v : v \in V, v = 01v_3 \dots\} = \{v : v \in V, v_1 = 0, v_2 = 1\},$$

and A_1^1 is devided into two coalitions

$$A_2^{10} = \{v : v \in V, v = 10v_3 \dots\} = \{v : v \in V, v_1 = 1, v_2 = 0\};$$
$$A_2^{11} = \{v : v \in V, v = 11v_3 \dots\} = \{v : v \in V, v_1 = 1, v_2 = 1\}.$$

The preferences of these coalitions have to be compatible with the preferences of the larger coalitions, defined at the previous step. For example,

$$f(A_1^0) = f(A_1^{00}) \cap f(A_2^{01}).$$

For this purpose, dividing a coalition into two smaller ones, we define their preferences in two mutually exclusive ways. We take the first of indifferent alternatives (in the given case x_2) and make it either more, or less preferable to others, remaining indifferent. If the last upper index of the smaller coalition is 0, it is declared more preferable, otherwise it is declared less preferable. Thus, the 2-level preference $(x_1,\ x_2\dots)$ splits into two 3-level preferences $(x_1,\ x_2,\ x_3\dots)$ and $(x_1,\ x_3\dots\ ,\ x_2)$, where $x_3\dots$ denotes the class of indifferent alternatives, consisting of x_3 and all subsequent ones. For every individual $v = v_1\dots v_n\dots$ define its preference as the limit of our construction, putting

$$f(v) = \bigcup_{n=1}^{\infty} f(A_n^{v_1\dots v_n}),$$

where the indicies $v_1\dots v_n$ coincide with the first n terms of the sequence v.

We shall prove that $f(v)$ is a strict order on X for every $v \in V$. Let

$$v = v_1\dots v_i\dots v_j\dots v_k\dots\ .$$

We shall show that $f(v)$ is asymmetric. Assume the contrary, i.e. that there are $x_i, x_j \in X$ such that $(x_i, x_j) \in f(v)$ and $(x_j, x_i) \in f(v)$, where, say, $i < j$ (note that $(x_i, x_i) \notin f(v)$ by definition). We obtain that the former implies $v_i = 0$, but the latter $v_i = 1$, which is impossible.

Now we are going to verify that $f(v)$ is negatively transitive. Suppose that $(x_i, x_j) \notin f(v)$ and $(x_j, x_k) \notin f(v)$. We shall show that $(x_i, x_k) \notin f(v)$. Consider all possible cases.

1. Let $i < j < k$, or $i < k < j$. Then $(x_i, x_j) \notin f(v)$ implies $(x_j, x_i) \notin f(v)$, which is possible if only $v_1 = 1$, consequently, $(x_k, x_i) \in f(v)$, hence, by asymmetry $(x_i, x_k) \notin f(v)$.

2. Now let $k < i < j$, or $k < j < i$. Then $(x_j, x_k) \notin f(v)$ implies $(x_k, x_j) \notin f(v)$, which is possible if only $v_k = 0$, consequently, $(x_k, x_i) \in f(v)$, hence, $(x_i, x_k) \notin f(v)$.

3. The case $j < i < k$ is impossible because $(x_k, x_i) \notin f(v)$ implies $(x_j, x_i) \in f(v)$, which could be if only $v_j = 0$, whence $(x_j, x_k) \in f(v)$ against the assumption.

4. The case $j < k < i$ is also impossible because $(x_j, x_k) \notin f(v)$ implies $(x_k, x_j) \in f(v)$, which could be if only $v_j = 1$, whence $(x_i, x_j) \in f(v)$ against the assumption.

Thus $f(v)$ is asymmetric and negatively transitive. By our definition for every two $x_i, x_j \in X$ it holds either $(x_i, x_j) \in f(v)$, or $(x_j, x_i) \in f(v)$, therefore, $f(v)$ is a strict order

It is clear that $f(v') \neq f(v'')$ for every unequal $v', v'' \in V$. We shall verify the measurability condition. Take two positive integers $m < n$. By our construction $(x_m, x_n) \in f(v)$ if and only if $v_m = 0$. Then

$$\{v : v \in V,\ (x_m, x_n) \in f(v)\} = \bigcup_{v_1=0,1;\ \dots\ ;\ v_{m-1}=0,1} A_m^{v_1 \dots v_{m-1} 0}.$$

The constituents of the last finite union are coalitions from the algebra, consequently, the union is also a coalition, as required. Since

$$\{v : v \in V,\ (x_n, x_m) \in f(v)\} = V \setminus \{v : v \in V,\ (x_m, x_n) \in f(v)\} \in \mathcal{A},$$

the measurability condition is satisfied.

Thus $f(v)$ is a situation, adopting continuum values (preferences). We conclude that after reduction of the model to a countable set of individuals most values (preferences) are lost. However, they can be reconstructed by continuity of situations, extended to eliminated individuals. It resembles the property of a continuous real-value function, which can be reconstructed by its restriction to a dense subset of the domain of definition.

To end the chapter we mention that our examples based on the Cantor discontinuum should not be regarded as artificial. Recall that the Cantor discontinuum is a *universal space* for all countable Boolean algebras, i.e. every countable Boolean algebra is up to isomorphism is a field of clopen sets of its certain closed subset (Sikorski 1964, p. 24; Engelking 1977, p. 115–116). It means that every algebraic collective choice model with a countable coalition algebra can be realized on the Cantor discontinuum.

Chapter 7

Interpretation of Dictator as Representative

7.1 Introductory Remarks

The lack of dictator in the infinite model implies that the part of properly dictatorial decisions is small if the number of individuals is large. Consequently, the denomination of dictator is justified in rare cases which can be considered as non-typical. Therefore, the interpretation of the model based on the common understanding of the dictator is not precise. On the other hand, the fact that a dictator can be taken into and away from the infinite model, not affecting its properties, indicates at the subsidiary character of the concept of a dictator itself. As shown in chapter 5, the dictator coincides with the upper level of deciding hierarchy, which can be unattainable in the infinite model. In contrast to the dictator, the deciding hierarchy is invariant with respect to isomorphisms of the model, finite and infinite as well. Moreover, since the function of the dictator is shared by the coalitions of the deciding hierarchy, his personal contribution to decision-making becomes to a great extent limited. Thus the dictator appears to be not so much opposed to other individuals, from which its prohibition was postulated originally.

The definition of a dictator doesn't specify, whether he compels other individuals to accept his choice, or the collective preference is formed in the first turn, and only afterwards an individual, sharing it, is found out. Nevertheless, the interpretation of the concept of a dictator in Arrow's model depends on what we put first—dictatorial or collective preference. The former possibility corresponds to our understanding of dictatorship in a common sense; the latter meets the interpretation of a dictator as a representative of the collective. The present chapter is devoted to the analysis of the latter possibility—to the interpretation of a dictator as a representative. We show that a dictator can be appointed to express a majority preference in most cases, although we allow him to contradict it in secondary decisions, or in unexpected situations To formalize the above reasons, we introduce three measures, with which we specify the weight of coalitions, the significance of decisions, and the expectation of individual preferences. By means of these measures we define quantitative indicators of representativeness of dictators, characterizing their capabilities to express the collective preference. For arbitrary measures we prove the existence of the dictators, representing a majority on average, and the dictators, representing a majority more often than in a half of all possible cases. In the second part of the chapter we examine the case of so called independent individuals and derive simple approximation formulas for the indicators of representativeness.

The obtained results substantiate the interpretation of some dictators in Arrow's model as representatives of the collective. It weakens the categoricity of the conclusions about the impossibility of rational collective choice, and in a sense we can even speak about the overcoming Arrow's paradox. Arrow's paradox can be considered as the result of an excess of information in the model, which comes to contradiction with itself. In turn an excess of information can be caused either by an excess of rules with which the contradictive information is deduced, or by an extended understanding of basic concepts, as in the naive set theory. The first of these possibilities is meant in the traditional interpretation of Arrow's paradox, proposing to overcome it by eliminating one of Arrow's axiom. Our results give arguments in favour of another possibility. The consideration of indicators of representativeness reveals that some dictators don't meet their denomination. Refining the concept of a dictator, we come to a new understanding of Arrow's paradox. In this connection we refer to the set theory, the paradoxes of which were overcome by refining the concept of a set itself.

In the light of such an interpretation and owing to their extreme simplicity, the dictatorial rules of decision-making can be acceptable even for practical purposes. The main prerequisite for an appropiate choice of a dictator is the reliability of prediction of individual preferences. If the prediction is wrong, the chosen representative can express no majority preference and turns out to be a dictator in a common sense of the word.

Finally note applications of our approach to multicriteria decision-making. A dictator-representative is associated with a partial criterium, which can serve for a global one. For example, in certain situations the price can be regarded as a general indicator of quality for a particular kind of goods.

The results of this chapter are published in Russian in (Tanguiane 1989a, 1990a).

7.2 Indicators of Representativeness

We shall restrict our consideration to the models with finite, or countable Boolean algebras, which by virtue of the limit theorem 6.3.3 are the only reasonable idealizations of the finite case. Recall that Stone representations of countable Boolean algebras are closed subsets of Cantor discontinuum (Sikorsky 1964, p. 25–26; Aleksandroff 1977, p. 287–290).

It is known that when a countable Boolean algebra is realized on its Stone compactum, there always exists a probability measure

$$\mu : \mathcal{A}_\sigma \rightarrow [0;1],$$

where $\mathcal{A}_\sigma$ is the σ-algebra generated by the given Boolean algebra (Sikorski 1964, p. 201). We use the measure μ to characterize the *weight of coalitions and individuals.* By $\mu(A)$ we denote the weight of coalition $A \in \mathcal{A}_\sigma$, by $\mu(v)$ we denote the weight of individual $v \in V$ (since $v \in \mathcal{A}_\sigma$). Since we refer to a probability measure, the weight of coalitions can be understood as the percent of the total number of individuals. Obviously, the collective V has the weight 100%, and the weight of a majority should be no less than 50%.

7.2.1. PROPOSITION (About the Existence of a Measure on the Set of Situations). *If the set of alternatives is finite and the coalition Boolean algebra is finite (countable), then the set of situations F is finite (countable). Consequently, there exists a probability measure on the set of all subsets of F, which can be defined by means of a mapping*

$$\nu : F \rightarrow [0;1],$$

satisfying the normalizing condition

$$\sum_{f \in F} \nu(f) = 1.$$

PROOF. Since the set of alternatives is finite, the set of all preferences is also finite. By virtue of the measurability condition and the finitness of the set of alternatives, each situation determines a finite partitioning of the set of individuals into coalitions of individuals with identical preferences. Therefore, each situation is a mapping of a finite partitioning of the set of individuals into a finite set of preferences. When a finite partitioning is fixed, the number of such mappings is finite. Since the number of finite partitionings of a finite (countable) algebra is finite (countable), we obtain that the number of situations is finite (countable), as required.

For a given situation $f \in F$ we interpret the value $\nu(f)$ as the *probability of situation* f. For each subset $G \subset F$ define its probability to be

$$\nu(G) = \sum_{f \in G} \nu(f).$$

If $\nu(f) > 0$ the situation f is called *possible.* Note that by means of measure ν we can also restrict the universality axiom A2, eliminating out of consideration certain combinations of individual preferences.

If the set of alternatives X is finite, then we can define a probability measure on the set of all subsets of the set $X \times X$ by means of a mapping

$$\xi : X \times X \to [0; 1],$$

satisfying the normalizing condition

$$\sum_{(x,y) \in X \times X} \xi(x, y) = 1.$$

For a given pair of alternatives (x, y) we interpret the value $\xi(x, y)$ as the *significance of decision* on pair (x, y). Another interpretation of $\xi(x, y)$ is the probability that the decision "x is preferred to y" is considered. If $\xi(x, y) > 0$ the pair of alternatives (x, y) is called *significant.* Taking into account the asymmetry of preferences, we don't consider pairs of the form (x, x), putting $\xi(x, x) = 0$ for all $x \in X$.

Consider the sample space

$$\Omega = X \times X \times F,$$

provided with the probability measure

$$\mathsf{P} = \xi \otimes \nu,$$

defined to be the product of measures ξ and ν. A *simple event* is therefore "a pair of alternatives and a situation"

$$\omega = (x, y, f).$$

It is called *significant* if

$$\mathsf{P}(\omega) = \xi(x, y)\, \nu(f) > 0.$$

Each simple event $\omega = (x, y, f)$ determines a division of the collective V into two coalitions (one of which may be empty) by preferences on the pair (x, y) under the situation f. We denote them by

$$A_\omega = A_{xyf} = \{v : v \in V,\ (x, y) \in f(v)\}; \tag{7.2.1}$$
$$A_\omega^c = A_{xyf}^c = \{v : v \in V,\ (x, y) \notin f(v)\}.$$

The first coalition is formed of the individuals who prefer x to y under the situation f. Another coalition consists of the individuals who don't prefer x to y under the situation f. Fix an individual v. Since he belongs to one of these coalitions, we can consider him as a representative of the coalition to which he belongs and which preference on the given pair of alternatives under the given situation he shares. The measure of his representativeness is the weight of the given coalition. We denote it by

$$m(v,\omega) = m(v,x,y,f) = \begin{cases} \mu(A_\omega) & \text{if } v \in A_\omega, \\ \mu(A_\omega^c) = 1 - \mu(A_\omega) & \text{if } v \in A_\omega^c, \end{cases} \tag{7.2.2}$$

and call the *representativeness of individual v for event ω*. Note that since $\mu(V) = 1$, the value $m(v,\omega)$ is the part (percent) of the individuals represented by v for event ω.

Now suppose that simple events (considered pairs of alternatives and situations) are taken randomly. In this case the individual v represents a certain coalition for each simple event, and for each simple event he has a certain magnitude of representativeness, associated with the weight of the represented coalition. This way we define a random variable on Ω. We call it the *representativeness of individual v* and denote by

$$m(v) = m(v,\omega) = m(v,x,y,f).$$

If we suppose that individual v is also taken randomly, we define a random variable on $V \times \Omega$ (with probability measure $\mu \otimes \mathsf{P}$), which we denote by

$$m = m(v,\omega) = m(v,x,y,f)$$

and call the *representativeness (of random dictator)*.

Sometimes we shall fix some arguments, e.g. we shall consider random variable $m(v,x,y)$, where only f will be random. In our designations we omit the arguments which are treated as random, and write down the ones which are treated as parameters.

To characterize the representativeness of individuals, we introduce three *indicators of representativeness.*

7.2.2. DEFINITION. The *average representativeness of individual v for pair of alternatives (x,y)* is the mathematical expectation

$$\mathsf{E}m(v,x,y) = \sum_{f\in F} \nu(f)\, m(v,x,y,f).$$

The *average representativeness of individual v* is the mathematical expectation

$$\mathsf{E}m(v) = \sum_{\omega\in\Omega} \mathsf{P}(\omega)\, m(v,\omega) = \sum_{(x,y)\in X\times X} \xi(x,y)\, \mathsf{E}m(v,x,y). \tag{7.2.3}$$

The *average representativeness (of random dictator)* is the mathematical expectation

$$\mathsf{E}m = \sum_{v\in V}\sum_{\omega\in\Omega}\mu(v)\,\mathsf{P}(\omega)\,m(v,\omega) = \sum_{v\in V}\mu(v)\,\mathsf{E}m(v),$$

or, if V is uncountable and $\mathsf{E}m(v)$ is a measurable function of v, then

$$\mathsf{E}m = \int_V d\mu(v)\,\mathsf{E}m(v).$$

Note that the random choice of dictator is supposed to be realized with respect to the probability measure μ on V, therefore, weighty individuals have better chances to be chosen.

7.2.3. Definition. The *majority representativeness of individual v for pair of alternatives (x, y)* is the probability of situations when the individual v represents a majority with respect to the pair of alternatives (x, y), or the mathematical expectation of rounded representativeness of v for fixed (x, y), i.e.

$$\begin{aligned}\mathsf{M}m(v,x,y) &= \nu\{f : f\in F,\ m(v,x,y,f)\geq 1/2\}\\ &= \sum_{f\in F}\nu(f)\,\mathrm{int}(m(v,x,y,f)+1/2),\end{aligned}$$

where the function int(.) retains the integer part of its argument. The *majority representativeness of individual v* is the probability of the event when the individual v represents a majority, or the mathematical expectation of rounded representativeness of v, i.e.

$$\begin{aligned}\mathsf{M}m(v) &= \sum_{\omega\in\Omega}\mathsf{P}(\omega)\,\mathrm{int}(m(v,\omega))+1/2)\\ &= \sum_{(x,y)\in X\times X}\xi(x,y)\,\mathsf{M}m(v,x,y).\end{aligned} \tag{7.2.4}$$

The *majority representativeness (of random dictator)* is the mathematical expectation

$$\begin{aligned}\mathsf{M}m &= \sum_{v\in V}\sum_{\omega\in\Omega}\mu(v)\,\mathsf{P}(\omega)\,\mathrm{int}(m(v,\omega))+1/2)\\ &= \sum_{v\in V}\mu(v)\,\mathsf{M}m(v),\end{aligned}$$

or, if V is uncountable and $\mathsf{M}m(v)$ is a measurable function of v, then

$$\mathsf{M}m = \int_V d\mu(v)\,\mathsf{M}m(v).$$

7.2.4. DEFINITION. The *strict majority representativeness of individual v for pair of alternatives* (x, y) is the probability of the situations when the individual v represents a strict majority with respect to the pair of alternatives (x, y), or the mathematical expectation of rounded representativeness of v for fixed (x, y) with 0.5 rounded down to 0, i.e.

$$\begin{aligned}\overline{\mathsf{M}}m(v,x,y) &= \nu\{f : f \in F,\ m(v,x,y,f) > 1/2\}\\ &= \sum_{f\in F} \nu(f)\,[-\mathrm{int}(-m(v,x,y,f)+1/2)].\end{aligned}$$

The *strict majority representativeness of individual* v is the probability of the event when the individual v represents a strict majority, or the mathematical expectation

$$\begin{aligned}\overline{\mathsf{M}}m(v) &= \sum_{\omega\in\Omega} \mathsf{P}(\omega)\,[-\mathrm{int}(-m(v,\omega))+1/2)]\\ &= \sum_{(x,y)\in X\times X} \xi(x,y)\,\overline{\mathsf{M}}m(v,x,y).\end{aligned}$$

The *strict majority representativeness (of random dictator)* is the mathematical expectation

$$\begin{aligned}\overline{\mathsf{M}}m &= \sum_{v\in V}\sum_{\omega\in\Omega} \mu(v)\,\mathsf{P}(\omega)\,[-\mathrm{int}(-m(v,\omega))+1/2)]\\ &= \sum_{v\in V} \mu(v)\,\overline{\mathsf{M}}m(v),\end{aligned}$$

or, if V is uncountable and $\overline{\mathsf{M}}m(v)$ is a measurable function of v, then

$$\overline{\mathsf{M}}m = \int_V d\mu(v)\,\overline{\mathsf{M}}m(v).$$

Since $\mathrm{int}(a+1/2)$ and $-\mathrm{int}(-a+1/2)$ are nothing else but two ways of rounding number a, satisfying the inequality

$$-\mathrm{int}(-a+1/2) \leq \mathrm{int}(a+1/2),$$

we always have

$$\overline{\mathsf{M}}m(v,x,y) \le \mathsf{M}m(v,x,y), \tag{7.2.5}$$
$$\overline{\mathsf{M}}m(v) \le \mathsf{M}m(v),$$
$$\overline{\mathsf{M}}m \le \mathsf{M}m,$$

The defined indicators of representativeness are used to distinguish between dictators with regard to their capabilities to express preferences of other individuals.

7.2.5. DEFINITION. An individual $v^* \in V$ is called an *optimal dictator with respect to the average (majority, strict majority) representativeness* if for all $v \in V$ it holds

$$\mathsf{E}m(v^*) \ge \mathsf{E}m(v)$$
$$(\mathsf{M}m(v^*) \ge \mathsf{M}m(v),$$
$$\overline{\mathsf{M}}m(v^*) \ge \overline{\mathsf{M}}m(v)).$$

An individual v is called a *dictator-representative with resepect to the average (majority, strict majority) representativeness* if the value of the given indicator is not less than 50%, i.e.

$$\mathsf{E}m(v) \ge 1/2$$
$$(\mathsf{M}m(v) \ge 1/2,$$
$$\overline{\mathsf{M}}m(v) \ge 1/2),$$

otherwise he is called a *proper dictator with respect to the given indicator.*

7.3 Representativeness of Optimal and Random Dictators

Now we are going to prove the existence of dictators-representatives with respect to the average representativeness. We show that with the only exception for the model where the collective is always divided by preferences into equal coalitions and, consequently, all individuals have the average representativeness 50%, an optimal dictator has the average representativeness strictly greater than 50%, i.e. on average he represents a strict majority. Moreover, the same is true not only for optimal but on average for randomly chosen dictators.

7.3.1. THEOREM (About the Average Representativeness of Optimal and Random Dictators). *Let the set of alternatives X be finite, the coalition*

Boolean algebra $\mathcal{A}$ be finite or countable, and also suppose that it is realized on its Stone compactum V. Then, whatever the measures μ on V and P on Ω are, the average representativeness $\mathsf{E}m$ is defined, $\mathsf{E}m(v)$ is a continuous function of v, attaining its maximum on compactum V at some point v^*, and

$$\mathsf{E}m(v^*) \geq \mathsf{E}m \geq 1/2.$$

The precise equality

$$\mathsf{E}m = 1/2$$

holds if and only if for every significant simple event $\omega = (x, y, f)$ the coalitions of individuals, preferring and not preferring x to y under the situation f, have equal weights, i.e. $\mu(A_\omega) = 1/2$. The dispersion of the representativeness of the optimal dictator v^* satisfies the inequality

$$\mathsf{D}m(v^*) \leq 1/16 - (\mathsf{E}m(v^*) - 3/4)^2 \leq 1/16,$$

and also

$$\mathsf{D}m = 1/16 - (\mathsf{E}m - 3/4)^2 \leq 1/16.$$

PROOF. By (7.2.2) for every fixed ω the function $m(v, \omega)$ adopts one or two values, being constant on clopen A_ω and A_ω^c. Therefore, $m(v, \omega)$ is continuous with respect to v for every fixed $\omega \in \Omega$. Since the series (7.2.3)

$$\mathsf{E}m(v) = \sum_{\omega \in \Omega} \mathsf{P}(\omega)\, m(v, \omega),$$

formed of continuous non-negative functions, is majorized on compactum V by the convergent series

$$\sum_{\omega \in \Omega} \mathsf{P}(\omega) = 1, \qquad (7.3.1)$$

it converges uniformly, and its sum $\mathsf{E}m(v)$ is a continuous function on compactum V with the maximum

$$\mathsf{E}^* = \mathsf{E}m(v^*)$$

at some point $v^* \in V$.

Since $\mathsf{E}m(v)$ is a continuous function on compactum V (with countable base $\mathcal{A}$, consequently, metrizable), it is integrable (in the case of finite or countable V it is summable with the weights $\mu(v)$, nevertheless we shall use the sign of integral), and

$$\begin{aligned}
\mathsf{E}m &= \int_V d\mu(v) \sum_{\omega\in\Omega} \mathsf{P}(\omega)\, m(v,\omega) \\
&= \int_V d\mu(v)\, \mathsf{E}m(v) \\
&\leq \mathsf{E}m(v^*) \int_V d\mu(v) \\
&= \mathsf{E}m(v^*) \\
&= \mathsf{E}^*.
\end{aligned}$$

Since the series of continuous functions under the sign of integral converges uniformly, the order of summation and integration can be reversed, whence

$$\mathsf{E}^* \geq \mathsf{E}m = \sum_{\omega\in\Omega} \mathsf{P}(\omega) \int_V d\mu(v)\, m(v,\omega). \tag{7.3.2}$$

Taking into account (7.2.2), we have

$$\begin{aligned}
\int_V d\mu(v)\, m(v,\omega) &= \int_{A_\omega} d\mu(v)\, m(v,\omega) + \int_{A_\omega^c} d\mu(v)\, m(v,\omega) \\
&= \mu^2(A_\omega) + (1-\mu(A_\omega))^2 \\
&= 1/2 + 2(\mu(A_\omega) - 1/2)^2.
\end{aligned}$$

Substitute the obtained value of the integral into (7.3.2) and get

$$\mathsf{E}^* \geq \mathsf{E}m = \sum_{\omega\in\Omega} \mathsf{P}(\omega)\, [1/2 + 2(\mu(A_\omega) - 1/2)^2] \geq 1/2, \tag{7.3.3}$$

where the last inequality is strict if and only if $\mu(A_\omega) \neq 1/2$ for some significant event $\omega \in \Omega$.

To estimate the dispersion $\mathsf{D}m(v^*)$, note that by virtue of (7.2.2) for every $v \in V$ and $\omega \in \Omega$ we have

$$(\mu(A_\omega) - 1/2)^2 = (m(v,\omega) - 1/2)^2,$$

whence, according to (7.3.3),

$$\sum_{\omega\in\Omega} \mathsf{P}(\omega)\, m(v^*,\omega) \geq \sum_{\omega\in\Omega} \mathsf{P}(\omega)\, [1/2 + 2(m(v^*,\omega) - 1/2)^2].$$

It is equivalent to

$$\sum_{\omega\in\Omega} \mathsf{P}(\omega)\, m^2(v^*,\omega) \leq \frac{3}{2} \sum_{\omega\in\Omega} \mathsf{P}(\omega)\, m(v^*,\omega) - 1/2 = \frac{3}{2}\mathsf{E}^* - 1/2, \tag{7.3.4}$$

and we obtain

$$\mathsf{D}m(v^*) = \mathsf{E}m^2(v^*) - \mathsf{E}m(v^*)^2 \le \frac{3}{2}\mathsf{E}^* - 1/2 - \mathsf{E}^{*2} = 1/16 - (\mathsf{E}^* - 3/4)^2.$$

Finally, to calculate the dispersion $\mathsf{D}m$, note that with the reference to (7.2.2) and (7.3.3) we have

$$\begin{aligned}
\mathsf{E}m^2 &= \int_V d\mu(v) \sum_{\omega\in\Omega} \mathsf{P}(\omega)\, m^2(v,\omega) \\
&= \sum_{\omega\in\Omega} \mathsf{P}(\omega) \int_V d\mu(v)\, m^2(v,\omega) \\
&= \sum_{\omega\in\Omega} \mathsf{P}(\omega)\, [\int_{A_\omega} d\mu(v)\, \mu^2(A_\omega) + \int_{A_\omega^c} d\mu(v)\, \mu^2(A_\omega^c)] \\
&= \sum_{\omega\in\Omega} \mathsf{P}(\omega)\, [\mu^3(A_\omega) + (1-\mu(A_\omega))^3] \\
&= \sum_{\omega\in\Omega} \mathsf{P}(\omega)\, [1/4 + 3(\mu(A_\omega) - 1/2)^2] \\
&= -\frac{1}{2} + \frac{3}{2}\mathsf{E}m.
\end{aligned}$$

Hence,

$$\mathsf{D}m = \mathsf{E}m^2 - (\mathsf{E}m)^2 = -\frac{1}{2} + \frac{3}{2}\mathsf{E}m - (\mathsf{E}m)^2 = 1/16 - (\mathsf{E}m - 3/4)^2 \le 1/16,$$

as required.

A similar result is valid for the majority representativeness.

7.3.2. THEOREM (About the Majority Representativeness of Optimal and Random Dictators). *Let the set of alternatives X be finite, the coalition Boolean algebra $\mathcal{A}$ be finite or countable, and also suppose that it is realized on its Stone compactum V. Then, whatever the measures μ on V and P on Ω are, the majority representativeness $\mathsf{M}m$ is defined, $\mathsf{M}m(v)$ is a continuous function of v, attaining its maximum on compactum V at some point v^*, and*

$$\mathsf{M}m(v^*) \ge \mathsf{M}m > 1/2.$$

If for every significant simple event $\omega = (x, y, f)$ the coalition of individuals, preferring x to y under the situation f, has the weight other than $1/2$, i.e. $\mu(A_\omega) \ne 1/2$, then the same is also true for the strict majority representativeness.

PROOF. By (7.2.2) for every fixed ω the function $m(v,\omega)$ is constant on clopen A_ω and A^c_ω, consequently, the function $\mathrm{int}(m(v,\omega)+1/2)$ is also constant on A_ω and A^c_ω. Therefore, $\mathrm{int}(m(v,\omega)+1/2)$ is continuous with respect to v for every fixed $\omega \in \Omega$. Since the series (7.2.4)

$$\mathsf{M}m(v) = \sum_{\omega\in\Omega} \mathsf{P}(\omega)\,\mathrm{int}(m(v,\omega)+1/2),$$

formed of continuous non-negative functions, is majorized on compactum V by the convergent series (7.3.1), it converges uniformly, and its sum $\mathsf{M}m(v)$ is a continuous function on compactum V with the maximum

$$\mathsf{M}^* = \mathsf{M}m(v^*)$$

at some point $v^* \in V$.

Since $\mathsf{M}m(v)$ is a continuous function on compactum V (with countable base $\mathcal{A}$, consequently, metrizable), it is integrable (in the case of finite or countable V it is summable with the weights $\mu(v)$, nevertheless we shall use the sign of integral), and

$$\begin{aligned}\mathsf{M}m &= \int_V d\mu(v) \sum_{\omega\in\Omega} \mathsf{P}(\omega)\,\mathrm{int}(m(v,\omega)+1/2)\\ &= \int_V d\mu(v)\,\mathsf{M}m(v)\\ &\leq \mathsf{M}m(v^*)\int_V d\mu(v)\\ &= \mathsf{M}m(v^*)\\ &= \mathsf{M}^*.\end{aligned}$$

Since the series of continuous functions under the sign of integral converges uniformly, the order of summation and integration can be reversed, whence

$$\mathsf{M}^* \geq \mathsf{M}m = \sum_{\omega\in\Omega} \mathsf{P}(\omega) \int_V d\mu(v)\,\mathrm{int}(m(v,\omega)+1/2). \tag{7.3.5}$$

For every simple event $\omega = (x,y,f)$ denote the coalition of individuals, belonging to the non-strict majorities with respect to ω, by

$$M_\omega = M_{xyf} = \begin{cases} A_\omega & \text{if } \mu(A_\omega) > 1/2,\\ V & \text{if } \mu(A_\omega) = 1/2,\\ A^c_\omega & \text{if } \mu(A_\omega) < 1/2.\end{cases} \tag{7.3.6}$$

It is easy to see that for every $\omega \in \Omega$ we have

$$\mathrm{int}(m(v,\omega)+1/2) = \begin{cases} 1 & \text{if } v \in M_\omega,\\ 0 & \text{if } v \notin M_\omega.\end{cases}$$

Therefore,

$$\int_V d\mu(v)\,\mathrm{int}(m(v,\omega)+1/2) = \int_{M_\omega} d\mu(v) = \mu(M_\omega).$$

Substitute it into (7.3.5) and, taking into account that $\mu(M_\omega) > 1/2$ for every $\omega \in \Omega$, get

$$\mathsf{M}^* \geq \mathsf{M}m = \sum_{\omega\in\Omega} \mathsf{P}(\omega)\,\mu(M_\omega) > 1/2, \tag{7.3.7}$$

as required.

To ascertain the statement of the theorem for the strict majority representativeness, note that if for every significant simple event $\omega = (x, y, f)$ the coalition of individuals, preferring x to y under the situation f, has the weight other than 1/2, then the majority representativeness coincides with the strict majority representativeness.

Although it is difficult to interpret the dispersion of the rounded representativeness $\mathrm{int}(m + 1/2)$, we can estimate it formally. Note that $\mathrm{int}(m + 1/2)$ equals to 0, or 1. Therefore,

$$[\mathrm{int}(m+1/2)]^2 = \mathrm{int}(m+1/2),$$

whence

$$\mathsf{D}\,\mathrm{int}(m+1/2) = \mathsf{M}m^2 - (\mathsf{M}m)^2 = \mathsf{M}m - (\mathsf{M}m)^2 = 1/4 - (\mathsf{M}m - 1/2)^2.$$

Taking into account (7.3.7), we obtain

$$\mathsf{D}\,\mathrm{int}(m+1/2) < 1/4.$$

For the dictator v^*, optimal with respect to the majority representativeness, we obtain similarly

$$\mathsf{D}\,\mathrm{int}(m(v^*)+1/2) = 1/4 - (\mathsf{M}m(v^*) - 1/2)^2 < 1/4.$$

We mention that the additional assumption of theorem 7.3.2, concerning the strict majority representativeness, is essential. Indeed, when the collective is divided by preferences into equal coalitions, no coation forms a strict majority. If it holds for all significant simple events $\omega \in \Omega$ we get $\overline{\mathsf{M}}m(v) = 0$ for all $v \in V$ (on the contrary, in this case $\mathsf{M}m(v) = 1$ for all $v \in V$).

In the light of the above two theorems, justifying the two approaches to the definition of optimal dictator, the question arises, whether a dictator, optimal with respect to one indicator, is at the same time optimal with respect to another? The following example shows that the general answer to this question is negative.

At first, however, we make a remark on the future examples. We shall define only the situations which distinguish individuals with respect to their preferences on some significant pairs of alternatives. We shall not mention not-possible situations and non-significant pairs of alternatives, since they don't contribute to the indicators of representativeness. We shall also avoid constant situations (when all individuals have the same preference), equally contributing to the indicators of representativeness of all individuals, not affecting the choice of optimal dictators. Thus, in our examples we reduce the sets of alternatives and situations to some sufficient minima. We often consider only two alternatives regardless of Arrow's axiom A2, supposing that the model can always be extended.

7.3.3. EXAMPLE (The Inconsistency of the Two Approaches to the Appointment of Optimal Dictator). Let $X = \{x, y\}$ and $\xi(x, y) = 1$ (we could take $X = \{x, y, z\}$, but under $\xi(x, y) = 1$ it would be the same). Let the set of individuals V be divided into three coalitions V_1, V_2, and V_3 with the weights

$$\mu(V_1) = 0.44,$$
$$\mu(V_2) = \mu(V_3) = 0.28.$$

Fix two preferences $P = \{(x, y)\}$ and $\emptyset$ (the indifference). Define three situations f_1, f_2, f_3 on V, putting

$$f_1(v) = \begin{cases} P & \text{if } v \in V_1, \\ \emptyset & \text{if } v \notin V_1, \end{cases} \quad \nu(f_1) = 0.52;$$

$$f_2(v) = \begin{cases} P & \text{if } v \in V_2, \\ \emptyset & \text{if } v \notin V_2, \end{cases} \quad \nu(f_2) = 0.24;$$

$$f_3(v) = \begin{cases} P & \text{if } v \in V_3, \\ \emptyset & \text{if } v \notin V_3, \end{cases} \quad \nu(f_3) = 0.24.$$

These situations are shown in fig. 57, where the coalitions V_1, V_2, V_3 are designated by rectangulars, proportional to their weight. The black rectangulars are the coalitions of individuals with the preference P; the white rectangulars correspond to the coalitions, consisting of indifferent individuals. For every $v_1 \in V_1$, $v_2 \in V_2$ and $v_3 \in V_3$ we have

$$m(v_1, x, y, f_1) = 0.44, \quad m(v_2, x, y, f_1) = 0.56, \quad m(v_3, x, y, f_1) = 0.56,$$
$$m(v_1, x, y, f_2) = 0.72, \quad m(v_2, x, y, f_2) = 0.28, \quad m(v_3, x, y, f_2) = 0.72,$$
$$m(v_1, x, y, f_3) = 0.72, \quad m(v_2, x, y, f_3) = 0.72, \quad m(v_3, x, y, f_3) = 0.28.$$

Hence,

$$\mathsf{E}m(v_1) = \sum_{i=1}^{3} \nu(f_i)\, m(v_1, x, y, f_i)$$

	V_1	V_2	V_3	$\nu(f)$	$\mu(A_{xyf})$	$\mu(A^c_{xyf})$
$\mu(V_i)$	0.44	0.28	0.28			
f_1				0.52	0.44	0.56
f_2				0.24	0.28	0.72
f_3				0.24	0.28	0.72

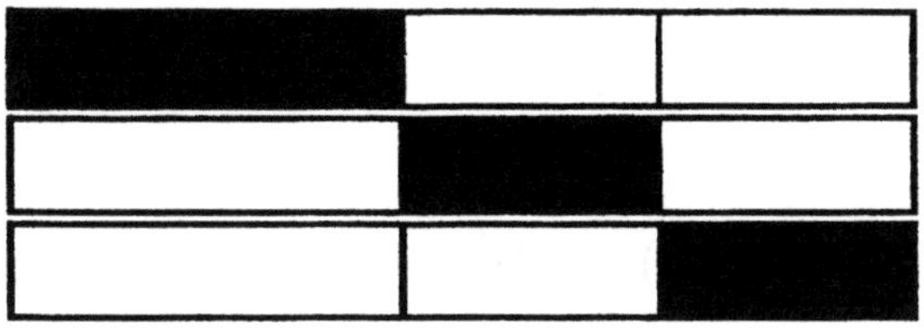

Fig. 57

$$
\begin{aligned}
&= 0.52 \times 0.44 + 0.24 \times 0.72 + 0.24 \times 0.72 \\
&= 0.5744,
\end{aligned}
$$

and similarly

$$
\begin{aligned}
\mathsf{E}m(v_2) &= 0.5312, \\
\mathsf{E}m(v_3) &= 0.5312.
\end{aligned}
$$

Thus the individuals from coalition V_1 have the maximal average representativeness. On the other hand, for every $v_1 \in V_1$ we have

$$\mathsf{M}m(v_1) = \nu\{f : f \in F,\ m(v_1, x, y, f) \geq 1/2\} = \nu(f_2) + \nu(f_3) = 0.48.$$

Similarly, for every $v_2 \in V_2$, and $v_3 \in V_3$ we obtain

$$
\begin{aligned}
\mathsf{M}m(v_2) &= \nu(f_1) + \nu(f_3) = 0.76; \\
\mathsf{M}m(v_3) &= \nu(f_1) + \nu(f_2) = 0.76,
\end{aligned}
$$

i.e. the maximal majority representativeness is inherent in the individuals from coalitions V_2 and V_3. Therefore, the dictators optimal with respect to average, or majority representativeness, are not equal.

The above example shows that even for two alternatives a dictator optimal with respect to the average representativeness, doesn't represent a majority in a half of situations. For the general case we can only prove that in a half of simple events he represents considerable large coalitions.

7.3.4. Proposition. *Under the assumptions of theorem* 7.3.1 *we have*

$$\mathsf{P}\{\omega : \omega \in \Omega,\ m(v^*, \omega) < (3 - \sqrt{2})/4\} < 1/2,$$

where v^* is the dictator optimal with respect to the average representativeness.

PROOF. From the inequality (7.3.4) we obtain

$$\sum_{\omega\in\Omega} \mathsf{P}(\omega)\,[(m(v^*,\omega)-3/4)^2-1/16]\le 0,$$

whence

$$\sum_{\omega\in\Omega} \mathsf{P}(\omega)\,(m(v^*,\omega)-3/4)^2\le 1/16. \tag{7.3.8}$$

Taking into account the inequality $m(v^*,\omega)\le 1$, we obtain

$$m(v^*,\omega)-3/4\le 1/4,$$

therefore,

$$\begin{aligned}
\sum_{\omega\in\Omega:m(v^*,\omega)<(3-\sqrt{2})/4} \mathsf{P}(\omega) &= \sum_{\omega\in\Omega:m(v^*,\omega)-3/4<-\sqrt{2}/4} \mathsf{P}(\omega)\\
&= \sum_{\omega\in\Omega:(m(v^*,\omega)-3/4)^2>1/8} \mathsf{P}(\omega)\\
&< 8 \sum_{\omega\in\Omega:(m(v^*,\omega)-3/4)^2>1/8} \mathsf{P}(\omega)\,(m(v^*,\omega)-3/4)^2\\
&\le 8\sum_{\omega\in\Omega} \mathsf{P}(\omega)\,(m(v^*,\omega)-3/4)^2.
\end{aligned}$$

Taking into account (7.3.8), we obtain the desired inequality.

Let us show with an example that the above estimation cannot be improved.

7.3.5. EXAMPLE. Alter the specifications in example 7.3.3, putting

$$\begin{aligned}
&\mu(V_1)=\mu,\\
&\mu(V_2)=\mu(V_3)=(1-\mu)/2,\\
&\nu(f_1)=\nu,\\
&\nu(f_2)=\nu(f_3)=(1-\nu)/2.
\end{aligned}$$

Then for $v_1\in V_1$, $v_2\in V_2$ and $v_3\in V_3$ we obtain similarly to example 7.3.3:

$$\begin{aligned}
&\mathsf{E}m(v_1)=\mu\nu+(1+\mu)\,(1-\nu)/2,\\
&\mathsf{E}m(v_2)=\mathsf{E}m(v_3)=(1-\mu)\,\nu+(1-\nu)/2.
\end{aligned}$$

Therefore, the dictator optimal with respect to the average representativeness belongs precisely to the coalition V_1 if and only if

$$\mu\nu+(1+\mu)\,(1-\nu)/2>(1-\mu)\,\nu+(1-\nu)/2,$$

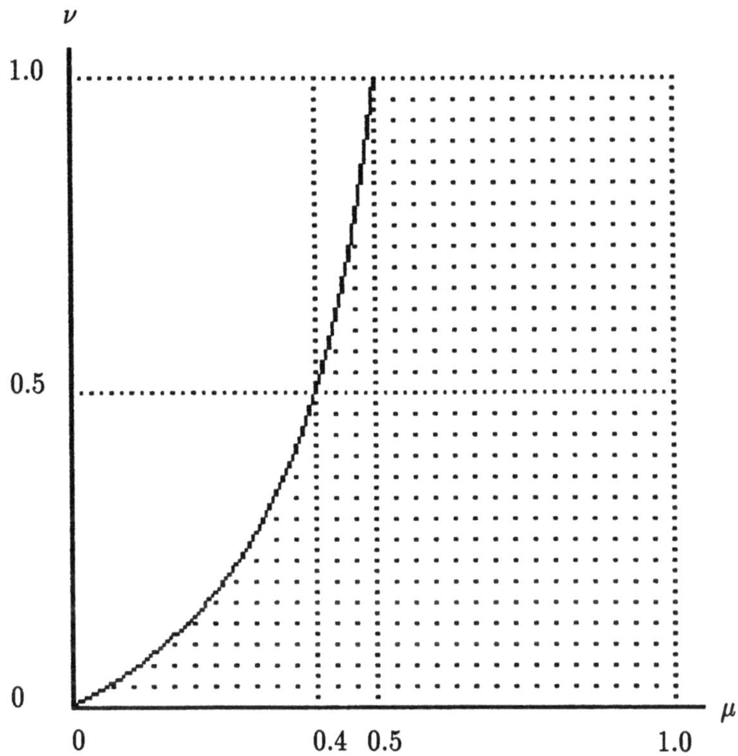

Fig. 58

which is equivalent to the inequality

$$(\mu - 2/3)(\nu + 1/3) > -2/9.$$

The pairs (μ, ν), satisfying the above condition, are shown in fig. 58 by the dotted domain. If in addition $\mu < 1/2$ and $\nu > 1/2$ (cf. with fig. 57), then the dictator $v_1 \in V_1$ optimal with respect to the average representativeness represents a minority (with the weight μ) more often than in a half of situations (with the probability ν). One can take (μ, ν), satisfying the above inequalities, with μ as close to 0.4 as desired. Thus a coalition which has the weight close to 0.4 can be deciding more often than in a half of situations. Since the constant from the statement of proposition 7.3.4 is approximated as follows

$$(3 - \sqrt{2})/4 \approx 0.3965 \approx 0.4,$$

the given example proves the accuracy of the estimation of proposition 7.3.4.

7.4 Overcoming Arrow's Paradox

The obtained results substantiate the interpretation of optimal dictators as representatives of the collective. Therefore, a general prohibition of dictatorship cannot be assumed as quite evident. Indeed, the idea of the dictator means that his decisions contradict interests of other individuals. If he expresses opinions of large coalitions, his interpretation as a representative is more precise. The distinction between proper dictators and dictators-representatives is formalized in definition 7.2.5. To be doubtless, the prohibition should relate to proper dictators only but not to dictators-representatives. In other words, we refine the concept of a dictator to a proper dictator. Taking into account these arguments, reformulate axiom A5.

A5a. (*Prohibition of Proper Dictators*). There is no proper dictator with respect to the average representativeness, i.e. the individual $v \in V$ such that $\mathsf{E}m(v) < 1/2$ and $f(v) = \sigma(f)$ for all situations $f \in F$.

7.4.1. THEOREM (The Overcoming Arrow's Paradox). *Let the set of alternatives and the set of individuals be finite. Let all combinations of individual preferences be possible (i.e. let the coalition Boolean algebra consist of all subsets of the set of individuals). Then axioms* A1–A5a *are consistent.*

PROOF. Under our assumptions the Stone compactum of the given Boolean algebra is the set of individuals V. By theorem 7.3.1 take the optimal dictator-representative $v^* \in V$, and by theorem 5.3.1 determine the aggregating operator σ with the dictator v^*. We obtain that there exists an aggregating operator with no proper dictator, as required.

The above theorem is also valid for a countable coalition Boolean algebra realized on its Stone compactum, i.e. for an infinite set of individuals. The countability of coalition algebra is essential:

(a) to provide the existence of a measure ν on F (proposition 7.2.1);

(b) to provide the existence of a σ-additive measure μ on V, necessary for integration in proofs of theorems 7.3.1 and 7.3.2 (for that purpose V is also assumed to be a Stone compactum).

Note that by Fishburn's theorem 5.4.6 Arrow's axioms are consistent if there is a free ultrafilter in the coalition Boolean algebra. If all its ultrafilters are fixed and the coalition algebra separates every two individuals (is a reduced field of sets), then the given Boolean algebra is realized on its Stone compactum (Sikorski 1964, Example 8A). Therefore, the question about the consistency of Arrow's axioms is brought to the case of Stone compactum of individuals, interpreted by Kirman and Sondermann as filled up with "invisible" agents. The analysis of Arrow's paradox we accomplish with a revision of the theorem of Kirman and Sondermann.

7.4.2. THEOREM (The Overcoming Paradox of Kirman and Sondermann). *Let the set of alternatives be finite, the coalition Boolean algebra be infinite and countable, and also suppose that it is realized on its Stone compactum. Then axioms* A1–A5a *are consistent.*

In the light of our consideration one can ask why our approach to overcoming Arrow's paradox wasn't proposed earlier. The cause is probably in different understanding of deciding coalitions as consisting of the individuals sharing the dictatorial preference. Identifying the dictator's representativeness with the weight of such deciding coalitions, we can see that it is too small to interpret dictators as representatives. In contrast to that, we define deciding coalitions with respect to pairs of alternatives. This way we account the representativeness in the most complete form. We can say that we account even partial coincidences in preferences, whereas they have been ignored under the established definition. To compare the two definitions of deciding coalitions, we introduce a concept of homogeneous representativeness.

7.4.3. DEFINITION. Let the set of alternatives X be finite. Enumerate the preferences on X by indicies $j = 1, \ldots, J$, where J is the number of preferences on X, i.e. let

$$\mathcal{P} = \{P_1, \ldots, P_j, \ldots, P_J\}.$$

For every situation $f \in F$ denote the coalition of individuals with the jth preference P_j under the situation f by

$$A_{jf} = \{v : v \in V,\ f(v) = P_j\}.$$

Define a random variable on the product $V \times F$. For each $v \in V$ and each $f \in F$ consider the coalition of individuals, having the same preference as v has, i.e. the coalition A_{jf} to which v belongs. Its weight, denoted by

$$\tilde{m} = \tilde{m}(v, f) = \mu(f^{-1}f(v)),$$

we call the *homogeneous representativeness of individual v for situation f.* The *average homogeneous representativeness of individual v* is the mathematical expectation

$$\mathsf{E}\tilde{m}(v) = \sum_{f\in F} \nu(f)\,\tilde{m}(v,f).$$

The *average homogeneous representativeness* is the mathematical expectation

$$\mathsf{E}\tilde{m} = \sum_{v\in V}\sum_{f\in F} \mu(v)\,\nu(f)\,\tilde{m}(v,f) = \sum_{v\in V} \mu(v)\,\mathsf{E}\tilde{m}(v),$$

or, if V is uncountable and $\mathsf{E}\tilde{m}(v)$ is a measurable function of v, then

$$\mathsf{E}\tilde{m} = \int_V d\mu(v)\,\mathsf{E}\tilde{m}(v).$$

Note an almost evident property of the introduced indicator of representativeness. Since always

$$\tilde{m}(v,f) \leq m(v,x,y,f)$$

and

$$\sum_{(x,y)\in X\times X} \xi(x,y) = 1,$$

consequently,

$$\begin{aligned}
\mathsf{E}\tilde{m}(v) &= \sum_{f\in F}\sum_{(x,y)\in X\times X} \nu(f)\,\xi(x,y)\,\tilde{m}(v,f)\\
&\leq \sum_{f\in F}\sum_{(x,y)\in X\times X} \nu(f)\,\xi(x,y)\,m(v,x,y,f)\\
&= \mathsf{E}m(v),
\end{aligned}$$

we have

$$\mathsf{E}\tilde{m}(v) \leq \mathsf{E}m(v);$$
$$\mathsf{E}\tilde{m} \leq \mathsf{E}m.$$

The difference between the average representativeness and the average homogeneous representativeness can be considerable. The deciding coalitions defined with respect to pairs of alternatives can be large even if individual preferences are all different. In this case the deciding coalitions defined with respect to the equality of preferences consist of single individuals. It is illustrated by the following example.

7.4.4. EXAMPLE. Let $X = \{x, y, z\}$; $V = \{v_1, v_2, v_3\}$; $\mu(v_1) = \mu(v_2) = \mu(v_3) = 1/3$. Define the situation

$$f(v) = \begin{cases} \{(x,y),(y,z),(x,z)\} & \text{if } v = v_1, \\ \{(x,z),(y,z)\} & \text{if } v = v_2, \\ \{(x,y),(x,z)\} & \text{if } v = v_3, \end{cases} \qquad \nu(f) = 1.$$

It is easy to see that

$$\begin{array}{lll} m(v_1,x,y,f) = 2/3, & m(v_2,x,y,f) = 1/3, & m(v_3,x,y,f) = 2/3, \\ m(v_1,x,z,f) = 1, & m(v_2,x,z,f) = 1, & m(v_3,x,z,f) = 1, \\ m(v_1,y,x,f) = 1, & m(v_2,y,x,f) = 1, & m(v_3,y,x,f) = 1, \\ m(v_1,y,z,f) = 2/3, & m(v_2,y,z,f) = 2/3, & m(v_3,y,z,f) = 1/3, \\ m(v_1,z,x,f) = 1, & m(v_2,z,x,f) = 1, & m(v_3,z,x,f) = 1, \\ m(v_1,z,y,f) = 1, & m(v_2,z,y,f) = 1, & m(v_3,z,y,f) = 1. \end{array}$$

Let $\xi(a,b) = 1/6$ for every $a, b \in X$, $a \neq b$. Summing up the above columns with coefficients 1/6, we get

$$\mathsf{E}m(v_1) = 16/18, \quad \mathsf{E}m(v_2) = 15/18, \quad \mathsf{E}m(v_3) = 15/18.$$

Since the three individuals have different preferences under the only possible situation f, we obtain

$$\mathsf{E}\tilde{m}(v_1) = \mathsf{E}\tilde{m}(v_2) = \mathsf{E}\tilde{m}(v_3) = 1/3.$$

Thus the difference between the two indicators of representativeness is considerable. By the way note that the average representativeness is more selective. Indeed, the optimal dictator with respect to average representativeness is individual v_1, whereas the three individuals are indistinguishable with respect to the average homogeneous representativeness.

To estimate the lower bound of the average homogeneous representativeness we formulate the following proposition, which is analogous to theorem 7.3.1.

7.4.5. PROPOSITION (About the Average Homogeneous Representativeness of Optimal and Random Dictators). *Let the set of alternatives X be finite, the coalition Boolean algebra $\mathcal{A}$ be finite or countable, and also suppose that it is realized on its Stone compactum V. Then, whatever the measures μ on V and ν on F are, the average homogeneous representativeness $\mathsf{E}\tilde{m}$ is defined, $\mathsf{E}\tilde{m}(v)$ is a continuous function of v, attaining its maximum on compactum V at some point v^*, and*

$$\mathsf{E}\tilde{m}(v^*) \geq \mathsf{E}\tilde{m} \geq 1/J.$$

The precise equality

$$\mathsf{E}\tilde{m}(v^*) = 1/J$$

holds if and only if for every possible situation f the collective V is divided by preferences into J coalitions, having equal weight, i.e. for every $j = 1, \ldots, J$ it holds $\mu(A_{jf}) = 1/J$.

PROOF. Since for every fixed situation f the function $\tilde{m}(v, f)$ is constant on every clopen A_{jf}, it is continuous with respect to v. Since the series

$$\mathsf{E}\tilde{m}(v) = \sum_{f \in F} \nu(f)\, \tilde{m}(v, f),$$

formed of continuous non-negative functions, is majorized on compactum V by the convergent series

$$\sum_{f \in F} \nu(f) = 1,$$

it converges uniformly, and its sum $\mathsf{E}\tilde{m}(v)$ is a continuous function on compactum V with a maximum at some point $v^* \in V$.

Since $\mathsf{E}\tilde{m}(v)$ is a continuous function on compactum V (with countable base $\mathcal{A}$, consequently, metrizable), it is integrable (in the case of finite, or countable V it is summable with the weights $\mu(v)$, nevertheless we shall use the sign of integral), and

$$\begin{aligned}
\mathsf{E}\tilde{m} &= \int_V d\mu(v) \sum_{f \in F} \nu(f)\, \tilde{m}(v, f) \\
&= \int_V d\mu(v)\, \mathsf{E}\tilde{m}(v) \\
&\leq \mathsf{E}\tilde{m}(v^*) \int_V d\mu(v) \\
&= \mathsf{E}\tilde{m}(v^*).
\end{aligned}$$

Since the series of continuous functions under the sign of integral converges iniformly, the order of summation and integration can be reversed, whence

$$\mathsf{E}\tilde{m}(v^*) \geq \mathsf{E}\tilde{m}(v) = \sum_{f \in F} \nu(f) \int_V d\mu(v)\, \tilde{m}(v, f). \tag{7.4.1}$$

By definition 7.4.3

$$\int_V d\mu(v)\, \tilde{m}(v, f) = \sum_{j=1}^{J} \int_{A_{jf}} d\mu(v)\, \tilde{m}(v, f) = \sum_{j=1}^{J} \mu^2(A_{jf}). \tag{7.4.2}$$

Since it is always

$$\sum_{j=1}^{J} \mu(A_{jf}) = 1;$$
$$0 \leq \mu(A_{jf}) \leq 1, \; j = 1, \ldots, J,$$

we can estimate sum (7.4.2) by the method of Lagrange multipliers, applied to the problem of finding the minimum of the function

$$\sum_{j=1}^{J} \mu_j^2$$

under the restrictions

$$\sum_{j=1}^{J} \mu_j = 1;$$
$$0 \leq \mu_j \leq 1, \; j = 1, \ldots, J.$$

One can see that the desired minimum equals to $1/J$. It is attained if and only if all $\mu_j = 1/J$. Substitute the obtained estimation of integral (7.4.2) in (7.4.1) and get

$$\mathsf{E}\tilde{m}(v^*) \geq \mathsf{E}\tilde{m} \geq 1/J,$$

where the last inequality is strict if and only if $\mu(A_{jf}) \neq 1/J$ for some possible situation f and some j. Conversely, if $\mu(A_{jf}) = 1/J$ for all possible situations f and all j, the average homogeneous representativeness $\mathsf{E}\tilde{m}(v)$ of every individual $v \in V$ equals to $1/J$, consequently, $\mathsf{E}\tilde{m}(v^*) = 1/J$, as required.

The above proposition implies that the attainable lower bound of average homogeneous representativeness of optimal dictators equals $1/J$. If the number of alternatives is K, then the number of strict (linear) orders is $K!$, consequently, $1/J < 1/K!$ decreases rapidly with the increase in the number of alternatives. Therefore, the average homogeneous representativeness cannot be used to justify the interpretation of dictators as representatives.

To end the section, note that we could justify the interpretation of a dictator as a representative and overcome Arrow's paradox, referring not to average but majority representativeness. However, a dictator can be a representative with respect to one indicator, not being a representative with respect to another. Further we shall overcome this objectionable ambiguity in the understanding of optimal representatives under additional assumptions.

7.5 Independence of Individuals

In the rest of the chapter we consider finite sets of independent individuals.

7.5.1. DEFINITION. Let the set of alternatives X be finite. Enumerate the preferences on X by indicies $j = 1, \dots, J$, where J is the number of preferences on X, i.e. let

$$\mathcal{P} = \{P_1, \dots, P_j, \dots, P_J\}.$$

Denote the probability that individual v has preference P_j by

$$p_j(v) = \nu\{f : f \in F,\ f(v) = P_j\}.$$

Individuals $v_1, \dots, v_i, \dots, v_n$ are said to be *independent* if for arbitrary preferences $P_{j_1}, \dots, P_{j_i}, \dots, P_{j_n}$, not necessary pairwise different, it holds

$$\nu\{f : f \in F,\ f(v_1) = P_{j_1},\ \dots,\ f(v_i) = P_{j_i},\ \dots,\ f(v_n) = P_{jn}\} = \prod_{i=1}^{n} p_{j_i}(v_i).$$

For independent individuals we use the following designations. Fix a pair of alternatives (x, y). The *preference probability of individual v on a pair of alternatives (x,y)* is defined to be the probability that the individual v prefers x to y. This probability is denoted by

$$p_{xy}(v) = \nu\{f : f \in F,\ (x, y) \in f(v)\}.$$

Sometimes we shall use the *probability distance* from 1/2, defined to be

$$d_{xy}(v) = p_{xy}(v) - 1/2.$$

The *mean probability* that an "average" individual prefers x to y we denote by

$$p_{xy} = \sum_{v \in V} \mu(v)\, p_{xy}(v). \tag{7.5.1}$$

Its *indicator* is defined to be

$$\delta_{xy} = \begin{cases} 0 & \text{if } p_{xy} < 1/2, \\ 1/2 & \text{if } p_{xy} = 1/2, \\ 1 & \text{if } p_{xy} > 1/2. \end{cases}$$

To simplify the formulation of further results, define the *characteristic of individual v* to be

$$c_{xy}(v) = \begin{cases} p_{xy}(v) - 1/2 & \text{if } p_{xy} \neq 1/2, \\ 0 & \text{if } p_{xy} = 1/2. \end{cases} \tag{7.5.2}$$

The *mean characteristic* and its *sign* denote, respectively, by

$$c_{xy} = p_{xy} - 1/2,$$
$$s_{xy} = \text{sgn } c_{xy} = 2(\delta_{xy} - 1/2).$$

Since we shall refer mostly to probabilities $p_{xy}(v)$ but not $p_j(v)$, let us formulate the following corollary of the above definition.

7.5.2. PROPOSITION (The Independence of Individuals for Pairs of Alternatives). *Let individuals $v_1, \ldots, v_n$ be independent. Then for every pair of alternatives (x, y) it holds*

$$\nu\{f : f \in F,\ (x,y) \in f(v_1),\ \ldots,\ (x,y) \in f(v_n)\} = \prod_{i=1}^{n} p_{xy}(v_i).$$

PROOF. Define the characteristic functions of preferences P_j, putting

$$\chi_j(x,y) = \begin{cases} 1 & \text{if } (x,y) \in P_j, \\ 0 & \text{if } (x,y) \notin P_j. \end{cases}$$

For every pair of alternatives (x, y) and every individual v we have, obviously,

$$p_{xy}(v) = \nu\{f : f \in F,\ (x,y) \in f(v)\} = \sum_{j=1}^{J} \chi_j(x,y)\, p_j(v).$$

For every collection of individuals $v_1, \ldots, v_n$ we obtain similarly

$$\nu\{f : f \in F,\ (x,y) \in f(v_1),\ \ldots,\ (x,y) \in f(v_n)\} =$$
$$= \sum_{j_1=1}^{J} \cdots \sum_{j_n=1}^{J} \chi_{j_1}(x,y) \ldots \chi_{j_n}(x,y)\, \nu\{f : f \in F, f(v_1) = P_{j_1}, \ldots, f(v_n) = P_{j_n}\}.$$

Therefore, by virtue of independence of individuals we have

$$\begin{aligned} \nu\{f : f \in F,\ (x,y) \in f(v_1),\ \ldots,\ (x,y) \in f(v_n)\} &= \\ = \sum_{j_1=1}^{J} \cdots \sum_{j_n=1}^{J} \chi_{j_1}(x,y) \ldots \chi_{j_n}(x,y)\, p_{j_1}(v_1) \ldots p_{j_n}(v_n) & \\ = \prod_{i=1}^{n} \sum_{j_i=1}^{J} \chi_{j_i}(x,y)\, p_{j_i}(v_i) & \\ = \prod_{i=1}^{n} p_{xy}(v_i), & \end{aligned}$$

as required.

Now let us explain why we restrict our consideration to finite sets of independent individuals.

7.5.3. PROPOSITION (On the Degeneration of a Probability Model into a Deterministic One). *Let the set of alternatives be finite and the coalition Boolean algebra be infinite and countable. Suppose that every finit collection of individuals is independent. Then $p_j(v)$ are continuous functions of v for all j, and either $p_j(v) = 0$, or $p_j(v) = 1$ at every non-isolated point $v \in V$. The same is also valid for all $p_{xy}(v)$.*

PROOF. At first we show that if v is a non-isolated point of V, then either $p_j(v) = 0$, or $p_j(v) = 1$. Assume the contrary, i.e. that there exists a non-isolated point $v \in V$ such that $0 < p_j(v) < 1$. Then there exist possible situations f_1, f_2 such that $f_1(v) = P_j$, $f_2(v) = P_k$ for some preferences $P_k \neq P_j$. Hence, A_{jf_1} and A_{kf_2} (see definition 7.4.3) are clopen neighborhoods of point v. Since v is not isolated and V has countable base $\mathcal{A}$, there exists a sequence

$$\{v_n\} \subset A_{jf_1} \cap A_{kf_2} \setminus \{v\},$$

converging to v. Taking into account the independence of individuals, for every positive integer n we have

$$1 \geq \prod_{i=1}^{n} p_j(v_i) \geq \nu(f_1) > 0,$$
$$1 \geq \prod_{i=1}^{n} (1 - p_j(v_i)) \geq \prod_{i=1}^{n} p_k(v_i) \geq \nu(f_2) > 0,$$

whence

$$\lim_{n\to\infty} p_j(v_n) = 1,$$
$$\lim_{n\to\infty} (1 - p_j(v_n)) = 1,$$

which is contradiction.

Now let us show that $p_j(v)$ is continuous with respect to v. Since V has countable base $\mathcal{A}$, it sufficies to verify that the convergence of sequence $\{v_n\}$ to non-isolated point v implies the convergence of $\{p_j(v_n)\}$ to $p_j(v)$. As we have proved, either $p_j(v) = 0$, or $p_j(v) = 1$. Consider the former case, when $\nu\{f : f \in F,\ f(v) \neq P_j\} = 1$, which implies that there exists a possible situation g such that $g(v) = P_k$ for some preference $P_k \neq P_j$. Hence A_{kg} is a clopen neighborhood of point v. Without loss of generality we can assume that

$\{v_n\} \subset A_{kg}$. Taking into account the independence of individuals, for every positive integer n we have

$$1 \geq \prod_{i=1}^{n}(1 - p_j(v_i)) \geq \prod_{i=1}^{n} p_k(v_i)\ \nu(g) > 0,$$

whence

$$\lim_{n\to\infty}(1 - p_j(v_n)) = 1,$$

which gives the required convergence of $p_j(v_n)$ to 0. The case $p_j(v_n) = 1$ is considered similarly.

Since, obviously,

$$p_{xy}(v) = \sum_{j:(x,y)\in P_j} p_j(v),$$

we derive the desired properties of functions $p_{xy}(v)$ from the properties of functions $p_j(v)$.

By the way note that if $v_n \to v$, then $p_j(v_n)$ tends to $p_j(v)$ quite rapidly. Indeed, the convergence of infinite products in the above proof is equivalent to the convergence of the series

$$\sum_{n=1}^{\infty}(p_j(v_n) - p_j(v)).$$

Now we can formulate an important corollary.

7.5.4. Corollary (About the Only Possible Situation). *If an infinite set of individuals is provided with a countable atomless coalition Boolean algebra and the set of alternatives is finite, then the independence of all finite collections of individuals is equivalent to that only one situation is possible.*

Recall that a countable Boolean algebra is isomorphic to the field of clopen sets of a certain close subset of Cantor discontinuum (Aleksandroff 1977; Sikorski 1964, p. 28). Therefore, if an infinite model with a countable coalition algebra is realized on its Stone compactum, there are some accumulation points, where the condition of independence of individuals turns out to be the determination of preferences. We can draw analogy to stochastic processes, for which the independence of values is hardly consistent with the continuity of trajectories. Indeed, on the one hand, the measurability of situations is nothing else but their continuity (see section 5.6), on the other hand, situations can be regarded as random functions (mappings).

Summing up what has been said, we conclude that the condition of independence of individuals is meaningful only if their number is finite. Therefore, the case of a large number of individuals we shall study directly, not referring to the infinite case.

7.5.5. DEFINITION. A *sequence of models with increasing number of independent individuals* is defined as follows. Let $\mathcal{N}$ be an increasing subsequence of positive integers. For every $n \in \mathcal{N}$ denote the set of individuals of the nth model, consisting of n independent individuals, by

$$V = V(n) = \{v_1^n, \ldots, v_i^n, \ldots, v_n^n\}.$$

Let the weights of individuals decrease uniformly with n, i.e. let there exist a sequence of majorants

$$\alpha(n) \underset{n\to\infty}{\rightrightarrows} 0$$

restricting the individual weights in the nth model:

$$\mu(v_i^n) \leq \alpha(n), \ i = 1, 2, \ldots, n,$$

under the normalizing condition, holding for every $n \in \mathcal{N}$:

$$\mu(V(n)) = \sum_{i=1}^{n} \mu(v_i^n) = 1.$$

Let the ratios between the weights of individuals and the probabilities of their preferences be the same in all models, i.e. let for every $N \in \mathcal{N}$, all $n \geq N, n \in \mathcal{N}$, and all significant pairs of alternatives (x, y) be

$$\mu(v_1^n) : \ \ldots \ : \mu(v_N^n) = \mu(v_1^N) : \ \ldots \ : \mu(v_N^N);$$

$$p_{xy}(v_i^n) = p_{xy}(v_i^N), \ i = 1, \ldots, N.$$

The increase in the number of individuals, i.e. the choice of subsequence $\mathcal{N}$, is supposed to remain constant the values of average probabilities for each significant pair of alternatives (x, y) for all $n \in \mathcal{N}$:

$$p_{xy} = \sum_{i=1}^{n} \mu(v_i^n)\, p_{xy}(v_i^n).$$

Let us illustrate the above definition with an example. Its aim is to formalize the idea of a large collective, consisting of individuals with neglible weights. This collective is divided into n coalitions, having the weights $\mu_i, \ i = 1, \ldots, n$. We also suppose that individuals from the same coalition have equal preference probabilities.

7.5.6. EXAMPLE. Let collective $V(n)$ consist of n independent individuals with the weights μ_i, $i = 1, \ldots n$, and the preference probabilities $p_{ji} = p_j(v_i^n)$, $i = 1, \ldots, n$. To realize the increase in the number of individuals without changing their preference probabilities and the ratios of their weights, we successively double the set of individuals, refining their weights proportionally. Thus

$$\begin{aligned} \mathcal{N} &= \{mn : m = 1, 2, \ldots\}, \\ V(mn) &= \{v_1^{mn}, \ldots, v_n^{mn}, v_{n+1}^{mn}, \ldots, v_{2n}^{mn}, \ \ldots \ , v_{kn+i}^{mn}, \ \ldots \ , v_{mn}^{mn}\}, \end{aligned}$$

where for every $k = 0, \ldots, m-1$ and every $i = 1, \ldots, n$ it holds

$$\begin{aligned} \mu(v_{kn+i}^{mn}) &= \mu_i / m, \\ p_j(v_{kn+i}^{mn}) &= p_{ji}. \end{aligned}$$

Obviously, for all pairs of alternatives (x, y) we have

$$p_{xy}(v_{kn+i}^{mn}) = p_{xy}(v_i^n), \ i = 1, \ldots, n,$$

whence p_{xy} are invariable in all our models, as required.

7.6 Average Representativeness for Independent Individuals

Theorem 7.3.1 can be slightly strengthened if individuals are independent.

7.6.1. PROPOSITION (About the Average Representativeness of Optimal and Random Dictators). *Consider a model with a finite set of independent individuals under the assumptions of theorem* 7.3.1. *If there exists an individual v, having positive weight, $\mu(v) > 0$ such that $0 < p_{xy}(v) < 1$ for some significant pair of alternatives (x, y), then $\mathsf{Em} > 1/2$.*

PROOF. Let a pair (x, y) satisfy the assumption. Fix a possible situation f. Such a situation exists by virtue of the finitness of F and the normalizing condition $\sum_{f \in F} \nu(f) = 1$. Then the simple event $\omega = (x, y, f)$ determined by the pair (x, y) and the situation f is significant. If $\mu(A_\omega) \neq 1/2$ we obtain the required fact by theorem 7.3.1. Suppose that $\mu(A_\omega) = 1/2$. We are going to break the equality, changing the preference of the individual v on (x, y), and bring our consideration to the former case. Let $P_j = f(v)$. Since $0 < p_{xy}(v) < 1$ and $\mathcal{P}$ is finite, there exists preference P_k, differing from P_j on (x, y), i.e.

$$P_k \cap \{(x, y)\} \neq P_j \cap \{(x, y)\}$$

such that $p_k(v) \neq 0$. Define the modified situation, putting

$$g(v') = \begin{cases} f(v') & \text{if } v' \neq v, \\ P_k & \text{if } v' = v. \end{cases}$$

Since situation f is possible and the individuals are independent, situation g is also possible. Since $\mu(v) \neq 0$, we obtain $\mu(A_{xyg}) \neq 1/2$, as required.

Before we prove the main theorem of the section, we formulate two auxiliary propositions, which we also use in the sequel.

7.6.2. LEMMA. *Let a positive integer m and real numbers α, θ be such that*

$$0 < \theta \leq 1,$$
$$\theta/m \leq \alpha \leq 1.$$

Let also

$$\mu_1 + \ldots + \mu_m = \theta,$$

where

$$0 \leq \mu_i \leq 1, \; i = 1, \ldots, m.$$

Then

$$\theta^2 \leq \mu_1^2 + \ldots + \mu_m^2 < 3\alpha.$$

PROOF. Obviously, the level hypersurfaces of the function $\mu_1^2 + \ldots + \mu_m^2$ are concentric hyperspheres centered at the point $(0, \ldots, 0)$. Their intersection with the hyperplane

$$\Pi = \{(\mu_1, \ldots, \mu_m) : \mu_1 + \ldots + \mu_m = \theta\}$$

are also concentric hyperspheres (of lower dimension) centered at the point $(\theta/m, \ldots, \theta/m)$, where the minimum of the function $\mu_1^2 + \ldots + \mu_m^2$ is attained, being equal to

$$m\theta^2/m^2 = \theta^2/m$$

(to ascertain it use the method of Lagrange multipliers). By assumption $\alpha \geq \theta/m$, consequently, the point $(\theta/m, \ldots, \theta/m)$ is located inside the cube

$$\Lambda = \{(\mu_1, \ldots, \mu_m) : 0 \leq \mu_i \leq \alpha, \; i = 1, \ldots, m\}.$$

Therefore, the maximum of the function $\mu_1^2 + \ldots + \mu_m^2$ under the restriction $(\mu_1, \ldots, \mu_m) \in \Pi \cap \Lambda$ is attained at the points of intersection of edges of the cube

Λ with the hyperplan Π. The edges of the cube consist of points $(\mu_1, \ldots, \mu_m)$ such that all their coordinates except one equal to 0, or α. Therefore, the condition $\mu_1 + \ldots + \mu_m = \theta$ implies that the desired point of maximum of the function $\mu_1^2 + \ldots + \mu_m^2$ must have k coordintes equal to α, another $m - k - 1$ coordinates equal to 0, and one rest equal to $\theta - k\alpha$, where k satisfies the inequalities

$$k\alpha \leq \theta < (k+1)\alpha,$$

or, which is equivalent,

$$\theta/\alpha - 1 < k \leq \theta/\alpha.$$

Therefore,

$$\begin{aligned} \max_{(\mu_1,\ldots,\mu_m)\in\Pi\cap\Lambda} \mu_1^2 + \ldots + \mu_m^2 &= k\alpha^2 + (\theta - k\alpha)^2 \\ &= (k + k^2)\alpha^2 + \theta^2 - 2\theta k\alpha \\ &< (\theta/\alpha + \theta^2/\alpha^2)\alpha^2 + \theta^2 - 2\theta(\theta/\alpha - 1)\alpha \\ &= 3\alpha\theta \\ &\leq 3\alpha, \end{aligned}$$

as required.

7.6.3. LEMMA. *Let the set of individuals be finite and all individuals be independent. Fix $W \subset V$. For every simple event $\omega = (x, y, f)$ consider the coalitions $A_\omega = A_{xyf}$ (see (7.2.2) for the definition) and*

$$B_{W\omega} = B_{Wxyf} = A_\omega \setminus W = \{v : v \in V \setminus W,\ (x,y) \in f(v)\}.$$

Fix a pair of alternatives (x, y) and let $f \in F$ be random. Define random variables $\mu(A_{xy})$ and $\mu(B_{Wxy})$ to be the weights of the corresponding random coalitions (recall that we omit the indicies, associated with random variables). Then their mathematical expectations and dispersions are

$$\begin{aligned} \mathsf{E}\mu(A_{xy}) &= p_{xy}, \\ \mathsf{D}\mu(A_{xy}) &= \sum_{v\in V} \mu^2(v)\,(1/4 - d_{xy}^2(v)), \\ \mathsf{E}\mu(B_{Wxy}) &= p_{xy} - \sum_{w\in W} \mu(w)\,p_{xy}(w), \\ \mathsf{D}\mu(B_{Wxy}) &= \sum_{v\in V\setminus W} \mu^2(v)\,(1/4 - d_{xy}^2(v)). \end{aligned}$$

Consider a sequence of models with increasing number n of independent individuals. Then for every fixed k, all $W \subset V$, consisting of no more than k

elements, and all sufficiently large n we have

$$\begin{aligned}
\mathsf{D}\mu(A_{xy}) &\approx 0,\\
\mathsf{E}\mu(B_{Wxy}) &\approx p_{xy},\\
\mathsf{D}\mu(B_{Wxy}) &\approx 0,
\end{aligned}$$

where the accuracy of approximation increases with n regardless of the choice of W.

PROOF. Fix a pair of alternatives (x, y). Put each individual $v \in V$ into correspondence with a Bernoulli random variable on F (with the probability measure ν) defined to be

$$\eta(v) = \begin{cases} 1 & \text{if } (x,y) \in f(v), \\ 0 & \text{if } (x,y) \notin f(v). \end{cases} \tag{7.6.1}$$

Obviously,

$$\begin{aligned}
\nu\{f : f \in F,\ \eta(v) = 1\} &= p_{xy}(v),\\
\nu\{f : f \in F,\ \eta(v) = 0\} &= 1 - p_{xy}(v).
\end{aligned}$$

In our designations we have

$$\mu(A_{xy}) = \sum_{v \in V} \mu(v)\, \eta(v),$$

consequently, by independence of individuals we obtain

$$\begin{aligned}
\mathsf{E}\mu(A_{xy}) &= \sum_{v\in V} \mu(v)\, \mathsf{E}\eta(v) = \sum_{v\in V} \mu(v)\, p_{xy}(v) = p_{xy};\\
\mathsf{D}\mu(A_{xy}) &= \sum_{v\in V} \mu^2(v)\, \mathsf{D}\eta(v)\\
&= \sum_{v\in V} \mu^2(v)\, p_{xy}(v)\,(1 - p_{xy}(v))\\
&= \sum_{v\in V} \mu^2(v)\, [1/4 - (p_{xy}(v) - 1/2)^2]\\
&= \sum_{v\in V} \mu^2(v)\, (1/4 - d_{xy}^2(v)).
\end{aligned}$$

Similarly,

$$\begin{aligned}
\mathsf{E}\mu(B_{Wxy}) &= \sum_{v\in V} \mu(v)\, p_{xy}(v) - \sum_{w\in W} \mu(w)\, p_{xy}(w)\\
&= p_{xy} - \sum_{w\in W} \mu(w)\, p_{xy}(w)\\
\mathsf{D}\mu(B_{Wxy}) &= \sum_{v\in V\setminus W} \mu^2(v)\, (1/4 - d_{xy}^2(v)).
\end{aligned}$$

Now consider a sequence of models with increasing number n of independent individuals. Since by definition 7.5.5 we have $\mu(v) \leq \alpha(n) \underset{n\to\infty}{\longrightarrow} 0$ for all $v \in V(n)$, by lemma 7.6.2 we obtain

$$\sum_{v\in V(n)} \mu^2(v) < 3\alpha(n),$$

whence

$$\mathsf{D}\mu(B_{Wxy}) \leq \mathsf{D}\mu(A_{xy}) \leq \sum_{v\in V(n)} \mu^2(v)/4 < 3\alpha(n)/4 \underset{n\to\infty}{\longrightarrow} 0.$$

Since

$$\Big| \sum_{w\in W} \mu(w)\, p_{xy}(w) \Big| \leq \sum_{w\in W} \mu(w) \leq k\,\alpha(n),$$

we obtain

$$\mathsf{E}\mu(B_{Wxy}) \underset{n\to\infty}{\longrightarrow} p_{xy},$$

as required.

7.6.4. THEOREM (About the Average Representativeness for Independent Individuals). *Let the set of alternatives be finite. Consider a sequence of models with increasing number n of independent individuals. Then*

$$\begin{aligned}
\mathsf{E}m(v) &= 1/2 + \mu(v)/2 + 2 \sum_{(x,y)\in X\times X} \xi(x,y)\,[c_{xy}\, c_{xy}(v) - \mu(v)\, d^2_{xy}(v)] \\
&\approx 1/2 + 2 \sum_{(x,y)\in X\times X} \xi(x,y)\, c_{xy}\, c_{xy}(v); && (7.6.2) \\
\mathsf{E}m &= 1/2 + \sum_{v\in V} \mu^2(v)/2 + 2 \sum_{(x,y)\in X\times X} \xi(x,y)\,[c^2_{xy} - \sum_{v\in V} \mu^2(v)\, d^2_{xy}(v)] \\
&\approx 1/2 + 2 \sum_{(x,y)\in X\times X} \xi(x,y)\, c^2_{xy}, && (7.6.3)
\end{aligned}$$

where the accuracy of approximation increases with n (regardless of the choice of v in the first formula).

PROOF. Taking into account the independence of individuals, for fixed $W = \{v\}$, $(x,y) \in X \times X$ by lemma 7.6.3 we have

$$\begin{aligned}
\mathsf{E}m(v,x,y) &= p_{xy}(v)\, \mathsf{E}(\mu(v) + \mu(B_{vxy})) + (1 - p_{xy}(v))\, \mathsf{E}(\mu(V) - \mu(B_{vxy})) \\
&= p_{xy}(v)\, \mu(v) + p_{xy}\, \mathsf{E}\mu(B_{vxy}) + (1 - p_{xy}(v))\, (1 - \mathsf{E}\mu(B_{vxy})) \\
&= p_{xy}(v)\, \mu(v) + 1/2 + 2(p_{xy}(v) - 1/2)\, (\mathsf{E}\mu(B_{vxy}) - 1/2) \\
&= p_{xy}(v)\, \mu(v) + 1/2 + 2(p_{xy}(v) - 1/2)\, (p_{xy} - 1/2) -
\end{aligned}$$

$$\begin{aligned}
&-2(p_{xy}(v) - 1/2)\, p_{xy}(v)\, \mu(v) \\
=\; & 1/2 + 2c_{xy}\, d_{xy}(v) + 2\mu(v)\, p_{xy}(v)\, (1 - p_{xy}(v)) \\
=\; & 1/2 + 2c_{xy}\, c_{xy}(v) + 2\mu(v)\, [1/4 - (p_{xy}(v) - 1/2)^2] \\
=\; & 1/2 + 2c_{xy}\, c_{xy}(v) + \mu(v)/2 - 2\mu(v)\, d^2_{xy}(v).
\end{aligned}$$

Since the number of alternatives is finite, by virtue of the finitness of sum (7.2.3) we obtain the required approximation (7.6.2). To prove (7.6.3), note that for a fixed pair $(x, y) \in X \times X$ we have

$$\begin{aligned}
\mathsf{E}(\mu(A_{xy}) - 1/2)^2 &= \mathsf{E}(\mu^2(A_{xy}) - \mu(A_{xy}) + 1/4) \\
&= \mathsf{D}\mu(A_{xy}) + [\mathsf{E}\mu(A_{xy})]^2 - \mathsf{E}\mu(A_{xy}) + 1/4 \\
&= \mathsf{D}\mu(A_{xy}) + p^2_{xy} - p_{xy} + 1/4 \\
&= \mathsf{D}\mu(A_{xy}) + (p_{xy} - 1/2)^2 \\
&= \mathsf{D}\mu(A_{xy}) + c^2_{xy}.
\end{aligned}$$

Substituting it in (7.3.3), we obtain

$$\begin{aligned}
\mathsf{E}m &= \sum_{(x,y)\in X\times X} \xi(x, y) \sum_{f\in F} \nu(f)\, [1/2 + 2(\mu(A_{xyf}) - 1/2)^2] \\
&= \sum_{(x,y)\in X\times X} \xi(x, y)\, [1/2 + 2\mathsf{E}(\mu(A_{xyf}) - 1/2)^2] \\
&= 1/2 + 2 \sum_{(x,y)\in X\times X} \xi(x, y)\, [\mathsf{D}\mu(A_{xy}) + c^2_{xy}].
\end{aligned}$$

By lemma 7.6.3 we obtain the required formula (7.6.3).

The next proposition follows from the above theorem.

7.6.5. PROPOSITION (The Location of Optimal Dictator for a Single Pair of Alternatives). *Consider a model with n independent individuals, having equal weights $1/n$, and let only one pair of alternatives be significant, i.e. $\xi(x, y) = 1$ for some $x, y \in X, x \neq y$. Then*

(a) if $c_{xy} = 0$, then the individual v^* with $d_{xy}(v)$ the most close to 0 has the highest average representativeness;

(b) if $c_{xy} < 0$ and $n \geq 1/\mid c_{xy} \mid$, then the individual v^* with the least $d_{xy}(v)$ has the highest average representativeness;

(c) if $c_{xy} > 0$ and $n \geq 1/\mid c_{xy} \mid$, then the individual v^* with the greatest $d_{xy}(v)$ has the highest average representativeness.

Proof. Since $\xi(x,y) = 1$, rewrite (7.6.2) in the following form

$$\begin{aligned} \mathsf{E}m(v) &= 1/2 + \mu(v)/2 - 2\mu(v)\,[d_{xy}^2(v) - d_{xy}(v)\,c_{xy}/\mu(v)] \\ &= -2\mu(v)\,[d_{xy}(v) - \frac{c_{xy}}{2\mu(v)}]^2 + \frac{c_{xy}^2}{2\mu(v)} + \frac{1+\mu(v)}{2}. \end{aligned}$$

Note that if c_{xy} is fixed, we can consider the above expression as a function of $d = d_{xy}(v)$ and $\mu = \mu(v)$, which we denote $\mathsf{E}(d,\mu)$. Since by assumption $\mu = \mu(v)$ is constant on V, the function $\mathsf{E}(d,\mu)$ of variable d is an inverted parabola with the only maximum at the point

$$d = \frac{c_{xy}}{2\mu(v)}.$$

Therefore if $c_{xy} = 0$, then the maximum of $\mathsf{E}m(v)$ is attained at the point v^*, where $d_{xy}(v)$ is most close to 0.

If $c_{xy} \neq 0$ and $\mu(v) \leq\mid c_{xy}\mid$, i.e. $n \geq 1/\mid c_{xy}\mid$, then the maximum of $\mathsf{E}(d,\mu)$ is attained outside the interval $-1/2 < d < 1/2$. Since $\mid d_{xy}(v)\mid \leq 1/2$, the maximum of $\mathsf{E}m(v)$ is attained at the least, or at the greatest $d_{xy}(v)$, depending on whether $c_{xy} < 0$, or $c_{xy} > 0$, respectively.

Let us discuss the assumptions of proposition 7.6.5. Since it is a corollary of theorem 7.6.4, our discussion also relates to the theorem. First of all examine formula (7.6.2).

According to (7.6.2), the average representativeness of every individual v depends only on his own specifications—his weight $\mu(v)$ and the vector

$$\boldsymbol{d}(v) = \{d_{xy}(v)\},$$

where the coordinate indicies are significant pairs of alternatives (x,y). The mean vector

$$\boldsymbol{c} = \{c_{xy}\}$$

is always constant. To comment on the properties of $\mathsf{E}m(v)$, consider the case of one-dimensional vector $\boldsymbol{d}(v)$, i.e. when $\xi(x,y) = 1$ for some $x \neq y$.

The level curves of the function $\mathsf{E} = \mathsf{E}(d,\mu)$ for $c = c_{xy} = 0.1, 0.2, \ldots, 0.9$ are shown in fig. 59. These curves are calculated by the formula derived from (7.6.2):

$$\mu = \frac{\mathsf{E}/2 - 1/4 - cd}{1/4 - d^2} \tag{7.6.4}$$

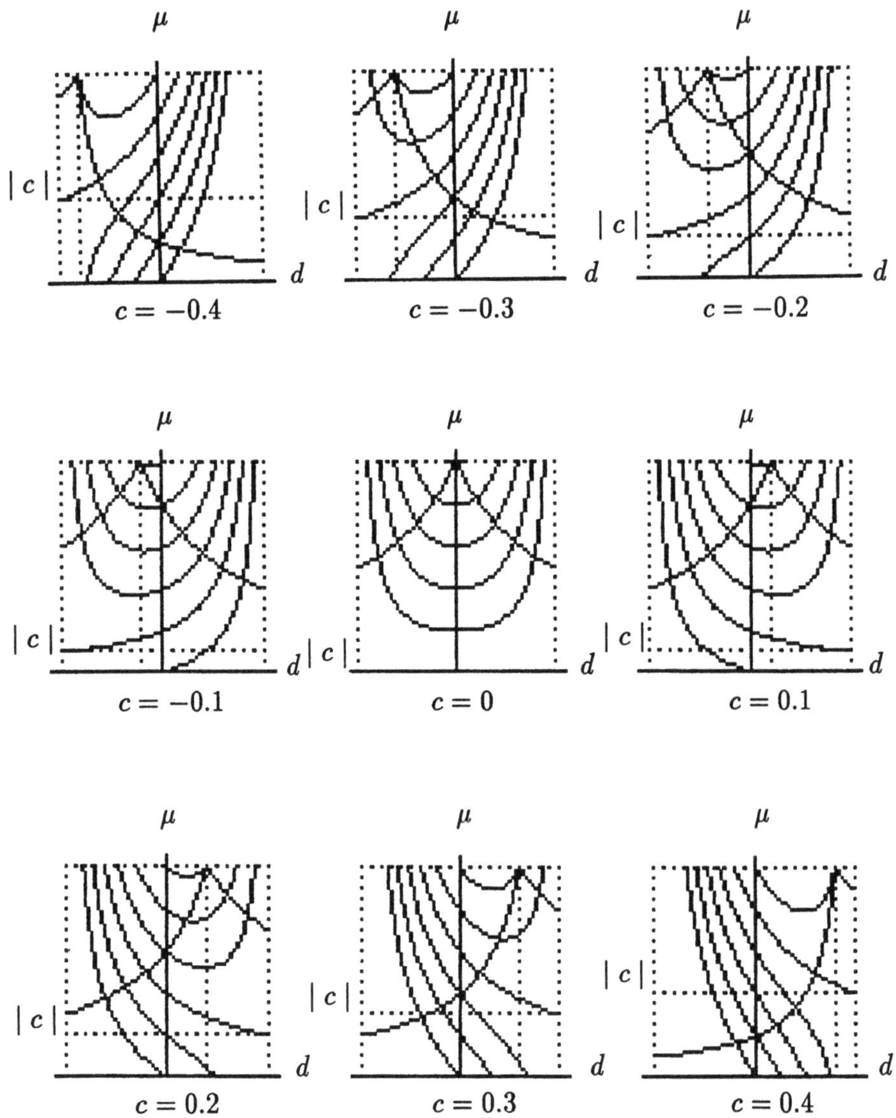
μ
|c|
d
c = −0.4
μ
|c|
d
c = −0.3
μ
|c|
d
c = −0.2
μ
|c|
d
c = −0.1
μ
|c|
d
c = 0
μ
|c|
d
c = 0.1
μ
|c|
d
c = 0.2
μ
|c|
d
c = 0.3
μ
|c|
d
c = 0.4

Fig. 59

for the levels $\mathsf{E} = 0.5, 0.6, \ldots, 1.0$. The domain of admissible pairs (d, μ) is drawn around in each graph of fig. 59. It is determined by the condition

$$c = \mu d + \sum_{v':v' \in V, v' \neq v} \mu(v')\, d(v') = \mu d + (1-\mu)\, d',$$

where d' is the mean value of $d(v')$, consequently,

$$-1/2 \leq d' \leq 1/2,$$

whence

$$-1/2 \leq d' = \frac{c - \mu d}{1 - \mu} \leq 1/2,$$

which is equivalent to the following restrictions

$$\mu \leq \frac{1/2 - c}{d - 1/2},$$
$$\mu \leq \frac{1/2 + c}{d + 1/2}.$$

The horizontal dottet lines in the graphs of fig. 59 indicate at the critical values of individual weights $\mu = | c |$, above which proposition 7.6.5 doesn't hold. Indeed, if all individuals have the same weight $\mu = 1/n$, then the condition $n \geq 1/ | c |$ turns out to be $\mu \leq | c |$. The equality of individual weights means that the pairs (d, μ), associated with the individuals, are placed along the horizontal line $\mu = 1/n$, where n is the number of individuals. As one can see in fig. 59, when the number of individuals is insufficient, i.e. when $\mu = \mu(v)$ is higher than the critical value, the maximum of function $\mathsf{E}(d, \mu)$ is not attained at the extreme values of $d = d(v)$. The only exception is the case $c = 0$, when the level curves are symmetric, and therefore the maximum of $\mathsf{E}(d, \mu)$ for fixed μ is attained at $d = 0$ regardless of the value of μ.

Also note the symmetry of graphs, when the magnitudes of c are symmetric relative to 0. It follows from (7.6.4), where μ depends on $| d |$ and the sign of cd. It meets our definition of representativeness, which takes into account the coincidences of individual preferences on pairs of alternatives, making no difference, whether a pair (x, y) does, or doesn't belong to them. In particular, it implies that the representativeness remains the same, if for a given pair (x, y) we invert the probabilities $p_{xy}(v)$ of all individuals $v \in V$ to $1 - p_{xy}(v)$, i.e. if we change the signs of all $d_{xy}(v)$.

Now let us show that the independence of individuals is essential in the formulation of proposition 7.6.5.

7.6.6. EXAMPLE. Let $V = \{1, \dots, 10\}$ and $\mu(v) = 0.1$ for all $v \in V$. Let $\xi(x, y) = 1$ for two different $x, y \in X$. Define two situations f_1 and f_2, putting

$$\begin{aligned} f_1(v) = &\ \{(x,y)\} \quad \text{if } v = 1, \dots, 10, \qquad \nu(f_2) = 0.4; \\ f_2(v) = &\begin{cases} \{(x,y)\} & \text{if } v = 1, \dots, 4, \\ \emptyset & \text{if } v = 5, \dots, 10, \end{cases} \qquad \nu(f_2) = 0.6. \end{aligned} \tag{7.6.5}$$

By definition of average representativeness,

$$\begin{aligned} \mathsf{E}m(1) &= \nu(f_1)\, m(1, x, y, f_1) + \nu(f_2)\, m(1, x, y, f_2) = 0.4 \times 1 + 0.6 \times 0.4 = 0.64, \\ \mathsf{E}m(5) &= \nu(f_1)\, m(5, x, y, f_1) + \nu(f_2)\, m(5, x, y, f_2) = 0.4 \times 1 + 0.6 \times 0.6 = 0.76. \end{aligned}$$

Obviously, the first four individuals have the same average representativeness, which is also valid for the rest six. Therefore, individuals $5, \dots, 10$ are optimal dictators with respect to the average representativeness. However, by proposition 7.6.5 it would be individuals $1, \dots, 4$. Really,

$$\begin{aligned} p_{xy}(1) &= \dots = p_{xy}(4) = 1, \\ p_{xy}(5) &= \dots = p_{xy}(10) = 0.4, \end{aligned}$$

whence $c_{xy} = 0.14$. Since $\mu(v) = 0.1 \leq | c_{xy} |$, by proposition 7.6.5 the optimal dictator would be the individual v with the greatest $d_{xy}(v)$, say, the first one. The contradiction arises because the individuals are not independent:

$$0.4 = \nu(f_1) \neq 1.0^4 \times 0.4^6.$$

Now we show that the requirement for a sufficiently large number of individuals is essential in the formulation of propositin 7.6.8.

7.6.7. EXAMPLE. Let $V = \{1, 2, 3\}$ and $\mu(v) = 1/3$ for all $v \in V$. Let $\xi(x, y) = 1$ for two different $x, y \in X$. Suppose that the individuals are independent and have preferences $\{(x, y)\}$, or $\emptyset$. Let

$$d_{xy}(1) = -0.2,\ d_{xy}(2) = -0.1,\ d_{xy}(3) = -0.4,$$

whence $c_{xy} = 0.1$. By (7.6.2) we have

$$\mathsf{E}m(1) = 0.6,\ \mathsf{E}m(2) = 0.68,\ \mathsf{E}m(3) = 0.64,$$

consequently, individual 2 is the optimal dictator. However, since $c_{xy} > 0$, by proposition 7.6.5 it would be individual 3 with the greatest $d_{xy}(v)$. The contradiction arises, because the number of individuals is insufficient:

$$n < 1/| c_{xy} | = 10.$$

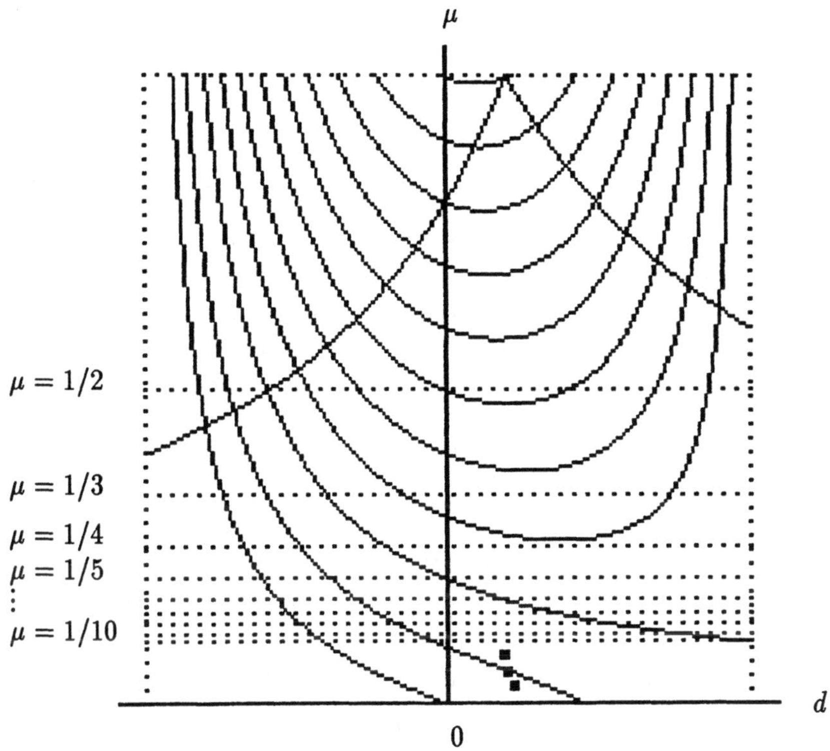

Fig. 60

The given example is illustrated by fig. 60 with the level curves of $\mathsf{E} = \mathsf{E}(d, \mu)$ for the levels $\mathsf{E} = 0.50, 0.55, \ldots, 1.00$. One can see in fig. 60 that the maximum of the function $\mathsf{E}(d, \mu)$ along the line $\mu = 1/3$ is attained not at the right-hand point $d = 0.5$ but close to $d = 0.1$. The same is observed for $n = 4, \ldots, 9$ (the corresponding dotted lines $\mu = 1/n$ are also shown in fig. 60). The maximum of $\mathsf{E}(d, \mu)$ is attained at the right-hand end of the interval $-1/2 < d < 1/2$ if only $n \geq 10$. Then the individual with the greatest $d = d_{xy}(v)$ is the optimal dictator.

To end the section, we show that the equality of individual weights is essential in the formulation of proposition 7.6.5.

7.6.8. Example. Let $V = \{1, \ldots, 20\}$ and

$$\mu(1) = \ldots = \mu(18) = 1/20, \quad \mu(19) = 1/40, \quad \mu(20) = 3/40.$$

Let $\xi(x,y) = 1$ for two different $x, y \in X$. Suppose that the individuals are independent and have preferences $\{(x,y)\}$, or $\emptyset$. Put

$$d_{xy}(1) = \ldots = d_{xy}(18) = 0.1, \quad d_{xy}(19) = 0.13, \quad d_{xy}(20) = 0.09,$$

whence $c_{xy} = 0.1$. By (7.6.2) we have

$$\mathsf{E}m(1) = \ldots = \mathsf{E}m(18) = 0.544, \quad \mathsf{E}m(19) = 0.537655, \quad \mathsf{E}m(20) = 0.554285,$$

consequently, individual 20 is the optimal dictator. The individuals are independent, their weights are sufficiently small ($\mu(v) \leq 3/40 < 0.1 = | c_{xy} |$), and $c_{xy} > 0$. By proposition 7.6.5 the optimal dictator would be individual 19 with the greates $d_{xy}(v)$. It is not true because for unequal weights of individuals the function $\mathsf{E}m(v)$ depends both on $d_{xy}(v)$ and $\mu(v)$. The given phenomenon is seen in fig. 60. The pairs (d, μ) associated with the individuals are shown by small squares. They are located around the point $(0.1, 1/20)$. Although individual 19 has the greates value $d_{xy}(v)$, its weight $\mu(v)$ is too small, and the point

$$(d_{xy}(19), \mu(19)) = (0.13, 1/40)$$

is below the level curve of $\mathsf{E}(d, \mu)$, passing through $(0.1, 1/20)$, whereas the point

$$(d_{xy}(20), \mu(20)) = (0.09, 3/40)$$

is located above the mentioned level curve.

7.7 Approximation of Majority Representativeness

Before we prove the main theorem of the section, we introduce and recall some designations and formulate four auxiliary propositions.

For every simple event $\omega = (x, y, f)$ denote the coalitions:

(a) of the *non-strict majorities* by

$$M_\omega = M_{xyf} = \begin{cases} A_\omega & \text{if } \mu(A_\omega) > 1/2, \\ V & \text{if } \mu(A_\omega) = 1/2, \\ A_\omega^c & \text{if } \mu(A_\omega) < 1/2; \end{cases}$$

(b) of the *strict majority* by

$$\overline{M}_\omega = \overline{M}_{xyf} = \begin{cases} A_\omega & \text{if } \mu(A_\omega) > 1/2, \\ \emptyset & \text{if } \mu(A_\omega) = 1/2, \\ A_\omega^c & \text{if } \mu(A_\omega) < 1/2; \end{cases}$$

(c) of the *non-strict minorities* by

$$\overline{M}^c_\omega = \overline{M}^c_{xyf} = \begin{cases} A_\omega & \text{if } \mu(A_\omega) < 1/2, \\ V & \text{if } \mu(A_\omega) = 1/2, \\ A^c & \text{if } \mu(A_\omega) > 1/2; \end{cases}$$

(d) of the *non-strict minority* (other than $\overline{M}^c_\omega$) by

$$L_\omega = L_{xyf} = \begin{cases} A_\omega & \text{if } \mu(A_\omega) \leq 1/2, \\ A^c_\omega & \text{if } \mu(A_\omega) > 1/2; \end{cases}$$

(e) of the *strict minority* by

$$\overline{L}_\omega = \overline{L}_{xyf} = M^c_{xyf} = \begin{cases} A_\omega & \text{if } \mu(A_\omega) < 1/2, \\ \emptyset & \text{if } \mu(A_\omega) = 1/2, \\ A^c_\omega & \text{if } \mu(A_\omega) > 1/2. \end{cases}$$

Fix $(x, y) \in X \times X$ and let $f \in F$ be random. Define random variables

$$\mu(M_{xy}),\ \mu(\overline{M}_{xy}),\ \mu(\overline{M}^c_{xy}),\ \mu(L_{xy}),\ \mu(\overline{L}_{xy})$$

to be the weight of the listed coalitions, respectively. Their mathematical expectations we denote by

$$\mathsf{E}\mu(M_{xy}),\ \mathsf{E}\mu(\overline{M}_{xy}),\ \mathsf{E}\mu(\overline{M}^c_{xy}),\ \mathsf{E}\mu(L_{xy}),\ \mathsf{E}\mu(\overline{L}_{xy}).$$

7.7.1. LEMMA. *Consider a sequence of models with increasing number n of independent individuals. Then for every positive integer k we have*

$$\mathsf{E}\mu^k(L_{xy}) \underset{n\to\infty}{\rightrightarrows} (1/2- \mid c_{xy} \mid)^k \approx (\mathsf{E}\mu(L_{xy}))^k.$$

PROOF. By definition of L_{xyf} we have

$$\begin{aligned} \mathsf{E}\mu^k(L_{xy}) &= \sum_{0\leq z<1/2} z^k\, \nu\{f : f \in F,\ \mu(A_{xyf}) = z\} + \\ &\quad +2^{-k}\, \nu\{f : f \in F,\ \mu(A_{xyf}) = 1/2\} + \\ &\quad + \sum_{1/2<z\leq 1} (1-z)^k\, \nu\{f : f \in F,\ \mu(A_{xyf}) = z\}. \qquad (7.7.1) \end{aligned}$$

By lemma 7.6.3 we obtain that $\mu(A_{xy})$ is a weighted sum of independent Bernoulli random variables. Its mathematical expectation and dispersion tend with increase in n to p_{xy} and 0, respectively. By virtue of Chebyshev inequality it implies that for arbitrary small $\epsilon > 0$ and all sufficiently large n the random variable $\mu(A_{xy})$ is almost completely concentrated within the ϵ-neighborhood of p_{xy}. Therefore,

$$\mathsf{E}\mu^k(L_{xy}) \underset{n\to\infty}{\rightrightarrows} \begin{cases} (p_{xy})^k & \text{if } p_{xy} < 1/2, \\ 2^{-k} & \text{if } p_{xy} = 1/2, \\ (1-p_{xy})^k & \text{if } p_{xy} > 1/2, \end{cases}$$

as required.

7.7.2. Lemma. *Consider a sequence of models with increasing number n of independent individuals. Fix a pair of alternatives (x, y) such that $p_{xy} \neq 1/2$. Then for every positive integer k, all sufficiently large n, all $W \subset V = V(n)$, consisting of no more than k elements, and all $t \in [0; \mu(W)]$ we have in designations of lemma 7.6.3:*

$$\nu\{f : f \in F, \mu(B_{Wxyf}) \geq 1/2 - t\} \approx \nu\{f : f \in F, \mu(B_{Wxyf}) > 1/2 - t\} \approx \delta_{xy},$$
$$\nu\{f : f \in F, \mu(B_{Wxyf}) \leq 1/2 - t\} \approx \nu\{f : f \in F, \mu(B_{Wxyf}) < 1/2 - t\} \approx$$
$$\approx 1 - \delta_{xy},$$

where the accuracy of approximation increases with n regardless of the choice of W and t. Besides,

$$\mathsf{E}\mu^k(M_{xy}) \approx \mathsf{E}\mu^k(\overline{M}_{xy}) \approx (1/2 + | c_{xy} |)^k,$$
$$\mathsf{E}\mu^k(\overline{L}_{xy}) \approx \mathsf{E}\mu^k(\overline{M}^c_{xy}) \approx (1/2 - | c_{xy} |)^k.$$

Proof. By lemma 7.6.3 we obtain that $\mu(B_{Wxyf})$ is a weighted sum of independent Bernoulli random variables with mathematical expectation and dispersion, tending with increase in n to p_{xy} and 0, respectively. Since by assumption and definition 7.5.5 we have $\mu(W) \leq k\alpha(n) \underset{n\to\infty}{\rightrightarrows} 0$, we can apply Chebyshev inequality to estimate the above probabilities. For example, if $p_{xy} < 1/2$, we obtain

$$\nu\{f : f \in F,\ \mu(B_{Wxyf}) \geq 1/2 - t\} \underset{n\to\infty}{\rightrightarrows} 0,$$
$$\nu\{f : f \in F,\ \mu(B_{Wxyf}) \leq 1/2 - t\} \underset{n\to\infty}{\rightrightarrows} 1$$

for all $W \subset V = V(n)$, consisting of no more than k elements and all $t \in [0; \mu(W)]$, as required. The rest probabilities are estimated similarly.

To approximate the mathematical expectations of the lemma we also apply Chebyshev inequality to expressions like (7.7.1). For example,

$$\begin{aligned}\mathsf{E}\mu^k(M_{xy}) &= \sum_{0\leq z<1/2} (1-z)^k \,\nu\{f : f\in F,\ \mu(A_{xyf}) = z\} \\ &\quad +\nu\{f : f\in F,\ \mu(A_{xyf}) = 1/2\} \\ &\quad + \sum_{1/2<z\leq 1} z^k \,\nu\{f : f\in F,\ \mu(A_{xyf}) = z\}. \end{aligned} \tag{7.7.2}$$

Since by assumption $p_{xy} \neq 1/2$, we have, following the arguments of the previous lemma,

$$\mathsf{E}\mu^k(M_{xy}) \underset{n\to\infty}{\rightrightarrows} \begin{cases} (1-p_{xy})^k & \text{if } p_{xy} < 1/2, \\ (p_{xy})^k & \text{if } p_{xy} > 1/2, \end{cases}$$

as required. The rest mathematical expectations are considered similarly.

7.7.3. LEMMA. *Consider a sequence of models with increasing number n of independent individuals, having comparable weights, i.e. $\mu(v) \sim O(n^{-1})$ for all $v \in V = V(n)$. Fix a pair of alternatives (x, y) such that $p_{xy} = 1/2$. Suppose that there exist coalitions of positive weight, consisting of individuals whose probabilites $p_{xy}(v)$ are separated from 0 and 1 by $\epsilon(n) \sim O(n^{1+\epsilon})$ for some positive $\epsilon > 0$, i.e.*

$$\mu\{v : v \in V(n),\ \epsilon(n) \leq p_{xy}(v) \leq 1-\epsilon(n)\} \geq \theta > 0.$$

Then the statement of lemma 7.7.2 is also valid for the pair of alternatives (x, y).

PROOF. In order to approximate the probabilities from lemma 7.7.2, we apply the central limit theorem to $\mu(B_{Wxy})$, which is a weighted sum of Bernoulli random variables (see the proof of lemma 7.6.3 for details). Let us verify Lyapunov condition. The sum of the third absolute central moments of these variables is

$$\begin{aligned} C &= \sum_{v\in V\setminus W} \mu^3(v)\,[(1-p_{xy}(v))^3\, p_{xy}(v) + p^3_{xy}(v)\,(1-p_{xy}(v))] \\ &= \sum_{v\in V\setminus W} \mu^3(v)\,(1-p_{xy}(v))\,p_{xy}(v)\,[1/2 + 2(p_{xy}(v)-1/2)^2] \\ &\leq O(n^{-1}) \sum_{v\in V\setminus W} \mu^2(v)\,(1-p_{xy}(v))\,p_{xy}(v) \\ &= O(n^{-1})\,\mathsf{D}\mu(B_{Wxy}). \end{aligned}$$

By lemmas 7.6.2 and 7.6.3 we have

$$\begin{aligned}
\mathsf{D}\mu(B_{Wxy}) &= \sum_{v\in V\setminus W} \mu^2(v)\, p_{xy}(v)\,(1-p_{xy}(v)) \\
&\geq \sum_{v\in V\setminus W:\epsilon(n)\leq p_{xy}(v)\leq 1-\epsilon(n)} \mu^2(v)\,\epsilon(n)\,(1-\epsilon(n)) \\
&\sim O(n^{-1+\epsilon}) \sum_{v\in V\setminus W:\epsilon(n)\leq p_{xy}(v)\leq 1-\epsilon(n)} \mu^2(v) \\
&\geq O(n^{-1+\epsilon})\frac{(\theta-\mu(W))^2}{n-k} \\
&\sim O(n^{-2+\epsilon}).
\end{aligned}$$

Now we can estimate Lyapunov ratio

$$\frac{C}{(\mathsf{D}\mu(B_{Wxy}))^{3/2}} \leq \frac{O(n^{-1})}{(\mathsf{D}\mu(B_{Wxy}))^{1/2}} \leq \frac{O(n^{-1})}{O(n^{-2+\epsilon})^{1/2}} \sim O(n^{-\epsilon/2}) \underset{n\to\infty}{\rightrightarrows} 0.$$

Therefore, we can apply the central limit theorem. Hence,

$$\nu\{f : f\in F,\ \mu(B_{Wxyf}) \geq 1/2 - t\} \approx \frac{1}{\sqrt{2\pi}}\int_z^\infty e^{-t^2/2}dt,$$

where

$$z = \frac{1/2 - t - \mathsf{E}\mu(B_{Wxy})}{\sqrt{\mathsf{D}\mu(B_{Wxy})}}.$$

By definition 7.5.5 we have $\mu(W)\underset{n\to\infty}{\rightrightarrows} 0$, consequently, by lemma 7.6.3 we obtain $\mathsf{E}\mu(B_{Wxy})\underset{n\to\infty}{\rightrightarrows} 1/2$. Therefore, $z\underset{n\to\infty}{\rightrightarrows} 0$ uniformly for all $t\in[0;\mu(W)]$. Hence,

$$\nu\{f : f\in F,\ \mu(B_{Wxyf}) \geq 1/2 - t\}\underset{n\to\infty}{\rightrightarrows} 1/2$$

uniformly for all $W\subset V = V(n)$, consisting of no more than k elements and all $t\in[0;\mu(W)]$, as required. The rest probabilities of the lemma are considered similarly.

In particular, since $A_{xyf} = B_{\emptyset xyf}$, we have

$$\begin{aligned}
&\nu\{f : f\in F,\ \mu(A_{xyf}) = 1/2 - t\} = \\
&= 1 - \nu\{f : f\in F,\ \mu(A_{xyf}) < 1/2 - t\} - \\
&\quad -\nu\{f : f\in F,\ \mu(A_{xyf}) > 1/2 - t\}\underset{n\to\infty}{\rightrightarrows} 0.
\end{aligned}$$

Now we can approximate the mathematical expectations of the lemma. Consider the sum (7.7.2). By virtue of the central limit theorem the term indexed by $z = 1/2$ is negligible for large n. Therefore, we can follow the proofs of lemmas 7.7.1–7.7.2 and obtain the required approximation. The other approximations of the lemma are considered similarly.

7.7.4. PROPOSITION. *Let the set of alternative X be finite. Consider a sequence of models with increasing number n of independent individuals. Let $p_{xy} \neq 1/2$ for all significant pairs of alternatives (x, y). Then for all sufficiently large n we have*

$$\mathsf{M}m(v) \approx \overline{\mathsf{M}}m(v) \approx 1/2 + \sum_{(x,y)\in X\times X} \xi(x,y)\, s_{xy}c_{xy}(v), \tag{7.7.3}$$

$$\mathsf{M}m \approx \overline{\mathsf{M}}m \approx 1/2 + \sum_{(x,y)\in X\times X} \xi(x,y) \mid c_{xy} \mid, \tag{7.7.4}$$

where the accuracy of approximation increases with n regardless of the choice of v in the first formula.

PROOF. Fix $W = \{v\}$ and a significant pair of alternatives $(x, y) \in X \times X$. Taking into account the independence of individuals, by virtue of lemma 7.7.2 we have

$$\begin{aligned} \mathsf{M}m(v,x,y) &= p_{xy}(v)\, \nu\{f : f \in F,\ \mu(B_{vxyf}) \geq 1/2 - \mu(v)\} + \\ &\quad +(1 - p_{xy}(v))\, \nu\{f : f \in F,\ \mu(B_{vxyf}) \leq 1/2\} \qquad (7.7.5) \\ &\approx p_{xy}(v)\delta_{xy} + (1 - p_{xy}(v))\,(1 - \delta_{xy}) \\ &= 1/2 + 2(\delta_{xy} - 1/2)\,(p_{xy}(v) - 1/2) \\ &= 1/2 + s_{xy}c_{xy}(v). \end{aligned}$$

The case of $\overline{\mathsf{M}}m(v, x, y)$ differs only in that the inequalities in (7.7.5) are strict. Since the set of alternatives is finite, by virtue of (7.2.4) we obtain (7.7.3). To prove (7.7.4) use (7.3.7) and lemma 7.7.2:

$$\begin{aligned} \mathsf{M}m &= \sum_{(x,y)\in X\times X} \xi(x,y) \sum_{f\in F} \nu(f)\, \mu(M_{xyf}) \\ &= \sum_{(x,y)\in X\times X} \xi(x,y)\, \mathsf{E}\mu(M_{xy}) \\ &\approx \sum_{(x,y)\in X\times X} \xi(x,y)\,(1/2+ \mid c_{xy} \mid) \\ &= 1/2 + \sum_{(x,y)\in X\times X} \xi(x,y) \mid c_{xy} \mid, \end{aligned}$$

as required. The mathematical expectation $\overline{\mathsf{M}}m$ is approximated similarly, referring to $\mathsf{E}\mu(\overline{M}_{xy})$.

7.7.5. THEOREM (About the Majority Representativeness for Independent Individuals). *Let the set of alternatives be finite. Consider a sequence of models with increasing number n of independent individuals, having comparable weights, i.e. $\mu(v) \sim O(n^{-1})$ for all $v \in V(n)$. Suppose that for every significant pair of alternatives (x, y) such that $p_{xy} = 1/2$ there exist coalitions of positive weight, consisting of individuals whose probabilities $p_{xy}(v)$ are neither too small, nor too high, i.e.*

$$\mu\{v : v \in V(n),\ \epsilon(n) \leq p_{xy}(v) \leq 1 - \epsilon(n)\} \geq \theta > 0,$$

where $0 < \epsilon(n) \sim O(n^{-1+\epsilon})$ for some $\epsilon > 0$. Then for sufficiently large n we have

$$\begin{aligned} \mathsf{M}m(v) &\approx \overline{\mathsf{M}}m(v) \approx 1/2 + \sum_{(x,y)\in X\times X} \xi(x,y) s_{xy}\, c_{xy}(v), \\ \mathsf{M}m &\approx \overline{\mathsf{M}}m \approx 1/2 + \sum_{(x,y)\in X\times X} \xi(x,y) \mid c_{xy} \mid, \end{aligned}$$

where the accuracy of approximation increases with n regardless of the choice of v in the first formula.

PROOF. Follow the proof of proposition 7.7.4. If $p_{xy} = 1/2$ for a significant pair of alternatives (x, y), refer to lemma 7.7.3.

The next proposition is an obvious corollary of the above theorem.

7.7.6. PROPOSITION (Location of Optimal Dictator for a Single Pair of Alternatives). *Consider a sequence of models with increasing number n of independent individuals, having comparable weights, i.e. $\mu(v) \sim O(n^{-1})$ for all $v \in V(n)$, and let only one pair of alternatives (x, y) be significant, i.e. $\xi(x, y) = 1$ for some different $x, y \in X$. Then for sufficiently large n we have:*

(a) if $c_{xy} < 0$, then the individual v^* with the least $d_{xy}(v)$ has the almost maximal (strict) majority representativeness, i.e. for arbitrary small $\epsilon >$ 0 and sufficiently large n it holds

$$\begin{gathered} \mathsf{M}m(v^*) > \max_{v\in V} \mathsf{M}m(v) - \epsilon \\ (\overline{\mathsf{M}}m(v^*) > \max_{v\in V} \overline{\mathsf{M}}m(v) - \epsilon); \end{gathered}$$

(b) if $c_{xy} > 0$, then the individual v^* with the greatest $d_{xy}(v)$ has the almost maximal (strict) majority representativeness;

(c) *if* $c_{xy} = 0$ *and there exist coalitions of positive weight of individuals whose* $d_{xy}(v)$ *are neither too small, nor too high, i.e.*

$$\mu\{v : v \in V(n),\ \epsilon(n) \leq p_{xy}(v) \leq 1 - \epsilon(n)\} \geq \theta > 0,$$

where $0 < \epsilon(n) \sim O(n^{-1+\epsilon})$ *for some* $\epsilon > 0$, *then every individual has the (strict) majority representativeness close to* $1/2$.

Now let us comment on the assumptions of proposition 7.7.6, meaning that our discussion relates to theorem 7.7.5 as well. First of all we show that the independence of individuals is essential.

7.7.7. EXAMPLE. Modify example 7.6.6. Let V be a finite set of n individuals, having equal weights $\mu(v) = 1/n$ for all $v \in V$, where n is sufficiently large. Let $V = V_1 \cup V_2$, $\mu(V_1) = 0.4$, $\mu(V_2) = 0.6$. Let $(x, y) \in X \times X$, $x \neq y$, be the only significant pair of alternatives. Define three situations f_1, f_2, and f_3, putting

$$f_1(v) = \{(x,y)\} \text{ for all } v \in V, \quad \nu(f_1) = 0.4;$$
$$f_2(v) = \begin{cases} \{(x,y)\} & \text{if } v \in V_1, \\ \emptyset & \text{if } v \in V_2, \end{cases} \quad \nu(f_2) = 0.55;$$
$$f_3(v) = \begin{cases} \emptyset & \text{if } v \in V_1, \\ \{(x,y)\} & \text{if } v \in V_2, \end{cases} \quad \nu(f_3) = 0.05.$$

It is easy to see that for every $v_1 \in V_1$ and $v_2 \in V_2$ we have

$$\mathsf{M}m(v_1) = \overline{\mathsf{M}}m(v_1) = \nu(f_1) = 0.4,$$
$$\mathsf{M}m(v_2) = \overline{\mathsf{M}}m(v_2) = \nu(f_1) + \nu(f_2) + \nu(f_3) = 1,$$

whence $v_2 \in V_2$ are the optimal dictators with respect to the (strict) majority representativeness. However, by proposition 7.7.6 it would be the individuals $v_1 \in V_1$. Indeed, for every $v_1 \in V_1$ and $v_2 \in V_2$ we have

$$p_{xy}(v_1) = 0.95, \quad p_{xy}(v_2) = 0.45,$$

consequently,

$$p_{xy} = 0.4 \times 0.95 + 0.6 \times 0.45 = 0.65,$$

whence $c_{xy} > 0$, and $v_1 \in V_1$ would be the optimal dictator. It is not true because the individuals are not independent.

Now we show that the requirement for a large number of individuals is essential in the assumptions of proposition 7.7.6.

7.7.8. EXAMPLE. Revert to example 7.6.7. To evaluate the (strict) majority representativeness of each individual, it sufficies to substract from 1 the probability of situations when the given individual belongs to a minority, i.e. when his preference differs from the preferences of the other two individuals. Thus

$$\begin{aligned}\mathsf{M}m(1) &= 1 - 0.3 \times (1-0.6) \times (1-0.9) - (1-0.3) \times 0.6 \times 0.9 = 0.61,\\ \mathsf{M}m(2) &= 1 - (1-0.3) \times 0.6 \times (1-0.9) - 0.3 \times (1-0.6) \times 0.9 = 0.85,\\ \mathsf{M}m(3) &= 1 - (1-0.3) \times (1-0.6) \times 0.9 - 0.3 \times 0.6 \times (1-0.9) = 0.73,\end{aligned}$$

whence individual 2 is the optimal dictator with respect to the (strict) majority representativeness. It contradicts the statement of proposition 7.7.6, by which the optimal dictator would be individual 3 with the greatest $c_{xy}(3) = 0.4$. The contradiction arises because the number of individuals is insufficient.

Finally, let us show that if $c_{xy} = 0$, then the existence of weighty coalitions, consisting of individuals with preference probabilities separable from 0 and 1, is essential in the assumptions of proposition 7.7.6.

7.7.9. EXAMPLE. Let $V = V_1 \cup V_2$, where each V_i consists of n individuals with the same weight $1/(2n)$. Let $(x, y) \in X \times X$, $x \neq y$, be the only significant pair of alternatives. Suppose that all individuals are independent and have preferences $\{(x, y)\}$, or $\emptyset$. For all $v_1 \in V_1$ and $v_2 \in V_2$ put

$$p_{xy}(v_1) = \epsilon(n), \; p_{xy}(v_2) = 1 - \epsilon(n),$$

where $0 < \epsilon(n) \underset{n\to\infty}{\longrightarrow} 0$. Evaluate the strict majority representativeness of $v_1 \in V_1$ by formula (7.7.5) adapted for the strict majority representativeness:

$$\begin{aligned}\overline{\mathsf{M}}m(v_1) &= \epsilon(v)\, \nu\{f : f \in F,\; \mu(B_{v_1xyf}) > 1/2 - 1/(2n)\} + \\ &\quad +(1-\epsilon(n))\, \nu\{f : f \in F,\; \mu(B_{v_1xyf}) < 1/2\}.\end{aligned}$$

Since the weight of each individual equals $1/(2n)$, we have

$$\begin{aligned}\nu_n &= \nu\{f : f \in F,\; \mu(B_{v_1xyf}) > 1/2 - 1/(2n)\}\\ &= \nu\{f : f \in F,\; \mu(B_{v_1xyf}) \geq 1/2\}.\end{aligned}$$

Since the individuals are independent, obviously,

$$\nu_n > \nu\{f : f \in F,\; (x, y) \in f(v_2) \text{ for all } v_2 \in V_2\} = (1 - \epsilon(n))^n.$$

Therefore, for large n, when $\epsilon(n)$ is small,

$$\begin{aligned}\overline{\mathsf{M}}m(v_1) &= \epsilon(v)\,\nu_n + (1-\epsilon(n))\,(1-\nu_n)\\ &\approx 1-\nu_n\\ &< 1-(1-\epsilon(n))^n\\ &\approx n\,\epsilon(n).\end{aligned}$$

Thus if $\epsilon(n) \sim O(n^{-1-\epsilon})$ for some $\epsilon > 0$, then $\overline{\mathsf{M}}m(v_1) \underset{n\to\infty}{\longrightarrow} 0$.

If $\epsilon(n) \sim O(n^{-1})$ take, say, $\epsilon(n) = 1/(8n)$ and obtain $\overline{\mathsf{M}}m(v_1) < 1/4$ for all sufficiently large n.

Both of these possibilities are inconsistent with proposition 7.7.6. Indeed, since $s_{xy} = 0$, by proposition 7.7.6 we should have $\overline{\mathsf{M}}m(v_1) \underset{n\to\infty}{\longrightarrow} 1/2$.

7.8 Geometric Interpretation of Dictators

Let $\boldsymbol{p}(v)$ be the *vector of preference probabilities of individual* $v \in V$, i.e.

$$\boldsymbol{p}(v) = \{p_{xy}(v)\},$$

where coordinate indicies are the pairs of alternatives $(x,y) \in X \times X$. Therefore, $\boldsymbol{p}(v)$ is a vector of Euclidean space of dimension $\mid X \times X \mid = \mid X \mid^2$. Actually we shall consider only significant pairs of alternatives (x,y); hence, the dimension of $\boldsymbol{p}(v)$ is lower. Define the vectors of the same dimension

$$\begin{aligned}\boldsymbol{p} &= \{p_{xy}\} &&\text{— the mean probability vector,}\\ \boldsymbol{\delta} &= \{\delta_{xy}\} &&\text{— the indicator vector,}\\ \boldsymbol{c}(v) &= \{c_{xy}(v)\} &&\text{— the characteristic vector of individual } v,\\ \boldsymbol{c} &= \{c_{xy}\} &&\text{— the mean characteristic vector,}\\ \boldsymbol{s} &= \{s_{xy}\} &&\text{— the sign vector.}\end{aligned}$$

By $\boldsymbol{\Xi}$ denote a diagonal matrix of size $\mid X \mid^2 \times \mid X \mid^2$, with the diagonal elements $\xi(x,y)$:

$$\boldsymbol{\Xi} = \begin{pmatrix} \xi(x,y) & 0 & \dots & 0 & \\ 0 & \xi(x,y) & 0 & \dots & 0 \\ \dots & \dots & \dots & \dots & \dots \\ 0 & \dots & & 0 & \xi(z,y) \end{pmatrix}$$

If we consider only significant pairs of alternatives, then the actual size of the above matrix is less than $\mid X \mid^2 \times \mid X \mid^2$. Finally, denote the scalar product of vectors of the considered vector space by

$$\langle\, ,\, \rangle.$$

The approximations (7.6.2) and (7.7.3) look in our designations as follows:

$$\mathsf{E}m(v) \approx 1/2 + 2\langle \boldsymbol{\Xi c}, \boldsymbol{c}(v)\rangle, \tag{7.8.1}$$

$$\mathsf{M}m(v) \approx \overline{\mathsf{M}}m(v) \approx 1/2 + \langle \boldsymbol{\Xi s}, \boldsymbol{c}(v)\rangle. \tag{7.8.2}$$

It means that within the accuracy of approximation the individual, whose vector $\boldsymbol{c}(v)$ provides the maximal projection onto the vector $\boldsymbol{c}$ under the linear transform $\boldsymbol{\Xi}$, is the optimal dictator with respect to the average representativeness. Similarly, the optimal dictator with respect to the (strict) majority representativeness is the individual v, whose vector $\boldsymbol{c}(v)$ provides the maximal projection onto the vector $\boldsymbol{s}$ under the linear transform $\boldsymbol{\Xi}$.

The definition of the sign vector $\boldsymbol{s}$ implies that the angle between vectors $\boldsymbol{s}$ and $\boldsymbol{c}$ is less than 45^0. Indeed, each coordinate of the vector $\boldsymbol{s}$ has the same sign as of the vector $\boldsymbol{c}$. Therefore, $\boldsymbol{s}$ and $\boldsymbol{c}$ belong to the same multidimensional angle, bounded by the coordinate hyperplanes (quadrant if these vectors are two-dimensional). Considering the non-zero coordinates of $\boldsymbol{s}$ only, we see that $\boldsymbol{s}$ is the bisectrix of the associated multidimensional angle (see example 7.8.3 and fig. 61). Since all elements of the diagonal matrix $\boldsymbol{\Xi}$ are non-negative, the vectors $\boldsymbol{\Xi c}$, $\boldsymbol{\Xi s}$ are also located in the same multidimensional angle as $\boldsymbol{c}$ and $\boldsymbol{s}$. Therefore, the angles between all these vectors cannot exceed 90^0. When all significant pairs of alternatives (x, y) have equal significance $\xi(x, y) = 1/m$ for some m, the angle between $\boldsymbol{\Xi c}$ and $\boldsymbol{\Xi s}$ doesn't exceed 45^0, as the angle between $\boldsymbol{c}$ and $\boldsymbol{s}$.

The positive half-spaces, determined by the hyperplanes passing through 0 with normals $\boldsymbol{\Xi c}$ and $\boldsymbol{\Xi s}$, have a non-empty intersection, containing the whole multidimensional angle mentioned. Since these hyperplanes, within the accuracy of approximation, separate the characteristic vectors $\boldsymbol{c}(v)$ of dictators-representatives from that of proper dictators, we obtain the following theorem.

7.8.1. THEOREM (A Condition of Consistency of Two Definitions of Optimal Dictators and Dictators-Representatives). *Under the assumptions of theorem* 7.7.5 *the following statements are valid witin the accuracy of approximations, provided by theorems* 7.6.4 *and* 7.7.5:

(a) an individual v is a dictator-representative with respect to average and (strict) majority representativeness simultaneously if and only if

$$\langle \boldsymbol{\Xi c}, \boldsymbol{c}(v)\rangle \geq 0, \tag{7.8.3}$$

$$\langle \boldsymbol{\Xi s}, \boldsymbol{c}(v)\rangle \geq 0; \tag{7.8.4}$$

(b) if vectors $\boldsymbol{\Xi c}$ and $\boldsymbol{\Xi s}$ are collinear, then the optimal dictator with respect to one indicator of representativeness is also optimal with respect to another indicator.

The following proposition is an obvious corollary of the above theorem.

7.8.2. PROPOSITION (The Consistency of Two Definitions of Optimal Dictators and Dictators-Representativeness for a Single Pair of Alternatives). *Under the assumptions of proposition 7.7.6 the following statements are valid within the accuracy of approximation provided by propositions 7.6.4 and 7.7.6 for sufficiently large number n of independent individuals:*

(a) an individual is a dictator-representative with respect to the average representativeness if and only if he is a dictator-representative with respect to the (strict) majority representativeness;

(b) if an individual is an optimal dictator with respect to one indicator of representativeness, then he is an optimal dictator with respect to another indicator.

Let us show that the collinearity of vectors $\boldsymbol{\Xi c}$ and $\boldsymbol{\Xi s}$ in the formulation of theorem 7.8.1 is essential.

7.8.3. EXAMPLE. Consider a set V of n independent individuals, having equal weights, $\mu(v) = 1/n$, where n is sufficiently large. Let $V = V_1 \cup V_2$, where $\mu(V_1) = \mu(V_2) = 2^{-1}$. Suppose that $X = \{x, y, z\}$ and $\xi(x, y) = \xi(x, z) = 2^{-1}$. Fix four preferences

$$P_1 = \emptyset, \quad P_2 = \{(x,y)\}, \quad P_3 = \{(x,z)\}, \quad P_4 = \{(x,y),(x,z)\}$$

and for every $v_1 \in V_1$, $v_2 \in V_2$ put

$$\begin{array}{llll} p_1(v_1) = 0.02, & p_2(v_1) = 0, & p_3(v_1) = 0.68, & p_4(v_1) = 0.30 \\ p_1(v_2) = 0.06, & p_2(v_2) = 0.90, & p_3(v_2) = 0, & p_4(v_2) = 0.04. \end{array}$$

It is easy to see that

$$\begin{array}{llll} p_{xy}(v_1) = 0.30, & p_{xz}(v_1) = 0.98, & \text{i.e. } \boldsymbol{c}(v_1) = (-0.20, 0.48), & \\ p_{xy}(v_2) = 0.94, & p_{xz}(v_2) = 0.04, & \text{i.e. } \boldsymbol{c}(v_2) = (0.44, -0.46), & \\ p_{xy} \;\; = 0.62, & p_{xz} \;\; = 0.51, & \text{i.e. } \boldsymbol{c} \;\; = \;\; (0.12, 0.01), & \boldsymbol{s} = (1,1). \end{array}$$

The vectors $\boldsymbol{c}(v_1)$, $\boldsymbol{c}(v_2)$, $2\boldsymbol{c}$, and $2^{-1}\boldsymbol{s}$ are shown in fig. 61. Since all the assumptions of theorems 7.6.4 and 7.7.5 are satisfied, we have

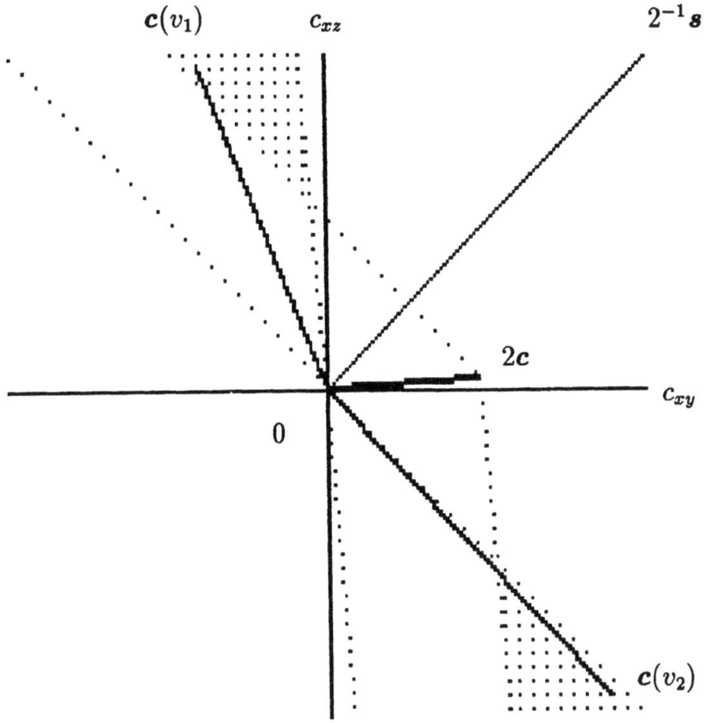

Fig. 61

$$\mathsf{E}m(v_1) \approx 1/2 + c_{xy}c_{xy}(v_1) + c_{xz}c_{xz}(v_1) = 0.4808,$$
$$\mathsf{M}m(v_1) \approx 1/2 + 2^{-1}s_{xy}c_{xy}(v_1) + 2^{-1}s_{xz}c_{xz}(v_1) = 0.6400,$$

and similarly

$$\mathsf{E}m(v_2) \approx 0.5482,$$
$$\mathsf{M}m(v_2) \approx 0.4900.$$

We see that every individual, being an optimal dictator with respect to one indicator of representativeness, is not even a dictator-representative with respect to another. To show it clearly, two dotted lines, passing through 0 with the normals $\boldsymbol{c}$ and $\boldsymbol{s}$, respectively, are drawn in fig. 61. These lines separate the space of characteristic vectors $\boldsymbol{c}(v)$ into the half-planes of that of proper dictators, and dictators-representatives with respect to each indicator (cf. with (7.8.3) and (7.8.4)). The dotted domains correspond to the vectors $\boldsymbol{c}(v_1)$, $\boldsymbol{c}(v_2)$

which are inconsistent with the system of inequalities (7.8.3)–(7.8.4) for the given vector $\boldsymbol{c}$, binding $\boldsymbol{c}(v_1)$, $\boldsymbol{c}(v_2)$ by virtue of (7.5.1) as follows:

$$\boldsymbol{c} = 2^{-1}\boldsymbol{c}(v_1) + 2^{-1}\boldsymbol{c}(v_2),$$

which is equivalent to

$$\boldsymbol{c}(v_1) + \boldsymbol{c}(v_2) = 2\boldsymbol{c}.$$

We can conclude that the inconsistency of the two definitions of dictators-representative (with respect to the two indicators) arises in rather specific cases, if the following conditions hold simultaneously:

(a) the angle between the vectors $\boldsymbol{c}$ and $\boldsymbol{s}$ is close to 45^0;

(b) the absolute value of the vector $\boldsymbol{c}$ is small (otherwise the dotted domain is outside the domain of admissible characteristic vectors),

(c) the individual preferences are antipodal: $p_{xy}(v_1)$ are small for $v_1 \in V_1$, whereas $p_{xy}(v_2)$ are great for $v_2 \in V_2$, and conversely, $p_{xz}(v_1)$ are great for $v_1 \in V_1$, whereas $p_{xz}(v_2)$ are small for $v_2 \in V_2$.

To satisfy the above conditions, the characteristic vectors $\boldsymbol{c}(v)$ must have a quite special localization. When they are widely scattered, we can expect the existence of the desired dictator-representative with respect to both indicators. In any case, an individual v with the characteristic vector $\boldsymbol{c}(v)$ from the same multidimensional angle as $\boldsymbol{c}$, is surely the desired one.

7.9 Numerical Estimation of Representativeness

We have introduced the indicators $\mathsf{E}m, \mathsf{M}m$, and $\overline{\mathsf{M}}m$ to characterize randomly chosen individuals and to estimate the lower bound of representativeness of optimal dictators. According to (7.3.3), (7.3.7), and its modification for the strict majority representativeness,

$$\begin{aligned}
\mathsf{E}m &= \sum_{\omega\in\Omega} \mathsf{P}(\omega)\,[1/2 + 2(\mu(A_\omega) - 1/2)^2],\\
\mathsf{M}m &= \sum_{\omega\in\Omega} \mathsf{P}(\omega)\,\mu(M_\omega),\\
\overline{\mathsf{M}}m &= \sum_{\omega\in\Omega} \mathsf{P}(\omega)\,\mu(\overline{M}_\omega).
\end{aligned}$$

The above expressions depend on divisions of V into A_ω and A_ω^c, and the greater the deviations from $\mu(A_\omega) = 0.5$ are, the higher are the indicators of representativeness. Since any knowledge about the individuals and their preferences results in deviations of the associated probability measures from uniform distributions, the worst case is the lack of information, implying the uniformity of the probability measures.

Using this observation, we estimate the lower bound of representativeness of optimal dictators. In the present section we restrict ourselves to the set of alternatives X, consisting of 3 elements only. As shown in example 6.3.5, there are precisely 19 preferences on X, and each pair of different alternatives belongs to 6 preferences from 19. We shall consider a model with a few independent individuals; for large models we have approximations, given by theorems 7.6.4 and 7.7.5.

Consider a sequence of models with the sets of individuals denoted by $V(n)$, each consisting of n independent individuals with equal weights $1/n$, $n = 2, 3, \ldots$. For each model define two versions of measure ξ :

(a) $\xi(x, y) = 1$ for some fixed pair of two different alternatives (x, y),

(b) $\xi(x, y) = 1/6$ for each pair of different alternatives (x, y).

The former is destined to characterize the representativeness on a single pair of alternatives (cf. with the measure of dictatorship on a single pair of alternatives in example 6.3.5 denoted by d). The latter is used to estimate the lower bound of representativeness of optimal dictators when all pairs of alternatives are equisignificant (recall that the pairs of the form (x, x) are not taken into account by the asymmetry of preferences, and 6 is the number of the rest pairs).

In the light of the above reasons we consider equidistributed preferences. If $\xi(x, y) = 1$ for some fixed pair of different alternatives, it means that actually we consider two preferences $\{(x, y)\}$ and $\emptyset$, consequently, put $p = p_{xy}(v) = 1/2$ for each $v \in V(n)$, $n = 2, 3, \ldots$. If $\xi(x, y) = 1/6$ for every pair of different alternatives (x, y), it means that we can consider 19 preferences, consequently, put $p = p_{xy}(v) = 6/19$ for each pair of different alternatives (x, y) and all $v \in V(n)$, $n = 2, 3, \ldots$. For both our cases for a fixed pair of unequal alternatives $(x, y) \in X \times X$ and any fixed individual $v \in V(n)$ we have

$$\begin{aligned} \mathsf{E}m &= \sum_{v' \in V(n)} \mu(v') \, \mathsf{E}m(v') = \\ &= \mathsf{E}m(v) = \sum_{(x', y') \in X \times X} \xi(x', y') \, \mathsf{E}m(v, x', y') = \\ &= \mathsf{E}m(v, x, y). \end{aligned}$$

Similarly,

$$\mathsf{M}m = \mathsf{M}m(v) = \mathsf{M}m(v, x, y),$$
$$\overline{\mathsf{M}}m = \overline{\mathsf{M}}m(v) = \mathsf{M}m(v, x, y).$$

Put $d = p - 1/2$. By (7.6.2), taking into account that $\mu(v) = 1/n$, we have for the nth model

$$\mathsf{E}m = \mathsf{E}m(v, x, y) = 1/2 + 1/(2n) + 2d^2(1 - 1/n).$$

Put $q = 1 - p$. By analogy with Bernoulli scheme we derive from (7.7.5)

$$\begin{aligned}
\mathsf{M}m &= \mathsf{M}m(v, x, y) \\
&= p\,\nu\{f : f \in F, \mu(B_{vxyf}) \geq 1/2 - 1/n\} + q\,\nu\{f : f \in F, \mu(B_{vxyf}) \leq 1/2\} \\
&= p \sum_{n/2-1 \leq k \leq n-1} C_{n-1}^k p^k q^{n-1-k} + q \sum_{0 \leq k \leq n/2} C_{n-1}^k p^k q^{n-1-k} \\
&= p \sum_{0 \leq k \leq n/2} C_{n-1}^{n-1-k} p^{n-1-k} q^k + q \sum_{0 \leq k \leq n/2} C_{n-1}^k p^k q^{n-1-k} \\
&= \sum_{0 \leq k \leq n/2} C_{n-1}^k (p^{n-k} q^k + p^k q^{n-k}).
\end{aligned}$$

Similarly, substituting strict inequalities for the non-strict ones in (7.7.5), we get

$$\overline{\mathsf{M}}m = \overline{\mathsf{M}}m(v, x, y) = \sum_{0 \leq k < n/2} C_{n-1}^k \,(p^{n-k} q^k + p^k q^{n-k}).$$

The values computed by the above formulas are presented by table 7.9.1. Let us make a few remarks.

1. One can see the convergence of the indicators of representativeness to the limits established by theorems 7.6.4 and 7.7.5. These limits are indicated at the bottom of the table. However, the convergence is rather slow, therefore, the approximations given by the mentioned theorems must be used with care.

2. Majority and strict majority representativeness are equal for the models with odd number of individuals. It follows from the fact that majority and strict majority are the same, when individuals have equal weights and their number is odd.

3. If the number of individuals is even, majority and strict majority are different, implying the difference in majority and strict majority representativeness. Note that $\mathsf{M}m$ increases, yet $\overline{\mathsf{M}}m$ decreases, comparing with the proceeding odd number of individuals $2n + 1$. It is explained

7.9.1. TABLE. Lower Bound of Representativeness (in %) of Optimal Dictators for Independent Individuals and 3 Alternatives.

Number of individuals	$\xi(x,y) = 1,\ p_{xy}(v) = 1/2$			$\xi(x,y) = 1/6,\ p_{xy}(v) = 6/19$		
n	$\mathsf{E}m(v)$	$\mathsf{M}m(v)$	$\overline{\mathsf{M}}m(v)$	$\mathsf{E}m(v)$	$\mathsf{M}m(v)$	$\overline{\mathsf{M}}m(v)$
2	75.00	100.00	50.00	78.39	100.00	56.79
3	66.67	75.00	75.00	71.19	78.39	78.39
4	62.50	87.50	50.00	67.59	87.73	59.72
5	60.00	68.75	68.75	65.43	73.72	73.72
6	58.33	81.25	50.00	63.99	81.79	61.62
7	57.14	65.63	65.63	62.96	71.71	71.72
8	56.25	77.34	50.00	62.19	78.25	62.99
9	55.56	63.67	63.67	61.59	70.62	70.62
10	55.00	74.61	50.00	61.11	75.89	64.03
11	54.55	62.30	62.30	60.72	69.96	69.96
12	54.17	72.56	50.00	60.39	74.23	64.83
13	53.85	61.28	61.28	60.11	69.53	69.53
14	53.57	70.95	50.00	59.87	73.01	65.47
15	53.33	60.47	60.47	59.67	69.24	69.24
16	53.13	69.64	50.00	59.49	72.09	65.98
17	52.94	59.82	59.82	59.33	69.04	69.04
18	52.78	68.55	50.00	59.19	71.39	66.40
19	52.63	59.27	59.27	59.06	68.89	68.89
20	52.50	67.62	50.00	58.95	70.83	66.73
21	52.38	58.81	58.81	58.84	68.78	68.78
22	52.27	66.82	50.00	58.75	70.39	67.01
23	52.17	58.41	58.41	58.67	68.70	68.70
24	52.08	66.12	50.00	58.59	70.04	67.24
25	52.00	58.06	58.06	58.52	68.64	68.64
26	51.92	65.50	50.00	58.45	69.76	67.43
27	51.85	57.75	57.75	58.39	68.59	68.59
28	51.79	64.94	50.00	58.33	69.53	67.59
29	51.72	57.47	57.47	58.28	68.56	68.56
30	51.67	64.45	50.00	58.23	69.23	67.72
31	51.61	57.22	57.22	58.18	68.53	68.53
32	51.56	63.99	50.00	58.14	69.19	67.83
33	51.52	57.00	57.00	58.10	68.51	68.51
34	51.47	63.58	50.00	58.06	69.06	67.92
35	51.43	56.79	56.79	58.02	68.49	68.49
36	51.39	63.21	50.00	57.99	68.96	68.00
37	51.35	56.60	56.60	57.95	68.48	68.48
38	51.32	62.86	50.00	57.92	68.87	68.07
39	51.28	56.43	56.43	57.89	68.47	68.47
40	51.25	62.54	50.00	57.87	68.80	68.12
41	51.22	56.27	56.27	57.84	68.46	68.46
42	51.19	62.24	50.00	57.82	68.74	68.17
43	51.16	56.12	56.12	57.79	68.45	68.45
44	51.14	61.96	50.00	57.77	68.69	68.20
45	51.11	55.98	55.98	57.75	68.45	68.45
46	51.09	61.70	50.00	57.73	68.65	68.24
47	51.06	55.85	55.85	57.71	68.44	68.44
48	51.04	61.46	50.00	57.69	68.61	68.26
...						
	50.00	50.00	50.00	56.79	68.42	68.42

by the following. In the model with $2n+1$ individuals, dictator v^{2n+1} represents both a majority and a strict majority if at least n individuals of the rest $2n$ share his preference. In the model with $2n+2$ individuals, dictator v^{2n+2} represents a non-strict majority if at least n of the rest $2n+1$ individuals share his preference, the probability of which is obviously greater:

$$\mathsf{M}m(v^{2n+2}) > \mathsf{M}m(v^{2n+1}).$$

To represent a strict majority in this case, dictator v^{2n+2} has to share the preference of at least $n+1$ of the rest $2n+1$ individuals. To prove the inequality

$$\overline{\mathsf{M}}m(v^{2n+2}) < \overline{\mathsf{M}}m(v^{2n+1}),$$

we use the analogy with Bernoulli scheme. By S_{2n} and S_{2n+1} denote, respectively, the number of successes in $2n$ and $2n+1$ trials. Since $2n+1$ is odd and $2n+2$ is even, we can apply the above reasons to (7.7.5), adapted for the strict majority representativeness. Hence,

$$\overline{\mathsf{M}}m(v^{2n+1}) = \overline{\mathsf{M}}m(v^{2n+1}, x, y) = p\,\nu\{S_{2n} \geq n\} + q\,\nu\{S_{2n} \leq n\} \quad (7.9.1)$$

and

$$\overline{\mathsf{M}}m(v^{2n+2}) = \overline{\mathsf{M}}m(v^{2n+2}, x, y) = p\,\nu\{S_{2n+1} \geq n+1\} + q\,\nu\{S_{2n+1} \leq n\}. \quad (7.9.2)$$

Note that

$$\begin{aligned} \nu\{S_{2n+1} \geq n+1\} &= \nu\{S_{2n} \geq n+1\} + \nu\{S_{2n} = n\}\,p \\ &= \nu\{S_{2n} \geq n\} + \nu\{S_{2n} = n\}\,p - \nu\{S_{2n} = n\} \\ &= \nu\{S_{2n} \geq n\} - \nu\{S_{2n} = n\}\,q, \end{aligned}$$

whence

$$\nu\{S_{2n} \geq n\} > \nu\{S_{2n+1} \geq n+1\}. \quad (7.9.3)$$

Similarly,

$$\begin{aligned} \nu\{S_{2n+1} \leq n\} &= \nu\{S_{2n} \leq n-1\} + \nu\{S_{2n} = n\}\,q \\ &= \nu\{S_{2n} \leq n\} - \nu\{S_{2n} = n\} + \nu\{S_{2n} = n\}\,q \\ &= \nu\{S_{2n} \leq n\} - \nu\{S_{2n} = n\}\,p, \end{aligned}$$

whence

$$\nu\{S_{2n} \leq n\} > \nu\{S_{2n+1} \leq n\}. \quad (7.9.4)$$

Applying (7.9.3) and (7.9.4) to (7.9.1) and (7.9.2), we come to the required inequality

$$\overline{\mathsf{M}}m(v^{2n+1}) > \overline{\mathsf{M}}m(v^{2n+2}).$$

4. Finally, our consideration proves that the estimation of representativeness, given by theorems 7.3.1 and 7.3.2, cannot be improved even for the case of independent individuals. Indeed, we can construct a model with sufficiently large number of individuals n, for which $\mathsf{E}m$, $\mathsf{M}m$, $\mathsf{E}m(v)$, and $\mathsf{M}m(v)$ are close to $1/2$ for all $v \in V$.

7.10 Notes on Interpretation

Let us comment on some peculiarities of the concept of representativeness with which we have analysed our collective choice model and revised Arrow's paradox.

We have introduced two indicators of representativeness (three, including the strict majority representativeness). We use the mathematical expectation of deciding coalition as the basic indicator in theorems 7.4.1 and 7.4.2 about overcoming the paradoxes of Arrow and Kirman and Sondermann. There are two reasons in favour of the average representativeness to be the basic indicator. According to proposition 7.3.4, an optimal dictator with respect to the average representativeness expresses the preferences of quite weighty coalitions more often than in a half of simple events. It hints at his capability to be a dictator-representative with respect to the majority representativeness as well. Another reason is that we have a precise formula for the average representativeness (7.6.2), but for the majority representativeness we have only an approximation (7.7.3). However, as shown in example 7.3.3, there are cases when the optimal dictator with respect to the average representativeness represents a minority in most simple events. To analyse these possibilities we introduce the second indicator—the majority representativeness, which also allows making an appointment of optimal dictator.

Generally speaking, to choose an approach to the definition of optimal dictator, one needs additional reasons. For example, if a dictator is to be appointed for a long period of time when he is supposed to express varing preferences of other individuals, the average representativeness seems to meet the problem better. The majority representativeness can be used for a single decision because the optimal dictator expresses the majority preference with higher probability. Certainly, it is no more than a conditional contraposition.

The desired equivalence of the two approaches to the appointment of optimal dictator, or at least dictator-representative, is obtained for two alternatives and a large number of independent individuals. As mentioned in section 7.8, in most practical cases the two approaches can be consistent under rather general assumptions.

In the case of a large number of independent individuals some remarkable peculiarities of the interaction of the optimal dictator with the collective are revealed. By virtue of the law of large numbers, the collective preference is almost determined, being close to the mean vector $\boldsymbol{c}$ of the "average" individual. By theorem 7.6.4 the maximum average representativeness is attained for the individual v whose preference is "close" to the preference of the "average" individual, providing the scalar product $\langle \boldsymbol{\Xi c}, \boldsymbol{c}(v)\rangle$ with maximum. A similar situation is observed for the majority representativeness. The majority preference is also nearly determined by general tendencies in the individual preferences described by the sign vector $\boldsymbol{c}$, showing whether an "average" individual is inclined to prefer one alternative to another, or not. By theorem 7.7.5 the maximum majority representativeness is attained for the individual v whose preference is "close" to the majority preference, maximizing the scalar product $\langle \boldsymbol{\Xi c}, \boldsymbol{s}(v)\rangle$. The matrix $\boldsymbol{\Xi}$ in the scalar products mentioned introduces corrections caused by the account of significance of decisions.

The interaction of the optimal dictator with the collective is influenced by the degree of definitness of prediction for individual preferences. By theorems 7.6.4 and 7.7.5, if the prediction is indefinite, i.e. p_{xy} are close to $1/2$, then the representativeness of optimal dictators is lowest, being close to $1/2$. The representativeness of optimal dictators increases with the increase in the degree of definitness of prediction, i.e. with removing p_{xy} from $1/2$. Therefore, the degree of definitness (reliability) of prediction of individual preferences results in whether the optimal dictator is an acceptable representative, or, on the contrary, meets the common use of the word "dictator". That is of prime importance in applications, where dictatorial rules of decision-making can be used to replace a set of factors by a single representative.

However, assuming the existence of probability measure P on Ω, we don't specify how it can be constructed numerically, e.g. revealed from statistical data. Nevertheless, random dictators, chosen with respect to measure μ on V only, have sufficiently good properties with respect to measure P, i.e. we obtain good results regardless of the way, how the measure P is defined. In a sense, we can draw analogy to the method of marks (chapter 4). The main assumption there is the existence of a measure of preference which is roughly represented by marks. It is noteworthy that the sums of marks approximate the sums of unknown estimates of alternatives. Since the measure is not used directly, its existence is of theoretical rather than practical importance. Our case is quite similar, and the measure P can be considered as an auxiliary concept.

On the other hand, the probabilities $p_{xy}(v)$ can be interpreted as indicators of the individual interest, expressing the degree of preference. Such an interpretation is similar to that of lotteries in Neumann–Morgenstern utility theory. Therefore, methods of revealing preferences can help in numerical determination of the probabilities $p_{xy}(v)$ and, indirectly, the measure ν on the set of situations. Furthermore, if the probabilities $p_{xy}(v)$ are interpreted as indicators of the individual interest, then the vector $\boldsymbol{p}$ can be interpreted as the average collective interests. In this case the optimal dictator is the individual whose interest is "closer" to the interest of the collective than the interest of any other individual is. In the interaction of collective and individual interests we see parallels with the theory of economic equilibrium, cooperative games, etc.

Chapter 8

Representation of Collective by Few Individuals

8.1 Introductory Remarks

As shown in the previous chapter, single individuals can represent the collective, i.e. make decisions, mostly meeting a majority preference. Thus we revised the prohibition of dictatorship and justified such an indirect way of realization of collective will as giving powers to the elected representative.

However, even for an optimal representative, the part of events when his preference contradicts that of a majority can be significant. In this connection the question arises, whether it is possible to take a few representatives and to delimitate their competence so that the decisions of the resulting "cabinet" would meet a majority preference for all, or almost for all events. Certainly, this way of decision-making is a considerable idealization. In reality the delimitation of competence can be unrealizable, or ignored by the cabinet members. Moreover, the personal responsibility doesn't contradict collective forms of decision-making, not provised in our approach. The given scheme relates rather to discussions, referendums, inquests, when a limited group of representatives is expected to demonstrate all opinions prevailing in the collective.

The formulated problem relates to multicriteria choice as well. Indeed, the appointment of a cabinet corresponds to the selection of a few partial criteria, which can serve alternately for a global one. In other words, we speak about the reduction of the set of partial criteria to a certain representative minimum.

In the given chapter the results obtained for single representatives are generalized to cabinets. In particular, we show that for every positive integer k there exists a cabinet of k members such that the part of the events when it represents a majority is greater than $1 - 2^{-k}$. For example, it is always possible to choose a cabinet of 7 members, representing a majority in at least

$1 - 2^{-7} > 99\%$ of events, and of 10 members, representing a majority in at least $1 - 2^{-10} > 99.9\%$ of events. Concerning multicriteria decision-making, it means that when the reliability of decisions is limited by the reliability of information, say, by 99–99.9%, it is not necessary to take into account the totality of data, since 7–10 properly selected factors can be quite sufficient. It also meets the experimentally established human capabilities to take into account not more than 7–9 factors in decision-making (Larichev 1979). In a sense this property is analoguous to that of computing, when there is no need to perform 64-bit arithmetics, if the accuracy of data is within 8 digits. It implies that certain decsion-making problems can be solved by simple means, not requiring powerful computers and large data bases.

The concept of a cabinet contributes to the solution of the problem about the consistency of two definitions of optimal representation—with respect to average, or majority representativeness. As shown in the previous chapter, the dictators, optimal with respect to both indicators at the same time, exist under special assumptions, but general case is ambiguous in understanding of optimal representation. We show that the desired unambiguity can be achieved in cabinets. We prove that with the increase in their size the two definitions of optimal representation tend to become equivalent.

The results of the present chapter are published in Russian in (Tangiane 1989b).

8.2 Cabinets and Indicators of Their Representativeness

First of all let us give a strict definition of a cabinet.

8.2.1. DEFINITION. By a *cabinet* with k members we understand both a set of *cabinet members* $W = \{v_1, \ldots, v_k\} \subset V$, or a k-tuple $W = \{v_1, \ldots, v_k\} \in V^k$, where k-tuples are considered to be invariant with respect to permutations of elements and eliminations of repeated elements. We suppose that for every simple event $\omega = (x, y, f)$ cabinet W accepts or rejects the decision "x is preferred to y", entrusting it to the member with the highest representativenss for the given event. Therefore, the *representativeness of cabinet* W is defined to be the random variable

$$\begin{aligned} m_k &= m_k(W) = m_k(v_1, \ldots, v_k) = m_k(W, \omega) = m_k(W, x, y, f) \\ &= \max_{i=1,\ldots,k} m(v_i, \omega). \end{aligned}$$

Entrusting certain dicisions to certain cabinet members, we mean that the samle space of "decisions under situations" is divided into "domains of competence" of the cabinet members, where they make decisions as dictators. Since the aim of the cabinet is to represent a majority preference, the delimitation of "competence" is realized to maximize its representativeness.

To characterize the representativeness of cabinets, we use the indicators introduced earlier for single individuals.

8.2.2. DEFINITION. The *average representativeness of cabinet W for pair of alternatives* (x,y) is the mathematical expectation

$$\mathsf{E}m_k(W,x,y) = \sum_{f\in F} \nu(f)\, m_k(W,x,y,f).$$

The *average representativeness of cabinet W* is the mathematical expectation

$$\mathsf{E}m_k(W) = \sum_{\omega\in\Omega} \mathsf{P}(\omega)\, m_k(W,\omega) = \sum_{(x,y)\in X\times X} \xi(x,y)\, \mathsf{E}m_k(W,x,y). \qquad (8.2.1)$$

The *average representativeness (of random cabinet with k members)* is the mathematical expectation

$$\begin{aligned} \mathsf{E}m_k &= \sum_{(v_1,\ldots,v_k)\in V^k} \sum_{\omega\in\Omega} \mu(v_1)\ldots\mu(v_k)\, \mathsf{P}(\omega)\, m_k(v_1,\ldots,v_k,\omega) \\ &= \sum_{(v_1,\ldots,v_k)\in V^k} \mu(v_1)\ldots\mu(v_k)\, \mathsf{E}m_k(v_1,\ldots,v_k). \end{aligned}$$

If V is uncountable and $\mathsf{E}m_k(v_1,\ldots,v_k)$ is a measurable function of $v_1,\ldots,v_k$, then

$$\mathsf{E}m_k = \int_{V^k} d\mu(v_1)\ldots d\mu(v_k)\, \mathsf{E}m_k(v_1,\ldots,v_k).$$

Note that the random choice of a cabinet is realized as an independent choice of its members with respect to the probability measure μ on V, therefore, the weighty individuals have better chances to be chosen. By definition 8.2.1, if some member is chosen several times, it means that the cabinet can be reduced without any loss in its representativeness.

8.2.3. DEFINITION. The *majority representativeness of cabinet W for pair of alternatives* (x,y) is the probability of the situations when the cabinet W represents a majority with respect to the pair of alternatives (x,y), or the mathematical expectation of rounded representativeness of W for fixed (x,y), i.e.

$$\begin{aligned}\mathsf{M}m_k(W,x,y) &= \nu\{f : f \in F,\ m_k(W,x,y,f) \geq 1/2\} \\ &= \sum_{f\in F} \nu(f)\,\mathrm{int}(m_k(W,x,y,f)+1/2).\end{aligned}$$

The *majority representativeness of cabinet W* is the probability of the events when the cabinet W represents a majority, or the mathematical expectation of rounded representativeness of W, i.e.

$$\mathsf{M}m_k(W) = \sum_{\omega\in\Omega} \mathsf{P}(\omega)\,\mathrm{int}(m_k(W,\omega)+1/2) = \sum_{(x,y)\in X\times X} \xi(x,y)\,\mathsf{M}m_k(W,x,y). \tag{8.2.2}$$

The *majority representativeness (of random cabinet with k members)* is defined to be the mathematical expectation

$$\begin{aligned}\mathsf{M}m_k &= \sum_{(v_1,\ldots,v_k)\in V^k}\sum_{\omega\in\Omega} \mu(v_1)\ldots\mu(v_k)\,\mathsf{P}(\omega)\,\mathrm{int}(m_k(v_1,\ldots,v_k,\omega)+1/2) \\ &= \sum_{(v_1,\ldots,v_k)\in V^k} \mu(v_1)\ldots\mu(v_k)\,\mathsf{M}m_k(v_1,\ldots,v_k).\end{aligned}$$

If V is uncountable and $\mathsf{M}m_k(v_1,\ldots,v_k)$ is a measurable function of $v_1,\ldots,v_k$, then

$$\mathsf{M}m_k = \int_{V^k} d\mu(v_1)\ldots d\mu(v_k)\,\mathsf{M}m_k(v_1,\ldots,v_k).$$

8.2.4. DEFINITION. The *strict majority representativeness of cabinet W for pair of alternatives* (x,y) is the probability of the situations when the cabinet W represents a strict majority with respect to the pair of alternatives (x,y), or the mathematical expectation of rounded representativeness of W for fixed (x,y) with 0.5 rounded down to 0, i.e.

$$\begin{aligned}\overline{\mathsf{M}}m_k(W,x,y) &= \nu\{f : f \in F,\ m_k(W,x,y,f) > 1/2\} \\ &= \sum_{f\in F} \nu(f)\,[-\mathrm{int}(-m_k(W,x,y,f)+1/2)].\end{aligned}$$

The *strict majority representativeness of cabinet W* is the probability of the events when the cabinet W represents a strict majority, or the mathematical expectation

$$\begin{aligned}\overline{\mathsf{M}}m_k(W) &= \sum_{\omega\in\Omega} \mathsf{P}(\omega)\,[-\mathrm{int}(-m_k(W,\omega)+1/2)] \\ &= \sum_{(x,y)\in X\times X} \xi(x,y)\,\overline{\mathsf{M}}m_k(W,x,y).\end{aligned}$$

The *strict majority representativeness (of random cabinet with k members)* is defined to be the mathematical expectation

$$\begin{aligned}\overline{\mathsf{M}}m_k &= \sum_{(v_1,\ldots,v_k)\in V^k} \sum_{\omega\in\Omega} \mu(v_1)\ldots\mu(v_k)\,\mathsf{P}(\omega)\,[-\mathrm{int}(-m_k(v_1,\ldots,v_k,\omega)+1/2)] \\ &= \sum_{(v_1,\ldots,v_k)\in V^k} \mu(v_1)\ldots\mu(v_k)\,\overline{\mathsf{M}}m_k(v_1,\ldots,v_k).\end{aligned}$$

If V is uncountable and $\overline{\mathsf{M}}m_k(v_1,\ldots,v_k)$ is a measurable function of $v_1,\ldots,v_k$, then

$$\overline{\mathsf{M}}m_k = \int_{V^k} d\mu(v_1)\ldots d\mu(v_k)\,\overline{\mathsf{M}}m_k(v_1,\ldots,v_k).$$

8.2.5. DEFINITION. A cabinet $W^* = (v_1^*,\ldots,v_k^*) \in V^k$ is called *optimal with respect to the average (majority, strict majority) representativeness,* if it has the greatest average (majority, strict majority) representativeness among the cabinets with the same number of members, i.e. for all $W \in V^k$ it holds

$$\begin{gathered}\mathsf{E}m_k(W^*) \geq \mathsf{E}m_k(W) \\ (\mathsf{M}m_k(W^*) \geq \mathsf{M}m_k(W) \\ \overline{\mathsf{M}}m_k(W^*) \geq \overline{\mathsf{M}}m_k(W)).\end{gathered}$$

Before we go on with the study of properties of cabinets, note that for every cabinet W it holds, similar to (7.2.5),

$$\begin{gathered}\overline{\mathsf{M}}m_k(W,x,y) \leq \mathsf{M}m_k(W,x,y), \\ \overline{\mathsf{M}}m_k(W) \leq \mathsf{M}m_k(W), \\ \overline{\mathsf{M}}m_k \leq \mathsf{M}m_k.\end{gathered}$$

8.2.6. PROPOSITION (The Monotonicy of Representativeness with Respect to the Cabinet Size). *If two cabinets $W', W'' \subset V$ with k' and k'' members, respectively, satisfy the inclusion $W' \subset W''$, then*

$$\begin{gathered}\mathsf{E}m_{k'}(W') \leq \mathsf{E}m_{k''}(W''), \\ \mathsf{M}m_{k'}(W') \leq \mathsf{M}m_{k''}(W''), \\ \overline{\mathsf{M}}m_{k'}(W') \leq \overline{\mathsf{M}}m_{k''}(W'').\end{gathered}$$

PROOF. By definition 8.2.1 for every simple event $\omega \in \Omega$ we have

$$m_{k'}(W', \omega) = \max_{w \in W'} m(w, \omega) \leq \max_{w \in W''} m(w, \omega) = m_{k''}(W'', \omega),$$

which implies the required inequalities.

8.2.7. PROPOSITION (On the Saturation of Cabinet). *If a cabinet W with k members has the weight $\mu(W) \geq 1/2$, then for every cabinet W' with k' members we have*

$$\begin{aligned} \mathsf{E}m_{k'}(W') &\leq \mathsf{E}m_k(W), \\ \mathsf{M}m_{k'}(W') &\leq \mathsf{M}m_k(W), \\ \overline{\mathsf{M}}m_{k'}(W') &\leq \overline{\mathsf{M}}m_k(W). \end{aligned}$$

PROOF. Since $\mu(W) \geq 1/2$, the larger coalition A_ω, or A_ω^c has a non-empty intersection with W for every simple event ω. Therefore, $m_k(W)$ adopts the maximal of two possible values for every simple event ω, whence we obtain the desired inequalities.

To characterize the saturation of cabinets, we introduce the following definition.

8.2.8. DEFINITION. Recall that for every simple event ω by $\mu(L_\omega)$ we denote the weight of a non-strict minority with respect to ω (see section 7.7). The *maximal value of average representativeness* for cabinets is defined to be

$$\mathsf{E}m(V) = \sum_{\omega \in \Omega} \mathsf{P}(\omega)\,(1 - \mu(L_\omega)).$$

The *maximal value of majority representativeness* for cabinets is defined to be 1.

Let us comment on the above definition. If a cabinet consists of all individuals $v \in V$, then it represents a majority for all simple events ω, having the representativeness $1 - \mu(L_\omega)$. Hence, the average representativeness of V is maximal. It explains the designation $\mathsf{E}m(V)$, where the number of individuals is omitted, since our reasons are also applicable to an infinite set of individuals. Similarly, we can define

$$\mathsf{M}m(V) = \sum_{\omega \in \Omega} \mathsf{P}(\omega)\,\mathrm{int}(1 - \mu(L_\omega) + 1/2),$$

and, since $\mu(L_\omega) \leq 1/2$ for all $\omega \in \Omega$, obtain

$$\mathsf{M}m(V) = \sum_{\omega\in\Omega} \mathsf{P}(\omega) = 1.$$

8.2.9. PROPOSITION (A Test for the Saturation of Cabinet). *Let W be a cabinet with k members. Then the following conditions are equivalent:*

1. $\mathsf{E}m_{k'}(W') \leq \mathsf{E}m_k(W)$ *for any cabinet W' of arbitrary size k'.*
2. $\mathsf{M}m_{k'}(W') \leq \mathsf{M}m_k(W)$ *for any cabinet W' of arbitrary size k'.*
3. $\mathsf{E}m_{k+1}(W \cup \{v\}) = \mathsf{E}m_k(W)$ *for any individual $v \in V$.*
4. $\mathsf{M}m_{k+1}(W \cup \{v\}) = \mathsf{M}m_k(W)$ *for any individual $v \in V$.*
5. $\mathsf{E}m_k(W) = \mathsf{E}m(V)$.
6. $\mathsf{M}m_k(W) = 1$.

PROOF. Since implications $6 \Rightarrow 2 \Rightarrow 4$ and $5 \Rightarrow 1 \Rightarrow 3$ are obvious, it is sufficient to prove implications $3 \Rightarrow 6$ and $4 \Rightarrow 5$.

At first let us prove that condition 3 implies condition 6. For our purpose it sufficies to show that for every significant simple event ω there exists $w \in W$ such that $m(w,\omega) \geq 1/2$. Assume the contrary, i.e. that there is a significant simple event ω such that $m(w,\omega) < 1/2$ for all $w \in W$. It means that W is contained in the coalition A_ω, or A^c_ω, which weight is strictly less than $1/2$. Fix v from the opposite coalition with the weight strictly greater than $1/2$. Then

$$m(v,\omega) > 1/2 > m(w,\omega) \tag{8.2.3}$$

for all $w \in W$. Since ω is significant,

$$\begin{aligned} \mathsf{E}m_{k+1}(W \cup \{v\}) &= \sum_{\omega\in\Omega} \mathsf{P}(\omega) \max_{w\in W\cup\{v\}} m(w,\omega) \\ &> \sum_{\omega\in\Omega} \mathsf{P}(\omega) \max_{w\in W} m(w,\omega) \\ &= \mathsf{E}m_k(W), \end{aligned}$$

against condition 3. The obtained contradiction proves that $\mathsf{M}m_k(W) = 1$.

Now let us show that condition 4 implies condition 5. By definition 8.2.8 to prove condition 5 it sufficies to show that for every significant simple event

ω there exists $w \in W$ such that $m(w,\omega) \geq 1/2$. Assume the contrary and, repeating the above proof, obtain (8.2.3) for some significant simple event ω and all $w \in W$. Hence,

$$\begin{aligned} \mathsf{M}m_{k+1}(W \cup \{v\}) &= \sum_{\omega\in\Omega} \mathsf{P}(\omega)\,\mathrm{int}(\max_{w\in W\cup\{v\}} m(w,\omega) + 1/2) \\ &> \sum_{\omega\in\Omega} \mathsf{P}(\omega)\,\mathrm{int}(\max_{w\in W} m(w,\omega) + 1/2) \\ &= \mathsf{M}m_k(W), \end{aligned}$$

against condition 4. The obtained contradiction proves condition 5.

The last two propositions clarify the behaviour of indicators of representativeness of enlarging cabinets. Cabinets can be enlarged in such a way that the indicators of representativeness increase strictly with their size. If no new member can provide the increase in one of the indicators, then any increase in any indicator is impossible. In particular, it means that sufficiently large cabinets are optimal with respect to both indicators of representativeness. We can expect that the consistency of our two definitions of optimal representation arises not abruptly but as a trend, inherent in cabinet's enlargement. We shall revert to this question in section 8.6.

8.3 Representativeness of Optimal and Random Cabinets

In this section we generalize theorems 7.3.1 and 7.3.2 about the existence of dictators-representatives to cabinets with k members. We show that the indicators or representativeness of optimal cabinets tend to their maximal values at a speed of exponent 2^{-k}. Moreover, the same is true not only for optimal but on average for randomly chosen cabinets.

8.3.1. THEOREM (About the Average Representativeness of Optimal and Random Cabinets). *Let the set of alternatives X be finite, the coalition Boolean algebra $\mathcal{A}$ be finite or countable, and also suppose that it is realized on its Stone compactum V. Then, whatever the measures μ on V and P on ω are, the average representativeness $\mathsf{E}m_k$ is defined for every positive integer k, the function $\mathsf{E}m_k(v_1,\ldots,v_k)$ is continuous with respect to $(v_1,\ldots,v_k) \in V^k$, attaining its maximum on V^k at some point $W^* = (v_1^*,\ldots,v_k^*)$, and*

$$\mathsf{E}m_k(W^*) \geq \mathsf{E}m_k \geq 1/2.$$

The precise equality

$$\mathsf{E}m_k(W^*) = \mathsf{E}m_k = 1/2$$

holds if and only if for every significant simple event $\omega = (x, y, f)$ *the coalitions of individuals, preferring and not preferring* x *to* y *under the situation* f*, have equal weights, i.e.* $\mu(A_\omega) = 1/2$*. The saturation of optimal and random cabinets with* k *members is characterized by the inequalities*

$$\mathsf{E}m_k(W^*) \geq \mathsf{E}m_k \geq \mathsf{E}m(V) - 2^{-k}k^k(k+1)^{-k-1} > \mathsf{E}m(V) - 2^{-k}k^{-1}e^{-1}.$$

PROOF. Recall that for every simple event $\omega \in \Omega$ by L_ω we denote the coalition of a non-strict minority (see section 7.7 for the definition). For every $\omega \in \Omega$ denote by L^k_ω the set of $(v_1, \dots, v_k) \in V^k$ such that all $v_i \in L_\omega$. Note that for every fixed $\omega \in \Omega$ by definition 8.2.1 we have

$$m_k(v_1, \dots, v_k, \omega) = \begin{cases} \mu(L_\omega) & \text{if } (v_1, \dots, v_k) \in L^k_\omega, \\ 1 - \mu(L_\omega) & \text{if } (v_1, \dots, v_k) \in V^k \setminus L^k_\omega. \end{cases} \tag{8.3.1}$$

We see that for every fixed ω the function $m_k(v_1, \dots, v_k, \omega)$ is constant on clopen subsets of V^k, consequently, it is continuous. Since the series (8.2.2)

$$\mathsf{E}m_k(W) = \sum_{\omega \in \Omega} \mathsf{P}(\omega)\, m_k(W, \omega),$$

formed of continuous non-negative functions, is majorized on compactum V^k by convergent series (7.3.1), it converges uniformly, and its sum $\mathsf{E}m_k(W)$ is a continuous function on compactum V^k with the maximum

$$\mathsf{E}^* = \mathsf{E}m_k(W^*)$$

at some $W^* \in V^k$.

Since $\mathsf{E}m_k(W)$ is a continuous function on compactum V^k (with countable base $\mathcal{A}^k$, consequently, metrizable), it is integrable (in the case of finite or countable V it is summable with the weights $\mu(v_1) \dots \mu(v_k)$, nevertheless we shall use the sign of integral), and

$$\begin{aligned} \mathsf{E}m_k &= \int_{V^k} d\mu(v_1) \dots d\mu(v_k) \sum_{\omega \in \Omega} \mathsf{P}(\omega)\, m_k(v_1, \dots, v_k, \omega) \\ &= \int_{V^k} d\mu(v_1) \dots d\mu(v_k)\, \mathsf{E}m_k(v_1, \dots, v_k) \\ &\leq \mathsf{E}^* \int_{V^k} d\mu(v_1) \dots d\mu(v_k) \\ &= \mathsf{E}^*. \end{aligned}$$

Since the series of continuous functions under the sign of integral converges uniformly, the order of summation and integration can be reversed, whence

$$\mathsf{E}^* \geq \mathsf{E}m_k = \sum_{\omega\in\Omega} \mathsf{P}(\omega) \int_{V^k} d\mu(v_1)\dots d\mu(v_k)\, m_k(v_1,\dots,v_k,\omega). \tag{8.3.2}$$

Taking into account (8.3.1), we have

$$\begin{aligned}
&\int_{V^k} d\mu(v_1)\dots d\mu(v_k)\, m_k(v_1,\dots,v_k,\omega) = \\
&= \int_{L^k_\omega} d\mu(v_1)\dots d\mu(v_k)\, m_k(v_1,\dots,v_k,\omega) + \\
&\quad + \int_{V^k\setminus L^k_\omega} d\mu(v_1)\dots d\mu(v_k)\, m_k(v_1,\dots,v_k,\omega) \\
&= \mu^{k+1}(L_\omega) + (1-\mu^k(L_\omega))\,(1-\mu(L_\omega)) \qquad (8.3.3)\\
&= 1/2 + 2(1/2 - \mu(L_\omega))\,(1/2-\mu^k(L_\omega)).
\end{aligned}$$

Since $\mu(L_\omega) \leq 1/2$ for every $\omega \in \Omega$, we obtain that the integrals in (8.3.2) are always not less than 1/2, whence we get the first inequality of the theorem.

Further, by definition 8.2.8 and formulas (8.3.2) and (8.3.3) we have

$$\begin{aligned}
\mathsf{E}m(V) - \mathsf{E}m_k &= \sum_{\omega\in\Omega} \mathsf{P}(\omega)\,[1-\mu(L_\omega) - \mu^{k+1}(L_\omega) - (1-\mu^k(L_\omega))\,(1-\mu(L_\omega))] \\
&= \sum_{\omega\in\Omega} \mathsf{P}(\omega)\,\mu^k(L_\omega)\,(1-2\mu(L_\omega)) \qquad (8.3.4)\\
&\leq \max_{0\leq\mu\leq 1/2} \mu^k(1-2\mu).
\end{aligned}$$

Equating to 0 the first derivate of the function $\mu^k(1-2\mu)$, we obtain that its maximum is attained at

$$\mu = \frac{k}{2(k+1)},$$

where the function equals

$$2^{-k}\frac{k^k}{(k+1)^{k+1}} = 2^{-k}k^{-1}(1-\frac{1}{k+1})^{k+1}.$$

Note that the sequence

$$(1-\frac{1}{k+1})^{k+1} \underset{k\to\infty}{\longrightarrow} e^{-1}$$

increases with k. Substituting it to (8.3.4), we get the second inequality of the theorem.

Note that the maximum E^* of $\mathsf{E}m_k(v_1, \ldots, v_k)$ can be attained, when some v_i equal to each other, i.e. the actual size of optimal cabinet is less than k. By proposition 8.2.9 it means that the cabinet is saturated, and no enlargement can heighten its representativeness.

8.3.2. THEOREM (About the Majority Representativeness of Optimal and Random Cabinets). *Let the set of alternatives X be finite, the coalition Boolean algebra $\mathcal{A}$ be finite or countable, and suppose that it is realized on its Stone compactum V. Then, whatever the measures μ on V and P on Ω are, the majority representativeness $\mathsf{M}m_k$ is defined for every positive integer k, the function $\mathsf{M}m_k(v_1, \ldots, v_k)$ is continuous with respect to $(v_1, \ldots, v_k) \in V^k$, attaining its maximum on V^k at some point $W^* = (v_1^*, \ldots, v_k^*)$. The saturation of optimal and random cabinets with k members is characterized by the inequalities*

$$\mathsf{M}m_k(W^*) \geq \mathsf{M}m_k > 1 - 2^{-k}.$$

If for every significant simple event $\omega = (x, y, f)$ the coalitions of individuals, preferring and not preferring x and y under the situation f, have unequal weights, i.e. $\mu(A_\omega) \neq 1/2$, then the same is also valid for the strict majority representativeness.

PROOF. Recall that for every simple event ω by $\overline{L}_\omega$ we denote the coalition of a strict minority (see section 7.7 for the definition). Denote by $\overline{L}_\omega^k$ the set of $(v_1, \ldots, v_k) \in V^k$ such that all $v_i \in \overline{L}_\omega$. Note that for every fixed $\omega \in \Omega$ we have by definition 8.2.1

$$\operatorname{int}(m_k(v_1, \ldots, v_k, \omega) + 1/2) = \begin{cases} 0 & \text{if}(v_1, \ldots, v_k) \in \overline{L}_\omega^k, \\ 1 & \text{if}(v_1, \ldots, v_k) \in V^k \setminus \overline{L}_\omega^k. \end{cases} \tag{8.3.5}$$

We see that for every fixed ω the function $\operatorname{int}(m_k(v_1, \ldots, v_k, \omega) + 1/2)$ is constant on clopen subsets of V^k, consequently, it is continuous. Since the series (8.2.5)

$$\mathsf{M}m_k(W) = \sum_{\omega \in \Omega} \mathsf{P}(\omega) \operatorname{int}(m_k(w, \omega) + 1/2),$$

formed of continuous non-negative functions, is majorized on compactum V^k by convergent series (7.3.1), it converges uniformly, and its sum $\mathsf{M}m_k(W)$ is a continuous function on compactum V^k with the maximum

$$\mathsf{M}^* = \mathsf{M}m_k(W^*)$$

at some $W^* \in V^k$.

Since $\mathsf{M}m_k(W)$ is a continuous functin on compactum V^k (with countable base $\mathcal{A}^k$, consequently, metrizable), it is integrable (in the case of finite or countable V it is summable with the weights $\mu(v_1)\dots\mu(v_k)$, nevertheless we shall use the sign of integral), and

$$\begin{aligned}\mathsf{M}m_k(W) &= \int_{V^k} d\mu(v_1)\dots d\mu(v_k)\sum_{\omega\in\Omega}\mathsf{P}(\omega)\,\mathrm{int}(m_k(v_1,\dots,v_k,\omega)+1/2)\\ &= \int_{V^k} d\mu(v_1)\dots d\mu(v_k)\,\mathsf{M}m(v_1,\dots,v_k)\\ &\le \mathsf{M}^*\int_{V^k} d\mu(v_1)\dots d\mu(v_k)\\ &= \mathsf{M}^*.\end{aligned}$$

Since the series of continuous functions under the sign of integral converges uniformly, the order of summation and integration can be reversed, whence

$$\mathsf{M}^* \ge \mathsf{M}m_k(W) = \sum_{\omega\in\Omega}\mathsf{P}(\omega)\int_{V^k} d\mu(v_1)\dots d\mu(v_k)\,\mathrm{int}(m_k(v_1,\dots,v_k,\omega)+1/2).$$

By virtue of (8.3.5), and taking into account that always $\mu(\overline{L}_\omega) < 1/2$, we have

$$\begin{aligned}\mathsf{M}^* \ge \mathsf{M}m_k(W) &= \sum_{\omega\in\Omega}\mathsf{P}(\omega)\int_{V^k\setminus\overline{L}^k} d\mu(v_1)\dots d\mu(v_k)\\ &= \sum_{\omega\in\Omega}\mathsf{P}(\omega)\,(1-\mu^k(\overline{L}_\omega)) \qquad (8.3.6)\\ &> 1-2^{-k},\end{aligned}$$

as required.

To ascertain the statement of the theorem for the strict majority representativeness, note that if for every significant simple event $\omega = (x, y, f)$ the coalition of individuals, preferring x to y under the situation f, has the weight other than $1/2$, then the majority representativeness coincides with the strict majority representativeness.

Note that a dictator is nothing else but a trivial cabinet with a single member. Therefore, the remark following theorem 7.3.2 relates also to cabinets, and to prove theorem 8.3.2 for the strict majority representativeness we need the condition $\mu(A_\omega) \neq 1/2$ for all significant simple events ω.

At the end of the chapter we shall consider a numerical example, illustrating that the obtained estimations for $\mathsf{E}m_k(W^*)$, $\mathsf{E}m_k$, $\mathsf{M}m_k(W^*)$, and $\mathsf{M}m_k$ cannot be improved even for independent individuals.

8.4 Recurrent Construction of Cabinets

Finding optimal cabinets may require much calculations. To simplify the task, we propose a recurrent procedure to construct representative cabinets (not

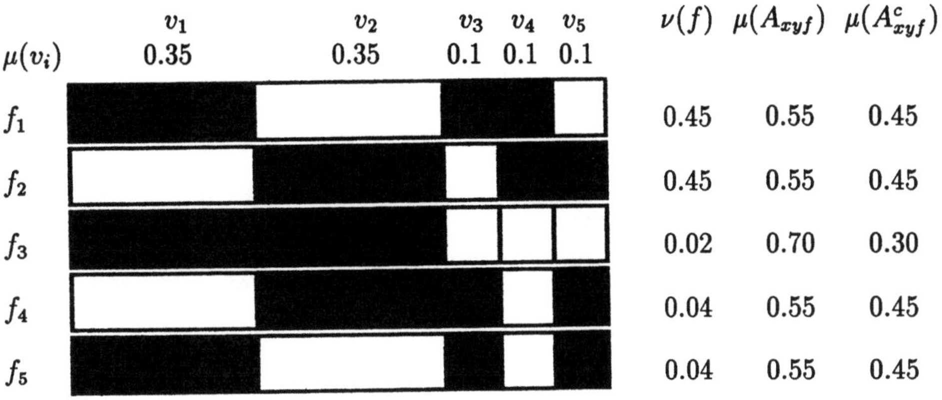

Fig. 62

optimal but satisfying an estimation of representativeness with the same exponent). At the first step the optimal dictator is found out. Next we take another individual, making most representative the resulting cabinet of two members, where the first one is already fixed. Then we adjoin the third member, etc.

First of all let us show that the described procedure doesn't guarantee the optimality of the obtained cabinet.

8.4.1. Example (The Non-Optimality of Recurrent Construction of a Cabinet). Consider a set V of 5 individuals, where $V = \{v_1, \ldots, v_5\}$;

$$\mu(v_1) = \mu(v_2) = 0.35,$$
$$\mu(v_3) = \mu(v_4) = \mu(v_5) = 0.1.$$

Let the only pair of alternatives be significant, i.e. put $\xi(x, y) = 1$ for some $x, y \in X, x \neq y$. By P denote the preference $\{(x, y)\}$. Suppose that the following 5 situations are possible:

$$f_1(v_1) = P,\ f_1(v_2) = \emptyset,\ f_1(v_3) = P,\ f_1(v_4) = P,\ f_1(v_5) = \emptyset,\ \nu(f_1) = 0.45;$$
$$f_2(v_1) = \emptyset,\ f_2(v_2) = P,\ f_2(v_3) = \emptyset,\ f_2(v_4) = P,\ f_2(v_5) = P,\ \nu(f_2) = 0.45;$$
$$f_3(v_1) = P,\ f_3(v_2) = P,\ f_3(v_3) = \emptyset,\ f_3(v_4) = \emptyset,\ f_3(v_5) = \emptyset,\ \nu(f_3) = 0.02;$$
$$f_4(v_1) = \emptyset,\ f_4(v_2) = P,\ f_4(v_3) = P,\ f_4(v_4) = \emptyset,\ f_4(v_5) = P,\ \nu(f_4) = 0.04;$$
$$f_5(v_1) = P,\ f_5(v_2) = \emptyset,\ f_5(v_3) = P,\ f_5(v_4) = \emptyset,\ f_5(v_5) = P,\ \nu(f_5) = 0.04.$$

Situations f_1–f_5 are shown conventionally in fig. 62, where the individuals are designated by rectangulars proportional to their weights. The black rectangulars are the individuals with the preference P; the white rectangulars are associated with the indifferent individuals. It is easy to see that the non-indifferent individuals form a majority in every situation. By definition of average representativeness

$$\begin{aligned}\mathsf{E}m(v_1) &= \\ &= \sum_{i=1}^{5} \nu(f_i)\, m(v_1, x, y, f_i) \\ &= 0.45 \times 0.55 + 0.45 \times 0.45 + 0.02 \times 0.7 + 0.04 \times 0.45 + 0.04 \times 0.55 \\ &= 0.504.\end{aligned}$$

Similarly,

$$\mathsf{E}m(v_2) = 0.504, \quad \mathsf{E}m(v_3) = 0.5, \quad \mathsf{E}m(v_4) = 0.537, \quad \mathsf{E}m(v_5) = 0.5.$$

Now let us consider various cabinets with two members, one of whom is individual v_4. By definition of average representativeness of a cabinet,

$$\begin{aligned}\mathsf{E}m_2(v_4, v_1) &= \\ &= \sum_{i=1}^{5} \nu(f_i) \max\{m(v_4, x, y, f_i), m(v_1, x, y, f_i)\} \\ &= 0.45 \times 0.55 + 0.45 \times 0.55 + 0.02 \times 0.7 + 0.04 \times 0.45 + 0.04 \times 0.55 \\ &= 0.549.\end{aligned}$$

Similarly,

$$\mathsf{E}m_2(v_4, v_2) = 0.549, \quad \mathsf{E}m_2(v_4, v_3) = 0.545, \quad \mathsf{E}m_2(v_4, v_5) = 0.545.$$

However,

$$\mathsf{E}m_2(v_1, v_5) = \mathsf{E}m_2(v_2, v_3) = 0.553,$$

whence no cabinet of two members, one of whom is individual v_4, is optimal with respect to the average representativeness.

The same is also valid for the majority representativeness. It is easy to ascertain that

$$\mathsf{M}m(v_1) = \mathsf{M}m(v_2) = 0.51, \quad \mathsf{M}m(v_3) = \mathsf{M}m(v_5) = 0.53, \quad \mathsf{M}m(v_4) = 0.9.$$

Hence, v_4 is the dictator optimal with respect to the majority representativeness. For the cabinets with two members, one of whom is v_4, we obtain

$$\mathsf{M}m_2(v_4, v_1) = \mathsf{M}m_2(v_4, v_2) = 0.96, \quad \mathsf{M}m_2(v_4, v_3) = \mathsf{M}m_2(v_4, v_5) = 0.98.$$

However,

$$\mathsf{M}m_2(v_1, v_5) = \mathsf{M}m_2(v_2, v_3) = 1,$$

whence no cabinet of two members, one of whom is v_4, is optimal with respect to the majority representativeness.

Thus we have proved that in general optimal cabinets, even with two members, cannot be constructed recurrently. Nevertheless, the discussed procedure gives satisfactory results. Before we formulate the main theorem of the section, we introduce a concept of conditional representativeness.

8.4.2. DEFINITION. The *conditional average representativeness of individual* v with respect to subset $U \subset \Omega$ of positive measure $\mathsf{P}(U) > 0$ is the conditional mathematical expectation

$$\mathsf{E}m(v \mid U) = \frac{\sum_{\omega \in U} \mathsf{P}(\omega)\, m(v, \omega)}{\mathsf{P}(U)}.$$

The *conditional majority representativeness of individual* v with respect to subset $U \subset \Omega$ of positive measure $\mathsf{P}(U) > 0$ is the conditional mathematical expectation

$$\mathsf{M}m(v \mid U) = \frac{\sum_{\omega \in U} \mathsf{P}(\omega)\, \mathrm{int}(m(v, \omega) + 1/2)}{\mathsf{P}(U)}.$$

Note that theorems 7.3.1 and 7.3.2 are valid for the conditional representativeness, i.e. for every subset $U \subset \Omega$ of positive measure $\mathsf{P}(U) > 0$ there exist individuals $v', v'' \in V$ such that

$$\mathsf{E}m(v' \mid U) \geq 1/2,$$
$$\mathsf{M}m(v'' \mid U) > 1/2.$$

8.4.3. THEOREM (About the Recurrent Construction of Cabinets). *Consider the following inductive construction of a cabinet* $W^k = \{v_1, \ldots, v_k\}$ *with* k *members.*

1^0. *Let* v_1 *be the optimal dictator with respect to the average representativeness, and let* U_1 *be the set of simple events when the cabinet* $W^1 = \{v_1\}$ *represents a strict minority, i.e.*

$$U_1 = \{\omega : \omega \in \Omega,\ m_1(W^1, \omega) < 1/2\}.$$

2⁰. *Suppose that we have already defined the members of cabinet* $W^k = \{v_1, \ldots, v_k\}$, *and the set of simple events, when the cabinet* W^k *represents a strict minority, i.e.*

$$U_k = \{\omega : \omega \in \Omega, m_k(W^k, \omega) < 1/2\}.$$

If $\mathsf{P}(U_k) > 0$, *we choose the* $(k+1)$*st cabinet member* v_{k+1} *who is the optimal dictator with respect to the conditional average representativeness with respect to* U_k, *which is equivalent to that*

$$\mathsf{E}m_{k+1}(v_1, \ldots, v_k, v_{k+1}) \geq \mathsf{E}m_{k+1}(v_1, \ldots, v_k, v)$$

for all $v \in V$. *If* $\mathsf{P}(U_k) = 0$, *we cease the construction (in this case, obviously,* $\mathsf{E}m_k(W^k) = \mathsf{E}m(V)$).

Then for the cabinet W^k *constructed by means of the described procedure we have*

$$\mathsf{E}m_k \geq \mathsf{E}m(V) - 2^{-k-2}.$$

For the cabinet W^k *constructed similarly, but with the reference to the majority representativeness,*

$$\mathsf{M}m_k(W^k) > 1 - 2^{-k}.$$

PROOF. We prove the theorem by induction on k.

1⁰. By theorem 8.3.1

$$\mathsf{E}m_1(W^1) \geq \mathsf{E}m(V) - 2^{-3}. \tag{8.4.1}$$

2⁰. Suppose that

$$\mathsf{E}m_k(W^k) \geq \mathsf{E}m(V) - 2^{-k-2}. \tag{8.4.2}$$

We are going to show that $\mathsf{E}m_{k+1}(W^{k+1}) \geq \mathsf{E}m(V) - 2^{-k-3}$. By our construction

$$\begin{aligned}
\mathsf{E}m_{k+1}(W^{k+1}) &= \sum_{\omega\in\Omega} \mathsf{P}(\omega)\, m_{k+1}(W^{k+1}, \omega) \\
&= \sum_{\omega\in\Omega\setminus U_k} \mathsf{P}(\omega)\, m_{k+1}(W^{k+1}, \omega) + \\
&\quad + \sum_{\omega\in U_k} \mathsf{P}(\omega)\, m_{k+1}(W^{k+1}, \omega) \\
&= \sum_{\omega\in\Omega\setminus U_k} \mathsf{P}(\omega)\, m_k(W^k, \omega) + \sum_{\omega\in U_k} \mathsf{P}(\omega)\, m(v_{k+1}, \omega)
\end{aligned}$$

$$\begin{aligned}
&= \sum_{\omega \in \Omega \setminus U_k} \mathsf{P}(\omega)\, m_k(W^k, \omega) + \sum_{\omega \in U_k} \mathsf{P}(\omega)\, m_k(W^k, \omega) - \\
&\quad - \sum_{\omega \in U_k} \mathsf{P}(\omega)\, m_k(W^k, \omega) + \sum_{\omega \in U_k} \mathsf{P}(\omega)\, m(v_{k+1}, \omega) \\
&= \mathsf{E}m_k(W^k) - \sum_{\omega \in U_k} \mathsf{P}(\omega)\, \mu(L_\omega) + \mathsf{E}m(v_{k+1} \mid U_k)\, \mathsf{P}(U_k).
\end{aligned}$$

By the remark before the theorem

$$\mathsf{E}m(v_{k+1} \mid U_k) \geq 1/2,$$

and, taking into account that

$$\mathsf{P}(U_k) = \sum_{\omega \in U_k} \mathsf{P}(\omega),$$

we obtain

$$\begin{aligned}
\mathsf{E}m_{k+1}(W^{k+1}) &\geq \mathsf{E}m_k(W^k) + \sum_{\omega \in U_k} \mathsf{P}(\omega)\, (1/2 - \mu(L_\omega)) \\
&= \mathsf{E}m_k(W^k) + 2^{-1} \sum_{\omega \in U_k} \mathsf{P}(\omega)\, (1 - 2\mu(L_\omega)). \qquad (8.4.3)
\end{aligned}$$

Since by our construction

$$\mathsf{E}m_k(W^k) = \sum_{\omega \in \Omega \setminus U_k} \mathsf{P}(\omega)\, (1 - \mu(L_\omega)) + \sum_{\omega \in U_k} \mathsf{P}(\omega)\, \mu(L_\omega)$$

and by definition 8.2.8

$$\mathsf{E}m(V) = \sum_{\omega \in \Omega \setminus U_k} \mathsf{P}(\omega)\, (1 - \mu(L_\omega)) + \sum_{\omega \in U_k} \mathsf{P}(\omega)\, (1 - \mu(L_\omega),$$

we have

$$\mathsf{E}m(V) - \mathsf{E}m_k(W^k) = \sum_{\omega \in U_k} \mathsf{P}(\omega)\, (1 - 2\mu(L_\omega)).$$

Substituting it into (8.4.3), and taking into account (8.4.2), we obtain

$$\begin{aligned}
\mathsf{E}m_{k+1}(W^{k+1}) &\geq \mathsf{E}m_k(W^k) + 2^{-1}(\mathsf{E}m(V) - \mathsf{E}m_k(W^k)) \\
&= 2^{-1}\mathsf{E}m(V) + 2^{-1}\mathsf{E}m_k(W^k) \\
&\geq 2^{-1}(\mathsf{E}m(V) + 2^{-1}(\mathsf{E}m(V) - 2^{-k-2}) \\
&= \mathsf{E}m(V) - 2^{-k-3},
\end{aligned}$$

as required.

Now suppose that the cabinet W^k is constructed similarly, but with the reference to the majority representativeness. Prove the second statement of the theorem also by induction on k.

1^0. By theorem 7.3.2

$$\mathsf{M}m_1(W^1) > 1 - 2^{-1}.$$

2^0. Suppose that

$$\mathsf{M}m_k(W^k) > 1 - 2^{-k}. \tag{8.4.4}$$

We are going to show that $\mathsf{M}m_{k+1}(W^{k+1}) > 1 - 2^{-k-1}$. By our construction and by definition of majority representativeness

$$\begin{aligned}
\mathsf{M}m_{k+1}(W^{k+1}) &= \mathsf{P}(\Omega \setminus U_{k+1}) \\
&= \mathsf{P}(\Omega \setminus U_k) + \mathsf{P}(U_k \setminus U_{k+1}) \\
&= \mathsf{M}m_k(W^k) + \mathsf{M}m(v_{k+1} \mid U_k)\,\mathsf{P}(U_k).
\end{aligned}$$

By the remark before the theorem

$$\mathsf{M}m(v_{k+1} \mid U_k) > 2^{-1},$$

and taking into account that

$$\mathsf{P}(U_k) = 1 - \mathsf{P}(\Omega \setminus U_k) = 1 - \mathsf{M}m_k(W^k),$$

we obtain, referring to (8.4.4),

$$\begin{aligned}
\mathsf{M}m_{k+1}(W^{k+1}) &> \mathsf{M}m_k(W^k) + 2^{-1}(1 - \mathsf{M}m_k(W^k)) \\
&= 2^{-1} + 2^{-1}\mathsf{M}m_k(W^k) \\
&> 2^{-1} + 2^{-1}(1 - 2^{-k}) \\
&= 1 - 2^{-k-1},
\end{aligned}$$

as required.

Thus we have shown that by the described recurrent procedure one can construct representative cabinets. Note that the steps of our construction can be traced on example 8.4.1.

8.5 Representativeness of Cabinets for Independent Individuals

In the present section we study the model with independent individuals (see section 7.5 for the definitions). We extend the results, obtained for single individuals to cabinets.

Denote the probabilities that all members of cabinet W prefer x to y, and don't prefer x to y, respectively, by

$$\begin{aligned} p_{xy}(W) &= \prod_{v \in W} p_{xy}(v), \\ q_{xy}(W) &= \prod_{v \in W} (1 - p_{xy}(v)). \end{aligned}$$

Note that in general

$$q_{xy}(W) \neq 1 - p_{xy}(W).$$

For further purposes define the *simplified sign vector*

$$\boldsymbol{ss} = \{ss_{xy}\},$$

for every pair of alternatives (x, y) putting

$$ss_{xy} = \begin{cases} -1 & \text{if } c_{xy} < 0, \\ 1 & \text{if } c_{xy} \geq 0. \end{cases}$$

For cabinet W define the vector

$$\boldsymbol{r}(W) = \{r_{xy}(W)\},$$

for every pair of alternatives (x, y) putting

$$r_{xy}(W) = \begin{cases} p_{xy}(W) & \text{if } p_{xy} < 1/2 \quad (c_{xy} < 0), \\ p_{xy}(W)/2 + q_{xy}(W)/2 & \text{if } p_{xy} = 1/2 \quad (c_{xy} = 0), \\ q_{xy}(W) & \text{if } p_{xy} > 1/2 \quad (c_{xy} > 0), \end{cases}$$

and the *characteristic vector*

$$\boldsymbol{c}(W) = \{c_{xy}(W)\},$$

for every pair of alternatives (x, y) putting

$$\begin{aligned} c_{xy}(W) &= ss_{xy}/2 - ss_{xy} r_{xy}(W) \\ &= \begin{cases} p_{xy}(W) - 1/2 & \text{if } p_{xy} < 1/2 \quad (c_{xy} < 0), \\ 1/2 - p_{xy}(W)/2 - q_{xy}(W)/2 & \text{if } p_{xy} = 1/2 \quad (c_{xy} = 0), \\ 1/2 - q_{xy}(W) & \text{if } p_{xy} > 1/2 \quad (c_{xy} > 0). \end{cases} \end{aligned}$$

Note that for a cabinet W with a single member v we have

$$q_{xy}(W) = 1 - p_{xy}(W),$$

whence

$$c_{xy}(W) = \begin{cases} p_{xy}(v) - 1/2 & \text{if } p_{xy} < 1/2, \\ 0 & \text{if } p_{xy} = 1/2, \\ p_{xy}(v) - 1/2 & \text{if } p_{xy} > 1/2, \end{cases}$$

i.e. the characteristic vector coincides with the earlier defined for individuals.

8.5.1. THEOREM (About the Average Representativeness of Cabinets for Independent Individuals). *Let the set of alternatives be finite. Consider a sequence of models with increasing number n of independent individuals. Then for all cabinets $W \subset V$ with k members and sufficientsly large n we have*

$$\begin{aligned} \mathsf{E}m_k(W) &\approx 1/2 + 2 \sum_{(x,y)\in X\times X} \xi(x,y)\, c_{xy}\, c_{xy}(W) \\ &= 1/2 + \sum_{(x,y)\in X\times X} \xi(x,y)\, c_{xy}\, [\mid c_{xy} \mid -2 \mid c_{xy} \mid r_{xy}(W)], \\ \mathsf{E}m_k &\approx 1/2 + \sum_{(x,y)\in X\times X} \xi(x,y)\, c_{xy}\, [\mid c_{xy} \mid -2 \mid c_{xy} \mid (1/2 - \mid c_{xy} \mid)^k], \end{aligned}$$

where the accuracy of approximation increases with n regardless of the choice of cabinet W in the first formula.

PROOF. For every simple event $\omega = (x, y, f)$ denote the members of cabinet W, preferring x to y under the situation f, by

$$W_\omega = W_{xyf} = \{v : v \in W,\ (x,y) \in f(v)\}. \tag{8.5.1}$$

Fix a pair of alternatives (x, y) and let $f \in F$ be random. To evaluate the mathematical expectation $\mathsf{E}m_k(W, x, y)$ we must take into account three possibilities:

(a) If all the cabinet members prefer x to y (with probability $p_{xy}(W)$), then the cabinet W represents itself and other individuals, preferring x to y (the coalition $W \cup B_{W_{xyf}}$ in the designations of lemma 7.6.3);

(b) if all the cabinet members don't prefer x to y (with probability $q_{xy}(W)$), then the cabinet W represents itself and other individuals, not preferring x to y (the coalition $V \setminus B_{W_{xyf}}$);

(c) if there are both cabinet members, preferring and not preferring x to y, then cabinet W represents the maximal coalition A_{xyf}, or A^c_{xyf}.

Since individuals are independent, we have

$$\begin{aligned}\mathsf{E}m_k(W,x,y) &= p_{xy}(W)\,[\mu(W)+\mathsf{E}\mu(B_{W_{xy}})] + q_{xy}(W)\,\mathsf{E}\mu(V\setminus B_{W_{xyf}}) + \\ &+ \sum_{0<t<\mu(W)} \nu\{f: f\in F,\ \mu(W_{xyf})=t\}\times \\ &\times \mathsf{E}\max\{t+\mu(B_{W_{xy}}), 1-t-\mu(B_{W_{xy}})\}. \qquad (8.5.2)\end{aligned}$$

By definition 7.5.5 $\mu(W) \underset{n\to\infty}{\rightrightarrows} 0$, and by lemma 7.6.3 the mathematical expectation and the dispersion of $\mu(B_{W_{xy}})$ tend with increase of n to p_{xy} and 0, respectively. By Chebyshev inequality we obtain that for a given $\epsilon > 0$ for all sufficiently large n for all $t \in [0;\mu(W)]$ the random variables $t+\mu(B_{W_{xy}})$ are almost completely concentrated within the ϵ-neighborhood of p_{xy}. Thus

$$\begin{aligned}\mu(W)+\mathsf{E}\mu(B_{W_{xy}}) &\underset{n\to\infty}{\rightrightarrows} p_{xy}, \\ \mu(W)+\mathsf{E}\mu(V\setminus B_{W_{xy}}) &\underset{n\to\infty}{\rightrightarrows} 1-p_{xy}, \\ \mathsf{E}\max\{t+\mu(B_{W_{xy}}), 1-t-\mu(B_{W_{xy}})\} &\underset{n\to\infty}{\rightrightarrows} \max\{p_{xy}, 1-p_{xy}\}\end{aligned}$$

uniformly with respect to all $t \in [0;\mu(W)]$. Since, obviously,

$$\sum_{0<t<\mu(W)} \nu\{f: f\in F,\ \mu(W_{xyf})=t\} = 1-p_{xy}(W)-q_{xy}(W),$$

we obtain from (8.5.2)

$$\begin{aligned}\mathsf{E}m_k(W,x,y) &\approx p_{xy}(W)\,p_{xy} + q_{xy}(W)\,(1-p_{xy}) \\ &\quad +(1-p_{xy}(W)-q_{xy}(W))\max\{p_{xy}, 1-p_{xy}\}.\end{aligned}$$

If $p_{xy} \le 1/2$, then

$$\max\{p_{xy}, 1-p_{xy}\} = 1-p_{xy},$$

whence

$$\begin{aligned}\mathsf{E}m_k(W,x,y) &\approx 2p_{xy}(W)\,p_{xy} - p_{xy}(W) - p_{xy} + 1 \\ &= 1/2 + 2(p_{xy}-1/2)\,(p_{xy}(W)-1/2) \\ &= 1/2 + 2c_{xy}\,c_{xy}(W).\end{aligned}$$

If $p_{xy} > 1/2$, then

$$\max\{p_{xy}, 1-p_{xy}\} = p_{xy},$$

whence

$$\begin{aligned}\mathsf{E}m_k(W,x,y) &\approx -2q_{xy}(W)\,p_{xy} + q_{xy}(W) + p_{xy} \\ &= 1/2 + 2(p_{xy}-1/2)\,(1/2-q_{xy}(W)) \\ &= 1/2 + 2c_{xy}\,c_{xy}(W).\end{aligned}$$

If $p_{xy} = 1/2$, then

$$\max\{p_{xy}, 1 - p_{xy}\} = 1/2,$$

whence

$$\mathsf{E}m_k(W, x, y) \approx 1/2 = 1/2 + 2c_{xy}c_{xy}(W).$$

Note that by definition of $c_{xy}(W)$ we have

$$2c_{xy}c_{xy}(W) = 2c_{xy}(ss_{xy}/2 - ss_{xy}r_{xy}(W)) = \mid c_{xy} \mid -2 \mid c_{xy} \mid r_{xy}(W).$$

Since the number of alternatives is finite, by virtue of the finitness of the sum in (8.2.1) we obtain the first of the desired approximations.

By (8.3.2) and (8.3.3)

$$\mathsf{E}m_k = \sum_{(x,y)\in X\times X} \xi(x,y) \sum_{f\in F} \nu(f) \, [1/2 + 2(1/2 - \mu(L_{xyf})) \, (1/2 - \mu^k(L_{xyf}))]. \tag{8.5.3}$$

By lemma 7.7.1 for all $k' \leq k+1$ we have

$$\sum_{f\in F} \nu(f) \, \mu^{k'}(L_{xyf}) = \mathsf{E}\mu^{k'}(L_{xy}) \underset{n\to\infty}{\rightrightarrows} (1/2 - \mid c_{xy} \mid)^{k'}. \tag{8.5.4}$$

Hence, since the number of alternatives is finite,

$$\begin{aligned} \mathsf{E}m_k \underset{n\to\infty}{\rightrightarrows} & \sum_{(x,y)\in X\times X} \xi(x,y) \, [1/2 + 2 \mid c_{xy} \mid (1/2 - (1/2 - \mid c_{xy} \mid)^k)] \\ &= 1/2 + \sum_{(x,y)\in X\times X} \xi(x,y) \, [\mid c_{xy} \mid -2 \mid c_{xy} \mid (1/2 - \mid c_{xy} \mid)^k], \end{aligned}$$

as required.

8.5.2. PROPOSITION. *Let the set of alternatives be finite. Consider a sequence of models with increasing number n of independent individuals. Suppose that $p_{xy} \neq 1/2$ for all significant pairs of alternatives (x, y). Then for all cabinets $W \subset V(n)$ with k members and sufficiently large n we have*

$$\begin{aligned} \mathsf{M}m_k(W) \approx \overline{\mathsf{M}}m_k(W) &\approx 1/2 + \sum_{(x,y)\in X\times X} \xi(x,y) \, ss_{xy} \, c_{xy}(W) \\ &= 1 - \sum_{(x,y)\in X\times X} \xi(x,y) \, r_{xy}(W), \\ \mathsf{M}m_k \approx \overline{\mathsf{M}}m_k &\approx 1 - \sum_{(x,y)\in X\times X} \xi(x,y) \, (1/2 - \mid c_{xy} \mid)^k, \end{aligned}$$

where the accuracy of approximation increases with n regardless of the choice of cabinet W in the first formula.

PROOF. Fix a significant pair of alternatives (x, y) and a cabinet W with k members. To evaluate its majority representativeness for the given pair of alternatives, we must take into account three possibilities:

(a) If all the cabinet members prefer x to y, then it represents a majority only when other individuals, preferring x to y, have the total weight not less than $1/2 - \mu(W)$;

(b) if no cabinet member prefers x to y, then the cabinet represents a majority only when other individuals, preferring x to y, have the total weight not greater than $1/2$;

(c) if there are both cabinet members, preferring and not preferring x to y, then the cabinet W always represents a majority.

Since individuals are independent, we have, applying lemma 7.7.2,

$$\begin{aligned}\mathsf{M}m_k(W,x,y) &= \nu\{f : f \in F,\ m_k(W,x,y,f) \geq 1/2\}\\ &= p_{xy}(W)\,\nu\{f : f \in F,\ \mu(B_{Wxyf}) \geq 1/2 - \mu(W)\} +\\ &\quad + q_{xy}(W)\,\nu\{f : f \in F,\ \mu(B_{Wxyf}) \leq 1/2\} +\\ &\quad + 1 - p_{xy}(W) - q_{xy}(W) \qquad (8.5.5)\\ &\approx p_{xy}(W)\,\delta_{xy} + q_{xy}(W)\,(1-\delta_{xy}) + 1 - p_{xy}(W) - q_{xy}(W)\\ &= 1 - p_{xy}(W)\,(1-\delta_{xy}) - q_{xy}(W)\,\delta_{xy}. \qquad (8.5.6)\end{aligned}$$

If $p_{xy} < 1/2$, then $\delta_{xy} = 0$, whence

$$\mathsf{M}m_k(W,x,y) \approx 1 - p_{xy}(W) = 1 - r_{xy}(W) = 1/2 + ss_{xy}\,c_{xy}(W).$$

If $p_{xy} > 1/2$, then $\delta_{xy} = 1$, whence

$$\mathsf{M}m_k(W,x,y) \approx 1 - q_{xy}(W) = 1 - r_{xy}(W) = 1/2 + ss_{xy}\,c_{xy}(W).$$

Since the number of alternatives is finite, by virtue of the finitness of sum (8.2.2) we obtain the first of required approximations for the majority representativeness. To prove it for the strict majority representativeness, substitute strict inequalitities for the non-strict ones in (8.5.5) and note that we must not account the situations when V is divided into equal coalitions. Therefore, for fixed (x, y) we have

$$\begin{aligned}&\overline{\mathsf{M}}m_k(W,x,y) =\\ &= p_{xy}(W)\,\nu\{f : f \in F,\ \mu(B_{Wxyf}) > 1/2 - \mu(W)\} +\\ &\quad + q_{xy}(W)\,\nu\{f : f \in F,\ \mu(B_{Wxyf}) < 1/2\} +\\ &\quad + \sum_{0<t<\mu(W)} \nu\{f : f \in F,\ \mu(W_{xyf}) = t\}\,\nu\{f : f \in F,\ \mu(B_{Wxyf}) \neq 1/2 - t\}.\end{aligned} \qquad (8.5.7)$$

Since W consists of k members, the summation index t in the above sum can adopt only finite number of values. Since

$$\begin{aligned}\nu\{f : f \in F,\ m_k(B_{Wxyf}) \neq 1/2 - t\} &= \nu\{f : f \in F,\ \mu(B_{Wxyf}) < 1/2 - t\} + \\ &+\nu\{f : f \in F,\ \mu(B_{Wxyf}) > 1/2 - t\}\end{aligned}$$

and

$$\sum_{0<t<\mu(W)} \nu\{f : f \in F,\ \mu(W_{xyf}) = t\} = 1 - p_{xy}(W) - q_{xy}(W),$$

by virtue of lemma 7.7.2 we come to the same approximation (8.5.6), as required.

Applying lemma 7.7.2 to (8.3.8), we obtain

$$\begin{aligned}\mathsf{M}m_k &= \sum_{(x,y)\in X\times X} \xi(x,y) \sum_{f\in F} \nu(f)\,(1 - \mu^k(\overline{L}_{xyf})) \\ &= 1 - \sum_{(x,y)\in X\times X} \xi(x,y)\,\mathsf{E}\mu^k(\overline{L}_{xy}) \\ &\approx 1 - \sum_{(x,y)\in X\times X} \xi(x,y)\,(1/2 - |\, c_{xy}\,|)^k.\end{aligned}$$

Finally, adapt (8.3.6) for the strict majority representativeness

$$\begin{aligned}\overline{\mathsf{M}}m_k &= \sum_{(x,y)\in X\times X} \xi(x,y) \sum_{f\in F} \nu(f)\,(1 - \mu^k(\overline{M}^c_{xyf})) \\ &= 1 - \sum_{(x,y)\in X\times X} \xi(x,y)\,\mathsf{E}\mu^k(\overline{M}^c_{xy}).\end{aligned}$$

By virtue of lemma 7.7.2 we obtain

$$\overline{\mathsf{M}}m_k \approx 1 - \sum_{(x,y)\in X\times X} \xi(x,y)\,(1/2 - |\, c_{xy}\,|)^k,$$

as required.

8.5.3. THEOREM (About the Majority Representativeness of Cabinets for Independent Individuals). *Let the set of alternatives be finite. Consider a sequence of models with increasing number n of independent individuals of comparable weight, i.e. $\mu(v) \sim O(n^{-1})$ for all $v \in V(n)$. Suppose that for every significant pair of alternatives (x,y) such that $p_{xy} = 1/2$ there exist coalitions of positive weight, consisting of the individuals whose probabilities $p_{xy}(v)$ are neither too small, nor too high, i.e.*

$$\mu\{v : v \in V(n),\ \epsilon(n) \leq p_{xy}(v) \leq 1 - \epsilon(n)\} \geq \theta > 0,$$

where $0 < \epsilon(n) \sim O(n^{1+\epsilon})$ *for some* $\epsilon > 0$. *Then for all cabinets* $W \subset V(n)$ *with* k *members and sufficiently large* n *we have*

$$\begin{aligned} \mathsf{M}m_k(W) \approx \overline{\mathsf{M}}m_k(W) &\approx 1/2 + \sum_{(x,y)\in X\times X} \xi(x,y)\, ss_{xy}\, c_{xy}(W) \\ &= 1 - \sum_{(x,y)\in X\times X} \xi(x,y)\, r_{xy}(W), \\ \mathsf{M}m_k \approx \overline{\mathsf{M}}m_k &\approx 1 - \sum_{(x,y)\in X\times X} \xi(x,y)\,(1/2- \mid c_{xy} \mid)^k, \end{aligned}$$

where the accuracy of approximation increases with n *regardless of the choice of cabinet* W *in the first formula.*

PROOF. Since $ss_{xy} = s_{xy}$ when $p_{xy} \neq 1/2$, by virtue of the previous proposition it sufficies to consider the significant pairs of alternatives (x, y) such that $p_{xy} = 1/2$. For these pairs the required approximations are obtained as in the above proof, but with the reference to lemma 7.7.3 instead of lemma 7.7.2.

Since the dictator is a trivial cabinet of a single member, all examples of sections 7.6–7.7, substantiating the assumptions of the theorems, are applicable to our consideration as well. Also note the validity of the geometric interpretation described in section 7.8. Cabinets with their characteristic vectors are opposed to the same "collective" vectors and meet the same optimization principles, as single dictators. Indeed, according to the results of the present section,

$$\begin{aligned} \mathsf{E}m_k(W) &\approx 1/2 + 2\langle \boldsymbol{\Xi c}, \boldsymbol{c}(W)\rangle, \\ \mathsf{M}m_k(W) &\approx \overline{\mathsf{M}}m_k(W) \approx 1/2 + \langle \boldsymbol{\Xi ss}, \boldsymbol{c}(W)\rangle. \end{aligned}$$

Since $\boldsymbol{c}(W) = \boldsymbol{c}(v)$ for a cabinet with a single member $W = \{v\}$, the only difference with (7.8.2) is the use of vector $\boldsymbol{ss}$ instead of $\boldsymbol{s}$. Recall that by (7.5.2) if $c_{xy} = 0$, then $c_{xy}(v) = 0$, therefore, we can substitute $\boldsymbol{ss}$ for $\boldsymbol{s}$ in (7.8.2). To justify the use of vector $\boldsymbol{s}$ in (7.8.2), we mention theorem 7.8.1 formulated in terms of collinearity of vectors $\boldsymbol{c}$ and $\boldsymbol{s}$.

8.6 Consistency of Two Definitions of Optimal Cabinets

In section 8.2 we have proved that average and majority representativeness of cabinets attain their maxima simultaneously with the increase in the cabinet size. Therefore, if a sufficiently large cabinet is optimal with respect to one indicator of representativeness, then it is almost optimal with respect to another. In the present section we show that this phenomenon is observed even for relatively small cabinets. Recall that for single dictators it is true only for one-dimensional space of preference probability vectors $\{p_{xy}(v)\}$, i.e. when only one pair of alternatives is significant (proposition 7.8.2). The consideration of cabinets, in other words, the increase in the dimension of the space of representatives, allows us to extend this result to the multidimensional space of preference probability vectors.

8.6.1. THEOREM (About the Consistency of the Two Definitions of Optimal Cabinets). *Let the set of alternatives be finite. Consider a sequence of models with increasing number n of independent individuals. Assume that $p_{xy} \neq 1/2$ for all significant pairs of alternatives (x,y). Let $W^*, W^{**} \subset V(n)$ be cabinets with k members, optimal with respect to average and majority representativeness, respectively. Then*

$$\begin{aligned} | \mathsf{E}m_k(W^*) - \mathsf{E}m_k(W^{**}) | &\leq 2\overline{C} \sum_{(x,y)\in X\times X} \xi(x,y)\,(1/2- | c_{xy} |)^k + \epsilon(n) \\ &< 2^{-k+1}\overline{C} + \epsilon(n), \\ | \mathsf{M}m_k(W^*) - \mathsf{M}m_k(W^{**}) | &\leq \frac{1}{\underline{C}} \sum_{(x,y)\in X\times X} \xi(x,y) \mid c_{xy} \mid (1/2- | c_{xy} |)^k + \epsilon(n) \\ &\leq 2^{-k-1}k^{-1}e^{-1}\underline{C}^{-1} + \epsilon(n), \end{aligned}$$

where

$$\overline{C} = \max_{(x,y)\in X\times X:\xi(x,y)>0} | c_{xy} |,$$
$$\underline{C} = \min_{(x,y)\in X\times X:\xi(x,y)>0} | c_{xy} |,$$

and $\epsilon(n) \underset{n\to\infty}{\longrightarrow} 0$ has the same exponent, as the accuracy of the approximation in theorem 8.5.1 *and proposition* 8.5.2.

PROOF. Note that equalities and inequalities in the following proof are used conventionally, within the accuracy of approximation provided by theorem 8.5.1 and proposition 8.5.2.

By proposition 8.5.2, and taking into accounting that $\mathsf{M}m_k(W^{**}) \geq \mathsf{M}m_k$, we have

$$\sum_{(x,y)\in X\times X} \xi(x,y)\, r_{xy}(W^{**}) \leq \sum_{(x,y)\in X\times X} \xi(x,y)\,(1/2- | c_{xy} |)^k.$$

Since always $r_{xy}(W) \geq 0$, we obtain

$$\sum_{(x,y)\in X\times X} \xi(x,y) \mid c_{xy} \mid r_{xy}(W^{**}) \;\leq\; \overline{C} \sum_{(x,y)\in X\times X} \xi(x,y)\, r_{xy}(W^{**})$$

$$\leq \overline{C} \sum_{(x,y)\in X\times X} \xi(x,y)\,(1/2-\mid c_{xy}\mid)^k.$$

By theorem 8.5.1, taking into account that W^* provides $\mathsf{E}m_k(W)$ with maximum and that always $r_{xy}(W) \geq 0$, we derive the first of the desired inequalities:

$$\begin{aligned}
0 &\leq \mathsf{E}m_k(W^*) - \mathsf{E}m_k(W^{**}) \\
&= 2 \sum_{(x,y)\in X\times X} \xi(x,y)\mid c_{xy}\mid r_{xy}(W^{**}) - 2 \sum_{(x,y)\in X\times X} \xi(x,y)\mid c_{xy}\mid r_{xy}(W^*) \\
&\leq 2 \sum_{(x,y)\in X\times X} \xi(x,y)\mid c_{xy}\mid r_{xy}(W^{**}) \\
&\leq 2\overline{C} \sum_{(x,y)\in X\times X} \xi(x,y)\,(1/2-\mid c_{xy}\mid)^k \\
&< 2^{-k+1}\overline{C}
\end{aligned}$$

(the last inequality is strict since by assumption $c_{xy} \neq 0$ for significant (x,y)).
By theorem 8.5.1, and taking into account that $\mathsf{E}m_k(W^*) \geq \mathsf{E}m_k$, we have

$$\sum_{(x,y)\in X\times X} \xi(x,y)\mid c_{xy}\mid r_{xy}(W^*) \leq \sum_{(x,y)\in X\times X} \xi(x,y)\mid c_{xy}\mid(1/2-\mid c_{xy}\mid)^k.$$

Since always $r_{xy}(W) \geq 0$, we have

$$\underline{C} \sum_{(x,y)\in X\times X} \xi(x,y)\,r_{xy}(W^*) \leq \sum_{(x,y)\in X\times X} \xi(x,y)\mid c_{xy}\mid r_{xy}(W^*),$$

which together with the previous inequality and the assumption $\underline{C} > 0$ gives

$$\sum_{(x,y)\in X\times X} \xi(x,y)\,r_{xy}(W^*) \leq \underline{C}^{-1} \sum_{(x,y)\in X\times X} \xi(x,y)\mid c_{xy}\mid(1/2-\mid c_{xy}\mid)^k.$$

By proposition 8.5.2, taking into account that W^{**} provides $\mathsf{M}m_k(W)$ with maximum and that always $r_{xy}(W) \geq 0$, we have

$$\begin{aligned}
0 &\leq \mathsf{M}m_k(W^{**}) - \mathsf{M}m_k(W^*) \\
&= \sum_{(x,y)\in X\times X} \xi(x,y)\,r_{xy}(W^*) - \sum_{(x,y)\in X\times X} \xi(x,y)\,r_{xy}(W^{**}) \\
&\leq \sum_{(x,y)\in X\times X} \xi(x,y)\,r_{xy}(W^*) \\
&\leq \underline{C}^{-1} \sum_{(x,y)\in X\times X} \xi(x,y)\mid c_{xy}\mid(1/2-\mid c_{xy}\mid)^k.
\end{aligned}$$

Estimate the last expression, as (8.3.4), and obtain the second desired inequality:

$$0 \leq \mathsf{M}m_k(W^{**}) - \mathsf{M}m_k(W^*) \leq \underline{C}^{-1}2^{-k-1}k^k(k+1)^{-k-1} \leq \underline{C}^{-1}2^{-k-1}k^{-1}e^{-1}.$$

Note that theorem 8.6.1 is valid for the strict majority representativeness as well, consequently, we can speak about the consistency of the three definitions of optimal cabinets. Also note that to prove the first inequality of the theorem, we don't use the assumption $p_{xy} \neq 1/2$ for all significant pairs of alternatives (x, y). However, if $\underline{C} = 0$ the second inequality cannot be proved in any form, since $\mid \mathsf{M}m_k(W^*) - \mathsf{M}m_k(W^{**}) \mid$ can remain significant for all k. Let us illustrate it with an example.

8.6.2. EXAMPLE (No Consistency of Two Definitions of Optimal Cabinets). Consider a sequence of models with increasing number n of independent individuals, having equal weights. Let two pairs of alternatives be significant, e.g. put $\xi(x, y) = \xi(y, z) = 1/2$. Let the collective be divided into 3 coalitions V_1, V_2, and V_3 and let

$$\mu(V_1) = \mu(V_2) = \mu(V_3) = 1/3.$$

Suppose that for every $v_1 \in V_1, v_2 \in V_2$, and $v_3 \in V_3$ we have

$$\begin{array}{llll} p_{xy}(v_1) = 1, & p_{xy}(v_2) = 0, & p_{xy}(v_3) = 1/2, & \text{whence } c_{xy} = 0; \\ p_{yz}(v_1) = 9/10, & p_{yz}(v_2) = 7/10, & p_{yz}(v_3) = 8/10, & \text{whence } c_{yz} = 3/10. \end{array}$$

Since all assumptions of theorems 8.5.1 and 8.5.3 are satisfied, we can evaluate the indicators of representativeness of cabinets by formulas from the mentioned theorems. Since $c_{xy} = 0$ and $\xi(x, y) = \xi(y, z) = 1/2$, the cabinet W^* optimal with respect to the average representativeness provides the minimum of $r_{yz}(W)$, whereas cabinet W^{**} optimal with respect to the majority representativeness provides the minimum of $r_{xy}(W) + r_{yz}(W)$. To consider all possible cabinets with k members, denote by W^{ijl} the cabinet with i members from V_1, j members from V_2, and l members from V_3, where $i + j + l = k$. Note that we write a letter index, when it it positive, otherwise we write 0. For example, W^{ij0} denotes that W consists of members from V_1 and V_2 only. The table below presents the values of $r_{xy}(W)$ and $r_{yz}(W)$.

	W^{k00}	W^{0k0}	W^{00k}	W^{ij0}	W^{i0l}	W^{0jl}	W^{ijl}
$r_{xy}(W)$	$\frac{1}{2}$	$\frac{1}{2}$	$\frac{1}{2^k}$	0	$\frac{1}{2^{l+1}}$	$\frac{1}{2^{l+1}}$	0
$r_{yz}(W)$	$\frac{1}{10^k}$	$\frac{3^k}{10^k}$	$\frac{2^k}{10^k}$	$\frac{3^j}{10^k}$	$\frac{2^l}{10^k}$	$\frac{3^j 2^l}{10^k}$	$\frac{3^j 2^l}{10^k}$

It is easy to see that cabinet W^{k00}, consisting of individuals from V_1 only, has the minimal value $r_{yz}(W)$. The minimal value $r_{xy}(W)+r_{yz}(W)$ is attained for cabinet W^{ij0}, when $j=1$ (then $i=k-1$). By formula from theorem 8.5.3 for sufficiently large n we have

$$\begin{aligned}
\mathsf{M}m_k(W^{(k-1)10}) - \mathsf{M}m_k(W^{(k00)}) &\approx 2^{-1}[r_{xy}(W^{k00}) + r_{yz}(W^{k00}) - \\
&\quad -r_{xy}(W^{(k-1)10}) - r_{yz}(W^{(k-1)10})] \\
&= 2^{-1}(1/2 + 1/10^k - 0 - 3/10^k) \\
&= 1/4 - 1/10^k \\
&\approx 1/4.
\end{aligned}$$

Thus an arbitrary large cabinet optimal with respect to the average representativeness can be far from being optimal with respect to the majority representativeness. Note that for every k we can take sufficiently large n to make the approximations of theorems 8.5.1 and 8.5.3 as accurate as needed.

8.7 Numerical Estimation of Representativeness of Cabinets

In the present section we extend the consideration of section 7.9 to cabinets. Similarly, we interpret the indicators of representativeness for a homogeneous model as the lower bounds of representativeness of optimal cabinets. Under the same assumptions, as in section 7.9, one can prove that

$$\begin{aligned}
\mathsf{E}m_k &= \mathsf{E}m_k(W) = \mathsf{E}m_k(W,x,y), \\
\mathsf{M}m_k &= \mathsf{M}m_k(W) = \mathsf{M}m_k(W,x,y), \\
\overline{\mathsf{M}}m_k &= \overline{\mathsf{M}}m_k(W) = \overline{\mathsf{M}}m_k(W,x,y),
\end{aligned}$$

where W is an arbitrary cabinet with k members and (x,y) is an arbitrary pair of different alternatives. Since all probabilities $p_{xy}(v)$ are equal, denote $p = p_{xy}(v)$ and put $q = 1-p$. By (8.5.2) we obtain

$$\begin{aligned}
\mathsf{E}m_k &= \mathsf{E}m_k(W,x,y) \\
&= \frac{1}{n}\{p^k\,[k+(n-k)p] + q^k\,[k+(n-k)q] + \\
&\quad + \sum_{0<t<k} C_k^t p^t q^{k-t}\,[\sum_{n/2-t\le z\le n-k} (z+t)\, C_{n-k}^z p^z q^{n-k-z} + \\
&\quad + \sum_{0\le z<n/2-t} (n-z-t)\, C_{n-k}^z p^z q^{n-k-z}]\}.
\end{aligned}$$

By (8.5.5) we obtain

$$\begin{aligned}
\mathsf{M}m_k &= \mathsf{M}m_k(W,x,y) \\
&= p^k \sum_{n/2-k\le i\le n-k} C^i_{n-k}p^iq^{n-k-i} + q^k \sum_{0\le i\le n/2} C^i_{n-k}p^iq^{n-k-i} + 1 - p^k - q^k \\
&= 1 - p^k \sum_{0\le i<n/2-k} C^i_{n-k}p^iq^{n-k-i} - q^k \sum_{n/2<i\le n-k} C^i_{n-k}p^iq^{n-k-i} \\
&= 1 - \sum_{0\le i<n/2-k} C^i_{n-k}(p^{k+i}q^{n-k-i} + p^{n-k-i}q^{k+i}).
\end{aligned}$$

To calculate the strict majority representativeness of cabinets with $k < n/2$ members, we refer to (8.5.7):

$$\begin{aligned}
\overline{\mathsf{M}}m_k &= \overline{\mathsf{M}}m_k(W,x,y) \\
&= p^k \sum_{n/2-k<i\le n-k} C^i_{n-k}p^iq^{n-k-i} + q^k \sum_{0\le i<n/2-k} C^i_{n-k}p^iq^{n-k-i} + \\
&\quad + \sum_{1\le i\le k-1} C^i_kp^iq^{k-i} \times \begin{cases} 1 & \text{if } n \text{ is odd,} \\ 1 - C^{n/2-i}_{n-k}p^{n/2-i}q^{n/2-k+i} & \text{if } n \text{ is even} \end{cases} \\
&= p^k \sum_{n/2-k<i\le n-k} C^i_{n-k}p^iq^{n-k-i} + q^k \sum_{n/2-k<i\le n-k} C^i_{n-k}p^{n-k-i}q^i + \\
&\quad +1 - p^k - q^k - \begin{cases} 0 & \text{if } n \text{ is odd,} \\ p^{n/2}q^{n/2}\sum_{1\le i\le k-1} C^i_nC^{n/2-i}_{n-k} & \text{if } n \text{ is even} \end{cases} \\
&= 1 - p^k \sum_{0\le i\le n/2-k} C^i_{n-k}p^iq^{n-k-i} - q^k \sum_{0\le i<n/2-k} C^i_{n-k}p^{n-k-i}q^i - \\
&\quad - \begin{cases} 0 & \text{if } n \text{ is odd,} \\ p^{n/2}q^{n/2}(C^{n/2}_n - C^0_kC^{n/2}_{n-k} - C^k_kC^{n/2-k}_{n-k}) & \text{if } n \text{ is even} \end{cases} \\
&= 1 - \sum_{0\le i\le n/2-k} C^i_{n-k}(p^{k+i}q^{n-k-i} + p^{n-k-i}q^{k+i}) - \\
&\quad - \begin{cases} 0 & \text{if } n \text{ is odd,} \\ p^{n/2}q^{n/2}(C^{n/2}_n - 2C^{n/2}_{n-k}) & \text{if } n \text{ is even.} \end{cases}
\end{aligned}$$

To calculate the strict majority representativeness of cabinets with $k \geq n/2$ members, note that such cabinets always represent a strict majority, except for the cases when the individuals, preferring and not preferring x to y, form coalitions of equal weight. Hence, we have for cabinets with $k \geq n/2$ members

$$\overline{\mathsf{M}}m_k = \overline{\mathsf{M}}m_k(W,x,y) = 1 - \begin{cases} 0 & \text{if } n \text{ is odd,} \\ p^{n/2}q^{n/2}C^{n/2}_n & \text{if } n \text{ is even.} \end{cases}$$

The computed values are tabulated in Appendix (tables A.2.1–A.2.6). Note that the first columns of these tables coincide with corresponding columns of table 7.9.1. We can say that tables A.2.1–A.2.6 provide table 7.9.1 with the third dimension—the size of representation.

The length of each line of the tables, i.e. the maximal size k of cabinet W considered for the given number of individuals n is restricted with regard to the monotonicity of representativeness (proposition 8.2.6) and the accuracy of calculations up to the 4th decimal. If $\mathsf{M}m_k(W) \geq 0.99995$ for some cabinet W, no further enlargement of the cabinet can improve its representativeness within the accepted accuracy. It relates also to the average representativeness (proposition 8.2.9). On the other hand, by theorem 8.3.2 we have

$$\mathsf{M}m_k(W) > 1 - 2^{-k}.$$

Hence, the inequality

$$\mathsf{M}m_k(W) \geq 0.99995$$

is always satisfied if $k \geq 15$. Thus the saturation of cabinets within our accuracy is attained for 15 members. Under the accuracy up to the 3rd decimal (within 0.0005) the saturation of cabinets is attained already for 11 members.

To estimate the saturation level for cabinets more precisely, one can also apply theorems 8.5.1 and 8.5.3. Note that for a model with a large number of independent individuals $r_{xy}(V) \approx 0$. For $\xi(x,y) = 1$, $p = 1/2$, and the accuracy of calculation 0.00005 we obtain the saturation conditions

$$\mathsf{E}m(V) - \mathsf{E}m_k(W) \approx 2 \sum_{(x,y)\in X\times X} \xi(x,y) \mid c_{xy} \mid r_{xy}(W) = 0 < 0.00005,$$

$$1 - \mathsf{M}m_k(W) \approx \sum_{(x,y)\in X\times X} \xi(x,y)\, r_{xy}(W) = 2^{-k} < 0.00005.$$

For $\xi(x,y) = 1/6$, $p = 6/19$, when $\mid c_{xy} \mid = \mid 6/19 - 1/2 \mid = 7/38$, we obtain similarly

$$\mathsf{E}m(V) - \mathsf{E}m_k(W) \approx 2\frac{7}{38}\left(\frac{6}{19}\right)^k = \frac{7}{19}\left(\frac{6}{19}\right)^k < 0.00005,$$

$$1 - \mathsf{M}m_k(W) \approx \left(\frac{6}{19}\right)^k < 0.00005.$$

The above inequalities determine the saturation levels of cabinets for the model with a large number of independent individuals for two versions of measure ξ. For the first version a single individual saturates the cabinet with respect to the average representativeness, but with respect to the majority representativeness 15 members may be needed. For the second version the saturation level is $k = 8$ with respect to the average representativeness, and $k = 9$ with respect to the majority representativeness.

The limit values of the representativeness of cabinets with k members for $n \to \infty$, calculated according to the approximation formulas given by theorems 8.5.1 and 8.5.3, are put at the bottom of each table. One can see that the lower bound of representativeness of optimal cabinets guaranteed by theorems 8.3.1 and 8.3.2 cannot be heightened. Finally, note that the right-hand end of each line of the tables presents the maximal value of indicator of representativeness specified by definition 8.2.8.

8.8 Notes on Interpretation

In comparison with the results concerning optimal dictators, we can draw conclusions about the advantages and the disadvantages of the collective representation in the form of cabinets. The advantages are:

(a) The possibility to attain high representativeness by means of limited sample groups of individuals (theorems 8.3.1 and 8.3.2).

(b) The overcoming of ambiguity in understanding the optimal representation, inherent in single representatives (theorem 8.6.1).

The disadvantages of the collective representation in comparison with single representatives (dictators) are caused both by the particular organization of cabinet, and some general principles.

As mentioned in section 8.1, the delimitation of competence between the cabinet members is to a certain extent an idealization, restricting the interpretation of the model. Besides, the cabinet lacks "consistent" preferences, since the orderings obtained by a majority rule are often intransitive. Since Condorcet it is known that the part of the situations, when a majority rule leads to intransitive orderings, increases rapidly with the increase in the number of alternatives and individuals. The same disadvantage, consequently, is inherent in the preference of a cabinet if it consists of more than one member. Since the "consistency" decreases with the enlargement of the cabinet, we come to a principal methodilogical alternative: Either eliminate the inconsistency in the cabinet preferences in predjudice of democracy (decrease the size of the cabinet, thus decreasing its representativeness), or allow the inconsistency in the cabinet preferences in favour of democracy (enlarge the cabinet, increasing its representativeness). This alternative cannot be avoided, and the choice of one of these possibilities should be made, taking into account of many factors outside the model.

Summing up what has been said, we conclude that the concept of a cabinet meets the task of representation of public opinion rather than modelling of decision-making. In this connection note that all the results of chapters 7 and 8 are valid not only for preferences, but also for arbitrary classes of binary relations on the set of alternatives—classifications, tolerances, etc., which can characterize individuals opinions.

Chapter 9

Representation of Collective by a Council

9.1 Introductory Remarks

The most questionable assumption in the concept of a cabinet is the delimitation of competence between its members, the prescription who and in which case represents the collective. As mentioned earlier, the interpretation of the model is also restricted by that no place for collective forms of decision-making is reserved in the concept of a cabinet. However, in reality any strict delimitation of powers is usually combined with collectivity, as in politics, where parlament procedures are based on joint decision-making, but government activities on the delimitation of responsibility between concrete executors.

In the light of what has been said, we are going to study a model of collective representation without delimitation of competence between its members. We refer to the council, making decisions by means of voting. We prove a series of propositions similar to that for cabinets: On the existence of optimal councils, on the asymptotics of representativeness of a council for a large number of independent individuals, on the consistency of different definitions of optimal councils. However, optimal councils have to be much larger than optimal cabinets, having the same representativeness. It means that the simplification in the internal organization of collective representation results in the loss of its efficiency. If we look at this from another standpoint, we come to the conclusion that the lack of information about the competence of members of representation can be compensated by their quantity, i.e. by the information about preferences of some other individuals. Therefore, the two models of collective representation—the cabinet and the council—should be regarded as complementary rather than mutually exclusive.

The results of this chapter are published in Russian in (Tanguiane 1990b).

9.2 Councils and Indicators of Their Representativeness

First of all let us formulate a strict definition of a council.

9.2.1. DEFINITION. By a *council* with k voters, where k is always supposed to be odd (in order to avoid vote balance), we understand both a set of *council voters* $\hat{W} = \{v_1, \dots, v_k\} \subset V$, or a k-tuple $\hat{W} = \{v_1, \dots, v_k\} \in V^k$, where k-tuples are considered to be invariant with respect to permutations of their elements. We distinguish the *set of council members* W, where each council member $v \in W$ is identified with a class of coinciding council voters $v \in \hat{W}$, meaning that a council member can have more than a single vote. A council member is reiterated in the set of council voters as many times as many votes he has. We suppose that for every simple event $\omega = (x, y, f)$ council $\hat{W}$ accepts or rejects the decision "x is preferred to y" under the situation f by a majority of votes. Therefore, the *representativeness of council* $\hat{W}$ is defined to be the random variable

$$\begin{aligned}\hat{m}_k(\hat{W}) &= \hat{m}_k(v_1, \dots, v_k) = \hat{m}_k(\hat{W}, \omega) = \hat{m}_k(\hat{W}, x, y, f) \\ &= \begin{cases} \mu(A_\omega) & \text{if } |\hat{W}_\omega| > k/2, \\ 1 - \mu(A_\omega) & \text{if } |\hat{W}_\omega| < k/2, \end{cases}\end{aligned}$$

where the set of council voters, preferring x to y under situation f, is

$$\hat{W}_\omega = \hat{W}_{xyf} = \{v : v \in \hat{W},\ (x, y) \in f(v)\},$$

and $|\hat{W}_\omega|$ designates their number. In other words, the representativeness of a council is the weight of the coalition whose preference it expresses.

To characterize the representativeness of councils, we use the indicators introduced earlier for single individuals and cabinets.

9.2.2. DEFINITION. The *average representativeness of council* $\hat{W}$ *for pair of alternatives* (x, y) is the mathematical expectation

$$\mathsf{E}\hat{m}_k(\hat{W}, x, y) = \sum_{f \in F} \nu(f)\, \hat{m}_k(\hat{W}, x, y, f).$$

The *average representativeness of council* $\hat{W}$ is the mathematical expectation

$$\begin{aligned}\mathsf{E}\hat{m}_k(\hat{W}) &= \sum_{\omega \in \Omega} \mathsf{P}(\omega)\, \hat{m}_k(\hat{W}, \omega) \\ &= \sum_{(x,y) \in X \times X} \xi(x, y)\, \mathsf{E}\hat{m}_k(\hat{W}, x, y). \qquad (9.2.1)\end{aligned}$$

The *average representativeness (of a random council with k voters)* is the mathematical expectation

$$\begin{aligned}\mathsf{E}\hat{m}_k &= \sum_{(v_1,\dots,v_k)\in V^k}\sum_{\omega\in\Omega}\mu(v_1)\dots\mu(v_k)\,\mathsf{P}(\omega)\,\hat{m}_k(v_1,\dots,v_k,\omega)\\ &= \sum_{(v_1,\dots,v_k)\in V^k}\mu(v_1)\dots\mu(v_k)\,\mathsf{E}\hat{m}_k(v_1,\dots,v_k).\end{aligned}$$

If V is uncountable and $\mathsf{E}\hat{m}_k(v_1,\dots,v_k)$ is a measurable function of $v_1,\dots,v_k$, then

$$\mathsf{E}\hat{m}_k = \int_{V^k} d\mu(v_1)\dots d\mu(v_k)\,\mathsf{E}\hat{m}_k(v_1,\dots,v_k).$$

Note that the random choice of a council is realized as an independent choice of its voters in accordance with the probability measure μ on V, therefore, the weighty individuals have better chances to be chosen and get several votes.

9.2.3. DEFINITION. The *majority representativeness of council $\hat{W}$ for pair of alternatives (x,y)* is the probability of the situations when the council $\hat{W}$ represents a majority with respect to the pair of alternatives (x,y), or the mathematical expectation of rounded representativeness of $\hat{W}$ for fixed (x,y), i.e.

$$\begin{aligned}\mathsf{M}\hat{m}_k(\hat{W},x,y) &= \nu\{f : f\in F,\ \hat{m}_k(\hat{W},x,y,f)\geq 1/2\}\\ &= \sum_{f\in F}\nu(f)\,\mathrm{int}(\hat{m}_k(\hat{W},x,y,f))+1/2).\end{aligned}$$

The *majority representativeness of council $\hat{W}$* is the probability of the event when the council $\hat{W}$ represents a majority, or the mathematical expectation of rounded representativeness of $\hat{W}$, i.e.

$$\begin{aligned}\mathsf{M}\hat{m}_k(\hat{W}) &= \sum_{\omega\in\Omega}\mathsf{P}(\omega)\,\mathrm{int}(\hat{m}_k(\hat{W},\omega)+1/2)\\ &= \sum_{(x,y)\in X\times X}\xi(x,y)\,\mathsf{M}\hat{m}_k(\hat{W},x,y). \qquad (9.2.2)\end{aligned}$$

The *majority representativeness (of a random council with k voters)* is defined to be the mathematical expectation

$$\begin{aligned}\mathsf{M}\hat{m}_k &= \sum_{(v_1,\dots,v_k)\in V^k}\sum_{\omega\in\Omega}\mu(v_1)\dots\mu(v_k)\,\mathsf{P}(\omega)\,\mathrm{int}(\hat{m}_k(v_1,\dots,v_k,\omega)+1/2)\\ &= \sum_{(v_1,\dots,v_k)\in V^k}\mu(v_1)\dots\mu(v_k)\,\mathsf{M}\hat{m}_k(v_1,\dots,v_k).\end{aligned}$$

If V is uncountable and $\mathsf{M}\hat{m}_k(v_1, \dots, v_k)$ is a measurable function of $v_1, \dots, v_n$, then

$$\mathsf{M}\hat{m}_k = \int_{V^k} d\mu(v_1) \dots d\mu(v_k)\, \mathsf{M}\hat{m}_k(v_1, \dots, v_k).$$

9.2.4. DEFINITION. The *strict majority representativeness of council* $\hat{W}$ *for pair of alternatives* (x, y) is the probability of the situations when the council $\hat{W}$ represents a strict majority with respect to the pair of alternatives (x, y), or the mathematical expectation of rounded representativeness of $\hat{W}$ for fixed (x, y), with 0.5 rounded down to 0, i.e.

$$\begin{aligned}\overline{\mathsf{M}}\hat{m}_k(\hat{W}, x, y) &= \nu\{f : f \in F,\ \hat{m}_k(\hat{W}, x, y, f) > 1/2\} \\ &= \sum_{f \in F} \nu(f)\, [-\mathrm{int}(-\hat{m}_k(\hat{W}, x, y, f)) + 1/2)].\end{aligned}$$

The *strict majority representativeness of council* $\hat{W}$ is the probability of the simple events when the council $\hat{W}$ represents a majority, or the mathematical expectation

$$\begin{aligned}\overline{\mathsf{M}}\hat{m}_k(\hat{W}) &= \sum_{\omega \in \Omega} \mathsf{P}(\omega)\, [-\mathrm{int}(-\hat{m}_k(\hat{W}, \omega) + 1/2)] \\ &= \sum_{(x,y) \in X \times X} \xi(x, y)\, \overline{\mathsf{M}}\hat{m}_k(\hat{W}, x, y).\end{aligned}$$

The *strict majority representativeness (of a random council with k voters)* is defined to be the mathematical expectation

$$\begin{aligned}\overline{\mathsf{M}}\hat{m}_k &= \sum_{(v_1, \dots, v_k) \in V^k} \sum_{\omega \in \Omega} \mu(v_1) \dots \mu(v_k)\, \mathsf{P}(\omega)\, [-\mathrm{int}(-\hat{m}_k(v_1, \dots, v_k, \omega) + 1/2)] \\ &= \sum_{(v_1, \dots, v_k) \in V^k} \mu(v_1) \dots \mu(v_k)\, \overline{\mathsf{M}}\hat{m}_k(v_1, \dots, v_k).\end{aligned}$$

If V is uncountable and $\overline{\mathsf{M}}\hat{m}_k(v_1, \dots, v_k)$ is a measurable function of $v_1, \dots, v_n$, then

$$\overline{\mathsf{M}}\hat{m}_k = \int_{V^k} d\mu(v_1) \dots d\mu(v_k)\, \overline{\mathsf{M}}\hat{m}_k(v_1, \dots, v_k).$$

9.2.5. DEFINITION. A council $\hat{W}^* = (v_1^*, \dots, v_k^*) \in V^k$ is called *optimal with respect to the average (majority, strict majority) representativeness* if it has the greatest average (majority, strict majority) representativeness among the councils with the same number of voters, i.e. for all $\hat{W} \in V^k$

$$\begin{gathered}\mathsf{E}\hat{m}_k(\hat{W}^*) \geq \mathsf{E}\hat{m}_k(\hat{W}) \\ (\mathsf{M}\hat{m}_k(\hat{W}^*) \geq \mathsf{M}\hat{m}_k(\hat{W}), \\ \overline{\mathsf{M}}\hat{m}_k(\hat{W}^*) \geq \overline{\mathsf{M}}\hat{m}_k(\hat{W})).\end{gathered}$$

9.2.6. DEFINITION. Recall that for every simple event ω by $\mu(L_\omega)$ we denote the weight of a non-strict minority with respect to ω (see section 7.7. for the definition). The *maximal value of average representativeness* for councils is defined to be

$$\mathsf{E}\hat{m}(V) = \sum_{\omega \in \Omega} \mathsf{P}(\omega)\,(1 - \mu(L_\omega)).$$

The *maximal value of majority representativeness* for councils is defined to be 1.

To justify the above definition, we refer to the reasons following definition 8.2.8.

Note that the properties of cabinets established by propositions 8.2.6, 8.2.7, and 8.2.9 cannot be extended to councils. Let us show with an example that an increase in the number of council voters can result in decrease in its representativeness, i.e. the indicators of representativeness of councils are not monotone functions of their size.

9.2.7. EXAMPLE (The Decrease in the Representativeness with the Council Enlargement). Suppose that a set of individuals V is divided into 5 coalitions V_i, having equal weights $\mu(V_i) = 1/5$, $i = 1, \dots, 5$. Let only one pair of alternatives be significant, i.e. $\xi(x,y) = 1$ for some pair $(x,y) \in X \times X$, where $x \neq y$. Let only such situations be possible, under which individuals of 3 coalitions from the 5 have the preference $\{(x,y)\}$ and others have the preference $\emptyset$ (the indifference). Obviously, there are precisely $C_5^3 = 10$ such situations f, and for each we can put $\nu(f) = 0.1$. Consider a council of 5 members, representing all the coalitions V_i, i.e. put $\hat{W}^* = \{v_1, \dots, v_5\}$, where $v_i \in V_i$, $i = 1, \dots, 5$. Then for every possible situation f the representativeness of the defined council is

$$\hat{m}_5(\hat{W}^*, x, y, f) = 3/5 = \max\{\mu(A_{xyf}), 1 - \mu(A_{xyf})\}.$$

Now consider an arbitrary council $\hat{W}$ of 7 voters. It is easy to show that some two of five coalitions V_i have a majority in $\hat{W}$. Indeed, if one of the coalitions V_i has 4 votes, the required is obvious. If one of the coalitions V_i has 3 votes, then there is another coalition with 1 vote. Finally, if no coalition has 3 or more votes, then at least one coalition from the five has 2 votes, and one coalition from the rest four has 2 votes as well. Let V_1 and V_2 be the coalitions which have 4 votes from 7. By f_0 denote the possible situation under which the individuals from $V_1 \cup V_2$ are indifferent. Then

$$\hat{m}_7(\hat{W}, x, y, f_0) = 2/5,$$

consequently,

$$\mathsf{E}\hat{m}_7(\hat{W}) < \mathsf{E}\hat{m}_5(\hat{W}^*)$$

and

$$\mathsf{M}\hat{m}_7(\hat{W}) < \mathsf{M}\hat{m}_5(\hat{W}^*).$$

Thus we have shown that an arbitrary council with 7 voters has lower indicators of representativeness than a certain council with 5 voters.

9.3 Representativeness of Optimal and Random Councils

In this section we extend theorems 7.3.1, 7.3.2, 8.3.1, and 8.3.5 about the representativeness of optimal and random dictators and cabinets to councils. We show that the average representativeness of optimal council tends to its maximal value at a speed of exponent $k^{-1/2}$, where k is the number of council voters. If the division of the collective by preferences into almost equal coalitions is hardly probable, then the indicators of representativeness of optimal councils tend to their maximal values at a speed of exponent k^{-1}. Moreover, it is true not only for optimal, but on average for randomly chosen councils.

At first we formulate an auxiliary proposition.

9.3.1. LEMMA. *Let the division of collective V by preferences into almost equal coalitions be hardly probable, i.e. for certain $C > 0$, $p \geq 1$ and all $t \in [0; 1/2)$ let it hold*

$$\mathsf{P}\{\omega : \omega \in \Omega,\ t \leq \mu(L_\omega) < 1/2\} \leq C\,(1/2 - t)^{2+p} \tag{9.3.1}$$

(see lemma 7.7.2 for the definition of L_ω). Then the sum (since Ω is countable)

$$S(p) = \sum_{t \in [0;1/2)} \frac{\mathsf{P}\{\omega : \omega \in \Omega,\ \mu(L_\omega) = t\}}{(1/2 - t)^p} \tag{9.3.2}$$

is finite. In particular,

$$S(1) < 0.8470\,C,$$
$$S(2) < 1.1314\,C.$$

PROOF. Since all terms of sum (9.3.2) are non-negative, they can be re-ordered and grouped, therefore

$$\begin{aligned} S(p) &= \sum_{n=2}^{\infty} \sum_{t\in[1/2-n^{-1};1/2-(n+1)^{-1})} \frac{\mathsf{P}\{\omega : \omega \in \Omega,\ \mu(L_\omega) = t\}}{(1/2-t)^p} \\ &\leq \sum_{n=2}^{\infty} \frac{C\,(n^{-1})^{2+p}}{(n+1)^{-p}} \\ &= C \sum_{n=2}^{\infty} \frac{(n+1)^p}{n^{2+p}} \\ &\sim C \sum_{n=2}^{\infty} O(n^{-2}) < \infty. \end{aligned}$$

Referring to Riemann dzeta-function

$$\zeta(p) = \sum_{n=1}^{\infty} n^{-p},$$

evaluated for some p in (Dwight 1961, formula 48), we obtain

$$\begin{aligned} S(1) &\leq C \sum_{n=2}^{\infty} \frac{n+1}{n^3} \\ &= C \sum_{n=2}^{\infty} (n^{-2} + n^{-3}) \\ &= C\,(\zeta(2) + \zeta(3) - 2) < 0.8470\,C, \\ S(2) &\leq C \sum_{n=2}^{\infty} \frac{(n+1)^2}{n^4} \\ &= C \sum_{n=2}^{\infty} (n^{-2} + 2n^{-3} + n^{-4}) \\ &= C\,(\zeta(2) + 2\zeta(3) + \zeta(4) - 4) < 1.1314\,C, \end{aligned}$$

as required.

9.3.2. THEOREM (About the Average Representativeness of Optimal and Random Councils). *Let the set of alternatives X be finite, the coalition Boolean algebra $\mathcal{A}$ be finite or countable, and also suppose that it is realized on its Stone compactum V. Then, whatever the measures μ on V and P on Ω are, the average representativeness $\mathsf{E}\hat{m}_k$ is defined for every odd k, the function $\mathsf{E}\hat{m}_k(v_1, \ldots, v_k)$ is continuous with respect to $(v_1, \ldots, v_k) \in V^k$, attaining its maximum on V^k at some point $\hat{W}^* = (v_1^*, \ldots, v_k^*)$, and*

$$\mathsf{E}\hat{m}_k(\hat{W}^*) \geq \mathsf{E}\hat{m}_k \geq 1/2.$$

The precise equality

$$\mathsf{E}\hat{m}_k(\hat{W}^*) = \mathsf{E}\hat{m}_k = 1/2,$$

holds if and only if for every significant simple event $\omega = (x, y, f)$ *the coalitions of individuals, preferring and not preferring* x *to* y *under situation* f, *have equal weights, i.e.* $\mu(A_\omega) = 1/2$. *The saturation of optimal and random councils with* k *voters is characterized by the inequalities*

$$\mathsf{E}\hat{m}_k(\hat{W}^*) \geq \mathsf{E}\hat{m}_k > \mathsf{E}\hat{m}(V) - (3\sqrt{k+2})^{-1}.$$

Moreover, if the division of the collective by preferences into almost equal coalitions is hardly probable, i.e.

$$\mathsf{P}\{\omega : \omega \in \Omega,\ t \leq \mu(L_\omega) < 1/2\} \leq C\,(1/2 - t)^3$$

for some $C > 0$ *and all* $t \in [0; 1/2)$, *then*

$$\mathsf{E}\hat{m}_k(\hat{W}^*) \geq \mathsf{E}\hat{m}_k > \mathsf{E}\hat{m}(V) - 0.0941\,C\,(k+2)^{-1}.$$

PROOF. Fix $\omega \in \Omega$. Define $U_\omega \subset V^k$ to be the set of councils $(v_1, \ldots, v_k) \in V^k$, expressing for the given simple event ω the preference of the non-strict minority, i.e. more than $k/2$ voters v_i of which belong to L_ω (see lemma 7.7.2 for the definition of L_ω). Note that by definition 9.2.1 for every fixed $\omega \in \Omega$ we have

$$\hat{m}_k(v_1, \ldots, v_k, \omega) = \begin{cases} \mu(L_\omega) & \text{if } (v_1, \ldots, v_k) \in U_\omega, \\ 1 - \mu(L_\omega) & \text{if } (v_1, \ldots, v_k) \in V^k \setminus U_\omega. \end{cases} \tag{9.3.3}$$

We see that for every fixed ω the function $\hat{m}_k(v_1, \ldots, v_k, \omega)$ is constant on clopen subsets of V^k, consequently, it is continuous. Since the series (9.2.1)

$$\mathsf{E}\hat{m}_k(\hat{W}) = \sum_{\omega \in \Omega} \mathsf{P}(\omega)\, \hat{m}_k(\hat{W}, \omega),$$

formed of continuous non-negative functions, is majorized on compactum V^k by convergent series (7.3.1), it converges uniformly, and its sum $\mathsf{E}\hat{m}_k(\hat{W})$ is a continuous function on compactum V^k with the maximum

$$\mathsf{E}^* = \mathsf{E}\hat{m}_k(\hat{W}^*)$$

at some $\hat{W}^* \in V^k$.

Since $\mathsf{E}\hat{m}_k(\hat{W})$ is a continuous function on compactum V^k (with countable base $\mathcal{A}^k$, consequently, metrizable), it is integrable (in the case of finite or countable V it is summable with the weights $\mu(v_1)\dots\mu(v_k)$, nevertheless we shall use the sign of integral), and

$$\begin{aligned}
\mathsf{E}\hat{m}_k &= \int_{V^k} d\mu(v_1)\dots d\mu(v_k) \sum_{\omega\in\Omega} \mathsf{P}(\omega)\, \hat{m}_k(v_1,\dots v_k,\omega) \\
&= \int_{V^k} d\mu(v_1)\dots d\mu(v_k)\, \mathsf{E}\hat{m}_k(v_1,\dots v_k) \\
&\le \mathsf{E}^* \int_{V^k} d\mu(v_1)\dots d\mu(v_k) \\
&= \mathsf{E}^*.
\end{aligned}$$

Since the series of continuous functions under the sign of integral converges uniformly, the order of summation and integration can be reversed, whence

$$\mathsf{E}^* \ge \mathsf{E}\hat{m}_k = \sum_{\omega\in\Omega} \mathsf{P}(\omega) \int_{V^k} d\mu(v_1)\dots d\mu(v_k)\, \hat{m}_k(v_1,\dots v_k,\omega). \tag{9.3.4}$$

Taking into account (9.3.3) and denoting the product measure on V^k by the same letter μ, we have

$$\begin{aligned}
\int_{V^k} d\mu(v_1)\dots d\mu(v_k)\, \hat{m}_k(v_1,\dots v_k,\omega) &= \\
&= \int_{U_\omega} d\mu(v_1)\dots d\mu(v_k)\, \hat{m}_k(v_1,\dots v_k,\omega) + \\
&\quad + \int_{V^k\setminus U_\omega} d\mu(v_1)\dots d\mu(v_k)\, \hat{m}_k(v_1,\dots v_k,\omega) \\
&= \mu(U_\omega)\,\mu(L_\omega) + (1-\mu(U_\omega))\,(1-\mu(L_\omega)) \\
&= 1/2 + 2(\mu(U_\omega)-1/2)\,(\mu(L_\omega)-1/2).
\end{aligned} \tag{9.3.5}$$

Note that by definition of U_ω we have

$$\mu(U_\omega) = \sum_{k/2<i\le k} C_k^i\, \mu^i(L_\omega)\,(1-\mu(L_\omega))^{k-i}. \tag{9.3.6}$$

Putting $t = \mu(L_\omega)$ and using the binomial representation of the incomplete beta function (4.2.3), for odd k we have

$$\mu(U_\omega) = I_t(\frac{k+1}{2}, \frac{k+1}{2}). \tag{9.3.7}$$

Recall that the incomplete beta function increases on $[0;1]$ and equals to $1/2$ at $t = 1/2$. Since $t = \mu(L_\omega) \le 1/2$, we obtain $\mu(U_\omega) \le 1/2$ for all $\omega \in \Omega$. Therefore, the two multipliers in (9.3.5) have the same sign, and we get

$$\int_{V^k} d\mu(v_1)\dots d\mu(v_k)\, \hat{m}_k(v_1,\dots v_k,\omega) \ge 1/2$$

for all $\omega \in \Omega$, which after the substitution into (9.3.4) gives the first inequality of the theorem. Note that the inequality is strict if and only if $t = \mu(L_\omega) \neq 1/2$ for some significant simple event $\omega \in \Omega$.

Let us prove the second inequality of the theorem. By definition 9.2.6 and formulas (9.3.4)–(9.3.5) we have

$$\begin{aligned} \mathsf{E}\hat{m}(V) - \mathsf{E}\hat{m}_k &= \sum_{\omega\in\Omega} \mathsf{P}(\omega)\,[1 - \mu(L_\omega) - 1/2 - 2(\mu(U_\omega) - 1/2)\,(\mu(L_\omega) - 1/2)] \\ &= \sum_{\omega\in\Omega} \mathsf{P}(\omega)\,(1 - 2\mu(L_\omega))\,\mu(U_\omega). \end{aligned}$$

Substituting t for $\mu(L_\omega)$, using (9.3.7), eliminating zero terms, indexed by $t = 0$ and $t = 1/2$, we obtain

$$\begin{aligned} \mathsf{E}\hat{m}(V) - \mathsf{E}\hat{m}_k &= \sum_{t\in[0;1/2]} \mathsf{P}\{\omega : \omega \in \Omega,\ \mu(L_\omega) = t\}\,(1-2t)\,I_t(\frac{k+1}{2}, \frac{k+1}{2}) \\ &= \sum_{t\in(0;1/2)} \mathsf{P}\{\omega : \omega \in \Omega,\ \mu(L_\omega) = t\}\,(1-2t)\,I_t(\frac{k+1}{2}, \frac{k+1}{2}). \end{aligned} \tag{9.3.8}$$

To estimate the above expression, note that $I_t(\frac{k+1}{2}, \frac{k+1}{2})$ can be considered as a continuous unimodal distribution function $F_\xi(t)$ of a beta-distributed random variable ξ, symmetrical with respect to $1/2$, having the mathematical expectation (refer to formulas (4.2.4) and (4.2.5))

$$\mathsf{E}\xi = 1/2$$

and the dispersion

$$\mathsf{D}\xi = \frac{(k+1)^2/2^2}{(k+1)^2(k+2)} = \frac{1}{4(k+2)}.$$

Applying strengthened Chebyshev inequality (Korn & Korn 1968, 18.3–14), for every $t < 1/2$ we have

$$I_t(\frac{k+1}{2}, \frac{k+1}{2}) \leq \frac{1}{2}\,\frac{4}{9}\,\frac{\mathsf{D}\xi}{(\mathsf{E}\xi - t)^2} = \frac{1}{18(1/2 - t)^2(k+2)}, \tag{9.3.9}$$

consequently,

$$(1-2t)\,I_t(\frac{k+1}{2}, \frac{k+1}{2}) \leq \frac{1}{9(1/2 - t)\,(k+2)}. \tag{9.3.10}$$

Hence, for every fixed $T \in (0; 1/2)$ and all $t \in [0; T)$ we obtain

$$(1-2t)\,I_t(\frac{k+1}{2}, \frac{k+1}{2}) \leq \frac{1}{9(1/2 - t)\,(k+2)} < \frac{1}{9(1/2 - T)\,(k+2)}. \tag{9.3.11}$$

Since for all $t \in [0; 1/2)$ we have

$$I_t(\frac{k+1}{2}, \frac{k+1}{2}) < 1/2,$$

for every fixed $T \in (0; 1/2)$ and all $t \in [T; 1/2)$ we obtain

$$(1-2t)\, I_t(\frac{k+1}{2}, \frac{k+1}{2}) < \frac{1-2t}{2} \leq 1/2 - T. \tag{9.3.12}$$

Putting T to satisfy the equation

$$1/2 - T = (3\sqrt{k+2})^{-1},$$

we obtain from (9.3.11) and (9.3.12)

$$(1-2t)\, I_t(\frac{k+1}{2}, \frac{k+1}{2}) < \max\{\frac{1}{9(1/2-T)(k+2)}, 1/2 - T\} = (3\sqrt{k+2})^{-1} \tag{9.3.13}$$

for all $t \in [0; 1/2)$. Applying it to (9.3.8), we obtain the second inequality of the theorem.

To prove the third inequality of the theorem, substitute (9.3.10) in (9.3.8) and use lemma 9.3.1:

$$\begin{aligned} \mathsf{E}\hat{m}(V) - \mathsf{E}\hat{m}_k &\leq \sum_{t \in (0;1/2)} \frac{\mathsf{P}\{\omega : \omega \in \Omega,\ \mu(L_\omega) = t\}}{9(k+2)\,(1/2 - t)} \\ &\leq \frac{1}{9(k+2)} S(1) \\ &< 0.0941\, C\, (k+2)^{-1}, \end{aligned}$$

as required.

In addition we mention that the exponent of the estimation (9.3.13) cannot be improved. Indeed, replace the incomplete beta function in (9.3.10) by its linear approximation at $t = 1/2$, which minorizes it for all $t \in [0; 1/2]$, and consider the resulting function

$$g(t) = (1-2t)\,[1/2 + \frac{2^{-k+1} k!}{(k/2 - 1/2)!^2}(t - 1/2)].$$

The graphs of the functions $1 - 2t$, $I_t(2,2) = I_t(\frac{k+1}{2}, \frac{k+1}{2})$ for $k = 3$, its linear approximation $\frac{1}{2} + \frac{3}{2}(t - \frac{1}{2})$, the product $(1-2t)\, I_t(2,2)$ and its minorant $g(t)$ are shown in fig. 63. Let us estimate the maximum of $g(t)$, minorizing the

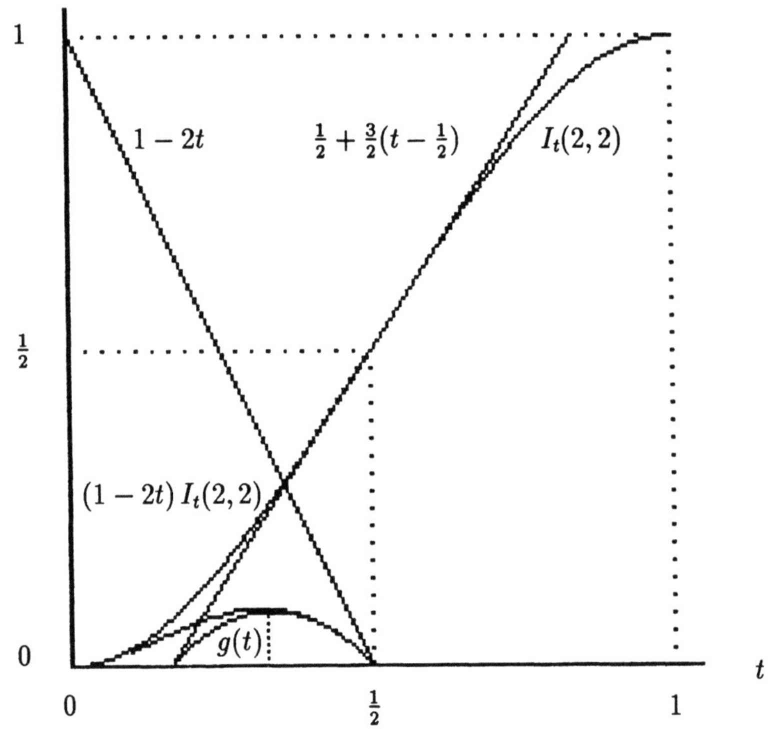

Fig. 63

maximum of $(1-2t)\,I_t(\frac{k+1}{2},\frac{k+1}{2})$. Substituting x for $1/2-t$ and equating the first derivate of $g(x)$ to 0, we obtain

$$g'(x)=[x-\frac{2^{-k+2}k!}{(k/2-1/2)!^2}x^2]'=1-\frac{2^{-k+3}k!}{(k/2-1/2)!^2}x=0,$$

whence the maximum of $g(x)$ is attained at the point

$$x^*=\frac{2^{k-3}(k/2-1/2)!^2}{k!}.$$

To estimate $g(x^*)$, we apply Stirling's formula

$$k!\approx k^k e^{-k}\sqrt{2\pi k}.$$

Thus

$$g(x^*)\quad=\quad\frac{2^{k-4}(k/2-1/2)!^2}{k!}$$

9.3.3. TABLE. The Maximal Deviation of the Average Representativeness of a Random Council with k Voters from the Maximal Value of Average Representativeness $\mathsf{E}\hat{m}_k(V) - \mathsf{E}\hat{m}_k$.

Number of voters k	The point t of maximum of $(2t-1)\,I_t(\frac{k+1}{2}, \frac{k+1}{2})$	Maximum value of $(2t-1)\,I_t(\frac{k+1}{2}, \frac{k+1}{2})$	Its estimation $(3\sqrt{k}+2)^{-1}$
1	0.2500	0.1250	0.1925
3	0.3150	0.0870	0.1491
5	0.3500	0.0706	0.1260
7	0.3700	0.0609	0.1111
9	0.3800	0.0543	0.1005
11	0.3900	0.0495	0.0925
13	0.4000	0.0458	0.0861
15	0.4050	0.0428	0.0808
17	0.4100	0.0403	0.0765
19	0.4150	0.0382	0.0727
21	0.4200	0.0364	0.0695
23	0.4250	0.0348	0.0667
25	0.4250	0.0335	0.0642
27	0.4300	0.0322	0.0619
29	0.4300	0.0311	0.0599
31	0.4350	0.0301	0.0580
33	0.4350	0.0292	0.0563
35	0.4350	0.0284	0.0548
37	0.4400	0.0276	0.0534
39	0.4400	0.0269	0.0521
41	0.4400	0.0263	0.0508
43	0.4450	0.0257	0.0497
45	0.4450	0.0251	0.0486
47	0.4450	0.0246	0.0476
49	0.4450	0.0241	0.0467
51	0.4500	0.0236	0.0458
53	0.4500	0.0232	0.0449
55	0.4500	0.0228	0.0442
57	0.4500	0.0224	0.0434
59	0.4500	0.0220	0.0427
61	0.4500	0.0216	0.0420
63	0.4550	0.0213	0.0413
65	0.4550	0.0209	0.0407
67	0.4550	0.0206	0.0401
69	0.4550	0.0203	0.0396
71	0.4550	0.0201	0.0390
73	0.4550	0.0198	0.0385
...			

$$\begin{aligned}
&\approx \frac{2^{k-4}(\frac{k-1}{2})^{k-1}e^{-k+1}2\pi\frac{k-1}{2}}{k^k e^{-k}\sqrt{2\pi k}} \\
&= \frac{2^{-7/2}(k-1)^k e}{k^k\sqrt{\pi k}} \\
&\approx 2^{-7/2}(1-1/k)^k e k^{-1/2}\pi^{-1/2} \\
&\approx 2^{-7/2}\pi^{-1/2}k^{-1/2},
\end{aligned}$$

as required. The inaccuracy of estimation (9.3.13) is seen from table 9.3.3.

The following theorem is similar to the proved one with the only difference that in a general case we don't observe any convergence of the majority representativeness of optimal councils to its maximal value with increase in the number of council voters.

9.3.4. THEOREM (About the Majority Representativeness of Optimal and Random Councils). *Let the set of alternatives X be finite, the coalition Boolean algebra $\mathcal{A}$ be finite or countable, and also suppose that it is realized on its Stone compactum V. Then, whatever the measures μ on V and P on Ω are, the majority representativeness $\mathsf{M}\hat{m}_k$ is defined for every odd k, the function $\mathsf{M}\hat{m}_k(v_1,\dots,v_k)$ is continuous with respect to $(v_1,\dots,v_k)\in V^k$, attaining its maximum on V^k at some point $\hat{W}^*=(v_1^*,\dots,v_k^*)$, and*

$$\mathsf{M}\hat{m}_k(\hat{W}^*) \geq \mathsf{M}\hat{m}_k > 1/2.$$

If the division of the collective by preferences into almost equal coalitions is hardly probable, i.e.

$$\mathsf{P}\{\omega : \omega\in\Omega,\ t\leq \mu(L_\omega) < 1/2\} \leq C\,(1/2-t)^4$$

for some $C>0$ and all $t\in[0;1/2)$, then the saturation of optimal and random councils with k voters is characterized by the inequalities

$$\mathsf{M}\hat{m}_k(\hat{W}^*) \geq \mathsf{M}\hat{m}_k > 1 - 0.0628\,C\,(k+2)^{-1}.$$

If for every significant simple event $\omega=(x,y,f)$ the coalitions of individuals, preferring and not preferring x to y under the situation f, have unequal weights, i.e. $\mu(A_\omega)\neq 1/2$, then the same is valid for the strict majority representativeness.

PROOF. Fix $\omega\in\Omega$. Define $\overline{U}_\omega\subset V^k$ to be the set of councils $(v_1,\dots,v_k)\in V^k$, expressing for the given simple event ω the preference of the strict minority, i.e. more than $k/2$ voters v_i of which belong to $\overline{L}_\omega$ (see section 7.7 for the definition of $\overline{L}_\omega$). Note that for every fixed $\overline{L}_\omega$ we have

$$\operatorname{int}(\hat{m}_k(v_1,\dots,v_k,\omega)+1/2) = \begin{cases} 0 & \text{if } (v_1,\dots,v_k)\in\overline{U}_\omega, \\ 1 & \text{if } (v_1,\dots,v_k)\in V^k\setminus\overline{U}_\omega. \end{cases} \tag{9.3.14}$$

We see that for every fixed ω the function $\operatorname{int}(\hat{m}_k(v_1,\dots,v_k,\omega)+1/2)$ is constant on clopen subsets of V^k, consequently, it is continuous. Since the series (9.2.2)

$$\mathsf{M}\hat{m}_k(\hat{W}) = \sum_{\omega\in\Omega} \mathsf{P}(\omega)\operatorname{int}(\hat{m}_k(\hat{W},\omega)+1/2),$$

formed of continuous non-negative functions, is majorized on compactum V^k by convergent series (7.3.1), it converges uniformly, and its sum $\mathsf{M}\hat{m}_k(\hat{W})$ is a continuous function on compactum V^k with the maximum

$$\mathsf{M}^* = \mathsf{M}\hat{m}_k(\hat{W}^*)$$

at some $\hat{W}^* \in V^k$.

Since $\mathsf{M}\hat{m}_k(\hat{W})$ is a continuous function on compactum V^k (with countable base $\mathcal{A}^k$, consequently, metrizable), it is integrable (in the case of finite or countable V it is summable with the weights $\mu(v_1)\dots\mu(v_1)$, nevertheless we shall use the sign of integral), and

$$\begin{aligned}
\mathsf{M}^* \geq \mathsf{M}\hat{m}_k &= \sum_{\omega\in\Omega} \mathsf{P}(\omega)\int_{V^k} d\mu(v_1)\dots d\mu(v_k)\operatorname{int}(\hat{m}_k(v_1,\dots v_k,\omega)+1/2)\\
&= \sum_{\omega\in\Omega} \mathsf{P}(\omega)\,(1-\mu(\overline{U}_\omega))\\
&= 1-\sum_{\omega\in\Omega} \mathsf{P}(\omega)\,\mu(\overline{U}_\omega). \qquad (9.3.15)
\end{aligned}$$

Following the proof of theorem 9.3.2 and taking into accounting that

$$\mu(\overline{L}_\omega) = \begin{cases} \mu(L_\omega) & \text{if } \mu(L_\omega) < 1/2,\\ 0 & \text{if } \mu(L_\omega) = 1/2,\end{cases}$$

we have

$$\mathsf{M}^* \geq \mathsf{M}\hat{m}_k = 1 - \sum_{t\in(0;1/2)} \mathsf{P}\{\omega : \omega\in\Omega,\ \mu(L_\omega)=t\}\, I_t\left(\frac{k+1}{2},\frac{k+1}{2}\right). \quad (9.3.16)$$

Since $I_t(\frac{k+1}{2},\frac{k+1}{2}) < 1/2$ for all $t \in (0;1/2)$, we obtain the first inequality of the theorem.

To prove the second inequality of the theorem, substitute (9.3.9) into (9.3.16) and use lemma 9.3.1:

$$\begin{aligned}
\mathsf{M}\hat{m}_k &\geq 1 - \sum_{t\in(0;1/2)} \frac{\mathsf{P}\{\omega:\omega\in\Omega,\ \mu(L_\omega)=t\}}{18(1/2-t)^2(k+2)}\\
&\geq 1 - \frac{1}{18(k+2)}S(2)\\
&> 1 - 0.0628\,C\,(k+2)^{-1},
\end{aligned}$$

as required.

To ascertain the statement of the theorem for the strict majority representativeness, note that if for each significant simple event $\omega = (x, y, f)$ the coalition of individuals, preferring x to y under the situation f, is a coalition, has the weight other than 1/2, then the majority representativeness coincides with the strict majority representativeness.

In conclusion we mention that a council optimal with respect to one indicator of representativeness can be not optimal with respect to another. To illustrate it, we refer to example 7.8.3. It is valid for our purpose, since a dictator is nothing else but a trivial council with a single voter.

9.4 Representativeness of Councils for Independent Individuals

In the present section we consider the model with independent individuals (see section 7.5 for definitions). For councils we obtain the results similar to that for single individuals and cabinets.

By $p_{xy}(\hat{W})$ denote the probability that council $\hat{W}$ prefers x to y. To define it strictly, refer to (7.6.1). Fix a pair of alternatives (x, y) and consider a collection of k Bernoulli random variable η_i, associated with k council voters v_i, such that

$$\eta_i = \begin{cases} 1 & \text{if } (x, y) \in f(v_i), \\ 0 & \text{if } (x, y) \notin f(v_i). \end{cases}$$

Put

$$p_{xy}(\hat{W}) = \nu\{f : f \in F, \sum_{i=1}^{k} \eta_i > k/2\}.$$

Obviously,

$$\nu\{\eta_i = 1\} = \nu\{f : f \in F, (x, y) \in f(v_i)\} = p_{xy}(v_i)$$

for all $i = 1, \ldots, k$. Note that if several council voters coincide, i.e. a certain council member has several votes, the associated random variables η_i are dependent.

For further purposes define the vector

$$\boldsymbol{r}(\hat{W}) = \{r_{xy}(\hat{W})\},$$

for every pair of alternatives (x, y) putting

$$r_{xy}(\hat{W}) = \begin{cases} p_{xy}(\hat{W}) & \text{if } p_{xy} < 1/2 \quad (c_{xy} < 0), \\ 1/2 & \text{if } p_{xy} = 1/2 \quad (c_{xy} = 0), \\ 1 - p_{xy}(\hat{W}) & \text{if } p_{xy} > 1/2 \quad (c_{xy} > 0), \end{cases}$$

and the *characteristic vector of council* $\hat{W}$

$$\mathbf{c}(\hat{W}) = \{c_{xy}(\hat{W})\},$$

where

$$c_{xy}(\hat{W}) = \begin{cases} p_{xy}(\hat{W}) - 1/2 & \text{if } p_{xy} \neq 1/2 \;\; (c_{xy} \neq 0), \\ 0 & \text{if } p_{xy} = 1/2 \;\; (c_{xy} = 0). \end{cases}$$

Note that the characteristic vector of a council, consisting of a single voter, equals to the characteristic vector of the given individual defined in (7.5.2).

9.4.1. THEOREM (About the Average Representativeness of Councils for Independent Individuals). *Let the set of alternatives be finite. Consider a sequence of models with increasing number n of independent individuals. Then for all councils* $\hat{W} \in V^k$ *with k voters and sufficiently large n we have*

$$\begin{aligned} \mathsf{E}\hat{m}_k(W) &\approx 1/2 + 2 \sum_{(x,y)\in X\times X} \xi(x,y)\, c_{xy}\, c_{xy}(\hat{W}) \\ &= 1/2 + \sum_{(x,y)\in X\times X} \xi(x,y)\, [\mid c_{xy} \mid -2 \mid c_{xy} \mid r_{xy}(\hat{W})], \\ \mathsf{E}\hat{m}_k &\approx 1/2 + \sum_{(x,y)\in X\times X} \xi(x,y)\, [\mid c_{xy} \mid -2 \mid c_{xy} \mid I_{1/2-|c_{xy}|}(\frac{k+1}{2}, \frac{k+1}{2})], \end{aligned}$$

where $I_t(p,q)$ *is the incomplete beta function, and the accuracy of approximation increases with n regardless of the choice of council* $\hat{W}$ *in the first formula.*

PROOF. Consider a simple event $\omega = (x, y, f)$. Recall that we distinguish between the set of council voters $\hat{W}_{xyf}$ and the set of council members W_{xyf}, preferring x to y under the situation f. Fix a pair of alternatives (x, y) and let $f \in F$ be random. Taking into account the independency of individuals, by the formula for the conditional mathematical expectation we have

$$\begin{aligned} &\mathsf{E}\hat{m}_k(\hat{W}, x, y) = \\ &= \nu\{f : f \in F, \mid \hat{W}_{xyf} \mid > k/2\}\, [\mathsf{E}(\mu(W_{xy}) \mid \mid \hat{W}_{xy} \mid > k/2) + \mathsf{E}\mu(B_{W_{xy}})] + \\ &\quad + \nu\{f : f \in F, \mid \hat{W}_{xyf} \mid < k/2\}\, [1 - \mathsf{E}(\mu(W_{xy}) \mid \mid \hat{W}_{xy} \mid < k/2) - \mathsf{E}\mu(B_{W_{xy}})] \end{aligned} \tag{9.4.1}$$

$$\begin{aligned} &= p_{xy}(\hat{W})\, [\mathsf{E}(\mu(W_{xy}) \mid \mid \hat{W}_{xy} \mid > k/2) + \mathsf{E}\mu(B_{W_{xy}})] \\ &\quad + (1 - p_{xy}(\hat{W}))\, [1 - \mathsf{E}(\mu(W_{xy}) \mid \mid \hat{W}_{xy} \mid < k/2) - \mathsf{E}\mu(B_{W_{xy}})]. \end{aligned} \tag{9.4.2}$$

By definition 7.5.7 $\mu(W) \underset{n\to\infty}{\Longrightarrow} 0$, and by lemma 7.6.2 $\mathsf{E}\mu(B_{W_{xy}}) \underset{n\to\infty}{\Longrightarrow} p_{xy}$. Hence,

$$\mathsf{E}\hat{m}_k(\hat{W}, x, y) \approx p_{xy}(\hat{W})\, p_{xy} + (1 - p_{xy}(\hat{W}))\, (1 - p_{xy})$$

$$\begin{aligned} &= 1/2 + 2(p_{xy} - 1/2)\,(p_{xy}(\hat{W}) - 1/2) \\ &= 1/2 + 2c_{xy}\,c_{xy}(\hat{W}) \\ &= 1/2 + | \, c_{xy} \, | - 2 \, | \, c_{xy} \, | \, r_{xy}(\hat{W}). \end{aligned}$$

Since the number of alternatives is finite, by virtue of (9.2.1) we obtain the first desired approximation.

By (9.3.4) and (9.3.5) we have

$$\mathsf{E}\hat{m}_k = \sum_{(x,y)\in X\times X} \xi(x,y) \sum_{f\in F} \nu(f)\,[1/2 + 2(\mu(U_{xyf}) - 1/2)\,(\mu(L_{xyf}) - 1/2)]. \tag{9.4.3}$$

By virtue of (9.3.6) the above expression is a polynomial of $\mu(L_{xyf})$, consequently, by lemma 7.7.1 the internal sum can be represented as a polynomial of

$$\mathsf{E}\mu(L_{xy}) \approx 1/2 - | \, c_{xy} \, | \, .$$

Taking into account (9.3.7), we obtain

$$\begin{aligned} \mathsf{E}\hat{m}_k &\approx \sum_{(x,y)\in X\times X} \xi(x,y)\,[1/2 + 2(I_{1/2-|c_{xy}|}(\frac{k+1}{2}, \frac{k+1}{2}) - 1/2)\,(-\, | \, c_{xy} \, |)] \\ &= \sum_{(x,y)\in X\times X} \xi(x,y)\,[1/2 + | \, c_{xy} \, | - 2 \, | \, c_{xy} \, | \, I_{1/2-|c_{xy}|}(\frac{k+1}{2}, \frac{k+1}{2})], \end{aligned}$$

as required.

9.4.2. PROPOSITION. *Let the set of alternatives be finite. Consider a sequence of models with increasing number n of independent individuals. Suppose that $p_{xy} \neq 1/2$ for all significant pairs of alternatives (x, y). Then for all councils $\hat{W} \in V^k$ with k voters and sufficiently large n we have*

$$\begin{aligned} \mathsf{M}\hat{m}_k(\hat{W}) \approx \overline{\mathsf{M}}\hat{m}_k(\hat{W}) &\approx 1/2 + \sum_{(x,y)\in X\times X} \xi(x,y)\, s_{xy}\, c_{xy}(\hat{W}) \\ &= 1 - \sum_{(x,y)\in X\times X} \xi(x,y)\, r_{xy}(\hat{W}), \\ \mathsf{M}\hat{m}_k \approx \overline{\mathsf{M}}\hat{m}_k &\approx 1 - \sum_{(x,y)\in X\times X} \xi(x,y)\, I_{1/2-|c_{xy}|}(\frac{k+1}{2}, \frac{k+1}{2}), \end{aligned}$$

where $I_t(p,q)$ is the incomplete beta function, and the accuracy of approximation increases with n regardless of the choice of council $\hat{W}$ in the first formula.

PROOF. Fix a significant pair of alternatives (x, y), and let $f \in F$ be random. Taking into account the independency of individuals, we have

$$\begin{aligned}
\mathsf{M}\hat{m}_k(\hat{W}, x, y) &= \nu\{f : f \in F,\ \hat{m}_k(\hat{W}, x, y) \geq 1/2\} \\
&= \nu\{f : f \in F, |\ \hat{W}_{xyf}\ | > k/2, \mu(W_{xyf}) + \mu(B_{W_{xyf}}) \geq 1/2\} + \\
&\quad + \nu\{f : f \in F, |\ \hat{W}_{xyf}\ | < k/2,\ \mu(W_{xyf}) + \mu(B_{W_{xyf}}) \leq 1/2\} \\
&= \sum_{t \in [0;\mu(W)]} \nu\{f : f \in F,\ |\ \hat{W}_{xyf}\ | > k/2,\ \mu(W_{xyf}) = t\} \times \\
&\quad \times \nu\{f : f \in F,\ \mu(B_{W_{xyf}}) \geq 1/2 - t\} + \\
&\quad + \sum_{t \in [0;\mu(W)]} \nu\{f : f \in F,\ |\ \hat{W}_{xyf}\ | < k/2,\ \mu(W_{xyf}) = t\} \times \\
&\quad \times \nu\{f : f \in F,\ \mu(B_{W_{xyf}}) \leq 1/2 - t\}. \qquad (9.4.4)
\end{aligned}$$

By lemma 7.7.2

$$\begin{aligned}
&\mathsf{M}\hat{m}_k(\hat{W}, x, y) \approx \\
&\approx \sum_{t \in [0;\mu(W)]} \nu\{f : f \in F,\ |\ \hat{W}_{xyf}\ | > k/2,\ \mu(W_{xyf}) = t\}\, \delta_{xy} + \\
&\quad + \sum_{t \in [0;\mu(W)]} \nu\{f : f \in F,\ |\ \hat{W}_{xyf}\ | < k/2,\ \mu(W_{xyf}) = t\}\, (1 - \delta_{xy}) \\
&= p_{xy}(\hat{W})\, \delta_{xy} + (1 - p_{xy}(\hat{W}))\, (1 - \delta_{xy}) \\
&= 1/2 + 2(\delta_{xy} - 1/2)\, (p_{xy}(\hat{W}) - 1/2) \\
&= 1/2 + 2 s_{xy}\, c_{xy}(\hat{W}) \\
&= 1 - r_{xy}(\hat{W}).
\end{aligned}$$

Since the number of alternatives is finite, by virtue of (9.2.2) we obtain the first of required approximations for the majority representativeness. To prove it for the strict majority representativeness, substitute strict inequalities for the non-strict ones in (9.4.4) and obtain the same approximation.

To prove the second approximation of the proposition, refer to (9.3.15):

$$\mathsf{M}\hat{m}_k = 1 - \sum_{(x,y) \in X \times X} \xi(x, y) \sum_{f \in F} \nu(f)\, \mu(\overline{U}_{xyf}). \qquad (9.4.5)$$

By definition of $\overline{U}_{xyf}$ we have similar to (9.3.6) and (9.3.7)

$$\mu(\overline{U}_{xyf}) = \sum_{k/2 < i \leq k} C_k^i\, \mu^i(\overline{L}_{xyf})\, (1 - \mu(\overline{L}_{xyf}))^{k-i} = I_{\mu(\overline{L}_{xyf})}(\frac{k+1}{2}, \frac{k+1}{2}). \qquad (9.4.6)$$

Therefore, (9.4.5) can be represented as a polynomial of $\mu(\overline{L}_{xyf})$, consequently, by lemma 7.7.2 the internal sum in (9.4.5) can be represented as a polynomial of

$$\mathsf{E}\mu(\overline{L}_{xyf}) \approx 1/2 - \mid c_{xy} \mid .$$

Thus we obtain

$$\sum_{f \in F} \nu(f)\, \mu(\overline{U}_{xyf}) \approx I_{1/2-|c_{xy}|}(\frac{k+1}{2}, \frac{k+1}{2}).$$

Since the number of alternatives is finite, we get the required approximation for the sum (9.4.5). To adapt our proof for the strict majority representativeness, it sufficies to substitute $\mu(\overline{M}^c_{xyf})$ for $\mu(\overline{L}_{xyf})$ in (9.4.6).

9.4.3. THEOREM (About the Majority Representativeness of Councils for Independent Individuals). *Let the set of alternatives be finite. Consider a sequence of models with increasing number n of independent individuals of comparable weight, i.e. $\mu(v) \sim O(n^{-1})$ for all $v \in V = V(n)$. Suppose that for every significant pair of alternatives (x, y) such that $p_{xy} = 1/2$ there exist coalitions of positive weight, consisting of the individuals whose probabilities $p_{xy}(v)$ are neither too small, nor too high, i.e.*

$$\mu\{v : v \in V(n),\ \epsilon(n) \leq p_{xy}(v) \leq 1 - \epsilon(n)\} \geq \theta > 0,$$

where $0 < \epsilon(n) \sim O(n^{-1+\epsilon})$ for some $\epsilon > 0$. Then for all councils $\hat{W} \in V^k$ with k voters and sufficiently large n we have

$$\begin{aligned} \mathsf{M}\hat{m}_k(\hat{W}) \approx \overline{\mathsf{M}}\hat{m}_k(\hat{W}) &\approx 1/2 + \sum_{(x,y) \in X \times X} \xi(x,y)\, s_{xy}\, c_{xy}(\hat{W}) \\ &= 1 - \sum_{(x,y) \in X \times X} \xi(x,y)\, r_{xy}(\hat{W}), \\ \mathsf{M}\hat{m}_k \approx \overline{\mathsf{M}}\hat{m}_k &\approx 1 - \sum_{(x,y) \in X \times X} \xi(x,y)\, I_{1/2-|c_{xy}|}(\frac{k+1}{2}, \frac{k+1}{2}), \end{aligned}$$

where $I_t(p, q)$ is the incomplete beta function, and the accuracy of approximation increases with n regardless of the choice of council $\hat{W}$ in the first formula.

PROOF. By virtue of the previous proposition it sufficies to prove the above approximations for $p_{xy} = 1/2$. For that purpose follow the proof of the previous proposition and apply lemma 7.7.3 instead of lemma 7.7.2.

Since a dictator is a trivial council with a single voter, all the examples of sections 7.6–7.7, substantiating the assumptions of the theorems, are applicable to our consideration as well. Also note the validity of the geometric interpretation described in section 7.8 and extended to cabinets in section 8.5.

Councils with their characteristic vectors are opposed to the same "collective" vectors and meet the same optimization principles as single dictators, or cabinets. Indeed, according to the results of the section,

$$\mathsf{E}\hat{m}_k(\hat{W}) \approx 1/2 + 2\langle \boldsymbol{\Xi} \boldsymbol{c}, \boldsymbol{c}(\hat{W})\rangle,$$
$$\mathsf{M}\hat{m}_k(\hat{W}) \approx \overline{\mathsf{M}}\hat{m}_k(\hat{W}) \approx 1/2 + \langle \boldsymbol{\Xi} \boldsymbol{s}, \boldsymbol{c}(\hat{W})\rangle.$$

The identity of geometric interpretation of optimal dictators, cabinets and councils clarifies the idea that the considered collective representations—the cabinet and the council—are kinds of "agents", interacting with the collective as single representatives.

9.5 Consistency of Two Definitions of Optimal Councils

In section 8.6 we have established that if the size of cabinets is sufficiently large, then our two definitions of optimal cabinets—with respect to average, or majority representativeness—are almost equivalent. In the present section we extend this result to councils.

9.5.1. PROPOSITION. *Let the set of alternatives be finite. Consider a sequence of models with increasing number n of independent individuals. Suppose that $p_{xy} \neq 1/2$ for all significant pairs of alternatives (x, y). Let $\hat{W}^*, \hat{W}^{**} \in V^k$ be two councils with k voters optimal with respect to average and majority representativeness, respectively. Then*

$$\begin{aligned}
&| \mathsf{E}\hat{m}_k(\hat{W}^*) - \mathsf{E}\hat{m}_k(\hat{W}^{**}) | \leq \\
&\quad \leq 2\overline{C} \sum_{(x,y)\in X\times X} \xi(x,y)\, I_{1/2-|c_{xy}|}\left(\frac{k+1}{2}, \frac{k+1}{2}\right) + \epsilon(n) \\
&\quad \leq \frac{\overline{C}}{9\underline{C}^2(k+2)} + \epsilon(n), \\
&| \mathsf{M}\hat{m}_k(\hat{W}^*) - \mathsf{M}\hat{m}_k(\hat{W}^{**}) | \leq \\
&\quad \leq \frac{1}{\underline{C}} \sum_{(x,y)\in X\times X} \xi(x,y) \mid c_{xy} \mid I_{1/2-|c_{xy}|}\left(\frac{k+1}{2}, \frac{k+1}{2}\right) + \epsilon(n) \\
&\quad \leq \frac{1}{18\underline{C}^2(k+2)} + \epsilon(n),
\end{aligned}$$

where $I_t(p, q)$ is the incomplete beta function,

$$\overline{C} = \max_{(x,y)\in X\times X: \xi(x,y)>0} | c_{xy} |,$$

$$\underline{C} = \min_{(x,y)\in X\times X:\xi(x,y)>0} | c_{xy} |,$$

and $\epsilon(n) \underset{n\to\infty}{\longrightarrow} 0$ *has the same exponent as the accuracy of approximation in theorem* 9.4.1 *and proposition* 9.4.2.

PROOF. Note that the equalities and inequalities in the following proof are used conventionally, within the accuracy of approximation provided by theorem 9.4.1 and proposition 9.4.2.

By proposition 9.4.2 and taking into account that $\mathsf{M}\hat{m}_k(\hat{W}^{**}) \geq \mathsf{M}\hat{m}_k$, we have

$$\sum_{(x,y)\in X\times X} \xi(x,y)\, r_{xy}(\hat{W}^{**}) \leq \sum_{(x,y)\in X\times X} \xi(x,y)\, I_{1/2-|c_{xy}|}(\frac{k+1}{2}, \frac{k+1}{2}),$$

Since always $r_{xy}(\hat{W}) \geq 0$, we have

$$\begin{aligned}\sum_{(x,y)\in X\times X} \xi(x,y) \mid c_{xy} \mid r_{xy}(\hat{W}^{**}) &\leq \overline{C} \sum_{(x,y)\in X\times X} \xi(x,y)\, r_{xy}(\hat{W}^{**})\\ &\leq \overline{C} \sum_{(x,y)\in X\times X} \xi(x,y)\, I_{1/2-|c_{xy}|}(\frac{k+1}{2}, \frac{k+1}{2}).\end{aligned}$$

Hence, by theorem 9.4.1 and taking into account that $\hat{W}^*$ provides $\mathsf{E}\hat{m}_k(\hat{W})$ with maximum and $r_{xy}(\hat{W}) \geq 0$, we have

$$\begin{aligned}0 &\leq \mathsf{E}\hat{m}_k(\hat{W}^*) - \mathsf{E}\hat{m}_k(\hat{W}^{**})\\ &= 2 \sum_{(x,y)\in X\times X} \xi(x,y) \mid c_{xy} \mid r_{xy}(\hat{W}^{**}) - 2 \sum_{(x,y)\in X\times X} \xi(x,y) \mid c_{xy} \mid r_{xy}(\hat{W}^{*})\\ &\leq 2 \sum_{(x,y)\in X\times X} \xi(x,y) \mid c_{xy} \mid r_{xy}(\hat{W}^{**})\\ &\leq 2\overline{C} \sum_{(x,y)\in X\times X} \xi(x,y)\, I_{1/2-|c_{xy}|}(\frac{k+1}{2}, \frac{k+1}{2}). \qquad (9.5.1)\end{aligned}$$

Since $c_{xy} \neq 0$ for all significant pairs of alternatives (x, y), by virtue of (9.3.9) we have

$$I_{1/2-|c_{xy}|}(\frac{k+1}{2}, \frac{k+1}{2}) \leq \frac{1}{18c_{xy}^2(k+2)} \leq \frac{1}{18\underline{C}^2(k+2)}. \qquad (9.5.2)$$

Substituting it in (9.5.1), we obtain the first desired inequality.

By theorem 9.4.1 and taking into account that $\mathsf{E}\hat{m}_k(\hat{W}) \geq \mathsf{E}\hat{m}_k$, we have

$$\sum_{(x,y)\in X\times X} \xi(x,y) \mid c_{xy} \mid r_{xy}(\hat{W}^*) \leq$$
$$\leq \sum_{(x,y)\in X\times X} \xi(x,y) \mid c_{xy} \mid I_{1/2-|c_{xy}|}(\frac{k+1}{2}, \frac{k+1}{2}).$$

Since always $r_{xy}(\hat{W}) \geq 0$, we have

$$\underline{C} \sum_{(x,y)\in X\times X} \xi(x,y)\, r_{xy}(\hat{W}^*) \leq \sum_{(x,y)\in X\times X} \xi(x,y) \mid c_{xy} \mid r_{xy}(\hat{W}^*),$$

which together with the previous inequality and our assumption $\underline{C} > 0$ gives

$$\sum_{(x,y)\in X\times X} \xi(x,y)\, r_{xy}(W^*) \leq \frac{1}{\underline{C}} \sum_{(x,y)\in X\times X} \xi(x,y) \mid c_{xy} \mid I_{1/2-|c_{xy}|}(\frac{k+1}{2}, \frac{k+1}{2}).$$

By proposition 9.4.2 and taking into account that $\hat{W}^{**}$ provides $\mathsf{M}\hat{m}_k(\hat{W})$ with maximum and $r_{xy}(\hat{W}) \geq 0$, we have

$$\begin{aligned}
0 &\leq \mathsf{M}\hat{m}_k(\hat{W}^{**}) - \mathsf{M}\hat{m}_k(\hat{W}^*) \\
&= \sum_{(x,y)\in X\times X} \xi(x,y)\, r_{xy}(\hat{W}^*) - \sum_{(x,y)\in X\times X} \xi(x,y)\, r_{xy}(\hat{W}^{**}) \\
&\leq \sum_{(x,y)\in X\times X} \xi(x,y)\, r_{xy}(\hat{W}^*) \\
&\leq \frac{1}{\underline{C}} \sum_{(x,y)\in X\times X} \xi(x,y) \mid c_{xy} \mid I_{1/2-|c_{xy}|}(\frac{k+1}{2}, \frac{k+1}{2}).
\end{aligned} \tag{9.5.3}$$

Since $c_{xy} \neq 0$ for all significant pairs of alternatives (x,y), by virtue of (9.3.10) we have

$$\mid c_{xy} \mid I_{1/2-|c_{xy}|}(\frac{k+1}{2}, \frac{k+1}{2}) \leq \frac{1}{18c_{xy}(k+2)} \leq \frac{1}{18\underline{C}(k+2)}. \tag{9.5.4}$$

Substituting it in (9.5.3), we obtain the second desired inequality.

9.5.2. THEOREM (About the Consistency of Two Definitions of Optimal Councils). *Let the set of alternatives be finite. Consider a sequence of models with increasing number n of independent individuals of comparable weight, i.e. $\mu(v) \sim O(n^{-1})$ for all $v \in V = V(n)$. Suppose that for every significant pair of alternatives (x,y) such that $p_{xy} = 1/2$ there exist coalitions of positive weight, consisting of the individuals whose probabilities $p_{xy}(v)$ are neither too small, nor too high, i.e.*

$$\mu\{v : v \in V(n),\ \epsilon(n) \leq p_{xy}(v) \leq 1 - \epsilon(n)\} \geq \theta > 0,$$

where $0 < \epsilon(n) \sim O(n^{-1+\epsilon})$ *for some* $\epsilon > 0$. *Let* $\hat{W}^*, \hat{W}^{**} \in V^k$ *be two councils with* k *voters optimal with respect to average and majority representativeness, respectively. Then*

$$\begin{aligned}
&| \mathsf{E}\hat{m}_k(\hat{W}^*) - \mathsf{E}\hat{m}_k(\hat{W}^{**}) | \leq \\
&\leq \; 2\overline{C} \sum_{(x,y)\in X\times X: c_{xy}\neq 0} \xi(x,y)\, I_{1/2-|c_{xy}|}\left(\frac{k+1}{2}, \frac{k+1}{2}\right) + \epsilon(n) \\
&\leq \; \frac{\overline{C}}{9\underline{C}^2(k+2)} + \epsilon(n), \\
&| \mathsf{M}\hat{m}_k(\hat{W}^*) - \mathsf{M}\hat{m}_k(\hat{W}^{**}) | \leq \\
&\leq \; \frac{1}{\underline{C}} \sum_{(x,y)\in X\times X: c_{xy}\neq 0} \xi(x,y) \mid c_{xy} \mid I_{1/2-|c_{xy}|}\left(\frac{k+1}{2}, \frac{k+1}{2}\right) + \epsilon(n) \\
&\leq \; \frac{1}{18\underline{C}^2(k+2)} + \epsilon(n),
\end{aligned}$$

where $I_t(p,q)$ *is the incomplete beta function,*

$$\begin{aligned}
\overline{C} &= \max_{(x,y)\in X\times X:\xi(x,y)>0} \mid c_{xy} \mid, \\
\underline{C} &= \min_{(x,y)\in X\times X:\xi(x,y)>0, c_{xy}\neq 0} \mid c_{xy} \mid,
\end{aligned}$$

and $\epsilon(n) \xrightarrow[n\to\infty]{} 0$ *has the same exponent as the accuracy of approximation in theorems* 9.4.1 *and* 9.4.3.

PROOF. By theorems 9.4.1 and 9.4.3 we have

$$\mathsf{E}\hat{m}_k(\hat{W},x,y) \approx \mathsf{M}\hat{m}_k(\hat{W},x,y) \approx \overline{\mathsf{M}}\hat{m}_k(\hat{W},x,y) \approx 1/2$$

for all councils $\hat{W}$ with k voters for every pair of alternatives (x,y) such that $p_{xy} = 1/2$. Consequently, for these pairs of alternatives

$$\begin{aligned}
| \mathsf{E}\hat{m}_k(\hat{W}^*,x,y) - \mathsf{E}\hat{m}_k(\hat{W}^{**},x,y) | &\approx 0, \\
| \mathsf{M}\hat{m}_k(\hat{W}^*,x,y) - \mathsf{M}\hat{m}_k(\hat{W}^{**},x,y) | &\approx 0.
\end{aligned}$$

Therefore, our problem is brought to the consideration of the pairs of alternatives (x,y) such that $p_{xy} \neq 1/2$, i.e. to the previous proposition.

Note that proposition 9.5.1 and theorem 9.5.2 are valid for the strict majority representativeness as well, consequently, we can speak about the consistency of our three definitions of optimal councils.

9.6 Numerical Estimation of Representativeness of Councils

In the present section we accomplish the consideration of sections 7.9 and 8.7. Following the same reasons, we interpret the indicators of representativeness for a homogeneous model as the lower bounds of representativeness of optimal councils. Under the same assumptions as in section 7.9 one can prove that

$$\begin{aligned} \mathsf{E}\hat{m}_k &= \mathsf{E}\hat{m}_k(\hat{W}) = \mathsf{E}\hat{m}_k(\hat{W},x,y), \\ \mathsf{M}\hat{m}_k &= \mathsf{M}\hat{m}_k(\hat{W}) = \mathsf{M}\hat{m}_k(\hat{W},x,y), \\ \overline{\mathsf{M}}\hat{m}_k &= \overline{\mathsf{M}}\hat{m}_k(\hat{W}) = \overline{\mathsf{M}}\hat{m}_k(\hat{W},x,y). \end{aligned}$$

where $\hat{W}$ is an arbitrary council with odd number of voters k, and (x,y) is an arbitrary pair of different alternatives. Since by assumption all the probabilities $p_{xy}(v)$ are equal, put $p = p_{xy}(v)$ and $q = 1-p$. For a council $\hat{W}$ with k members, having a single vote each, we obtain by (9.4.1)

$$\begin{aligned} &\mathsf{E}\hat{m}_k(\hat{W}) = \mathsf{E}\hat{m}_k(\hat{W},x,y) = \\ &= \frac{1}{n}\{\sum_{k/2<i\leq k} C_k^i p^i q^{k-i} \sum_{j=0}^{n-k} C_{n-k}^j p^j q^{n-k-j}(i+j) \\ &\quad + \sum_{0\leq i<k/2} C_k^i p^{k-i} q^i \sum_{j=0}^{n-k} C_{n-k}^j p^j q^{n-k-j}(n-i-j)\} \\ &= \frac{1}{n}\{\sum_{0\leq i<k/2} C_k^i p^{k-i} q^i \sum_{j=0}^{n-k} C_{n-k}^j p^j q^{n-k-j}(k-i+j) \\ &\quad + \sum_{0\leq i<k/2} C_k^i p^i q^{k-i} \sum_{j=0}^{n-k} C_{n-k}^j p^j q^{n-k-j}(n-i-j)\} \\ &= \frac{1}{n}\{\sum_{0\leq i<k/2} C_k^i \sum_{j=0}^{n-k} C_{n-k}^j [p^{k-i+j} q^{n-k+i-j}(k-i+j) + p^{i+j} q^{n-i-j}(n-i-j)]\}. \end{aligned}$$

By (9.4.3) we have

$$\begin{aligned} \mathsf{M}\hat{m}_k(\hat{W}) &= \mathsf{M}\hat{m}_k(\hat{W},x,y) = \\ &= \sum_{k/2<i\leq k} C_k^i p^i q^{k-i} \sum_{\substack{j\geq n/2-i \\ 0\leq j\leq n-k}} C_{n-k}^j p^j q^{n-k-j} + \sum_{0\leq i<k/2} C_k^i p^i q^{k-i} + \\ &\quad + \sum_{\substack{j\geq n/2-k+i \\ 0\leq j\leq n-k}} C_{n-k}^j p^{n-k-j} q^j \\ &= \sum_{0\leq i<k/2} C_k^i \sum_{\substack{j\geq n/2-k+i \\ 0\leq j\leq n-k}} C_{n-k}^j \left(p^{k-i+j} q^{n-k+i-j} + p^{n-k+i-j} q^{k-i+j}\right). \end{aligned}$$

The strict majority representativeness of council $\hat{W}$ is expressed similarly with the only difference that for even n, when a majority differs from a strict majority, the summation index j has to satisfy the strict inequality, as in the following formula:

$$\begin{aligned}\overline{\mathsf{M}}\hat{m}_k(\hat{W}) &= \overline{\mathsf{M}}\hat{m}_k(\hat{W},x,y) = \\ &= \sum_{0\leq i<k/2} C_k^i \sum_{\substack{j>n/2-k+i\\ 0\leq j\leq n-k}} C_{n-k}^j\,(p^{k-i+j}q^{n-k+i-j}+p^{n-k+i-j}q^{k-i+j}).\end{aligned}$$

The computed values are tabulated in Appendix (tables A.3.1–A.3.6). As in the case of cabinets, first columns of tables A.3 coincide with the columns of table 7.9.1 (because an optimal dictator is an optimal council with a single voter, or an optimal cabinet with a single member).

Note the monotone increase in the indicators of council reresentativeness along the lines of tables A.3, i.e. with the increase in the number of voters for a fixed number of individuals in the model. It is explained by the fact that the larger is the council, the more often a majority in the council overlaps with a majority in the collective. Such a trend is evident for a few individuals, when a minor enlargement of the council is relatively significant. Also note that the independence of individuals is essential here (cf. with example 9.2.7, where the representativeness is not monotone with respect to the council size).

Taking into account the monotone increase of indicators of representativeness along the lines of the tables, we cease enlarging the council, when its indicators of representativeness attain their maxima within the accepted accuracy of 0.5%. In the case of majority and strict majority representativeness this maximum equals 100%. The maximum of average representativeness we recognize by the maximum of the majority representativeness. When the majority representativeness equals to 100%, the council represents a majority for all simple events, whence its average representativeness is also maximal. Restricting the length of table lines, we don't use the theoretical estimation given by theorem 9.3.1 (cf. with that for cabinets). Indeed, according to theorem 9.3.1, to attain the maximal average representativeness within the accepted accuracy of 0.005, the number of council voters k has to satisfy the saturation inequality

$$(3\sqrt{k+2})^{-1} < 0.005,$$

whence

$$k \geq 4443,$$

which is inapplicable to the considered collectives up to 60 individuals.

The limit values of council representativeness for $n \to \infty$, calculated by the asymptotic formulas from theorems 9.4.1 and 9.4.3, are put at the bottom of tables A.3. With the help of table A.3.2 one can see that even for independent individuals the majority representativeness of optimal councils doesn't tend to 100% with the increase in the number of council voters, since the conditions of theorem 9.3.4 are not satisfied.

Finally, note that for odd n the right-hand ends of the lines of the tables display the maximal values of the corresponding indicators of representativeness (cf. definition 9.2.6).

9.7 Notes on Interpretation

Compare two forms of collective representation—the cabinet and the council. They allow overcoming the disadvantages inherent in single representatives—relatively low representativeness and ambiguity in the understanding of optimal representation. It is noteworthy that the properties of cabinets with k members and councils with k voters don't depend on the total number of individuals in the model but only on k. Let us discuss a few particular items.

1. Recall that the average representativeness of cabinet with k members and council with k voters tends to its maximal value at a speed of exponent 2^{-k} and $k^{-1/2}$, respectively. Such a great difference in the convergence speed can be explained by the following reasons. In the case of a cabinet the addition of a new member results in the increase in the representativeness of the cabinet for the simple events ω which form the domain of competence of the new member, and no other effect is observed. In the case of a council the contribution of a new voter is much more complex. On the one hand, to heighten the council representativeness for a given simple event ω, the total balance of votes must be changed, which can require a considerable number of additional votes. On the other hand, since votes belong to different individuals with different preferences, the change of the vote balance for a given simple event can change its balance for some other simple events. It can lower the council representatives for them, implying the total gain to be relatively small. To illustrate it, refer to example 9.2.7, where an arbitrary addition of two voters even results in the decrease in the council representativeness. Note that the number of coalitions in example 9.2.7 can be arbitrarily large, consequently, the decrease in the council representativeness one can observe for any number of voters. (It doesn't contradict theorem 9.3.2, because for a great number of the coalitions V_i the total number of situations is also great, and the probability of the situation f_0, when the council representativeness decreases, is small, resulting in a small decrease in the representativeness of the council.) Thus the addition of voters makes the

council representativeness increase and decrease in turn, and the general increase can be rather slow.

2. According to theorems 8.3.1, 8.3.2, 9.3.2, and 9.3.4, the estimations of indicators of representativeness are valid not only for optimal but on average for randomly chosen cabinets and councils. Recall that the random choice of cabinet members and council voters is realized so that an individual can be chosen several times. For a council it means that one member gets several votes, but for a cabinet it means that doubled members, not contributing to the representativeness of the cabinet, can be deleted. Therefore, a more natural assumption for cabinets is not to double the cabinet members. In other words, instead of sampling of individuals with replacement we can consider sampling without replacement. Under such an assumption the mathematical expectations of representativeness of randomly chosen cabinetis are even greater than the earlier defined $\mathsf{E}m_k, \mathsf{M}m_k$, and $\overline{\mathsf{M}}m_k$. The only case, when the mathematical expectations of representativeness of randomly chosen cabinets in the mentioned sense equal to $\mathsf{E}m_k, \mathsf{M}m_k$, and $\overline{\mathsf{M}}m_k$, is when the weight of every individual is 0, implying the probability of doubling members to be 0. It corresponds to the infinite model with an atomless measure on the set of individuals. Therefore, for the finite model the estimates of theorems 8.3.1 and 8.3.2 can be somewhat improved. Thus the efficiency of collective representation in the form of a cabinet in comparison with the council is much better for both variants of choice of its members (sampling with, or without replacement).

3. A remarkable peculiarity is the convergence of the indicators of representativeness of optimal councils and cabinets to some maximal values. It implies that all information about the preferences, prevailing in a large collective, is represented by a group of negligible weight. Moreover, that group can be chosen randomly. From the theoretical standpoint this conclusion can be regarded as a next paradox of collective choice. Its practical meaning is the validity of selective interrogations of public opinion, the possibility to reduce the number of specifications of alternatives in multicriteria decision-making.

4. The convergence of one indicator of representativeness to its maximum for enlarging cabinets and councils implies that the larger cabinets and councils represent a majority more often. That is the prerequisite for the consistency of different definitions of optimal representation for large cabinets and councils. Indeed, each simple event ω divides the whole collective into two coalitions A_ω and A^c_ω, which weights determine the

representativeness of cabinets, or councils, for the given simple event. An increase in an indicator of representativeness is observed, if for some simple event ω the greater coalition A_ω, or A_ω^c, is represented instead of the smaller one. Since this mechanism is quite universal, any new indicator of representativeness will fail to introduce something principally new. In fact, an increase in one such indicators will result in an increase of all others. Thus all concepts of optimal representativeness will tend to be equivalent.

5. Note that all the results of the present chapter, as well as the results of chapters 7 and 8, are valid not only for preferences, but for arbitrary binary relations on the set of alternatives. Therefore, we can apply our conclusions to the problem of representation of collective opinion, formalized by classifications, tolerances, etc.

Conclusions

1. We consider Arrow's paradox from the standpoint of historical development of collective choice. We examine two alternate approaches to overcome it. The first follows the traditional interpretation of Arrow's paradox. We reject one of Arrow's axioms—the universality condition, or independence of irrelevant alternatives. We also propose another approach—the refinement of the concept of dictator, implying the refinement of the axiom concerning its prohibition. This approach, analoguous to the overcoming of paradoxes in the set theory, was never applied to collective choice.

2. A collective choice model without the universality condition is studied on the example of an algorithm of aggregation of fixed independent preferences. We justify it by estimating the accuracy of approximation of collective preference obtained. We also prove a uniqueness theorem about the reconstruction of collective preference by some minimal information.

3. A collective choice model without the independence of irrelevant alternatives is studied on the example of method of marks. It allows taking into account the degree of preference in collective choice. We derive estimations of reliability of decisions obtained by the method of marks.

4. To study the general case, we formulate Arrow's model of aggregation of preferences in algebraic terms. We introduce a concept of deciding hierarchy and establish a bijection between the hierarchies and the aggregating operators. We prove a representation theorem, reducing the consideration of the model to the consideration of Stone compactum of the coalition Boolean algebra. On these grounds we explain several results, contradicting each other, from a single standpoint. In particular, the dictator turns out to be the top level of deciding hierarchy. Therefore, the existence of a dictator, implying the inconsistency of Arrow's axioms, depends on the existence of its top level. Since it can be unattainable in the infinite model, we have different results concerning the consistency of Arrow's axioms for the finite and infinite cases.

5. For a collective choice model with an infinite number of individuals we prove a limit theorem, clarifying in which sense the infinite model is an idealization of the finite model with a large number of individuals. For a model with a countable algebra of coalitions the equivalence of direct and sequential aggregation of preferences is established. In this way we bridge the finite and infinite models and fill up the corresponding gap in the theory of collective choice.

6. The existence of a deciding hierarchy with a dictator at its top level brings us to an understanding of a dictator as representative of deciding coalitions. To elaborate this idea, we define quantitative indicators, characterizing the capabilities of single individuals to represent the collective preference. Owing to the formalization of the idea of representativeness we manage to pose and solve a series of new problems. In particular, we distinguish between dictators-representatives and dictators in a proper sense and prove a theorem on the existence of an optimal dictator-representative, on average representing a majority. Moreover, restricting the prohibition of dictators to dictators in a proper sense, we revise and solve Arrow's paradox, since after this refinement Arrow's axioms become consistent.

7. The further study of the concept of representativeness is undertaken for cabinets and councils, understood as limited groups of individuals, making decisions on behalf of the whole collective. We prove that cabinets and councils can be as much representative as desired, and that for large cabinets and councils different definitions of optimal representation are almost equivalent. The properties of the three types of representation are summarized in table C.1.

8. One of the most important conclusions is that the collective chioce can be realized by means of representatives, single, or organized in certain structures. Their interaction with the represented collective has many common properties. On the other hand, the three types of representation are complementary in several respects. The cabinet and the council can provide high representativeness, but their preferences may lack "consistency", being intransitive. A dictator is not so representative as a cabinet or a council, but has an evident advantage in the "consistency" of his preference and the simplicity of its presentation. Therefore, the models of dictator, the cabinet, and the council should be used jointly, by analogy with the organization of political systems, where the power, being a form of expression of collective will, is shared by the president, the parlament, and the government.

TABLE C.1. Properties of optimal representations.

	Optimal dictator	Optimal cabinet with k members	Optimal council with k voters
Type of decision making	Dictatorial	Multi-dictatorial with delimited competence	Collective, by means of a majority rule
Transitivity of preference	Yes	No	No
Representative-ness	Not less than 50%	Not less than $100\% - C\,2^{-k}$	Not less than $100\% - C\,k^{-1}$
Effect from enlargement of representation	–	Monotone increase in representative-ness	Not monotone increase in representative-ness
Interaction with the collective (geometric interpretation)	Maximum scalar product of characteristic vectors	Maximum scalar product of characteristic vectors	Maximum scalar product of characteristic vectors
Consistency of different concepts of optimality	Under special conditions	Not less than $100\% - C\,2^{-k}$	Not less than $100\% - C\,k^{-1}$

9. Another important conclusion relates to the applications of our models to multicriteria decision making. It turns out that the totality of data, used commonly in decision making, is to a great extent redundant. Most of the necessary information is represented by a few partial criteria, or specifications of alternatives. Therefore, instead of processing the totality of available data, it sufficies to select a few partial criteria. It implies that certain decision making problems can be solved by simple means, not requiring powerful computers and large data bases.

10. Our consideration is aimed at the description of the interaction between representatives and the represented collective. The concept of representativeness, applied to single representatives and their limited groups, proved to be efficient for the analysis of collective choice problems with extensions to multicriteria decision making. We hope that it contributes to the development of a new scientific branch, which we call the mathematical theory of democracy.

Appendix

A.1.1–A.1.18. TABLES. Probabilities $\mathsf{P}\{\xi_{(m,k)} > \xi_{(m,l)}\}$ (in %) Computed by Formula from Theorem 4.3.1 for $m = 3, \dots, 20$.

A.1.1. TABLE $m = 3$.

$k-1$		
0	50	
1	80	50
$l-1$	0	1

A.1.2. TABLE $m = 4$.

$k-1$			
0	50		
1	79	50	
2	93	76	50
$l-1$	0	1	2

A.1.3. TABLE $m = 5$.

$k-1$				
0	50			
1	78	50		
2	92	74	50	
3	98	90	74	50
$l-1$	0	1	2	3

A.1.4. Table $m = 6$.

$k-1$ \ $l-1$	0	1	2	3	4
0	50				
1	77	50			
2	91	73	50		
3	97	88	72	50	
4	99	96	88	73	50

A.1.5. Table $m = 7$.

$k-1$ \ $l-1$	0	1	2	3	4	5
0	50					
1	77	50				
2	90	72	50			
3	97	87	70	50		
4	99	95	86	70	50	
5	100	99	95	87	70	50

A.1.6. Table $m = 8$.

$k-1$ \ $l-1$	0	1	2	3	4	5	6
0	50						
1	77	50					
2	90	72	50				
3	96	86	70	50			
4	99	94	84	69	50		
5	100	98	93	84	70	50	
6	100	99	98	94	86	72	50

A.1.7. Table $m = 9$.

$k-1$ \ $l-1$	0	1	2	3	4	5	6	7
0	50							
1	76	50						
2	90	71	50					
3	96	85	69	50				
4	99	93	83	68	50			
5	100	98	92	83	68	50		
6	100	99	97	92	83	69	50	
7	100	100	99	98	93	85	71	50

A.1.8. Table $m = 10$.

$k-1$									
0	50								
1	76	50							
2	89	71	50						
3	96	85	69	50					
4	98	93	83	68	50				
5	99	97	92	82	67	50			
6	100	99	97	91	82	68	50		
7	100	100	99	97	92	83	69	50	
8	100	100	100	99	97	93	85	71	50
$l-1$	0	1	2	3	4	5	6	7	8

A.1.9. Table $m = 11$.

$k-1$										
0	50									
1	76	50								
2	89	71	50							
3	95	84	68	50						
4	98	93	82	67	50					
5	99	97	91	81	67	50				
6	100	99	96	90	80	67	50			
7	100	100	99	96	90	81	67	50		
8	100	100	100	99	96	91	82	68	50	
9	100	100	100	100	99	97	93	84	71	50
$l-1$	0	1	2	3	4	5	6	7	8	9

A.1.10. Table $m = 12$.

$k-1$											
0	50										
1	76	50									
2	89	70	50								
3	95	84	68	50							
4	98	92	81	67	50						
5	99	97	90	80	66	50					
6	100	99	96	89	79	66	50				
7	100	100	98	95	89	79	66	50			
8	100	100	99	98	95	89	80	67	50		
9	100	100	100	99	98	96	90	81	68	50	
10	100	100	100	100	100	99	97	92	84	70	50
$l-1$	0	1	2	3	4	5	6	7	8	9	10

A.1.11. TABLE $m = 13$.

$k-1$												
0	50											
1	76	50										
2	89	70	50									
3	95	84	68	50								
4	98	92	81	66	50							
5	99	96	90	79	66	50						
6	100	98	95	89	79	65	50					
7	100	99	98	94	88	78	65	50				
8	100	100	99	98	94	88	79	66	50			
9	100	100	100	99	98	94	89	79	66	50		
10	100	100	100	100	100	99	98	95	81	68	50	
11	100	100	100	100	100	99	98	96	92	84	70	50
$l-1$	0	1	2	3	4	5	6	7	8	9	10	11

A.1.12. TABLE $m = 14$.

$k-1$													
0	50												
1	76	50											
2	89	70	50										
3	95	84	68	50									
4	98	92	81	66	50								
5	99	96	90	79	65	50							
6	100	98	95	88	78	65	50						
7	100	99	98	94	87	78	65	50					
8	100	100	99	97	94	87	78	65	50				
9	100	100	100	99	97	94	87	78	65	50			
10	100	100	100	100	99	97	94	88	79	66	50		
11	100	100	100	100	100	99	98	95	90	81	68	50	
12	100	100	100	100	100	100	99	98	96	92	84	70	50
$l-1$	0	1	2	3	4	5	6	7	8	9	10	11	12

A.1.13. TABLE $m = 15$.

$k-1$ \ $l-1$	0	1	2	3	4	5	6	7	8	9	10	11	12	13
0	50													
1	76	50												
2	89	70	50											
3	95	84	67	50										
4	98	92	81	66	50									
5	99	96	89	79	65	50								
6	100	98	95	88	78	64	50							
7	100	99	97	94	87	77	64	50						
8	100	100	99	97	93	86	77	64	50					
9	100	100	100	99	97	93	86	77	64	50				
10	100	100	100	100	99	97	93	87	78	65	50			
11	100	100	100	100	100	99	97	94	88	79	66	50		
12	100	100	100	100	100	100	99	97	95	89	81	67	50	
13	100	100	100	100	100	100	100	99	98	96	92	84	70	50

A.1.14. TABLE $m = 16$.

$k-1$ \ $l-1$	0	1	2	3	4	5	6	7	8	9	10	11	12	13	14
0	50														
1	76	50													
2	89	70	50												
3	95	83	67	50											
4	98	91	80	66	50										
5	99	96	89	78	65	50									
6	100	98	94	87	77	64	50								
7	100	99	97	93	86	76	64	50							
8	100	100	99	97	93	86	76	64	50						
9	100	100	100	99	97	92	86	76	64	50					
10	100	100	100	99	98	96	92	86	76	64	50				
11	100	100	100	100	99	98	96	93	86	77	65	50			
12	100	100	100	100	100	99	99	97	93	87	78	66	50		
13	100	100	100	100	100	100	100	99	97	94	89	80	67	50	
13	100	100	100	100	100	100	100	100	99	98	96	91	83	70	50

A.1.15. Table $m = 17$.

$k-1$																
0	50															
1	76	50														
2	89	70	50													
3	95	83	67	50												
4	98	91	80	66	50											
5	99	96	89	78	65	50										
6	100	98	94	87	77	64	50									
7	100	99	97	93	86	76	64	50								
8	100	100	99	96	92	85	75	63	50							
9	100	100	99	98	96	92	85	75	63	50						
10	100	100	100	99	98	96	92	85	75	64	50					
11	100	100	100	100	99	98	96	92	85	76	64	50				
12	100	100	100	100	100	99	98	96	92	86	77	65	50			
13	100	100	100	100	100	100	99	98	96	93	87	78	66	50		
14	100	100	100	100	100	100	100	99	99	97	94	89	80	67	50	
15	100	100	100	100	100	100	100	100	100	99	98	96	91	83	70	50
$l-1$	0	1	2	3	4	5	6	7	8	9	10	11	12	13	14	15

A.1.16. Table $m = 18$.

$k-1$																	
0	50																
1	76	50															
2	89	70	50														
3	95	83	67	50													
4	98	91	80	65	50												
5	99	96	89	78	64	50											
6	100	98	94	87	76	64	50										
7	100	99	97	93	86	76	63	50									
8	100	100	99	96	92	85	75	63	50								
9	100	100	99	98	96	91	84	75	63	50							
10	100	100	100	99	98	95	91	84	75	63	50						
11	100	100	100	100	99	98	95	91	84	75	63	50					
12	100	100	100	100	100	99	98	95	91	85	76	64	50				
13	100	100	100	100	100	100	99	98	96	92	86	76	64	50			
14	100	100	100	100	100	100	100	99	98	96	93	87	78	65	50		
15	100	100	100	100	100	100	100	100	99	99	97	94	89	80	67	50	
16	100	100	100	100	100	100	100	100	100	100	99	98	96	91	83	70	50
$l-1$	0	1	2	3	4	5	6	7	8	9	10	11	12	13	14	15	16

A.1.17. Table $m = 19$.

$k-1$ \ $l-1$	0	1	2	3	4	5	6	7	8	9	10	11	12	13	14	15	16	17
0	50																	
1	76	50																
2	89	70	50															
3	95	83	67	50														
4	98	91	80	65	50													
5	99	96	88	78	64	50												
6	100	98	94	87	76	64	50											
7	100	99	97	92	85	75	63	50										
8	100	100	99	96	91	84	75	63	50									
9	100	100	99	98	95	91	84	75	63	50								
10	100	100	100	99	98	95	90	84	74	63	50							
11	100	100	100	100	99	98	95	90	84	74	63	50						
12	100	100	100	100	100	99	97	95	90	84	75	63	50					
13	100	100	100	100	100	100	99	98	95	91	84	75	64	50				
14	100	100	100	100	100	100	100	99	98	95	91	85	76	64	50			
15	100	100	100	100	100	100	100	100	99	98	96	92	87	78	65	50		
16	100	100	100	100	100	100	100	100	100	99	99	97	94	88	80	67	50	
17	100	100	100	100	100	100	100	100	100	100	100	99	98	96	91	83	70	50

A.1.18. Table $m = 20$.

$k-1$ \ $l-1$	0	1	2	3	4	5	6	7	8	9	10	11	12	13	14	15	16	17	18
0	50																		
1	76	50																	
2	88	70	50																
3	95	83	67	50															
4	98	91	80	65	50														
5	99	95	88	77	64	50													
6	100	98	94	86	76	63	50												
7	100	99	97	92	85	75	63	50											
8	100	100	98	96	91	84	74	63	50										
9	100	100	99	98	95	90	83	74	62	50									
10	100	100	100	99	98	95	90	83	74	62	50								
11	100	100	100	100	99	97	94	90	83	74	62	50							
12	100	100	100	100	100	99	97	94	90	84	74	63	50						
13	100	100	100	100	100	99	99	97	94	90	83	74	63	50					
14	100	100	100	100	100	100	99	99	97	95	90	84	75	63	50				
15	100	100	100	100	100	100	100	100	99	98	95	91	85	76	64	50			
16	100	100	100	100	100	100	100	100	100	99	98	96	92	86	77	65	50		
17	100	100	100	100	100	100	100	100	100	100	99	98	97	94	88	80	67	50	
18	100	100	100	100	100	100	100	100	100	100	100	100	99	98	95	91	83	70	50

A.2.1. TABLE. Lower Bound of Average Representativeness (in %) of Optimal Cabinets with k Members for n Independent Individuals and One Significant Pair of Alternatives ($Em_k(W)$ for $\xi(x,y)=1,\ p_{xy}(v)=1/2$).

n \ k	1	2	3	4	5	6	7	8	9	10	11
2	75.00										
3	66.67	75.00									
4	62.50	68.75									
5	60.00	67.50	68.75								
6	58.33	64.58	65.63								
7	57.14	63.84	65.48	65.63							
8	56.25	62.11	63.48	63.67							
9	55.56	61.63	63.28	63.63	63.67						
10	55.00	60.47	61.95	62.27	62.30						
11	54.55	60.14	61.80	62.22	62.30	62.30					
12	54.17	59.29	60.82	61.20	61.27	61.28					
13	53.85	59.05	60.69	61.15	61.26	61.28	61.28				
14	53.57	58.41	59.93	60.36	60.45	60.47	60.47				
15	53.33	58.22	59.83	60.31	60.44	60.47	60.47	60.47			
16	53.13	57.71	59.22	59.67	59.79	59.81	59.82				
17	52.94	57.56	59.14	59.63	59.78	59.81	59.82	59.82			
18	52.78	57.14	58.63	59.10	59.23	59.27	59.27	59.27			
19	52.63	57.02	58.56	59.07	59.22	59.26	59.27	59.27			
20	52.50	56.67	58.13	58.61	58.76	58.80	58.81	58.81			
21	52.38	56.58	58.08	58.59	58.75	58.79	58.81	58.81	58.81		
22	52.27	56.28	57.71	58.20	58.35	58.39	58.41	58.41	58.41		
23	52.17	56.20	57.66	58.17	58.34	58.39	58.41	58.41	58.41		
24	52.08	55.94	57.34	57.83	57.99	58.04	58.05	58.06	58.06		
25	52.00	55.87	57.30	57.81	57.98	58.04	58.05	58.06	58.06		
26	51.92	55.64	57.02	57.51	57.68	58.73	57.74	57.75	57.75		
27	51.85	55.58	56.99	57.49	57.67	57.72	57.74	57.75	57.75	57.75	
28	51.79	55.38	56.74	57.22	57.39	57.45	57.47	57.47	57.47		
29	51.72	55.33	56.70	57.21	57.39	57.45	57.46	57.47	57.47	57.47	
30	51.67	55.15	56.48	56.97	57.14	57.20	57.22	57.22	57.22	57.22	

n \ k	1	2	3	4	5	6	7	8	9	10	11
31	51.61	55.11	56.45	56.95	57.13	57.19	57.21	57.22	57.22	57.22	
32	51.56	54.95	56.25	56.74	56.91	56.97	56.99	57.00	57.00	57.00	
33	51.52	54.91	56.23	56.72	56.90	56.97	56.99	56.99	57.00	57.00	
34	51.47	54.76	56.04	56.52	56.70	56.76	56.78	56.79	56.79	56.79	
35	51.43	54.73	56.02	56.51	56.69	56.76	56.78	56.79	56.79	56.79	
36	51.39	54.60	55.85	56.33	56.51	56.57	56.59	56.60	56.60	56.60	
37	51.35	54.56	55.83	56.32	56.50	56.57	56.59	56.60	56.60	56.60	56.60
38	51.32	54.44	55.68	56.15	56.33	56.40	56.42	56.43	56.43	56.43	
39	51.28	54.41	55.66	56.14	56.33	56.39	56.42	56.43	56.43	56.43	56.43
40	51.25	54.30	55.52	55.99	56.17	56.23	56.26	56.26	56.27	56.27	
41	51.22	54.28	55.50	55.98	56.16	56.23	56.26	56.26	56.27	56.27	56.27
42	51.19	54.18	55.37	55.84	56.02	56.08	56.11	56.12	56.12	56.12	
43	51.16	54.15	55.35	55.83	56.01	56.08	56.11	56.11	56.12	56.12	56.12
44	51.14	54.06	55.23	55.70	55.88	55.94	55.97	55.98	55.98	55.98	55.98
45	51.11	54.03	55.22	55.69	55.87	55.94	55.97	55.98	55.98	55.98	55.98
46	51.09	53.95	55.11	55.57	55.74	55.81	55.84	55.85	55.85	55.85	55.85
47	51.06	53.93	55.09	55.56	55.74	55.81	55.84	55.85	55.85	55.85	55.85
48	51.04	53.84	54.99	55.44	55.62	55.69	55.71	55.72	55.73	55.73	55.73
49	51.02	53.83	54.97	55.44	55.62	55.69	55.71	55.72	55.73	55.73	55.73
50	51.00	53.75	54.87	55.33	55.50	55.57	55.60	55.61	55.61	55.61	55.61
51	50.98	53.73	54.86	55.32	55.50	55.57	55.60	55.61	55.61	55.61	55.61
52	50.96	53.66	54.77	55.22	55.40	55.46	55.49	55.50	55.50	55.51	55.51
53	50.94	53.64	54.76	55.21	55.39	55.46	55.49	55.50	55.50	55.51	55.51
54	50.93	53.58	54.67	55.12	55.29	55.36	55.39	55.40	55.40	55.40	55.40
55	50.91	53.56	54.66	55.11	55.29	55.36	55.39	55.40	55.40	55.40	55.40
56	50.89	53.50	54.58	55.02	55.19	55.26	55.29	55.30	55.31	55.31	55.31
57	50.88	53.48	54.57	55.01	55.19	55.26	55.29	55.30	55.31	55.31	55.31
58	50.86	53.42	54.49	54.93	55.10	55.17	55.20	55.21	55.21	55.22	55.22
59	50.85	53.41	54.48	54.92	55.10	55.17	55.20	55.21	55.21	55.22	55.22
60	50.83	53.35	54.41	54.84	55.01	55.08	55.11	55.12	55.13	55.13	55.13
...											
	50.00	50.00	50.00	50.00	50.00	50.00	50.00	50.00	50.00	50.00	50.00

A.2.2. TABLE. Lower Bound of Majority Representativeness (in %) of Optimal Cabinets with k Members for n Independent Individuals and One Significant Pair of Alternatives ($\mathsf{M}m_k(W)$ for $\xi(x,y) = 1$, $p_{xy}(v) = 1/2$).

n \ k	1	2	3	4	5	6	7	8	9	10	11
2	100.00										
3	75.00	100.00									
4	87.50	100.00									
5	68.75	93.75	100.00								
6	81.25	96.88	100.00								
7	65.63	90.63	98.44	100.00							
8	77.34	94.53	99.22	100.00							
9	63.67	88.67	97.27	99.61	100.00						
10	74.61	92.77	98.44	98.80	100.00						
11	62.30	87.30	96.39	99.22	99.90	100.00					
12	72.56	91.41	97.75	99.56	99.95	100.00					
13	61.28	86.28	95.70	98.88	99.78	99.78	100.00				
14	70.95	90.31	97.17	99.32	99.88	99.99	100.00				
15	60.47	85.47	95.15	98.58	99.66	99.94	99.99	100.00			
16	69.64	89.40	96.66	99.09	99.80	99.97	100.00				
17	59.82	84.82	94.70	98.33	99.54	99.90	99.98	100.00			
18	68.55	88.64	96.23	98.88	99.71	99.94	99.99	100.00			
19	59.27	84.27	94.32	98.11	99.44	99.86	99.97	100.00			
20	67.62	87.98	95.85	98.69	99.63	99.91	99.98	100.00			
21	58.81	83.81	93.99	97.92	99.34	99.81	99.96	99.99	100.00		
22	66.82	87.41	95.51	98.51	99.55	99.88	99.97	99.99	100.00		
23	58.41	83.41	93.71	97.75	99.26	99.78	99.94	99.99	100.00		
24	66.12	86.91	95.21	98.36	99.48	99.85	99.96	99.99	100.00		
25	58.06	83.06	93.46	97.60	99.18	99.74	99.92	99.98	100.00		
26	65.50	86.47	94.94	98.21	99.41	99.82	99.95	99.99	100.00		
27	57.75	82.75	93.23	97.47	99.11	99.70	99.91	99.98	99.99	100.00	
28	64.94	86.07	94.70	98.08	99.34	99.79	99.94	99.98	100.00		
29	57.47	82.47	93.04	97.35	99.04	99.67	99.90	99.97	99.99	100.00	
30	64.45	85.71	94.47	97.96	99.28	99.76	99.93	99.98	99.99	100.00	

n \ k	1	2	3	4	5	6	7	8	9	10	11
31	57.22	82.22	92.86	97.24	98.78	99.64	99.88	99.96	99.99	100.00	
32	63.99	85.38	94.27	97.84	99.23	99.74	99.92	99.98	99.99	100.00	
33	57.00	82.00	92.69	97.14	98.92	99.61	99.87	99.96	99.99	100.00	
34	63.58	85.08	94.09	97.74	99.17	99.71	99.90	99.97	99.99	100.00	
35	56.79	81.79	92.54	97.04	98.87	99.59	99.86	99.95	99.99	100.00	
36	63.21	84.81	93.91	97.64	99.12	99.69	99.89	99.97	99.99	100.00	
37	56.60	81.60	92.41	96.96	98.82	99.56	99.84	99.95	99.98	99.99	100.00
38	62.86	84.56	93.76	97.55	99.07	99.66	99.88	99.96	99.99	100.00	
39	56.43	81.43	92.28	96.88	98.78	99.54	99.83	99.94	99.98	99.99	100.00
40	62.54	84.32	93.61	97.47	99.03	99.64	99.87	99.96	99.99	100.00	
41	56.27	81.27	92.16	96.80	98.73	99.51	99.82	99.94	99.98	99.99	100.00
42	62.24	84.10	93.47	97.39	98.99	99.62	99.86	99.95	99.98	100.00	
43	56.12	81.12	92.05	96.74	98.69	99.49	99.81	99.93	99.98	99.99	100.00
44	61.96	83.90	93.34	97.32	98.95	99.60	99.85	99.95	99.98	99.00	100.00
45	55.98	80.98	91.95	96.67	98.66	99.47	99.80	99.93	99.97	99.99	100.00
46	61.70	83.71	93.22	97.25	98.91	99.58	99.84	99.94	99.98	99.00	100.00
47	55.85	80.85	91.86	96.61	98.62	99.45	99.79	99.92	99.97	99.99	100.00
48	61.46	83.53	93.11	97.18	98.87	99.56	99.84	99.94	99.98	99.00	100.00
49	55.73	80.73	91.77	96.55	98.59	99.44	99.78	99.92	99.97	99.99	100.00
50	61.23	83.36	93.00	97.12	98.84	99.54	99.83	99.94	99.98	99.00	100.00
51	55.61	80.61	91.68	96.50	98.56	99.42	99.77	99.91	99.97	99.99	100.00
52	61.01	83.20	92.90	97.06	98.81	99.53	99.82	99.93	99.98	99.00	100.00
53	55.51	80.51	91.60	96.45	98.53	99.40	99.76	99.91	99.97	99.99	100.00
54	60.81	83.05	92.80	97.00	98.78	99.51	99.81	99.93	99.97	99.00	100.00
55	55.40	80.40	91.53	96.40	98.50	99.39	99.76	99.91	99.96	99.99	100.00
56	60.61	82.91	92.71	96.95	98.75	99.50	99.80	99.92	99.97	99.00	100.00
57	55.31	80.31	91.46	96.36	98.47	99.37	99.75	99.90	99.96	99.99	99.00
58	60.43	82.78	92.62	96.90	98.72	99.48	99.79	99.92	99.97	99.00	100.00
59	55.22	80.22	91.39	96.31	98.45	99.36	99.74	99.90	99.96	99.99	99.00
60	60.26	82.65	92.54	96.85	98.69	99.47	99.79	99.92	99.97	99.00	100.00
...	50.00	75.00	87.50	93.75	96.88	98.44	99.22	99.61	99.80	99.90	99.95

A.2.3. TABLE. Lower Bound of Strict Majority Representativeness (in %) of Optimal Cabinets with k Members for n Independent Individuals and One Significant Pair of Alternatives ($\overline{\mathsf{M}}m_k(W)$ for $\xi(x,y) = 1,\ p_{xy}(v) = 1/2$).

n \ k	1	2	3	4	5	6	7	8	9	10	11
2	100.00										
3	75.00	100.00									
4	87.50	100.00									
5	68.75	93.75	100.00								
6	50.00	65.63	68.75								
7	65.63	90.63	98.44	100.00							
8	50.00	67.19	71.88	72.66							
9	63.67	88.67	97.27	99.61	100.00						
10	50.00	68.16	73.83	75.20	75.39						
11	62.30	87.30	96.39	99.22	99.90	100.00					
12	50.00	68.85	75.20	77.00	77.39	77.44					
13	61.28	86.28	95.70	98.88	99.78	99.78	100.00				
14	50.00	69.36	76.22	78.37	78.93	79.04	79.05				
15	60.47	85.47	95.15	98.58	99.66	99.94	99.99	100.00			
16	50.00	69.76	77.03	79.45	80.16	80.33	80.36	80.36			
17	59.82	84.82	94.70	98.33	99.54	99.90	99.98	100.00			
18	50.00	70.09	77.68	80.33	81.16	81.39	81.44	81.45	81.45		
19	59.27	84.27	94.32	98.11	99.44	99.86	99.97	100.00			
20	50.00	70.36	78.23	81.07	82.01	82.29	82.36	82.38	82.38	82.38	
21	58.81	83.81	93.99	97.92	99.34	99.81	99.96	99.99	100.00		
22	50.00	70.60	78.69	81.69	82.73	83.06	83.15	83.18	83.18	83.18	83.18
23	58.41	83.41	93.71	97.75	99.26	99.78	99.94	99.99	100.00		
24	50.00	70.80	79.09	82.24	83.36	83.73	83.84	83.87	83.88	83.88	83.88
25	58.06	83.06	93.46	97.60	99.18	99.74	99.92	99.98	100.00		
26	50.00	70.97	79.44	82.71	83.91	84.32	84.45	84.49	84.50	84.50	84.50
27	57.75	82.75	93.23	97.47	99.11	99.70	99.91	99.98	99.99	100.00	
28	50.00	71.13	79.75	83.13	84.40	84.85	84.99	85.04	85.05	85.05	85.06
29	57.47	82.47	93.04	97.35	99.04	99.67	99.90	99.97	99.99	100.00	
30	50.00	80.03	83.51	84.84	85.32	85.48	85.53	85.55	85.55	85.55	85.55

n \ k	1	2	3	4	5	6	7	8	9	10	11
31	57.22	82.22	92.86	97.24	98.78	99.64	99.88	99.96	99.99	100.00	
32	50.00	71.39	80.28	83.85	85.23	85.74	85.92	85.98	86.00	86.00	86.00
33	57.00	82.00	92.69	97.14	98.92	99.61	99.87	99.96	99.99	100.00	
34	50.00	71.50	80.50	84.16	85.59	86.13	86.32	86.39	86.41	86.41	86.42
35	56.79	81.79	92.54	97.04	98.87	99.59	99.86	99.95	99.99	100.00	
36	50.00	71.60	80.71	84.40	85.92	86.48	86.69	86.76	86.78	86.79	86.79
37	56.60	81.60	92.41	96.96	98.82	99.56	99.84	99.95	99.98	99.99	100.00
38	50.00	71.70	80.90	84.69	86.22	86.81	87.02	87.10	87.13	87.14	87.14
39	56.43	81.43	92.28	96.88	98.78	99.54	99.83	99.94	99.98	99.99	100.00
40	50.00	71.79	81.07	84.93	86.49	87.10	87.34	87.42	87.45	87.46	87.46
41	56.27	81.27	92.16	96.80	98.73	99.51	99.82	99.94	99.98	99.99	100.00
42	50.00	71.87	81.23	85.15	86.75	87.38	87.62	87.71	87.75	87.76	87.76
43	56.12	81.12	92.05	96.74	98.69	99.49	99.81	99.93	99.98	99.99	100.00
44	50.00	71.94	81.38	85.35	86.99	87.64	87.89	87.99	88.02	88.03	88.04
45	55.98	80.98	91.95	96.67	98.66	99.47	99.80	99.93	99.97	99.99	100.00
46	50.00	72.01	81.52	85.54	87.21	87.88	88.14	88.24	88.28	88.29	88.30
47	55.85	80.85	91.86	96.61	98.62	99.45	99.79	99.92	99.97	99.99	100.00
48	50.00	72.07	81.65	85.62	87.42	88.11	88.38	88.48	88.52	88.54	88.54
49	55.73	80.73	91.77	96.55	98.59	99.44	99.78	99.92	99.97	99.99	100.00
50	50.00	72.14	81.77	85.89	87.61	88.32	88.60	88.71	88.75	88.76	88.77
51	55.61	80.61	91.68	96.50	98.56	99.42	99.77	99.91	99.97	99.99	100.00
52	50.00	72.19	81.89	86.05	87.80	88.52	88.81	88.92	88.96	88.98	88.99
53	55.51	80.51	91.60	96.45	98.53	99.40	99.76	99.91	99.97	99.99	100.00
54	50.00	72.25	81.99	86.19	87.97	88.70	89.00	89.12	89.17	89.18	89.19
55	55.40	80.40	91.53	96.40	98.50	99.39	99.76	99.91	99.96	99.99	100.00
56	50.00	72.30	82.10	86.33	88.13	88.88	89.19	89.31	89.36	89.38	89.38
57	55.31	80.31	91.46	96.36	98.47	99.37	99.75	99.90	99.96	99.99	99.00
58	50.00	72.35	82.19	86.46	88.29	89.05	89.36	89.49	89.54	89.56	89.56
59	55.22	80.22	91.39	96.31	98.45	99.36	99.74	99.90	99.96	99.99	99.00
60	50.00	72.39	82.28	86.59	88.43	89.21	89.53	89.66	89.71	89.73	89.74
...											
	50.00	75.00	87.50	93.75	96.88	98.44	99.22	99.61	99.80	99.90	99.95

A.2.4. TABLE. Lower Bound of Average Representativeness (in %) of Optimal Cabinets with k Members for n Independent Individuals and Equisignificant Preferences on Three Alternatives ($\mathsf{E}m_k(W)$ for $\xi(x,y) = 1/6$, $p_{xy}(v) = 6/19$).

n \ k	1	2	3	4	5	6	7	8	9	10	11
2	78.39										
3	71.19	78.39									
4	67.59	73.72									
5	65.43	72.79	73.72								
6	63.99	70.82	71.71								
7	62.96	70.28	71.56	71.71							
8	62.19	69.22	70.47	70.62							
9	61.59	68.88	70.35	70.59	70.62						
10	61.11	68.24	69.69	69.93	69.69						
11	60.72	68.00	69.60	69.91	69.95	69.96					
12	60.39	67.58	69.17	69.48	69.53	69.53					
13	60.11	67.41	69.10	69.46	69.52	69.53	69.53				
14	59.87	67.11	68.80	69.16	69.23	69.24	69.24				
15	59.67	66.98	68.75	69.14	69.22	69.24	69.24				
16	59.49	66.76	68.53	68.94	69.02	69.04	69.04				
17	59.33	66.67	68.49	68.92	69.02	69.03	69.04	69.04			
18	59.19	66.50	68.33	68.77	68.87	68.89	68.89				
19	59.06	66.42	68.30	68.76	68.86	68.89	68.89	89.89			
20	58.95	66.29	68.18	68.65	68.75	68.78	68.78	68.78			
21	58.84	66.23	68.15	68.63	68.75	68.78	68.78	68.78			
22	58.75	66.13	68.06	68.55	68.67	68.70	68.70	68.70			
23	58.67	66.08	68.04	68.54	68.66	68.69	68.70	68.70			
24	58.59	66.00	67.97	68.48	68.60	68.63	68.64	68.64			
25	58.52	65.95	67.95	68.47	68.60	68.63	68.64	68.64			
26	58.45	65.88	67.89	68.42	68.55	68.59	68.59	68.59			
27	58.39	65.85	67.87	68.41	68.55	68.58	68.59	68.59	68.59		
28	58.33	65.79	67.83	68.37	68.51	68.55	68.56	68.56			
29	58.28	65.76	67.81	68.36	68.51	68.55	68.56	68.56	68.56		
30	58.23	65.71	67.78	68.33	68.48	68.52	68.53	68.53			

n \ k	1	2	3	4	5	6	7	8	9	10	11
31	58.18	65.68	67.76	68.33	68.48	68.52	68.53	68.53	68.53		
32	58.14	65.64	67.73	68.30	68.46	68.50	68.51	68.51	68.51		
33	58.10	65.62	67.72	68.30	68.45	68.49	68.51	68.51	68.51		
34	58.06	65.59	67.69	68.28	68.44	68.48	68.49	68.49	68.49		
35	58.02	65.56	67.68	68.27	68.43	68.48	68.49	68.49	68.49		
36	57.99	65.53	67.66	68.26	68.42	68.46	68.47	68.48	68.48		
37	57.95	65.51	67.65	68.25	68.42	68.46	68.47	68.48	68.48		
38	57.92	65.49	67.64	68.24	68.41	68.45	68.46	68.47	68.47		
39	57.89	65.47	57.63	68.24	68.40	68.45	68.46	68.47	68.47		
40	57.87	65.45	67.61	68.22	68.39	68.44	68.45	68.46	68.46		
41	57.84	65.43	67.60	68.22	68.39	68.44	68.45	68.46	68.46		
42	57.82	65.41	67.59	68.21	68.39	68.43	68.45	68.45	68.45		
43	57.79	65.40	67.58	68.21	68.38	68.43	68.45	68.45	68.45		
44	57.77	65.38	67.57	68.20	68.38	68.43	68.44	68.44	68.45		
45	57.75	65.37	67.57	68.20	68.38	68.43	68.44	68.44	68.45		
46	57.73	65.35	67.56	68.19	68.37	68.42	68.44	68.44	68.44		
47	57.71	65.34	67.55	68.19	68.37	68.42	68.44	68.44	68.44		
48	57.69	65.32	67.54	68.18	68.37	68.42	68.43	68.44	68.44		
49	57.67	65.31	67.54	68.18	68.36	68.42	68.43	68.44	68.44		
50	57.65	65.30	67.53	68.18	68.36	68.41	68.43	68.43	68.43		
51	57.63	65.29	67.52	68.17	68.36	68.41	68.43	68.43	68.43		
52	57.62	65.28	67.52	68.17	68.36	68.41	68.43	68.43	68.43		
53	57.60	65.21	57.51	68.17	68.36	68.41	68.43	68.43	68.43		
54	57.59	65.26	67.51	68.16	68.35	68.41	68.42	68.43	68.43		
55	57.57	65.25	67.50	68.16	68.35	68.41	68.42	68.42	68.43		
56	57.56	65.24	67.50	68.16	68.35	68.41	68.42	68.43	68.43		
57	57.54	65.23	67.49	68.16	68.35	68.41	68.42	68.43	68.43		
58	57.53	65.22	67.49	68.15	68.35	68.40	68.42	68.43	68.43		
59	57.52	65.21	67.48	68.15	68.35	68.40	68.42	68.43	68.43		
60	57.51	65.20	67.48	68.15	68.35	68.40	68.42	68.42	68.43		
...											
	56.79	64.75	67.26	68.05	68.31	68.38	68.41	68.42	68.42	68.42	68.42

A.2.5. TABLE. Lower Bound of Majority Representativeness (in %) of Optimal Cabinets with k Members for n Independent Individuals and Equisignificant Preferences on Three Alternatives ($\mathsf{M}m_k(W)$ for $\xi(x,y) = 1/6$, $p_{xy}(v) = 6/19$).

n \ k	1	2	3	4	5	6	7	8	9	10	11
2	100.00										
3	78.39	100.00									
4	87.73	100.00									
5	73.72	95.33	100.00								
6	81.79	97.35	100.00								
7	71.71	93.31	98.99	100.00							
8	78.25	95.49	99.43	100.00							
9	70.62	92.22	98.34	99.78	100.00						
10	75.89	94.20	98.90	99.88	100.00						
11	69.96	91.57	97.91	99.59	99.95	100.00					
12	74.23	93.27	98.48	99.74	99.97	100.00					
13	69.53	91.14	97.63	99.45	99.90	99.99	100.00				
14	73.01	92.59	98.16	99.61	99.94	99.99	100.00				
15	69.24	90.85	97.43	99.35	99.86	99.98	100.00				
16	72.09	92.07	97.90	99.50	99.90	99.99	100.00				
17	69.04	90.64	97.29	99.27	99.82	99.96	99.99	100.00			
18	71.39	91.67	97.70	99.41	99.41	99.87	99.98	100.00			
19	68.89	90.50	97.19	99.21	99.79	99.95	99.99	100.00			
20	70.83	91.36	97.54	99.34	99.84	99.97	99.99	100.00			
21	68.78	90.39	97.11	99.16	99.77	99.94	99.99	100.00			
22	70.39	91.11	97.42	99.28	99.81	99.96	99.99	100.00			
23	68.70	90.31	97.05	99.13	99.75	99.94	99.98	100.00			
24	70.04	90.92	97.31	99.23	99.79	99.95	99.99	100.00			
25	68.64	90.25	97.01	99.10	99.74	99.93	99.98	100.00			
26	69.76	90.76	97.23	99.20	99.78	99.94	99.99	100.00			
27	68.59	90.20	96.98	99.08	99.73	99.92	99.98	99.99	100.00		
28	69.53	90.63	97.17	99.16	99.76	99.93	99.98	100.00			
29	68.56	90.17	96.95	99.07	99.72	99.92	99.98	99.99	100.00		
30	69.34	90.53	97.11	99.14	99.75	99.93	99.98	100.00			

31	68.53	90.14	96.93	99.06	99.71	99.92	99.98	99.99	100.00		
32	69.19	90.44	97.07	99.11	99.74	99.93	99.98	99.99	100.00		
33	68.51	90.12	96.92	99.05	99.71	99.91	99.97	99.99	100.00		
34	69.06	90.37	97.03	99.10	99.73	99.92	99.98	99.99	100.00		
35	68.49	90.10	96.90	99.04	99.70	99.91	99.97	99.99	100.00		
36	68.96	90.32	97.00	99.08	99.72	99.92	99.98	99.99	100.00		
37	68.48	90.08	96.89	99.03	99.70	99.91	99.97	99.99	100.00		
38	68.87	90.27	96.98	99.07	99.72	99.92	99.98	99.99	100.00		
39	68.47	90.07	96.88	99.03	99.70	99.91	99.97	99.99	100.00		
40	68.80	90.23	96.96	99.06	99.71	99.91	99.97	99.99	100.00		
41	68.46	90.07	96.88	99.02	99.70	99.91	99.97	99.99	100.00		
42	68.74	90.20	96.94	99.05	99.71	99.91	99.97	99.99	100.00		
43	68.45	90.06	96.87	99.02	99.69	99.91	99.97	99.99	100.00		
44	68.69	90.17	96.93	99.04	99.70	99.91	99.97	99.99	100.00		
45	68.45	90.05	96.87	99.02	99.69	99.90	99.97	99.99	100.00		
46	68.65	90.15	96.91	99.04	99.70	99.91	99.97	99.99	100.00		
47	68.44	90.05	96.87	99.02	99.69	99.90	99.97	99.99	100.00		
48	68.61	90.13	96.90	99.03	99.70	99.91	99.97	99.99	100.00		
49	68.44	90.04	96.86	99.01	99.69	99.90	99.97	99.99	100.00		
50	68.58	90.11	96.90	99.03	99.70	99.91	99.97	99.99	100.00		
51	68.43	90.04	96.86	99.01	99.69	99.90	99.97	99.99	100.00		
52	68.56	90.10	96.89	99.02	99.70	99.91	99.97	99.99	100.00		
53	68.43	90.04	96.86	99.01	99.69	99.90	99.97	99.99	100.00		
54	68.54	90.09	96.88	99.02	99.69	99.90	99.97	99.99	100.00		
55	68.43	90.04	96.86	99.01	99.69	99.90	99.97	99.99	100.00		
56	68.52	90.08	96.88	99.02	99.69	99.90	99.97	99.99	100.00		
57	68.43	90.04	96.86	99.01	99.69	99.90	99.97	99.99	100.00		
58	68.50	90.07	96.87	99.02	99.69	99.90	99.97	99.99	100.00		
59	68.43	90.03	96.86	99.01	99.69	99.90	99.97	99.99	100.00		
60	68.49	90.06	96.87	99.02	99.69	99.90	99.97	99.99	100.00		
...											
	68.42	90.03	96.85	99.01	99.69	99.90	99.97	99.99	100.00	100.00	100.00
n / k	1	2	3	4	5	6	7	8	9	10	11

A.2.6. TABLE. Lower Bound of Strict Majority Representativeness (in %) of Optimal Cabinets with k Members for n Independent Individuals and Equisignificant Preferences on Three Alternatives ($\overline{\mathsf{M}}m_k(W)$ for $\xi(x,y) = 1/6,\ p_{xy}(v) = 6/19$).

n \ k	1	2	3	4	5	6	7	8	9	10	11
2	56.79										
3	78.39	100.00									
4	59.72	71.99									
5	73.72	95.33	100.00								
6	61.62	77.17	79.83								
7	71.72	93.31	98.99	100.00							
8	62.99	80.24	84.17	84.74							
9	70.62	92.22	98.34	99.78	100.00						
10	64.03	82.34	87.04	88.01	88.13						
11	69.96	91.57	97.91	99.59	99.95	100.00					
12	64.83	83.87	89.08	90.33	90.57	90.60					
13	69.53	91.14	97.63	99.45	99.90	99.99	100.00				
14	65.47	85.04	90.61	92.06	92.39	92.45	92.46				
15	69.24	90.85	97.43	99.35	99.86	99.98	100.00				
16	65.98	85.96	91.79	93.39	93.79	93.87	93.89				
17	69.04	90.64	97.29	99.27	99.82	99.96	99.99	100.00			
18	66.40	86.68	92.71	94.42	94.88	94.99	95.01	95.01	95.01		
19	68.89	90.50	97.19	99.21	99.79	99.95	99.99	100.00			
20	66.73	87.26	93.45	95.24	95.74	95.87	95.90	95.90	95.90	95.90	
21	68.78	90.39	97.11	99.16	99.77	99.94	99.99	100.00			
22	67.01	87.73	94.04	95.90	96.43	96.58	96.61	96.62	96.62	96.62	96.62
23	68.70	90.31	97.05	99.13	99.75	99.94	99.98	100.00			
24	67.24	88.12	94.52	96.44	96.99	97.15	97.19	97.20	97.20	97.20	97.20
25	68.64	90.25	97.01	99.10	99.74	99.93	99.92	99.98	100.00		
26	67.43	88.43	94.91	96.87	97.45	97.61	97.66	97.67	97.67	97.67	97.67
27	68.59	90.20	96.98	99.08	99.73	99.92	99.98	99.99	100.00		
28	67.59	88.69	95.23	97.22	97.82	98.00	98.04	98.06	98.06	98.06	98.06
29	68.56	90.17	96.95	99.07	99.92	99.98	99.99	100.00			
30	67.72	88.91	95.49	97.52	98.13	98.31	98.36	98.38	98.38	98.38	98.38

n \ k	1	2	3	4	5	6	7	8	9	10	11
31	68.53	90.14	96.93	99.06	99.71	99.92	99.98	99.99	100.00		
32	67.83	89.09	95.71	97.76	98.38	98.57	98.62	98.64	98.64	98.64	98.64
33	68.51	90.12	96.92	99.05	99.71	99.91	99.97	99.99	100.00		
34	67.92	89.24	95.89	97.96	98.59	98.78	98.84	98.86	98.86	98.86	98.86
35	68.49	90.10	96.90	99.04	99.70	99.91	99.97	99.99	100.00		
36	68.00	89.36	96.05	98.13	98.77	98.96	99.02	99.04	99.04	99.04	99.04
37	68.48	90.08	96.89	99.03	99.70	99.91	99.97	99.99	100.00		
38	68.07	89.47	96.17	98.26	98.91	99.11	99.17	99.19	99.19	99.20	99.20
39	68.47	90.07	96.88	99.03	99.70	99.91	99.97	99.99	100.00		
40	68.12	89.55	96.28	98.38	99.03	99.24	99.30	99.31	99.32	99.32	99.32
41	68.46	90.07	96.88	99.02	99.70	99.91	99.97	99.99	100.00		
42	68.17	89.63	96.37	98.48	99.14	99.34	99.40	99.42	99.43	99.43	99.43
43	68.45	90.06	96.87	99.02	99.69	99.91	99.97	99.99	100.00		
44	68.20	89.69	96.44	98.56	99.22	99.43	99.49	99.51	99.51	99.52	99.52
45	68.45	90.05	96.87	99.02	99.69	99.90	99.97	99.99	100.00		
46	68.24	89.74	96.51	98.63	99.29	99.50	99.56	99.58	99.59	99.59	99.59
47	68.44	90.05	96.87	99.02	99.69	99.90	99.97	99.99	100.00		
48	68.26	89.78	96.56	98.69	99.35	99.56	99.63	99.65	99.65	99.65	99.65
49	68.44	90.04	96.86	99.01	99.69	99.90	99.97	99.99	100.00		
50	68.29	89.82	96.60	98.74	99.40	99.61	99.68	99.70	99.70	99.71	99.71
51	68.43	90.04	96.86	99.01	99.69	99.90	99.97	99.99	100.00		
52	68.31	89.85	96.64	98.78	99.45	99.66	99.72	99.74	99.75	99.75	99.75
53	68.43	90.04	96.86	99.01	99.69	99.90	99.97	99.99	100.00		
54	68.33	89.88	96.67	98.81	99.48	99.69	99.76	99.78	99.79	99.79	99.79
55	68.43	90.04	96.86	99.01	99.69	99.90	99.97	99.99	100.00		
56	68.34	89.90	96.70	98.84	99.51	99.73	99.79	99.81	99.82	99.82	99.82
57	68.43	90.04	96.86	99.01	99.69	99.90	99.97	99.99	100.00		
58	68.35	89.92	96.72	98.87	99.54	99.75	99.82	99.84	99.85	99.85	99.85
59	68.43	90.03	96.86	99.01	99.69	99.90	99.97	99.99	100.00		
60	68.36	89.94	96.74	98.89	99.56	99.77	99.84	99.86	99.87	99.87	99.87
...	68.42	90.03	96.85	99.01	99.69	99.90	99.97	99.99	100.00	100.00	100.00

A.3.1. TABLE. Lower Bound of Average Representativeness (in %) of Optimal Councils with k Voters for n Independent Individuals and One Significant Pair of Alternatives ($\mathsf{E}\hat{m}_k(\hat{W})$ for $\xi(x,y) = 1,\ p_{xy}(v) = 1/2$).

n \ k	1	3	5	7	9	11	13	15	17	19	21	23	25	27	29	31	33	35	37	39	41	43	45	47	49	51	53	55	57	59
2	75																													
3	67	75																												
4	63	69																												
5	60	65	69																											
6	58	63	66																											
7	57	61	63	66																										
8	56	59	62	64																										
9	56	58	60	62	64																									
10	55	58	59	61	62																									
11	55	57	59	60	61	62																								
12	54	56	58	59	60	61																								
13	54	56	57	58	59	60	61																							
14	54	55	57	58	59	60	60																							
15	53	55	56	57	58	59	60	60																						
16	53	55	56	57	58	58	59	60																						
17	53	54	56	56	57	58	59	59	60																					
18	53	54	55	56	57	58	58	59	59																					
19	53	54	55	56	56	57	58	58	59	59																				
20	53	54	55	55	56	57	57	58	58	59																				
21	52	54	54	55	56	56	57	57	58	58	59																			
22	52	54	54	55	56	56	57	57	58	58	59																			
23	52	53	54	55	55	56	56	57	57	58	58	58																		
24	52	53	54	55	55	56	56	57	57	57	58	58																		
25	52	53	54	54	55	55	56	56	57	57	57	58	58																	
26	52	53	54	54	55	55	56	56	56	57	57	57	58																	
27	52	53	53	54	55	55	55	56	56	57	57	57	57	58																
28	52	53	53	54	54	55	55	56	56	56	57	57	57	57																
29	52	53	53	54	54	55	55	55	56	56	56	57	57	57	57															
30	52	53	53	54	54	55	55	55	56	56	56	56	57	57	57															

n \ k	1	3	5	7	9	11	13	15	17	19	21	23	25	27	29	31	33	35	37	39	41	43	45	47	49	51	53	55	57	59
31	52	52	53	54	54	54	55	55	55	56	56	56	56	57	57	57														
32	52	52	53	53	54	54	55	55	55	56	56	56	56	57	57	57														
33	52	52	53	53	54	54	54	55	55	55	56	56	56	56	57	57	57													
34	51	52	53	53	54	54	54	55	55	55	55	56	56	56	56	57	57													
35	51	52	53	53	54	54	54	54	55	55	55	56	56	56	56	56	57	57												
36	51	52	53	53	53	54	54	54	55	55	55	55	56	56	56	56	56	57												
37	51	52	53	53	53	54	54	54	55	55	55	55	55	56	56	56	56	56	57											
38	51	52	52	53	53	54	54	54	54	55	55	55	55	56	56	56	56	56	56											
39	51	52	52	53	53	53	54	54	54	55	55	55	55	55	56	56	56	56	56	56										
40	51	52	52	53	53	53	54	54	54	54	55	55	55	55	55	56	56	56	56	56										
41	51	52	52	53	53	53	54	54	54	54	55	55	55	55	55	55	56	56	56	56	56									
42	51	52	52	53	53	53	53	54	54	54	54	55	55	55	55	55	55	56	56	56	56									
43	51	52	52	53	53	53	53	54	54	54	54	54	55	55	55	55	55	56	56	56	56	56								
44	51	52	52	52	53	53	53	54	54	54	54	54	55	55	55	55	55	55	56	56	56	56								
45	51	52	52	52	53	53	53	53	54	54	54	54	54	55	55	55	55	55	55	56	56	56	56							
46	51	52	52	52	53	53	53	53	54	54	54	54	54	55	55	55	55	55	55	55	56	56	56							
47	51	52	52	52	53	53	53	53	54	54	54	54	54	54	55	55	55	55	55	55	55	56	56	56						
48	51	52	52	52	53	53	53	53	53	54	54	54	54	54	55	55	55	55	55	55	55	55	56	56						
49	51	52	52	52	53	53	53	53	53	54	54	54	54	54	54	55	55	55	55	55	55	55	55	56	56					
50	51	52	52	52	52	53	53	53	53	54	54	54	54	54	54	54	55	55	55	55	55	55	55	55	56					
51	51	51	52	52	52	53	53	53	53	53	54	54	54	54	54	54	55	55	55	55	55	55	55	55	56	56				
52	51	51	52	52	52	53	53	53	53	53	54	54	54	54	54	54	54	55	55	55	55	55	55	55	55	56				
53	51	51	52	52	52	53	53	53	53	53	53	54	54	54	54	54	54	54	55	55	55	55	55	55	55	55	56			
54	51	51	52	52	52	53	53	53	53	53	53	54	54	54	54	54	54	54	55	55	55	55	55	55	55	55	55			
55	51	51	52	52	52	52	53	53	53	53	53	54	54	54	54	54	54	54	54	55	55	55	55	55	55	55	55	55		
56	51	51	52	52	52	52	53	53	53	53	53	53	54	54	54	54	54	54	54	54	55	55	55	55	55	55	55	55		
57	51	51	52	52	52	52	53	53	53	53	53	53	54	54	54	54	54	54	54	54	55	55	55	55	55	55	55	55	55	
58	51	51	52	52	52	52	53	53	53	53	53	53	53	54	54	54	54	54	54	54	54	55	55	55	55	55	55	55	55	
59	51	51	52	52	52	52	52	53	53	53	53	53	53	54	54	54	54	54	54	54	54	54	55	55	55	55	55	55	55	55
60	51	51	52	52	52	52	52	53	53	53	53	53	53	53	54	54	54	54	54	54	54	54	54	55	55	55	55	55	55	55
...																														
	50	50	50	50	50	50	50	50	50	50	50	50	50	50	50	50	50	50	50	50	50	50	50	50	50	50	50	50	50	50

A.3.2. TABLE. Lower Bound of Majority Representativeness (in %) of Optimal Councils with k Voters for n Independent Individuals and One Significant Pair of Alternatives ($\mathsf{M}\hat{m}_k(\hat{W})$ for $\xi(x,y) = 1,\ p_{xy}(v) = 1/2$).

n \ k	1	3	5	7	9	11	13	15	17	19	21	23	25	27	29	31	33	35	37	39	41	43	45	47	49	51	53	55	57	59
2	100																													
3	75	100																												
4	88	100																												
5	69	81	100																											
6	81	91	100																											
7	66	75	84	100																										
8	77	85	92	100																										
9	64	71	79	86	100																									
10	75	81	87	93	100																									
11	62	69	75	81	88	100																								
12	73	79	84	89	94	100																								
13	61	67	73	77	83	89	100																							
14	71	77	81	85	90	94	100																							
15	60	66	71	75	79	84	90	100																						
16	70	75	79	83	87	91	95	100																						
17	60	65	69	73	77	81	85	90	100																					
18	69	73	77	81	84	88	91	95	100																					
19	59	64	68	72	75	78	82	86	91	100																				
20	68	72	76	79	82	85	88	92	95	100																				
21	59	63	67	70	73	77	80	83	87	91	100																			
22	67	71	75	78	81	83	86	89	92	96	100																			
23	58	63	66	69	72	75	78	81	84	87	92	100																		
24	66	70	74	77	79	82	84	87	90	92	96	100																		
25	58	62	66	68	71	74	76	79	82	84	88	92	100																	
26	65	70	73	75	78	80	83	85	88	90	93	96	100																	
27	58	62	65	68	70	73	75	77	80	82	85	88	92	100																
28	65	69	72	74	77	79	81	84	86	88	90	93	96	100																
29	57	61	64	67	69	72	74	76	78	81	83	86	89	93	100															
30	64	68	71	74	76	78	80	82	84	86	89	91	93	96	100															

n \ k	1	3	5	7	9	11	13	15	17	19	21	23	25	27	29	31	33	35	37	39	41	43	45	47	49	51	53	55	57	59
31	57	61	64	66	69	71	73	75	77	79	81	84	86	89	93	100														
32	64	68	70	73	75	77	79	81	83	85	87	89	91	94	96	100														
33	57	61	63	66	68	70	72	74	76	78	80	82	84	87	89	93	100													
34	64	67	70	72	74	76	78	80	82	84	85	87	89	91	94	97	100													
35	57	60	63	65	67	69	71	73	75	77	79	81	83	85	87	90	93	100												
36	63	67	69	71	74	75	77	79	81	82	84	86	88	90	92	94	97	100												
37	57	60	63	65	67	69	71	72	74	76	78	79	81	83	85	87	90	93	100											
38	63	66	69	71	73	75	76	78	80	81	83	85	86	88	90	92	94	97	100											
39	56	60	62	64	66	68	70	72	73	75	77	78	80	82	84	86	88	90	94	100										
40	63	66	68	70	72	74	76	77	79	80	82	84	85	87	88	90	92	94	97	100										
41	56	59	62	64	66	68	69	71	73	74	76	77	79	81	82	84	86	88	91	94	100									
42	62	65	68	70	72	73	75	77	78	80	81	83	84	86	87	89	91	92	94	97	100									
43	56	59	62	64	66	67	69	71	72	74	75	76	78	79	81	83	84	86	88	91	94	100								
44	62	65	67	69	71	73	74	76	77	79	80	82	83	85	86	88	89	91	93	95	97	100								
45	56	59	61	63	65	67	68	70	71	73	74	76	77	79	80	82	83	85	87	89	91	94	100							
46	62	65	67	69	71	72	74	75	77	78	79	81	82	84	85	86	88	89	91	93	95	97	100							
47	56	59	61	63	65	66	68	69	71	72	74	75	76	78	79	81	82	84	85	87	89	91	94	100						
48	61	64	67	69	70	72	73	75	76	77	79	80	81	83	84	85	87	88	90	91	93	95	97	100						
49	56	59	61	63	65	66	68	69	70	72	73	74	76	77	78	80	81	82	84	85	87	89	91	94	100					
50	61	64	66	68	70	71	73	74	76	77	78	79	81	82	83	84	86	87	88	90	91	93	95	97	100					
51	56	58	61	63	64	66	67	69	70	71	72	74	75	76	78	79	80	81	83	84	86	87	89	92	94	100				
52	61	64	66	68	69	71	72	74	75	76	77	79	80	81	82	84	85	86	87	89	90	92	93	95	97	100				
53	56	58	60	62	64	65	67	68	69	71	72	73	74	76	77	78	79	81	82	83	85	86	88	90	92	94	100			
54	61	64	66	67	69	71	72	73	74	76	77	78	79	80	82	83	84	85	86	88	89	90	92	93	95	97	100			
55	55	58	60	62	64	65	67	68	69	70	72	73	74	75	76	77	78	80	81	82	83	85	86	88	90	92	95	100		
56	61	63	65	67	69	70	71	73	74	75	76	78	79	80	81	82	83	84	85	87	88	89	90	92	93	95	97	100		
57	55	58	60	62	63	65	66	67	69	70	71	72	73	74	76	77	78	79	80	81	83	84	85	87	88	90	92	95	100	
58	60	63	65	67	68	70	71	72	74	75	76	77	78	79	80	81	82	83	85	86	87	88	89	91	92	94	95	97	100	
59	55	58	60	62	63	65	66	67	68	69	71	72	73	74	75	76	77	78	79	81	82	83	84	85	87	88	90	92	95	100
60	60	63	65	67	68	69	71	72	73	74	75	76	78	79	80	81	82	83	84	85	86	87	88	90	91	92	94	95	97	100
...																														
	50	50	50	50	50	50	50	50	50	50	50	50	50	50	50	50	50	50	50	50	50	50	50	50	50	50	50	50	50	50

A.3.3. TABLE. Lower Bound of Strict Majority Representativeness (in %) of Optimal Councils with k Voters for n Independent Individuals and One Significant Pair of Alternatives ($\overline{\mathsf{M}}\hat{m}_k(\hat{W})$ for $\xi(x,y) = 1,\ p_{xy}(v) = 1/2$).

n \ k	1	3	5	7	9	11	13	15	17	19	21	23	25	27	29	31	33	35	37	39	41	43	45	47	49	51	53	55	57	59
2	50																													
3	75	100																												
4	50	63																												
5	69	81	100																											
6	50	59	69																											
7	66	75	84	100																										
8	50	58	65	73																										
9	64	71	79	86	100																									
10	50	57	63	69	75																									
11	62	69	75	81	88	100																								
12	50	56	61	66	71	77																								
13	61	67	73	77	83	89	100																							
14	50	56	60	65	69	73	79																							
15	60	66	71	75	79	84	90	100																						
16	50	55	59	63	67	71	75	80																						
17	60	65	69	73	77	81	85	90	100																					
18	50	55	59	62	66	69	73	77	81																					
19	59	64	68	72	75	78	82	86	91	100																				
20	50	55	58	62	65	68	71	74	78	82																				
21	59	63	67	70	73	77	80	83	87	91	100																			
22	50	54	58	61	64	67	69	72	75	79	83																			
23	58	63	66	69	72	75	78	81	84	87	92	100																		
24	50	54	58	60	63	66	68	71	73	76	80	84																		
25	58	62	66	68	71	74	76	79	82	84	88	92	100																	
26	50	54	57	60	62	65	67	70	72	75	77	80	85																	
27	58	62	65	68	70	73	75	77	80	82	85	88	92	100																
28	50	54	57	60	62	64	66	69	71	73	76	78	81	85																
29	57	61	64	67	69	72	74	76	78	81	83	86	89	93	100															
30	50	54	57	59	61	64	66	68	70	72	74	76	79	82	86															

n \ k	1	3	5	7	9	11	13	15	17	19	21	23	25	27	29	31	33	35	37	39	41	43	45	47	49	51	53	55	57	59
31	57	61	64	66	69	71	73	75	77	79	81	84	86	89	93	100														
32	50	54	56	59	61	63	65	67	69	71	73	75	77	80	82	86														
33	57	61	63	66	68	70	72	74	76	78	80	82	84	87	89	93	100													
34	50	53	56	59	61	63	65	66	68	70	72	74	76	78	80	83	86													
35	57	60	63	65	67	69	71	73	75	77	79	81	83	85	87	90	93	100												
36	50	53	56	58	60	62	64	66	68	69	71	73	75	76	79	81	83	87												
37	57	60	63	65	67	69	71	72	74	76	78	79	81	83	85	87	90	93	100											
38	50	53	56	58	60	62	64	65	67	69	70	72	74	75	77	79	81	84	87											
39	56	60	62	64	66	68	70	72	73	75	77	78	80	82	84	86	88	90	94	100										
40	50	53	56	58	60	62	63	65	66	68	70	71	73	74	76	78	80	82	84	87										
41	56	59	62	64	66	68	69	71	73	74	76	77	79	81	82	84	86	88	91	94	100									
42	50	53	56	58	59	61	63	64	66	67	69	70	72	73	75	77	78	80	82	85	88									
43	56	59	62	64	66	67	69	71	72	74	75	76	78	79	81	83	84	86	88	91	94	100								
44	50	53	55	57	59	61	62	64	65	67	68	70	71	73	74	76	77	79	81	83	85	88								
45	56	59	61	63	65	67	68	70	71	73	74	76	77	79	80	82	83	85	87	89	91	94	100							
46	50	53	55	57	59	61	62	64	65	66	68	69	71	72	73	75	76	78	79	81	83	85	88							
47	56	59	61	63	65	66	68	69	71	72	74	75	76	78	79	81	82	84	85	87	89	91	94	100						
48	50	53	55	57	59	60	62	63	65	66	67	69	70	71	73	74	75	77	78	80	81	83	86	89						
49	56	59	61	63	65	66	68	69	70	72	73	74	76	77	78	80	81	82	84	85	87	89	91	94	100					
50	50	53	55	57	59	60	62	63	64	66	67	68	69	71	72	73	74	75	77	79	80	82	84	86	89					
51	56	58	61	63	64	66	67	69	70	71	72	74	75	76	78	79	80	81	83	84	86	87	89	92	94	100				
52	50	53	55	57	58	60	61	63	64	65	66	68	69	70	71	73	74	75	76	78	79	71	82	84	86	89				
53	56	58	60	62	64	65	67	68	69	71	72	73	74	76	77	78	79	81	82	83	85	86	88	90	92	94	100			
54	50	53	55	57	58	60	61	62	64	65	66	67	68	70	71	72	73	74	76	77	78	79	81	83	84	86	89			
55	55	58	60	62	64	65	67	68	69	70	72	73	74	75	76	77	78	80	81	82	83	85	86	88	90	92	95	100		
56	50	53	55	57	58	60	61	62	63	65	66	67	68	69	70	71	72	74	75	76	77	79	80	81	83	85	87	89		
57	55	58	60	62	63	65	66	67	69	70	71	72	73	74	76	77	78	79	80	81	83	84	85	87	88	90	92	95	100	
58	50	53	55	56	58	59	61	62	63	64	65	67	68	69	70	71	72	73	74	75	76	78	79	80	82	83	85	87	90	
59	55	58	60	62	63	65	66	67	68	69	71	72	73	74	75	76	77	78	79	81	82	83	84	85	87	88	90	92	95	100
60	50	53	55	56	58	59	60	62	63	64	65	66	67	68	69	70	71	72	74	75	76	77	78	79	81	82	83	85	87	90
...																														
	50	50	50	50	50	50	50	50	50	50	50	50	50	50	50	50	50	50	50	50	50	50	50	50	50	50	50	50	50	50

A.3.4. TABLE. Lower Bound of Average Representativeness (in %) of Optimal Councils with k Voters for n Independent Individuals and Equisignificant Preferences on Three Alternatives ($\mathsf{E}\hat{m}_k(\hat{W})$ for $\xi(x,y) = 1/6,\ p_{xy}(v) = 6/19$).

n \ k	1	3	5	7	9	11	13	15	17	19	21	23	25	27	29	31	33	35	37	39	41	43	45	47	49	51	53	55	57	59
2	78																													
3	71	78																												
4	68	74																												
5	65	71	74																											
6	64	69	72																											
7	63	68	70	72																										
8	62	67	69	71																										
9	64	66	68	70	71																									
10	61	65	68	69	70																									
11	61	65	67	69	69	70																								
12	60	64	67	68	69	70																								
13	60	64	66	68	69	69	70																							
14	60	64	66	67	68	69	69																							
15	60	63	66	67	68	69	69	69																						
16	59	63	65	67	68	68	69	69																						
17	59	63	65	67	68	68	69	69	69																					
18	59	63	65	66	67	68	68	69	69																					
19	59	63	65	66	67	68	68	69	69	69																				
20	59	63	65	66	67	68	68	68	69	69																				
21	59	62	65	66	67	68	68	68	69	69	69																			
22	59	62	64	66	67	67	68	68	68	69	69																			
23	59	62	64	66	67	67	68	68	68	69	69	69																		
24	59	62	64	66	66	67	68	68	68	68	69	69																		
25	59	62	64	65	66	67	68	68	68	68	68	69	69																	
26	58	62	64	65	66	67	67	68	68	68	68	69	69																	
27	58	62	64	65	66	67	67	68	68	68	68	68	69	69																
28	58	62	64	65	66	67	67	68	68	68	68	68	69	69																
29	58	62	64	65	66	67	67	68	68	68	68	68	68	69	69															
30	58	62	64	65	66	67	67	68	68	68	68	68	68	68	69															

n \ k	1	3	5	7	9	11	13	15	17	19	21	23	25	27	29	31	33	35	37	39	41	43	45	47	49	51	53	55	57	59
31	58	62	64	65	66	67	67	68	68	68	68	68	68	68	69	69														
32	58	61	64	65	66	67	67	68	68	68	68	68	68	68	68															
33	58	61	63	65	66	67	67	67	68	68	68	68	68	68	68	68	69													
34	58	61	63	65	66	66	67	67	68	68	68	68	68	68	68	68														
35	58	61	63	65	66	66	67	67	68	68	68	68	68	68	68	68	68	68												
36	58	61	63	65	66	66	67	67	68	68	68	68	68	68	68	68	68													
37	58	61	63	65	66	66	67	67	68	68	68	68	68	68	68	68	68	68												
38	58	61	63	65	66	66	67	67	68	68	68	68	68	68	68	68	68	68												
39	58	61	63	65	66	66	67	67	68	68	68	68	68	68	68	68	68	68	68											
40	58	61	63	65	66	66	67	67	68	68	68	68	68	68	68	68	68	68												
41	58	61	63	64	65	66	67	67	67	68	68	68	68	68	68	68	68	68	68	68										
42	58	61	63	64	65	66	67	67	67	68	68	68	68	68	68	68	68	68	68											
43	58	61	63	64	65	66	67	67	67	68	68	68	68	68	68	68	68	68	68	68										
44	58	61	63	64	65	66	67	67	67	68	68	68	68	68	68	68	68	68	68											
45	58	61	63	64	65	66	67	67	67	68	68	68	68	68	68	68	68	68	68	68	68									
46	58	61	63	64	65	66	67	67	67	68	68	68	68	68	68	68	68	68	68	68										
47	58	61	63	64	65	66	67	67	67	68	68	68	68	68	68	68	68	68	68	68	68									
48	58	61	63	64	65	66	67	67	67	68	68	68	68	68	68	68	68	68	68	68										
49	58	61	63	64	65	66	67	67	67	68	68	68	68	68	68	68	68	68	68	68	68	68								
50	58	61	63	64	65	66	67	67	67	68	68	68	68	68	68	68	68	68	68	68	68									
51	58	61	63	64	65	66	67	67	67	68	68	68	68	68	68	68	68	68	68	68	68	68								
52	58	61	63	64	65	66	66	67	67	68	68	68	68	68	68	68	68	68	68	68	68									
53	58	61	63	64	65	66	66	67	67	68	68	68	68	68	68	68	68	68	68	68	68	68								
54	58	61	63	64	65	66	66	67	67	67	68	68	68	68	68	68	68	68	68	68	68	68								
55	58	61	63	64	65	66	66	67	67	67	68	68	68	68	68	68	68	68	68	68	68	68	68							
56	58	61	63	64	65	66	66	67	67	67	68	68	68	68	68	68	68	68	68	68	68	68								
57	58	61	63	64	65	66	66	67	67	67	68	68	68	68	68	68	68	68	68	68	68	68	68							
58	58	61	63	64	65	66	66	67	67	67	68	68	68	68	68	68	68	68	68	68	68	68								
59	58	61	63	64	65	66	66	67	67	67	68	68	68	68	68	68	68	68	68	68	68	68	68							
60	58	61	63	64	65	66	66	67	67	67	68	68	68	68	68	68	68	68	68	68	68	68								
...																														
	57	60	62	63	64	65	65	66	66	67	67	67	67	68	68	68	68	68	68	68	68	68	68	68	68	68	68	68	68	68

A.3.5. TABLE. Lower Bound of Majority Representativeness (in %) of Optimal Councils with k Voters for n Independent Individuals and Equisignificant Preferences on Three Alternatives ($\mathsf{M}\hat{m}_k(\hat{W})$ for $\xi(x,y) = 1/6$, $p_{xy}(v) = 6/19$).

n \ k	1	3	5	7	9	11	13	15	17	19	21	23	25	27	29	31	33	35	37	39	41	43	45	47	49	51	53	55	57	59
2	100																													
3	78	100																												
4	88	100																												
5	74	86	100																											
6	82	92	100																											
7	72	82	90	100																										
8	78	88	94	100																										
9	71	80	87	92	100																									
10	76	85	91	96	100																									
11	70	79	85	90	94	100																								
12	74	83	89	93	97	100																								
13	70	78	84	88	92	95	100																							
14	73	81	87	91	95	97	100																							
15	69	78	83	87	91	94	96	100																						
16	72	80	86	90	93	96	98	100																						
17	69	77	83	87	90	93	95	97	100																					
18	71	80	85	89	92	94	96	98	100																					
19	69	77	83	86	89	92	94	96	98	100																				
20	71	79	84	88	91	94	95	97	99	100																				
21	69	77	82	86	89	92	93	95	97	98	100																			
22	70	79	84	88	91	93	95	96	98	99	100																			
23	69	77	82	86	89	91	93	95	96	97	98	100																		
24	70	78	83	87	90	92	94	96	97	98	99	100																		
25	69	77	82	86	89	91	93	94	96	97	98	99	100																	
26	70	78	83	87	90	92	94	95	96	98	98	99	100																	
27	69	77	82	86	89	91	93	94	95	96	97	98	99	100																
28	70	78	83	87	89	92	93	95	96	97	98	99	99	100																
29	69	77	82	86	88	91	92	94	95	96	97	98	98	99	100															
30	69	77	83	86	89	91	93	95	96	97	98	98	99	99	100															

n \ k	1	3	5	7	9	11	13	15	17	19	21	23	25	27	29	31	33	35	37	39	41	43	45	47	49	51	53	55	57	59
31	69	77	82	86	88	91	92	94	95	96	97	97	98	99	99	100														
32	69	77	82	86	89	91	93	94	96	97	97	98	99	99	100															
33	69	77	82	85	88	91	92	94	95	96	97	97	98	98	99	99	100													
34	69	77	82	86	89	91	93	94	95	96	97	98	98	99	99	100														
35	68	76	82	85	88	90	92	94	95	96	97	97	98	98	99	99	99	100												
36	69	77	82	86	89	91	93	94	95	96	97	98	99	99	99	99	100													
37	68	76	82	85	88	90	92	94	95	96	96	97	98	98	99	99	99	100												
38	69	77	82	86	89	91	93	94	95	96	97	97	98	98	99	99	99	100												
39	68	76	82	85	88	90	92	94	95	96	96	97	98	98	98	99	99	99	100											
40	69	77	82	86	89	91	92	94	95	96	97	97	98	98	99	99	99	100												
41	68	76	82	85	88	90	92	94	95	96	96	97	98	98	98	99	99	99	99	100										
42	69	77	82	86	88	91	92	94	95	96	97	97	98	98	99	99	99	99	100											
43	68	76	82	85	88	90	92	93	95	96	96	97	97	98	98	99	99	99	99	100										
44	69	77	82	86	88	91	92	94	95	96	97	97	98	98	99	99	99	99	100											
45	68	76	82	85	88	90	92	93	95	96	96	97	97	98	98	99	99	99	99	99	100									
46	69	77	82	86	88	91	92	94	95	96	97	98	98	98	99	99	99	99	99	100										
47	68	76	82	85	88	90	92	93	95	96	96	97	97	98	98	99	99	99	99	99	100									
48	69	77	82	85	88	90	92	94	95	96	96	97	98	98	98	99	99	99	99	100										
49	68	76	82	85	88	90	92	93	95	95	96	97	97	98	98	99	99	99	99	99	99	100								
50	69	77	82	85	88	90	92	94	95	96	96	97	98	98	98	99	99	99	99	99	100									
51	68	76	82	85	88	90	92	93	95	95	96	97	97	98	98	98	99	99	99	99	99	100								
52	69	77	82	85	88	90	92	94	95	96	96	97	97	98	98	99	99	99	99	99	100									
53	68	76	82	85	88	90	92	93	95	95	96	97	97	98	98	98	99	99	99	99	99	100								
54	69	77	82	85	88	90	92	94	95	96	96	97	97	98	98	99	99	99	99	99	99	100								
55	68	76	82	85	88	90	92	93	95	95	96	97	97	98	98	98	99	99	99	99	99	99	100							
56	69	76	82	85	88	90	92	93	95	96	96	97	97	98	98	99	99	99	99	99	99	100								
57	68	76	82	85	88	90	92	93	95	95	96	97	97	98	98	98	99	99	99	99	99	99	100							
58	69	76	82	85	88	90	92	93	95	96	96	97	97	98	98	99	99	99	99	99	99	100								
59	68	76	82	85	88	90	92	93	95	95	96	97	97	98	98	98	99	99	99	99	99	99	100							
60	68	76	82	85	88	90	92	93	95	96	96	97	97	98	98	98	99	99	99	99	99	100								
...																														
	68	76	82	85	88	90	92	93	95	95	96	97	97	98	98	98	99	99	99	99	99	99	100	100	100	100	100	100	100	100

A.3.6. TABLE. Lower Bound of Strict Majority Representativeness (in %) of Optimal Councils with k Voters for n Independent Individuals and Equisignificant Preferences on Three Alternatives $(\overline{\mathsf{M}}\hat{m}_k(\hat{W})$ for $\xi(x,y)=1/6,\ p_{xy}(v)=6/19)$.

n \ k	1	3	5	7	9	11	13	15	17	19	21	23	25	27	29	31	33	35	37	39	41	43	45	47	49	51	53	55	57	59
2	57																													
3	78	100																												
4	60	72																												
5	74	86	100																											
6	62	72	80																											
7	72	82	90	100																										
8	63	72	79	85																										
9	71	80	87	92	100																									
10	64	73	79	84	88																									
11	70	79	85	90	94	100																								
12	65	73	79	84	87	91																								
13	70	78	84	88	92	95	100																							
14	65	74	79	84	87	90	92																							
15	69	78	83	87	91	94	96	100																						
16	66	74	80	84	87	90	92	94																						
17	69	77	83	87	90	93	95	97	100																					
18	66	75	80	84	87	89	91	93	95																					
19	69	77	83	86	89	92	94	96	98	100																				
20	67	75	80	84	87	89	91	93	94	96																				
21	69	77	82	86	89	92	93	95	97	98	100																			
22	67	75	80	84	87	90	91	93	94	95	97																			
23	69	77	82	86	89	91	93	95	96	97	98	100																		
24	67	75	81	84	87	90	91	93	94	95	96	97																		
25	69	77	82	86	89	91	93	94	96	97	98	99	100																	
26	67	75	81	85	87	90	91	93	94	95	96	97	98																	
27	69	77	82	86	89	91	93	94	95	96	97	98	99	100																
28	68	76	81	85	87	90	92	93	94	95	96	97	97	98																
29	69	77	82	86	88	91	92	94	95	96	97	98	98	99	100															

n / k	1	3	5	7	9	11	13	15	17	19	21	23	25	27	29	31	33	35	37	39	41	43	45	47	49	51	53	55	57	59
31	69	77	82	86	88	91	92	94	95	96	97	97	98	99	99	100														
32	68	76	81	85	88	90	92	93	94	95	96	97	97	98	98	99														
33	69	77	82	85	88	91	92	94	95	96	97	97	98	98	99	99	100													
34	68	76	81	85	88	90	92	93	94	95	96	97	97	98	98	98	99													
35	68	76	82	85	88	90	92	94	95	96	97	97	98	98	99	99	99	100												
36	68	76	81	85	86	90	92	93	94	95	96	97	97	98	98	98	99	99												
37	68	76	82	85	88	90	92	94	95	96	96	97	98	98	99	99	99	100												
38	68	76	81	85	88	90	92	93	94	95	96	97	97	98	98	98	98	99	99											
39	68	76	82	85	88	90	92	94	95	96	96	97	98	98	98	99	99	99	100											
40	68	76	81	85	88	90	92	93	94	95	96	97	97	98	98	98	99	99	99	99										
41	68	76	82	85	88	90	92	94	95	96	96	97	98	98	98	99	99	99	99	100										
42	68	76	81	85	88	90	92	93	94	95	96	97	97	98	98	99	99	99	99	99										
43	68	76	82	85	88	90	92	93	95	96	96	97	97	98	98	99	99	99	99	100										
44	68	76	81	85	88	90	92	93	94	95	96	97	97	98	98	98	99	99	99	99	99	100								
45	68	76	82	85	88	90	92	93	95	96	96	97	97	98	98	99	99	99	99	99	100									
46	68	76	81	85	88	90	92	93	94	95	96	97	97	98	98	98	99	99	99	99	99	99	100							
47	68	76	82	85	88	90	92	93	95	96	96	97	97	98	98	99	99	99	99	99	100									
48	68	76	81	85	88	90	92	93	94	95	96	97	97	98	98	98	99	99	99	99	99	99	100							
49	68	76	82	85	88	90	92	93	95	95	96	97	97	98	98	99	99	99	99	99	99	100								
50	68	76	81	85	88	90	92	93	94	95	96	97	97	98	98	98	99	99	99	99	99	99	100							
51	68	76	82	85	88	90	92	93	95	95	96	97	97	98	98	98	99	99	99	99	99	100								
52	68	76	81	85	88	90	92	93	94	95	96	97	97	98	98	98	99	99	99	99	99	99	99	100						
53	68	76	82	85	88	90	92	93	95	95	96	97	97	98	98	98	99	99	99	99	99	100								
54	68	76	81	85	88	90	92	93	94	95	96	97	97	98	98	98	99	99	99	99	99	99	99	100						
55	68	76	82	85	88	90	92	93	95	95	96	97	97	98	98	98	99	99	99	99	99	99	100							
56	68	76	81	85	88	90	92	93	94	95	96	97	97	98	98	98	99	99	99	99	99	99	99	100						
57	68	76	82	85	88	90	92	93	95	95	96	97	97	98	98	98	99	99	99	99	99	99	100							
58	68	76	81	85	88	90	92	93	94	95	96	97	97	98	98	98	99	99	99	99	99	99	99	100						
59	68	76	82	85	88	90	92	93	95	95	96	97	97	98	98	98	99	99	99	99	99	99	100							
60	68	76	81	85	88	90	92	93	94	95	96	97	97	98	98	98	99	99	99	99	99	99	99	100						
...																														
	68	76	82	85	88	90	92	93	95	95	96	97	97	98	98	98	99	99	99	99	99	99	100	100	100	100	100	100	100	100

References

Aleksandroff 1977

Александров П.С. Введение в теорию множеств и общую топологию. — М. : Наука, 1977. — 367 с. / German translation: *Einfuhrung in die Mengenlehre und die allgemeine Topologie.* — Berlin: Deutscher Verlag d. Wiss., 1984. — 336 g.

Aleksandroff & Urysohn 1929

Alexandroff P., Urysohn P. *Memoire sur les espaces topologiques compacts.* — Verhandelingen der Koninklijke Akademie van Wetenschappen te Amsterdam. Afd. Natuurkunde sectie 1. Dl. 14, No. 1. — Amsterdam, Koninkli jke Akademie, 1929. — viii, 96 pp.

Arkhangelskii & Ponomarev 1974

Архангельский А.В., Пономарев В.И. Основы общей топологии в задачах и упражнениях. — М.: Наука, 1974. — 423 с. / English translation: *Fundamentals of General Topology: Problems and Exercises.* — Dordrecht and Lancaster: Reidel, 1984. — xvi, 415 pp.

Armstrong 1980

Armstrong T.E. Arrow's Theorem with Restricted Coalition Algebras. — *Journal of Mathematical Economics.* — 1980. — Vol. 7, No. 1. — Pp. 55–75.

Armstrong 1985

Armstrong T.E. Precisely Dictatorial Social Welfare Functions. Erratum and Addendum to 'Arrow's Theorem with Restricted Coalition Algebras'. — *Journal of Mathematical Economics.* — 1985. — Vol. 14, No. 1. — Pp. 57–59.

Arrow 1951

Arrow K.J. *Social Choice and Individual Values.* — New York: Wiley, 1951. — 99 pp.

Aumann 1964
Aumann R.J. Markets with a Continuum of Traders. — *Econometrica.* — 1964. — Vol. 32, No. 1–2. — Pp. 39–45.

Aumann 1966
Aumann R.J. Existence of Competitive Equilibria in Markets with a Continuum of Traders. — *Econometrica.* — 1966. — Vol. 34, No. 1. — Pp. 1–17.

Aumann & Shapley 1974
Aumann R.J. and Shapley L.S. *Values of Non-Atomic Games.* — Princeton, NJ: Princeton University Press, 1974. — xi, 333 pp.

Black 1958
Black D. *The Theory of Committees and Elections.* — Cambridge: At the University Press, 1958. — xiii, 241 pp.

Cantor 1895
Cantor G. Beiträge zur Begründung der transfiniten Mengenlehre. — *Mathematische Annalen.* — 1895. — Vol. 46. — Pp. 481–512.

Copeland 1951
Copeland A.H. *A "Reasonable" Social Welfare Function.*— Mimeographed. — University of Michigan Seminar on Applications of Mathematics to Social Sciences. — 1951.

Debreu 1954
Debreu G. Representation of a Preference Ordering by a Numerical Function. — In: R.M.Thrall et al. (Eds.). *Decision Processes.* — New York: Wiley, 1954. — Pp. 159–165.

Debreu 1960
Debreu G. Topological Methods in Cardinal Utility Theory. — In: K. Arrow (Ed.). *Mathematical Methods in the Social Sciences, 1959, Stanford.* — Stanford: Stanford University Press, 1960. — Pp. 16–26.

Debreu 1964
Debreu G. Continuity Properties of Paretian Utility. — *International Economic Review.* — 1964. — Vol. 5, No. 3. — Pp. 285–293.

Douwen 1978
Douwen E. van. Existence and Applications of Remote Points. — *Bulletin of the American Mathematical Society.* — 1978. — Vol. 84, No. 1. — Pp. 161–163.

Dwight 1961
Dwight H.B. *Tables of Integrals and Other Mathematical Data,* 4th ed. — New York: MacMillan, 1961. — 336 pp.

Eilenberg 1941
Eilenberg S. Ordered Topological Spaces. — *American Journal of Mathematics.* — 1941. — Vol. 63, No. 1. — Pp. 39–45.

Engelking 1977
Engelking R. *General Topology.* — Warszawa: PWN, 1977. — 626 pp.

Fishburn 1967
Fishburn P. Methods of Estimating Additive Utilities. — *Management Science.* — 1967. — Vol. 7, No. 3. — Pp. 435–453.

Fishburn 1970a
Fishburn P. Arrow's Impossibility Theorem: Concise Proof and Infinite Voters. — *Journal of Economic Theory.* — 1970. — Vol. 2, No. 1. — P. 103–106.

Fishburn 1970b
Fishburn P. *Utility Theory for Decision Making.* — New York: Wiley, 1970. — xiv, 234 pp.

Fishburn 1973
Fishburn P. *The Theory of Social Choice.* — Princeton: Princeton University Press, 1973. — xii, 264 pp.

Fishburn 1983
Fishburn P. Utility Function on Ordered Convex Sets. — *Journal of Mathematical Economics.* — 1983. — Vol. 12, No. 3. — Pp. 221–232.

Fishburn 1987
Fishburn P. *Interprofile Conditions and Impossibility.* — Chur, etc.: Harwood Academic Publishers, 1987. — viii, 94 pp.

Fishburn & Keeney 1974
Fishburn P., Keeney R.L. Seven Independence Concepts and Continuous Multiattributer Utility Functions. — *Journal of Mathematical Psychology.* — 1974. — Vol. 11, No. 3. — Pp. 294–327.

Hadley 1964
Hadley G. *Nonlinear and Dynamic Programming.* — Reading, Mass.: Addison Wesley, 1964. — xi, 484 pp.

Keeney 1974
Keeney R.L. Multiplicative Utility Functions. — *Operations Research.* — 1974. — Vol. 22, No. 1. — Pp. 22–34.

Kelley 1955
Kelley J.L. *General Topology.* — New York: Van Nostrand, 1955. — xiv, 298 pp.

Kelly 1978
Kelly J.S. *Arrow Impossibility Theorems.* — New York: Academic Press, 1978. — xi, 194 pp.

Kendall & Stuart 1958
Kendall M., Stuart A. *The Advanced Theory of Statistics. Vol. 1.*— London: Ch. Griffin & Co. Lim., 1958. — 433 pp.

Kirman & Sondermann 1972
Kirman A., Sondermann D. Arrow's Theorem, Many Agents, and Invisible Dictators. *Journal of Economic Theory.* — 1972. — Vol. 5, No. 2. — Pp. 267–277.

Koopmans 1972
Koopmans T.C. Representation of Preference Ordering with Independent Components of Consumption. — In: McGuire C.B. and Radner R. (Eds.) *Decision and Organisation.* — Amsterdam: North-Holland Publishing Co., 1972. — Pp. 57–78.

Korn & Korn 1968
Korn G.A., Korn T.M. *Mathematical Handbook. For Scientists and Engeneers,* 2nd ed. — New York: McGraw-Hill, 1968. — xvii, 1130 pp.

Krantz Luce Suppes & Tversky 1971
Krantz, D.H., Luce R.D., Suppes, P., Tversky, A. *Foundations of Measurement. Vol. 1.* — New York: Academic Press, 1971. — 578 pp.

Larichev 1979
Ларичев О.И. Наука и искусство принятия решений. — М.: Наука, 1979. — 200 с.

Leontief 1947
Leontief W. Introduction to a Theory of the Internal Structure of Functional Relationships. — *Econometrica.* — 1947. — Vol. 15, No. 4. — Pp. 361–373.

Lyapunov & Malenkov 1962

Ляпунов А.А., Маленков А.Г. Логический анализ строения наследственной информации. — Проблемы кибернетики. — М.: Наука, 1962. — Вып. 8. — С. 293–308.

Mirkin 1974

Миркин Б.Г. Проблема группового выбора. — М.: Наука, 1974. — 256 с. / English translation: *Group Choice.* — Washington: A Halsted Press Book, 1979. — xxx, 252 pp.

Murakami 1966

Murakami Y. Formal Structure of Majority Decision. — *Econometrica.* — 1966. — Vol. 34, No. 3. — Pp.709–718.

Naumov 1978

Наумов Г.Е. Правило множителей для векторной задачи оптимизации с бесконечным множеством критериев. — Техническая кибернетика. — 1978. — № 2. — С. 36–38.

Neumann & Morgenstern 1944

Neumann J. von, Morgenstern O. *Theory of Games and Economic Behavior.* — Princeton: Princeton University Press, 1944. — xviii, 625 pp.

Pearson 1968

Pearson K. *Tables of the Incomplete Beta-Function,* 2nd ed. — London: published for the Biometrica Trustees by Cambridge, 1968. — xxxii, 505 p.

Ramsey 1931

Ramsey F.P. *The Foundations of Mathematics and Other Logical Essays.* — New York: Harcourt Brace Jovanovich Inc., 1931. — xviii, 292 pp.

Richter 1971

Richter K. Coalitions, Core and Competition. — *Journal of Economic Theory.* — 1971. — Vol. 3, No. 3. — Pp. 323–334.

Samuelson 1948

Samuelson P.A. *Foundations of Economic Analysis.*— Cambridge, Mass.: Harvard University Press, 1948. — 447 pp.

Schmitz 1977

Schmitz N. A Further Note on Arrow' Impossibility Theorem. — *Journal of Mathematical Economics.* — 1977. — Vol. 4, No. 3. — Pp. 189–196.

Shilov 1973
Shilov G.E. *Elementary Real and Complex Analysis.* — Cambridge, Mass.: M.I.T. Press, 1973. — xi, 516 pp.

Sikorski 1964
Sikorski R. *Boolean Algebras,* 2nd ed. — Berlin: Springer, 1964. — 237 pp.

Szpilrajn 1930
Szpilrajn E. Sur l'extension de l'ordre partiel. — *Fundamenta Mathematicae.* — 1930. — Vol. 16. — Pp. 386–389.

Tanguiane 1979a
Тангян А.С. Модель выявления потребительского предпочтения. — Экономика и математические методы. — 1979. — Т. 15, № 1. — С. 128–134.

Tanguiane 1979b
Тангян А.С. Модели социального выбора с конечным и бесконечным числом участников. — Препринт. — М.: ЦЭМИ АН СССР, 1979. — 53 с.

Tanguiane 1979c
Тангян А.С. Агрегирование в модели социального выбора. — Препринт. — М: ЦЭМИ АН СССР, 1979. — 64 с.

Tanguiane 1980a
Тангян А.С. Иерархическая модель группового выбора. — Экономика и математические методы. — 1980. — Т. 16, № 3. — С. 519–534.

Tanguiane 1980b
Тангян А.С. Практическое построение аддитивной целевой функции. — Препринт. — М.: ЦЭМИ АН СССР, 1980. — 52 с.

Tanguiane 1981a
Тангян А.С. Переход к бесконечному числу участников в модели группового выбора. — Экономика и математические методы. — 1981. — Т. 17, № 1. — С. 109–120.

Tanguiane 1981b
Тангян А.С. О теореме Эрроу для алгебры коалиций. — Экономика и математические методы. — 1981. — Т. 17, № 4. — С. 800–801.

Tanguiane 1981c
Tangyan A.S. On Construction of an Additive Goal Function. *Soviet Math. Dokl.* — 1981. — Vol. 24, No. 2. — Pp. 307–311.

Tanguiane 1982a

Тангян А.С. Последовательное агрегирование в модели группового выбора. — Экономика и математические методы. — 1982. — Т. 18, № 1. — С. 105–114.

Tanguiane 1982b

Тангян А.С. Оценка погрешности для аппроксимации аддитивной целевой функции. — Анализ нечисловых данных в системных исследованиях. — Сбор-ник трудов ВНИИ системных исследований. — 1982. — Вып. 10. — С. 124–131.

Tanguiane 1982c

Тангян А.С. Построение сепарабельной целевой функции. — Экономика и математические методы. — 1982. — Т. 18, № 5. — С. 890–899.

Tanguiane 1985

Тангян А.С. Оценка интенсивности предпочтений с помощью вероятностной модели Борда–Лапласа. — Экономика и математические методы. — 1985. — Т. 21, № 1. — С. 110–116.

Tanguiane 1988

Tangyan A.S. Representation of a Weak Ordering by a Numerical Function. — *Soviet Math. Dokl.*. — 1988. — Vol. 37, No. 1. — Pp. 222–225.

Tanguiane 1989a

Тангян А.С. Интерпретация диктатора в модели Эрроу как представителя коллектива. — Математическое моделирование. — 1989. — Т. 1, № 7. — С. 51–92.

Tanguiane 1989b

Тангян А.С. Модельколлективного представительства в условиях демократии. — Математическое моделирование. — 1989. — Т. 1, № 10. — С. 80–125.

Tanguiane 1990a

Тангян А.С. Оптимальное назначение диктатора в модели Эрроу. — Доклады АН СССР. — 1990. — Т. 310, № 6. — С. 1310–1314.

Tanguiane 1990b

Тангян А.С. Модель коллективного представительства типа совета. — Математическое моделирование. — 1990. — Т. 2, № 5. — С. 60–103.

Winterfeld & Fisher 1975

Winterfeldt D., Fisher G. Multiattribute Utility Theory: Models and Assessement Procedures. — In: D. Wendt and Ch. Vlek (Eds.). *Utility, Probability, and Human Decision Making. Selected Proceedings of an*

Interdisciplinary Research Conference. Rome 3–6 September, 1975. — Dordrecht, Holland, 1975. — Pp. 47–85.

Zolotarev 1986

Золотарев Б.М. Современная теория суммирования независимых случайных величин. — М.: Наука, 1986. — 415 с.

Index

Name Index

Subject Index

Designations